# PHILOSOPHY
## OF
## PLATO AND ARISTOTLE

# PHILOSOPHY
## OF
# PLATO AND ARISTOTLE

*Advisory Editor*
**GREGORY VLASTOS**
Princeton University

# PLATO'S REPUBLIC

## THE GREEK TEXT

*EDITED, WITH NOTES AND ESSAYS*

BY

## B. JOWETT

AND

## LEWIS CAMPBELL

VOL. II. ESSAYS

## ARNO PRESS
A New York Times Company
New York / 1973

Reprint Edition 1973 by Arno Press Inc.

Reprinted from a copy in
The University of Illinois Library

PHILOSOPHY OF PLATO AND ARISTOTLE
ISBN for complete set: 0-405-04830-0
See last pages of this volume for titles.

Manufactured in the United States of America

**Library of Congress Cataloging in Publication Data**

Plato.
    Plato's Republic.

    (Philosophy of Plato and Aristotle)
    Notes in English.
    Reprint of v. 2 only of the 1894 ed.
    I.  Jowett, Benjamin, ed.  II.  Campbell, Lewis,
1830-1908, ed.  ~~III.  Title.  IV.  Series.~~
PA4279.R4  1973        184        72-9295
ISBN 0-405-04846-7

15 1849

# PLATO'S REPUBLIC

*JOWETT AND CAMPBELL*

VOL. II.

*London*

HENRY FROWDE

OXFORD UNIVERSITY PRESS WAREHOUSE
AMEN CORNER, E.C.

*New York*

MACMILLAN & CO., 66 FIFTH AVENUE

# PLATO'S REPUBLIC

## THE GREEK TEXT

*EDITED, WITH NOTES AND ESSAYS*

BY THE LATE

## B. JOWETT, M.A.

MASTER OF BALLIOL COLLEGE
REGIUS PROFESSOR OF GREEK IN THE UNIVERSITY OF OXFORD
DOCTOR IN THEOLOGY OF THE UNIVERSITY OF LEYDEN

AND

## LEWIS CAMPBELL, M.A., LL.D.

HONORARY FELLOW OF BALLIOL COLLEGE
EMERITUS PROFESSOR OF GREEK IN THE UNIVERSITY OF
ST. ANDREWS

*IN THREE VOLUMES*

VOL. II. ESSAYS

Oxford

AT THE CLARENDON PRESS

1894

𝔒𝔵𝔣𝔬𝔯𝔡

PRINTED AT THE CLARENDON PRESS

BY HORACE HART, PRINTER TO THE UNIVERSITY

# CONTENTS OF VOL. II

———••———

# ESSAYS

BY

*THE LATE PROFESSOR JOWETT*

(UNFINISHED)

# ESSAY I

## ON THE TEXT OF GREEK AUTHORS, AND ESPECIALLY OF PLATO

I. THAT Greek MSS. are miswritten and misspelt in various degrees;—that glosses and marginal interpretations have crept into the text;—that particular letters or combinations of letters, as for example Α, Δ, Λ,—Γ, Τ,— Ε, Θ, Ο, C,—are often interchanged;—that contractions are another source of confusion;—that forms of words or usages which were allowed by Thucydides or Plato have sometimes received a more Attic impress from the hand of grammarians, or have decayed insensibly into the forms and usages of the common or Macedonian language;—that the writing is more regular and uniform than can be supposed to have proceeded from authors who lived in the days when grammar was only beginning to be studied;— that the texts of the Classics have passed through changes sometimes in the uncial sometimes in the cursive [or minuscule] stage;—that the copyists of many MSS. like modern editors had a love of emendation, which led them to improve upon the meaning or grammar of their author; —that emendation is often needed, and that many emendations are probably, almost certainly, right;—these general facts would hardly be disputed by any one who has a critical acquaintance with Greek authors.

But such general considerations do not justify the indiscriminate use of conjectural emendation. We have to distinguish the kind of mistake before we can determine whether it can be corrected. That mistakes often happen is a safe text ; the inference which is sometimes drawn that they are liable to happen equally in all authors and in all MSS., and that all therefore afford equal material for the conjectural art, is a very erroneous one. The kind of mistake may also vary from the interchange of Γ and T which is corrected at sight up to a degree of confusion in which grammar and sense are lost in anarchy. And where such mistakes are most numerous and complicated they are generally beyond the reach of human sagacity to amend. Unless new and better MSS. are discovered, the corruption must remain a corruption to the end of time. Nor can the most ingenious conjecture ever attain the certainty of a reading well supported by MS. authority. The verifying faculty is only the knowledge and moderation of the critic, who may indeed have acquired the power of seeing in the dark, or at least of seeing better than others, but who may also have found in lifelong studies only the material of his own self-deception. An art or kind of knowledge which is attractive and at the same time wanting in certain tests of truth is always liable to fall into the hands of projectors and inventors. It may be cultivated by many generations of scholars without their once making the discovery that they have been wasting their lives in a frivolous and unmeaning pursuit. From being subordinate and necessary it may come to be thought the crowning accomplishment of the scholar. But after all, to compare small things with great, ingenious conjectures are only like the hypotheses of physical science in the days when there were no experiments, which, while retaining their attractiveness, diverge further and further from the truth.

A sanguine temperament and sometimes even a good memory flush the mind and interfere with the exercise of the judgement. A little knowledge will furnish objections to an old reading or arguments in support of a new one. The inventor has a natural fondness for his own inventions and is ready to offer his reputation as a guarantee of their truth. He has got into a region in which the common sense of the many is unable to control him, and in which no one can demonstrate that he is only a visionary. And as learning or imitative talent or even genius for scholarship are often unaccompanied by philosophical power, which is the natural corrective of a lively fancy, the sanction of great names has not been wanting to great mistakes. There have been Atticists in modern as well as in ancient times, who have regarded grammar as a science of rules without exceptions, and who have assumed a greater clearness and accuracy than ever existed in the text of ancient authors. Metrical canons which are not universally true have been applied with the rigour and severity of a law of nature. It has been forgotten that there was a transitional age of language in which syntax and prosody had not yet become separate studies, and that in every age the subtlety of language far exceeds the minuteness of grammatical rules. Writers like Sophocles or Thucydides or Plato have been even divested of the peculiarities of their own style, in order to satisfy some more general notion of sense and Greek. Not the value of the correction but the name and reputation of the critic have been regarded. The authority of Bentley, Porson, and Hermann has obtruded on the text of the Classics many unfounded emendations which have been allowed to remain, as a homage to their reputation.

A just estimate of the value of emendations requires a consideration, (1) of the limits of the human faculties in this sort of divination. No definite measure can be given of them ; they must depend on the nature of the materials ; but often the real limits are in inverse proportion to the ingenuity and facility of scholars in making emendations : (2) there must be a consideration of the nature of MSS. In textual as in historical criticism the invention or imagination which has no foundation of facts can only build castles in the air. The emendations which lie on the surface have been generally made by previous editors, while the deeper corruptions are hardly ever remediable. And in proportion to the character of the MS. the necessity or possibility of emendation will greatly vary. No generalities about the frequency of mistakes, or the possibility of glosses, or the probability in favour of the more difficult reading can be set against the readings of MSS., which may be erroneous but cannot be corrected out of nothing. (3) There must be a consideration of authors as well as of MSS. The range of language in some is too wide or irregular or uncertain to admit even of a fair probability in the emendation of them. The Doric or Aeolic dialect is not so well known to us as the Attic; and again, conjectures in prose and verse stand on a different footing. Nor will any one say that he is as certain of the use of language in Pindar and Theocritus as in Sophocles and Euripides, or of the metre in a line of a chorus as of an Iambic or Trochaic verse, or that a fragment is equally within the range of emendation with a passage that has a context. Yet the method of conjecture which was practised by the first editors seems to have continued as a habit of mind among scholars, who do not always remember that the field for new conjectures is ever narrowing, and that the 'woods and pastures new' of fragments, to which they return, are the least likely to afford passages which can be corrected with certainty. Nothing can be more improbable than some of the conjectures of Madvig on Thucydides, when he discards a word because it is not found in later Greek and introduces a new word found in later Greek, but not in Thucydides.

Some idea of the limits of human ingenuity in restoring a text or an inscription, may be formed in this way: let a person try the experiment of emending the text of an English passage previously unknown to him miswritten for the purpose. (You may vary the conditions of prose or metre, or give a fragment without the context, or select from an author whose style is only known in short writings; or take some writing such as an epitaph which has regular lines and set forms of speech; the words too may be wrongly divided or written without stops and without accents or breathings as in the Uncial Greek MSS.) One person is quicker at guessing the riddle than another, but in any case the critic will soon be at fault, for the simple reason that he has no materials for conjecture. No divination or second sight or knowledge of style can supply one-half of a page from the other half, nor restore with certainty a single word or even letter unless absolutely required by the context, that is to say if any other word or letter would equally fit or make sense. The general meaning may in any of these cases be clear or probable; e.g. in the case of a torn letter, or of the Inscription of which Niebuhr attempts a restoration about the burning of the tribunes; but the precise words are really irrecoverable wherever more than one word or letter or combination of words and letters may amend the miswriting or bridge or fill up the vacant space. The problem is not of the nature of the discovery of a cipher, the secret of which is really contained in certain letters or symbols which have been artificially transposed, or of the interpretation of a hieroglyphic, the signs of which are known, although the mode of reading them or the language in which they were written has been lost. The case of an Inscription again is widely different from a MS., because an Inscription is formal and regular and may be compared with other Inscriptions which are sometimes verbatim or literatim the same. Hence a single letter in a particular place may sometimes restore a whole line, but why? because the letter is found in that place in a line which is preserved elsewhere. Nor, again, is the restoration of the text of an author analogous to the restoration of a ruined building or statue, the form or structure of which is simple and uniform, and the lost features of which may be restored from a very few

indications assisted by the analogy of buildings or statues
of the times. Such illustrations are misleading because
they are not *in pari materia,* and when applied to the
restoration of words they tend to obscure the real difficulty
which is the variety and flexibility of language. To take
an example : between two points in a line of Shakespeare
there is a lacuna or erasure or corruption of five letters
which admits of being filled up in twenty or thirty different
ways ; who can decide between them ? A truly Shakespearian word may be found by one of our critics whom we
may suppose to be playing at the game of emendation ; in
referring to the text the expression actually used may turn
out to be less Shakespearian, or more common, or the
reverse ; possibly a word not elsewhere occurring in any
extant play. Two very popular and familiar emendations
of Shakespeare will illustrate the point which I am dis-
cussing :

(1) *Henry V*, act ii, scene 3—

> 'His nose was as sharp as a pen
> On a *table* of green *fields*'   (Ff. ; om. in Qq.) ;

> 'And a' *babbled* of green fields '   (Cj. Theobald) :

or altering the other word,

> 'On a table of green *frieze.*'   (Collier MS.)

A third expedient, adopted by Pope, is to omit the whole
phrase 'And . . . fields,' with the Qq. Several other conjectures by scholars of repute, including Malone, have found
acceptance in their time.

(2) *Macbeth*, act v, scene 3—

> 'My *way* of life
> Is fall'n into the sere and yellow leaf.'

> 'My *May* of life.'   (Cj. Johnson.)

The change is slight and gives an attractive reading while
avoiding an apparent incongruity. But similar incon-
gruities arising from the condensation or crowding together
of imagery abound in the Shakespearian text and are not
always so easily got rid of :—e.g. 'to take arms against
a sea of troubles.'

The critic can only succeed when a particular word is absolutely demanded by the context, or where the error is reducible to some rule. He will more easily restore the terminations of words than their roots; mere misspellings in which the sound remains are found to occasion no difficulty to the practised eye. And much further we cannot go. The instance just given shows how in a very characteristic and remarkable passage it is impossible absolutely to decide about a single letter. Conjectural emendation is a kind of prophecy, and though there is a vast difference between the powers of one man and another while they remain within the legitimate field of knowledge, there is not much difference when they take to foretelling future events.

The argument from English to Greek and Latin scholarship is not really unfair, provided the difference be remembered between a language which has and which has not inflexions; the unfairness, however, is really in favour of English conjectural emendation. The practice of emending classical authors has come down from the revival of literature, and is fostered, at any rate in Englishmen, by the habit of Greek and Latin composition in early life. But every Englishman who applies his mind to the subject is a better judge of English than of Greek verse, for he is better acquainted with his native language than with a dead one. Even Bentley knew more of English than of Greek, and there is no paradox in saying that he was better qualified to edit Milton than to edit Homer—that is to say, not comparatively with others, but absolutely in reference to his own knowledge. In an evil hour he applied to an English poet the method or manner which he had acquired in editing the classics; and the result tends to detect his method and to raise a suspicion of his authority as an editor of the Greek and Latin classics. He finds a great deal of error in Milton; this he supposes to be due to the circumstance that Milton in his blindness dictated to his daughters ; a sort of general consideration introduced into the subject similar to the hypothesis of transposed leaves in Lucretius or Catullus. Bentley's Milton cannot be separated from Bentley's Horace ; the multitude of emendations in the one tends to shake our faith in the multitude of emendations in the other. The many will hardly trust, in what they are unable to understand, a judgement which is so wild and fanciful in what is within their own range. The lesson is instructive, as showing what is indeed sufficiently apparent otherwise, that great powers may often coexist with extravagance and want of common sense.

The English parallel may throw a further light on the problem which has been started. The text of Shakespeare presents many points of similarity with the text of an ancient author. The richness and obscurity of the language, the complexity of the meaning, the variety of readings, and the uncertainty which hangs over their origin, give rise to doubts like those which have tried the text of the classics. A harvest of emendations has sprung up ; Shakespeare has been treated in the same bold style by Warburton as Milton by Bentley. But the ingenuity of critics has not supplied a generally received version ; only in a very few instances have conjectures found their way into the text.

Two other general facts may be adduced which are of weight in estimating the value of emendation in classical authors. 1. First the absence of *emendations* in the New Testament ; there are ' old correctors ' of the Gospels and Epistles, but they are not scholars of the present or last century ; at least the important variations which occur in them are of an earlier date and spring from other causes ; and the few emendations which have been suggested by scholars have not found their way into the text. Lachmann, when he made the attempt in the preface to the second volume of his New Testament, met with very little success. [Of Cobet perhaps the same might have been said.] Nor does Bentley himself indulge in his bold 'meo periculo' style of criticism within the sacred precinct; it is from manuscript not from conjecture that he proposes to restore the text of the New Testament. Yet there are certainly a few passages in the New Testament which have as much apparent difficulty as the corruptions of classical authors. (It is true that in some respects the text of the New Testament is unlike that of other Greek writers, especially in the number of MSS. and versions.) The quotations in other writers are also numerous, but these create the new difficulty of an *embarras de richesses*. The circumstance that critical emendation has not been held a safe or certain path in the most important of all Greek writings is a proof that there is danger and uncertainty in the application of such a method to the text of Greek authors generally.

2. The tendency of criticism has of late years been adverse and not favourable to the use of conjecture. Manuscripts have been collated afresh and more precisely valued, and the result has rarely confirmed the previous conjectures of critics. There is no consensus of great critics in important emendations; those of Meineke and Ahrens are decried by Cobet; Porson has not generally been followed by Hermann in his corrections of the text. The ideas which inspired the last-named critic (Hermann) in his edition of Aeschylus are already out of date and certainly tend to undermine the authority of the great editor in Sophocles and Aristophanes. Madvig, the most prolific inventor of new emendations, who has laid down many sound principles which he fails to observe in practice, remarks that Bentley constantly violated the rules of his art, and that Hermann never had any; he also justly censures Dindorf in Ed. V of the Poetae Scenici for pretending to emend passages without regard to the MSS. Most persons will find that the need of conjecture diminishes as

their familiarity with an author increases; the peculiarities of his style become more apparent to them; they receive on the authority of MSS. expressions which their first thoughts would have set down as destitute of grammar and meaning; and the judgement and industry of Bekker have probably done more for the text of Greek writers than was effected by the vast powers of Bentley.

3. Lastly, some instruction may be gathered from observing the most palpable forms of delusion which prevail among conjectural critics. Their judgement is not equal to their invention; they are often deceived by parallel passages; any special knowledge which they possess of Greek dialects or metres or lexicographers tends unduly to form their opinion. They are apt to introduce a point which is not wanted, or to create a false emphasis, or to impair the due subordination of the word to the sentence or figure of speech. They are hasty in assuming that an author could not have used this or that expression or formation; and they think a regular and perfect phrase or figure or parallel better than an irregular one. They sometimes insist on uniformity of construction where uniformity is not required, or they miss the slight and subtle change from the 'oratio recta' to the 'oratio obliqua,' or conversely. A random statement of a lexicographer or grammarian or other ancient author is sometimes affirmed against the clearest evidence of the manuscript. Their perception of the context is often overpowered by their sense of some anomaly or obscurity. They do not always study an author from himself; the subtleties of which Plato and Sophocles are capable in the use of language or grammar are not made a separate matter of investigation. The transitional periods of grammar and language are confounded by them with those in which the uses of language are fixed. They do not fairly renounce impossible problems, but seem rather to find a stimulus to their imagination in hopeless corruptions of the text. They sometimes restore

an author from himself and argue from the use of a word in one passage to the use of the same word or phrase in another. Their own self-confidence in the most slippery of all arts is a reason why they should suspect themselves, and may well raise a suspicion in the mind of others ; 'meo periculo,' 'away with all this,' 'apage putidissimam interpolationem ;' the disdain of objectors ; the repeated promise to free a beautiful passage from deformities ; the improvements and re-writings of the text ; the 'nihil tam metuens quam ne de se diffidere videretur,' are not indeed inconsistent with a real knowledge and study of Greek, but they are doubtful proofs of the judgement or trustworthiness of the critic. The tendency appears to grow upon them with years ; their last performances are often a caricature of their earlier ones. They speak of an intuition which is peculiar to themselves ; which a person who is not similarly gifted might be more ready to acknowledge, if the intuition of one critic were not sometimes at variance with the intuition of another ; the older editors, as for example Casaubon in Polybius, frequently introduce emendations without distinguishing them from the text of the MS., and many late emendations, as of Hermann in Sophocles, are fast becoming established in the printed books without brackets or other signs of uncertainty. Nor does there seem any reason why the self-confidence of a discoverer should be accepted as a warrant of the truth of a discovery in restoring the text of the classics any more than in science or life.

II. The general purport of what I have been saying is that the more we reflect upon the nature of conjectural emendation of the classics—the more we put it to the test, or try it by the analogy of English—the more we think of the follies into which great scholars have been betrayed by the love of it—the narrower are the limits which we are disposed to assign to it. The nature of the

manuscripts has now to be considered.  At first sight the
accurate preservation or transmission of the words or ideas
of ancient writers during a period of 2000 years might be
deemed impossible.  Yet experience supplies many facts
which make this credible.  The text of the Vedas is
known to have remained unaltered since the fourth century
before Christ.  Unlike the Greek Scholiasts, the Vedic
commentaries of more than 2000 years ago have exactly
the same readings which are found in Vedic MSS. at
the present day.  This is the more remarkable when the
observation is also made that, owing to the material on
which they are written, they must have been frequently
copied : no Sanscrit MSS. have the antiquity of Greek
ones : and more remarkable still when it is considered that
the commentary is purely fanciful and stands in no relation
to the original text.  And there are many Greek MSS.,
such as the Paris A of the Republic of Plato, which are
remarkably good and gain in authority in proportion as
they are better known.  There is no probability therefore
of accuracy or inaccuracy in a Greek MS. prior to an
examination of the contents.  No general assumption that
copyists were ignorant or that 'mistakes often happen'
should be allowed antecedently to influence the mind.

Thus the question which we started returns from very
general considerations to very minute ones.  The greater
part of the science of textual criticism is contained in
the valuation of MSS.  That corruptions, confusion,
glosses, interchanges of letters, emendations of grammarians and copyists are to be found in Greek MSS.
will be readily allowed ; the point at issue is whether
a particular interchange of letters or the insertion of a
gloss or any other special corruption is incidental to the
writing of a certain scribe or of the copy which he used.
An editor may feel disposed to substitute OCIOC for
ΘEIOC ; he has to ask himself the question whether this
particular form of corruption occurs elsewhere in the MS.

Or he may feel a conviction that certain awkwardly introduced words are a gloss ; again, he will have reason to doubt the correctness of his conviction should no similar example of a gloss occur elsewhere in the same MS. Once more, he may feel disposed to adopt the better or easier reading—say of a late manuscript : his hand will be held if he finds that the manuscript which is his authority offers in many other places better and easier readings where other good MSS. are perplexed or obscure. For then the intelligibility of the copy is possibly due to the corrector and not to the original text. The student or editor has to consider not all the possible errors which may be thought likely to occur in Greek MSS., but those which he discovers in the manuscript which he is perusing. There is no error of which some copyists are not capable in times and places when Greek was becoming barbarized ; but the mass of Greek MSS. were written by moderately learned persons who were copying their own language. And the MSS. of the greater writers, with the exception of some passages of Aeschylus and Euripides, are as a fact extremely free from error, and would be thought still more so, if their correctness were measured by the style of the writer and not by an imaginary grammatical standard.

Some application of the doctrine of chances may serve as an illustration of the probabilities of error in MSS. (1) There is obviously a probability that the copyist will fail in difficult passages ; the mind and eye require great discipline before they can write exactly words or forms of words which are unintelligible or unknown or imperfectly known to them. (2) But there is no greater probability that the copyist will err in the violation of a canon of grammar or of prosody, unless indeed in cases where the usage or grammar or metre has changed in later literature, than in any other way. (3) Thus, let us suppose the case of a manuscript which contains in all

a hundred errors or miswritings; and further that no less
than twenty of these are found to consist in omissions of
ἄν, or uses of ἄν with the present indicative, or of τυγχάνω
as a verb of existence, or of οὐ μή with the present or
1st Aor. Act., or of unions of dissimilar tenses, or of words
of doubtful analogy, or of any other violations of supposed
laws of grammar—the question arises whether the proportion of grammatical errors which has been described
is not greater than can be accounted for on any rational
principle. Why should as many as $\frac{20}{100}$ of all the mistakes
which occur be found to affect the rules of grammarians?
Why, for example, should the copyists have been guilty of
forty errors which are violations of the celebrated law of the
Cretic in Tragic Iambic Verse? When it is remembered
that the refusal to admit a spondee which is broken into
two words in the fifth place is a sort of last refinement in
the structure of the verse, the probability appears to be
that such a law would be occasionally broken, rather than
uniformly observed.

There is a further consideration which seems to
strengthen this view of the subject. There are grammatical anomalies which are not found to exist equally in
earlier and later Greek writers. The usages of Demosthenes
are more regular than those of Thucydides or Plato. But
this cannot be attributed to the greater care or skill of
the transcribers; there is no reason why the words of
Demosthenes should have been preserved to us with more
accuracy than those of Plato. The only reason is that
the MSS. exhibit a real difference of usage in earlier and
later writers. Whether in historical or textual criticism,
in the New Testament or in classical authors, those inti-
mations which are opposed to the prevailing use or feeling
of an age witness to their own truth. Many reasons may
be given why the copyist should have altered the forms or
usages of Thucydides into those of his own age; but there
is no reason why he should have returned to older forms;

why for example he should have used εἰ with the subjunctive or omitted ἄν with the optative, except that such
apparent anomalies existed in the original copies. That
the traces of such anomalies in Plato or Thucydides or in
the Greek tragedians are already becoming faint is a fact
which agrees with the contemporary rise and progress
of grammatical studies. The golden age of Attic tragedy
was never completely purged of the remains of Epic
irregularity; that the anomalous uses which are found in
the MSS. retain this character is in some degree a proof
of their genuineness.

Another consideration distinct from the mere correctness
of a manuscript is antiquity. The superiority of the older
MS. is traceable to the circumstance that the copy is not
only nearer to the original but also to the Uncial MS.
A manuscript like Paris A, which is supposed to have been
written in the ninth century, or the Bodleian which bears
the date A.D. 896, retains many Uncial forms, and has
probably been transcribed from an Uncial MS. And the
observation may be worth making that another interval
of equal length would nearly reach back to the autograph
of Plato. Many chances of error are thus excluded. The
size of the character and the comparative absence of contractions prevents the letters from being minced into an
illegible scrawl. On the other hand the indications which
are afforded of the divisions of words by breathings and
accents or of sentences by stops are generally wanting in
the Uncial MSS. Nor in such matters can MSS. be held
to be of any authority. It is unfortunate also that in
minute questions of orthography an appeal has ever been
made to them. For such questions (1) are of little importance; the correct writing of ἐπεπόνθη or of κᾆτα adds
nothing to our appreciation of Greek authors and scarcely
anything to philology; (2) they can seldom be determined
precisely; the MSS. are constantly at variance with
one another and with the precepts of the grammarians;

(3) uniformity and etymology are better principles of spelling than are supplied either by the MSS. or by the Atticist grammarians; (4) there is no reason to suppose that the classical authors of an earlier period could have known or conformed to exact rules of orthography. Such inquiries have certainly been carried far enough and need no longer be suffered to detain us from more important subjects. They would be thought ridiculous if applied to the printed text of English authors of two or three centuries ago.

Besides the estimate of a particular manuscript as distinct from manuscripts in general, there remains a further estimate to be formed of the value of manuscript authority in a particular passage or word. There are peculiar causes which may lead to error in certain places; an entanglement in the meaning of a passage will often confuse the copyist's head or hand; he will be apt either to miswrite or amend the words at which he stumbles; and as common words are often substituted for uncommon ones, common forms will also take the place of uncommon or curious ones. Similar letters at the end of one word and the beginning of another; repetitions of syllables; similar beginnings in two successive sentences, are also a frequent cause of error or omission; the omission of a word is far more usual than the insertion of one. The omission of a word may often lead to the insertion of the same word in another order or in a clause which has a common government. Again, words written at the side sometimes find their way into the text, or two passages which are really similar are absolutely identified. (Of this many examples occur in the Gospels.) Among various readings that one is preferable of which the origin may be explained on some one of these principles or which seems to be the centre or kernel of the rest. Above all the similarities of certain Greek letters both in the Uncial and the Cursive hand render particular words much more liable than others to be misspelt; which first misspelling by rendering the passage unintelligible naturally introduces some further error. Two such lists, one of Uncial, the other of Cursive letters, should be present to the student's eye; the Uncial letters ΑΔΛ; ΓΤ; ЄΘΟϹ; ΗΝ; ΤΙ, Π, ΙΓΤ; Κ, ΙΣ; ΛΛ, ΑΛ, ΛΑ; ΝΙ, Μ; ΤΤ, ΙΤ, ΤΙ, ΙΓ; ΨΤ;—the Cursive letters which offer a second chance of error being λ, μ, ν; (β) υκ; ψ φ; α, ευ; τ ε. The use of Cursive [minuscule] letters together with Uncial letters is a stage of writing which must also be considered. A further source of error is the habit of contracting certain words both in Uncial and Cursive writing ΘΣ, ΠΡ, ΠΡΟΣ, ΑΝΩ, ΚΣ, ΙΗΛ, ΟΥΝΩ (θεός, πατήρ, πατρός, ἀνθρώπῳ, κύριος, Ἰσραήλ, οὐρανῷ), and the abbreviation of terminations.

The famous rule 'potior lectio difficilior,' seems to require some limitation. For there is plainly a degree of difficulty or obscurity which may render the acceptance of a reading improbable; nonsense which is just construable is not to be regarded as preferable to sense when offered by a MS. Some correction or alteration must be made in the rule. (1) First of all, not the more difficult reading is to be preferred, but the more remote one or the one least likely to have been invented. (2) But the question which is the more difficult reading can never be confined to this one point; repetitions of letters or syllables may tend to substitute the more remote or difficult reading for the simpler one. (3) The rule presupposes a certain degree of knowledge and intelligence in the copyist who makes the substitution, which does not always exist. (4) The meaning and agreement with the context or style of the author cannot be left out of sight in the comparative estimate of MSS.; nor lastly the character of the MS. which in some cases may be discovered to be valueless by the uniform adoption or insertion of easier readings. (5) A large allowance must be made for accident; the greater number of mistakes do not arise from the principle of the adoption of the easier reading but on no principle at all. This famous rule seems to be chiefly suggestive and certainly cannot be allowed to supersede in particular passages the estimate of the value of MSS. taken as a whole. The canon of the more difficult reading really points to one element among many in the consideration of the text. It is not enough to say, 'this is the more difficult reading and therefore the true one.' But 'this is the more difficult reading, which at the same time makes good sense and is in harmony with the general style.'

Lastly—(a) the Scholia, (β) quotations in other Greek authors, especially lexicographers and grammarians, (γ) Latin versions, may be reckoned among the occasional subsidia.

(a) The Scholia may be regarded as a witness to the genuineness of the text of Greek authors ; also as a living link with the past ; moreover in a few passages they have preserved a reading which is lost in the MSS. ; their language has also been tortured into the support of conjectural emendations, and the occurrence of a word in the explanation of the Scholiast has been an argument for the introduction of it into the text. It need scarcely be remarked that they are of every degree of antiquity and value and embrace observations of the most widely different kinds, learned and puerile, ethical and grammatical, according to the temper of the author. The value of each Scholiast, like that of each MS., must of course be judged alone, remembering, as is obvious in the Scholiasts on Homer, that he may often repeat or preserve the opinions of older or wiser writers than himself. Many of them, like the Scholiasts on Thucydides or on Aristotle, while deficient in grammatical knowledge and falling according to our standard into remarkable grammatical blunders, have a curious dialectical insight into the meaning of passages ; they are not unfrequently chargeable with the objection 'Too much logic,' or illogical logic. That with all Greek literature lying open before them, themselves the students

of an art which, commencing with the Sophists and Alexandrian grammarians, lived and flourished for above 1500
years, they should have added so little to our knowledge
either of the classics or of language generally, is a valuable
warning of the tendency of such studies when pursued in
a false and narrow spirit by those ὅσοι μὴ ἔχουσι φάρμακον
τὸ εἰδέναι αὐτὰ οἷά ἐστι. A labour which is wholly dispro-
portioned to the result is apt to infect the judgement and
to pervert the wider comparison of the other branches of
knowledge which is the safeguard against the errors of
exclusive study. A man will hardly be persuaded to form
a humble or uncertain estimate of the labour of many years
of his life. Nor can any mere servile and unreflecting toil
add much even to the stores of learning. No man who is
a mere scholar can ever be a great scholar, because scholarship is not separable from other branches of knowledge,
e.g. from history and philosophy. The school which is
represented by Niebuhr and K. O. Müller in Germany
were quite right in regarding antiquity as a whole; their
error lay not there, but in the introduction of theories and
conjectures in the place of facts and in not considering
the nature of evidence.

(β) Quotations in old Greek writers can only be used
with great hesitation as a means of correcting the text of
an author. The pre-Alexandrian readings of Homer cannot with any certainty be restored from Plato or Aristotle.
Quotations, in the strict sense of the term, are frequently
altered to suit the context or structure of the sentence;
moreover they often lose or change a word owing to a lapse
of memory in the author who cites them. The citations
of lexicographers, again, unless strongly supported by
internal reasons, are rarely to be set against the evidence
of the MSS. And although in the days of Suidas the
familiar knowledge of Greek literature was beginning to be
narrowed within the range of authors which have been preserved to us (any one who will be at the pains of counting

will find that the proportion of passages in Suidas which are from extant works or parts of works far exceeds the proportion which these works bear to the mass of Greek literature), yet the materials which were used by them were very large and the difficulty of accuracy proportionably increased.    Nor can the testimony of grammarians about the uses of forms or words in particular authors be safely trusted when opposed to the evidence of the MSS., because (1) they have probably attempted to impress an Attic character on earlier writers; or (2) they may have drawn their precepts from copies in which the original forms had been altered.

III.    One more general head remains to be considered; this is the different character of different authors or writings, under which the principal points for consideration seem to be the following :—First, the different ages of authors and our knowledge of contemporary literature.    No one, for example, would attempt to restore the poems of Homer to the earliest or original form or indeed to any other but that of the Alexandrian period.    Though there may be reason to think that the change which they have undergone is not great, there are no materials worth speaking of which would enable us to fix the text of the Iliad and Odyssey which was present to the eyes of Herodotus or of Plato. No critical ingenuity can penetrate the grammatical covering which the Alexandrian critics have interposed around them or distinguish the original from the restored forms of words.    Again, of Attic literature alone there were at least three periods; *first*, the antegrammatical or transitional, which includes Aeschylus and Sophocles, and in Attic prose may be admitted to descend as low as Plato.    *Secondly*, the age of orators, in which the language attained the perfection of grammatical and rhetorical accuracy.    *Thirdly*, the age of the Atticizers, who have an affectation of purism, and mix up with the imitation of an earlier age the uses and

forms of their own. The text of each of these classes of
authors has some peculiar features. The grammar in the
first period is less reducible to rule and the use of words
more audacious and inventive than in that of the second ;
there is more uncertainty in limiting the freedom of language ; the forms and constructions of the old Epic poetry
are not altogether banished from the tragedians ; in Thucydides, again, is felt the oppression of an age which is
beginning to philosophize and sometimes loses hold of
grammar in the attempt to arrange multifarious relations
of thought. The Tragic dialect is tinged by Homericism,
and the influence of Attic verse has not yet completely
harmonized the language of prose. These causes interfere
with the attainment of that perfect type of Attic regularity
which the grammarians of later ages found or made and
sought to impose upon earlier ones. And the greater the
liberty the greater also the difficulty not only of fixing the
limit of usage but of restoring by conjecture what has
become corrupted. The second may be regarded as the
normal period of Greek grammar. (2) These differences
of ages or periods of literature run into other differences of
individual style or character. One measure of language
must be applied to Aeschylus or Pindar ; another to
Sophocles ; a third to Euripides — one to Thucydides,
another to Xenophon ; one to narrative writings, another
to speeches or philosophical reflections. It is not by
a general knowledge of Greek, for example, that an idea
can be formed of how a particular author would have
written in certain passages, as far as such an idea can be
formed at all, but from the attentive study of the usages
of individual authors. The abruptness of Aeschylus, the
fanciful and tortuous associations and order of words in
Pindar, the novelties, subtleties, experiments, refinements
of Sophocles, the freedom in the use of cases and the substitution of a logical for a grammatical connexion which
characterizes the language of the two first extant tragedians

as well as of Thucydides, could not have been anticipated
from any general knowledge of the principles of Greek
grammar.   Each writer is characteristic in some degree in
his grammar as well as in his style.   The uses of grammar
like the meaning of words are (1) chronological in some
degree and require to be considered in chronological order ;
(2) they are individual and vary (though in a less degree)
with the character and subject matter of an author.   And
these considerations tend to impose a check on those who
are ready to maintain with authority what an author may
or may not have written.

Peculiarities of dialect and metre remain to be briefly
considered.   As to the first (1) we obviously possess no
means of determining the forms or uses of the Doric and
Aeolic with the precision of the Attic ; the remains of their
literature are small and the notices of the grammarians
comparatively unfrequent.   (2) It is difficult to decide the
limits of that common Doric dialect which the Tragic
writers retained in their choruses, and which in a still more
Doricized form is the language of Pindar.   (3) The dialects
themselves were never subjected to the influence of grammarians ; nor equally with the Attic to the influence of
writing.   (4) The Tragic dialect, again, always retained
some degree of metrical licence and also of Epic usage,
which are seen in the double forms—μόνος, μοῦνος: κεῖνος,
ἐκεῖνος, &c., and in the occasional omission of the augment.
(5) General distinctions between the earlier and later Attic
forms cannot be always determined with certainty on the
debateable ground of Plato and Aristophanes.   But the
general rule may be laid down that, e.g. ἀπαλλαχθείς and
not ἀπαλλαγείς would be commonly found in writers before
400 B.C.   (6) That any distinction has been preserved is
a testimony to the incorruptness of the MSS., which indeed
contrasts with the changes in English books: no reprint of an
English book of three centuries since, if not a professed fac-
simile, would retain the antiquated spelling of the original.

The other question of the extent of metrical licence has also an important bearing on the doctrine of emendation. Metre is a help to the emender's art, and whatever may be the uncertainty of emendations in metre it is less than of emendations in prose. For one datum which the metre gives is wanting in prose. Still the metre also introduces a new element of difficulty. For supposing the laws of the metre to be known the language must conform to those laws ; and what are the laws of metre must be gathered partly from the writings of metricians and grammarians, partly from an induction of the facts. This subject may be divided for the sake of convenience into two heads : (1) the more exact metres of the dialogue, (2) the laxer metres of the choruses. It is remarkable that great precision has been attained in the conventional quantity of words and that in either kind of metre there is rarely a suspicion of difference or error.

1. The metres of the dialogue have general and inviolate rules about the admissibility of feet; they have also precepts which relate to the divisions and composition of feet. Whether these latter are of the same inviolable nature as the former is doubtful ; they seem to be not so much metrical canons as unconscious refinements of the ear. The fact that some of them, as for example the rule that trisyllabic feet shall be included in single words, do not apply equally to all the tragedians, tends to show that they are not matters of rule but of ear. In the latter case they would be general rather than universal, and the lines which do not conform to them would not therefore be held to be corrupt. The probability of such rules being universal evidently depends partly on the nature of the rule, chiefly on the number of exceptions. The law of the Cretic, which has been already mentioned, may be cited as an example of a rule with several exceptions, while the rarity of the Anapaest in the third place of the Tragic Iambic would probably justify the inference that the

exception is only a corruption of the text. Again, is it not probable that some syllables may have had common or different quantities which have generally been held to be of a fixed or uniform one; if words such as φάρη, ὑμῖν and ἡμῖν are admitted to have had two quantities, may not νεαρός also have been common or uncertain? Such an inference seems a fair one where the exceptional quantity is strongly supported by the MSS. even in a single passage. It agrees generally with the fact that in the termination -ινος there are two quantities; we say χειμερῖνός, but also ὀρθρῖνός and ὀπωρῖνός.

2. The choruses of the Greek plays have a rhythmical rather than a metrical character; that is to say, the metre is hardly enough defined to be distinguishable from rhythm. Many of the metres used in them admit of such numerous exchanges of feet, and the transitions from one rhythm to another are so frequent, that there would generally be great uncertainty as to the corruption of a line in which the metre alone appeared to be at fault. There is more guidance however afforded by the correspondence of strophe and antistrophe. Still doubts will remain; (*a*) are the quantities of words absolutely certain? (*b*) has the beat of the verse no effect on them? (*c*) is no Homeric licence ever admitted? (*d*) are the corresponding feet exactly known? Such doubts are only suggested here; the tendency of them is to abate our confidence in the discovery of corruptions in the choruses of which the metre is taken as the proof.

In conclusion, let me observe that though I have endeavoured to show how small the power of divination is, and though I deeply lament that the lives of so many ingenious men should be thrown away in such a fruitless task, and though I think that the supposed corruptions of the text have been greatly exaggerated through this very 'cacoethes' or 'lues emendandi,' yet I am far from maintaining that the Greek classics are in general free from corruption or that there can never be any place for conjectural criticism. But a passage must be proved corrupt first before it is made the subject of the emender's art : and the emendation must be the least possible (for no other has any chance of being true); it must follow the letters of the MSS., it must accord with the style and language of the author.

IV. The principles or suggestions offered for consideration in the preceding pages may now be illustrated from Plato. The text of the Republic will be conveniently treated under three heads, (1) the MSS. and recensions of the text, (2) the anomalies of language which affect the text, (3) the more remarkable conjectures, an examination of which will tend to illustrate the general principles which have been followed in this edition.

Of all the MSS. of Plato first and without a second is the Codex Parisiensis A. It contains the Cleitophon, Republic, Timaeus, Critias, Minos, Laws, Epinomis, Definitions, Epistles, the Dialogues 'De Justo' and 'De Virtute,' Demodocus, Sisyphus, Halcyon, Eryxias, Axiochus. It is written on parchment in double columns, the scholia being in small capitals, and has the annotation written at the end, ὠρθώθη ἡ βίβλος αὕτη ὑπὸ Κωνσταντίνου μητροπολίτου ἱεραπόλεως τοῦ καὶ ὠνησαμένου. 'This book was corrected by Constantine, metropolitan of Hierapolis, who was the purchaser of the book.' About the precise antiquity of the MS. there is some uncertainty; Bekker who is the highest authority on such subjects places the date as early as the ninth century on the ground that the writing is more ancient than that of the Bodleian or Clarkian MS. which has the date 896 written at the end. (In the latter which contains nearly every other dialogue the Republic and the Laws are wanting.) The Codex A is certainly one of the noblest of extant MSS. And considering the fate of other Greek authors we may congratulate ourselves on having the whole writings of Plato preserved in two MSS. of the ninth century.

The authority of Paris A may be justly said to balance that of all other MSS. put together. The successive editors of Plato—Stallbaum, Schneider, Baiter, Hermann, seem to estimate more and more highly the value of this MS. The last-named scholar has made a closer approximation to its text than was ever exhibited before. Nor is this high estimate exaggerated, as may indeed be shown by a simple test. Any one who will take the very slight trouble of comparing the recension of the First Book at the beginning of the Zurich edition with the text will find that after making allowance for differences of orthography the real substantial errors are exceedingly few, being in all not more than two or three. There is considerable variation in minute points, as for example (1) the first person of the pluperfect tense which has been Atticized in the first hand of the MS. ($\dot{\epsilon}\omega\rho\acute{a}\kappa\eta$, $\dot{\epsilon}\pi\epsilon\pi\acute{o}\nu\theta\eta$ A$^1$, $\dot{\epsilon}\omega\rho\acute{a}\kappa\epsilon\iota\nu$, $\dot{\epsilon}\pi\epsilon$-$\pi\acute{o}\nu\theta\epsilon\iota\nu$ A$^2$); (2) also in the forms of some substantives, e.g. $\dot{\omega}\phi\epsilon\lambda\acute{\iota}a$, $\epsilon\dot{v}\eta\theta\acute{\iota}a$: (3) in the use of the $\iota$ subscript which is most frequently adscribed; (4) most of all in the omission or addition of the aspirate, causing a frequent confusion of $a\dot{v}\tau\acute{o}s$ and $a\dot{v}\tau\acute{o}s$, &c.: and (5) not unfrequent confusion in accentuation. Whether $\ddot{o}\tau a\nu$ $\delta\acute{\epsilon}o\iota$ $\kappa.\tau.\lambda.$ 333 D, which is found in several other MSS., including Vat. $\Theta$, or $o\dot{v}\kappa o\hat{v}\nu$ followed by an optative without $\ddot{a}\nu$ (ib. E) be a mistake is uncertain. But after making these deductions there remain only about three passages which must be admitted to be substantial errors; these are 327 A $\ddot{\eta}\tau\tau\omega\nu$ for $\ddot{\eta}\tau\tau o\nu$, $o\ddot{\iota}o\nu$ $\tau\epsilon$ $\sigma\acute{v}$ probably for $o\ddot{\iota}o\nu$ $\gamma\epsilon$ $\sigma\acute{v}$ 336 E; the interchange between T and $\Gamma$ being of the commonest of MS. errors, and probably $\dot{a}\pi o\kappa\rho\acute{\iota}\nu\epsilon\sigma\theta a\iota$ for $\dot{a}\pi o\kappa\rho\iota\nu\epsilon\hat{\iota}\sigma\theta a\iota$ 337 C. (These last variations are cited on the authority of the Zurich edition; none of them are to be discovered in the collation of the Paris MS. made by Dübner for Didot, the various readings in which are almost confined to matters of orthography.)

On the other hand there are several probable corrections of the received text, e.g. ἐλλείπεται for ἐν λείπεται 327 C, probably the two examples of the omission of ἄν noted above (333 D, E), the explanatory ἀσύνδετον in which γάρ is wanting (ἐπειδὰν αἱ ἐπιθυμίαι for ἐπειδὰν γὰρ αἱ ἐπιθυμίαι 329 C), the substitution of πιαίνειν for ποιμαίνειν, all of which are supported by the canon of the more difficult reading.

Nearly the same result follows from the examination of the Second Book, in which several erasures and a somewhat greater number of errors are found, e. g. there are six omissions: (1) ἀδικία δ' ἐπαινεῖται 358 A, (2) the words αὖ μέγα δύνανται after αἱ τελεταί 366 A, (3) εἶναι after ὅσοι φατέ 366 E, (4) ἀλλὰ τὸ δοκεῖν 367 C which is inserted in the margin, (5) the words παρὰ τὸν βασιλέα 360 B which are also found in the margin, (6) καὶ τὴν ποικιλίαν 373 A. The number of these omissions tends to weaken the authority of the MS. in other cases of omission ; number (4) which is an antithetical clause and is added at the side also throws light on the character of the omission in number (1). The tendency to omission and especially to the omission of parallel clauses or words may be observed in several other passages of the MS., e. g 400 D τὸ εὐάρμοστον [καὶ ἀνάρμοστον]. Again there are errors of orthography, ὠφελίας for ὠφελείας 368 C, λύσειοι for λύσιοι 366 B, ἀμφωτέρων for ἀμφοτέρων 379 D, ἰαμβία 380 A, interchanges of υ for υ and of breathings and accents; also one or two of a more serious character, e.g. τῷ δικαίῳ for τῷ ἀδίκῳ 363 A, τῷ Γύγῃ τοῦ Λυδοῦ 359 D where the error of the other MSS. is retained. On the other hand it is possible that in ἐὰν καὶ μὴ δοκῶ 365 B, ἀποσχοίμην 367 D, this MS. has preserved the true reading.

[Professor Jowett's MS. here ends abruptly : for further observations on the text of the Republic see Essay II, pp. 67 ff. of this volume.]

# ESSAY II

## *THE KINGDOM OF EVIL*

### Book I. 352 D.

οἵ γε παμπόνηροι . . . πράττειν ἀδύνατοι. Plato argues
that there is no such thing as a kingdom of evil (compare
Matthew xii. 25, 26—'Every kingdom divided against itself
is brought to desolation; and every city or house divided
against itself shall not stand; and if Satan cast out Satan,
he is divided against himself: how shall then his kingdom
stand?'); also that there is no unmixed evil in the individual. Cp. Lys. 220 E, 221 A πότερον, . . . ἐὰν τὸ κακὸν ἀπόληται,
οὐδὲ πεινῆν ἔτι ἔσται οὐδὲ διψῆν, οὐδὲ ἄλλο οὐδὲν τῶν τοιούτων ;
. . . ἢ γελοῖον τὸ ἐρώτημα, ὅ τί ποτ' ἔσται τότε ἢ μὴ ἔσται ;
τίς γὰρ οἶδεν ; which raises the question of the connexion
of evil with the desires; and Crat. 403 E, where (as in the
Timaeus) evil is attributed to the accidents of the bodily
state.   Evil is elsewhere referred to necessities in the
nature of things (Theaet. 176 A), or to pre-existing
elements in the world (Polit. 273 C), or to the necessary
imperfection of secondary causes (Tim. 48 A), or to the
bodily constitution (Tim. 86).   The contradictory nature
of evil is again discussed in the Laws (i. 626 C, D), where
the argument that war is the natural condition of states
is carried back to individuals.   The connexion of virtue
and power is also observed by Aristotle, Pol. i. 6, § 3
τρόπον τινὰ ἀρετὴ τυγχάνουσα χορηγίας καὶ βιάζεσθαι δύναται
μάλιστα, καὶ ἔστιν ἀεὶ τὸ κρατοῦν ἐν ὑπεροχῇ ἀγαθοῦ τινός, ὥστε
δοκεῖν μὴ ἄνευ ἀρετῆς εἶναι τὴν βίαν, ἀλλὰ περὶ τοῦ δικαίου μόνον
εἶναι τὴν ἀμφισβήτησιν.   On the other hand in Rep. X. 610 E

evil is described as having an agonized and intensified existence—τὸν δ' ἔχοντα καὶ μάλα ζωτικὸν παρέχουσαν.

It has been asked in later ages whether evil is negative or positive, to be represented under the figure of decomposition or of death. It may be replied : (1) that there is no ideal of evil; Milton or Goethe give consistency to their creations by the addition of intellect and of will; (2) all evil has some admixture of good. But again, no limit can be assigned either to the persistency, or to the consequences of evil. The difficulty of this, as of many other questions, seems to arise out of the attempt to realize in the abstract a state or nature which is essentially concrete. Cp. note on IV. 444 B.

# ESSAY III

## *THE STATE AND THE INDIVIDUAL*

Book II. 369 a ff.

THE favourite analogy of the state and the individual is a figure of speech which lends a sort of elevation and interest to politics, and yet is only true partially and has frequently led to practical errors. Man is a microcosm, and 'the world is set in his heart,' and new aspects of either arise when they are reflected on each other. But the life and organization of the state are far inferior to the life and organization of the individual, nor do the virtues or parts of the one answer, as Plato supposes, to the virtues or parts of the other. The nation never attains the unity of a person and has therefore a lower degree of freedom and responsibility; a national will means the excess of the majority of wills, which often balance each other or are lost in circumstances, and thus pass into a sort of imperfect necessity. The famous expression of a 'national' or 'state' conscience is poetical and figurative only, for that consciousness which is essential to the idea of conscience in the individual becomes in a state only the aggregation of many individual consciousnesses which from sympathy or some action or tendency of circumstances are led to form the same reflection on themselves. And in judging collectively, the sense of right and wrong is apt to be blunted. When, again, a nation is said to 'rise as one man,' the very form of expression seems to imply that this unanimity is an exceptional condition, and that a nearer approach is

made to the unity of an individual at one time than at
another. On the other hand the nation lasts while 'the
individuals wither' : it gathers up and retains many more
elements than are found in any single person : it has no
natural term, and may have an endless growth. The
citizen of a state presupposes the state into which he is
born, the laws and institutions of which are the outward
barriers and limits within which his life is set, being a more
durable structure than that which he himself is. Lastly,
the sphere of the state is co-extensive with law and politics,
the sphere of the individual with morals and religion. The
exceptions to this opposition arise where individuals act
for nations, or where in the leaders of states the personal
character takes the place of the official and representative,
or where, as in the case of a treaty or agreement, there is
a definite act binding on nations just as much as on individuals. Nor must nations any more than individuals be
deemed incapable of acting from any higher motive than
interest ; nor are they mere organizations of individuals,
but they have also a national life.

Grave errors may arise in practice from the neglect of
these simple considerations. When politics are confounded
with ethics or the state identified with the individual, the
conditions of human society are ignored ; legislation has
a false aim : human law is superseded by a fiction of divine
law : there are aspirations after the ideal which degenerate
into feebleness and tyranny. The Utopias of ancient times
often fall into the theoretical errors of which the confusions
of spiritual and temporal, or erroneous theories of punishment in modern times are practical illustrations.

That the state was not a larger family or magnified
individual was clearly understood by Aristotle (Pol. i. 1).
In the political ideal of Plato the state and the individual
are in closer union (ἐγγύτερον ἀνδρὸς ἑνός) than in fact and
experience. In the same way, the lines which distinguish
the Church and the members of the Church fade away in

such expressions as—' The kingdom of Heaven is within you.'

The idea of the individual as distinct from the state or family is not one of the earliest but one of the latest of human conceptions, not having yet emerged in ancient times from the unity of the family which expanded into the state.

# ESSAY IV

## *VERACITY*

### Book II. 382 A ff.

Plato allows that a doctrine of economy or accommo-
dation may be necessary for men in certain cases, but not
for the Gods ; the accommodations attributed to the Gods
are really erroneous conceptions of the divine nature.
Falsehood is permitted by him : (1) in dealing with
enemies or madmen (I. 331 C); (2) for educational purposes,
provided the falsehood be a moral one (II. 377 A ff.) ;
(3) as an engine of state, to be used by the rulers only
(III. 389 B, 414 B).

Moral philosophy in modern times has a stricter rule.
Every one would agree that some points of divinity or
philosophy are liable to be imperfectly apprehended; also
that modes of thought vary in different ages and countries,
or in different individuals, according to their education and
natural powers. In the communication of one age with
another, some degree of error or inaccuracy thus arises
naturally. Nor would any one deny that instruction is
often best conveyed through fiction, or that the rule of
truth and falsehood is in a measure determined by the
relations of men to one another, or that received opinions,
however erroneous, cannot always be rudely and immediately set aside. But we refuse to admit that any man
under any circumstances may tell or preach a lie ; or that
the rulers of states and churches are privileged to introduce
artificial economies. Extreme cases, which are sometimes
put, of justifiable, or more strictly speaking, excusable
falsehood, may be fairly said to prove the rule.

# ESSAYS

BY

*PROFESSOR CAMPBELL*

# ESSAY I

## ON THE STRUCTURE OF PLATO'S REPUBLIC AND ITS RELATION TO OTHER DIALOGUES.

————•♦•————

### I

#### On the Composition of the Republic.

THE Republic parts naturally into five sections, which § 1. are marked off with elaborate forms of transition by Plato himself.

1. Book I, in which the question concerning Justice is propounded, and the views of Socrates and of the Sophist are dramatically set in opposition.

2. Books II, III, IV, in which the question is put more seriously, and partly answered through the institution of the ideal State.

3. Books V, VI, VII, developing further the ideal of the State, and expounding (*a*) the community of goods and of marriage, (*b*) the supremacy of the philosopher, (*c*) the education of the philosopher-kings, reaching up to Dialectic and to the Idea of Good.

4. Books VIII and IX, supplying the reverse picture of the declension of States and Individuals from ideal perfectness, and concluding with the ideal of evil, as embodied in the tyrannical man. This is forcibly contrasted with the kingdom of Righteousness, which each man may seek to establish 'within his own clear breast.'

5. The tenth Book forms an appendix or conclusion to the whole work, in which (1) ·the exclusion of the poets from education is reaffirmed, and (2) (as in the Gorgias) the rewards of another life are added to the blessedness of the just and misery of the wicked in this life as already set forth.

§ 2.    Parts 1 and 2 are intimately connected.

1. (B. I.)  In conversation with Cephalus, who bases happiness on a moral and religious ground, so implying that the just are happy, Socrates raises the question 'What is Justice?'  Polemarchus vainly tries to answer him. Thrasymachus interposes, and in arguing with him Socrates employs, (1) the analogy of the arts, especially of medicine and navigation; (2) the comparison of the Ruler to a Shepherd, suggested by an objection of Thrasymachus; (3) the notion of ξυμφέρον, utility or expediency, which recurs afterwards in various forms and applications; while (4) the extreme opposition of the tyrant to the true ruler is ironically hinted by anticipation.

2. (Bb. II, III.)  The remarks of Glaucon and Adeimantus having shown that the question is not thus disposed of, Socrates undertakes to give his own account of the matter. Observing that the nature of Justice is first to be studied in the large letters, for this purpose he 'creates the State.' The principle of 'one member one function' is first laid down, then the state of primitive simplicity imagined,—then the introduction of luxury occasions the necessity for soldiers, who in accordance with the first principle must be trained and organized as a standing army.  But the protectors of the State must not only be 'good haters' but true friends, and they must be chosen and educated accordingly.

The rules for their education, (1) in liberal culture, (2) in bodily exercises, are clearly set forth, with many pregnant observations scattered by the way; then the rulers are provisionally appointed, and the army is led out to its modest quarters, the whole people having been first imbued with the Phoenician 'lie.'

(B. IV.)  The objection of Adeimantus, that the highest class is not thus made the happiest, leads to reflexions on the desirableness of unity, the dangers of wealth and poverty, and other incidental topics, concluding with the establishment of religion on a national basis. Thus the still impending task of defining Justice is further delayed. But the time for it arrives at last, and amidst various references to the opening of the inquiry, Socrates calls for a 'light.' He then suggests the method of residues, by which in the discussion of the four cardinal virtues Justice is held in reserve. When her turn arrives, the importance of the critical moment is marked by the new image of huntsmen clustering round an impenetrable thicket. And when Justice in the State has been discovered, much yet remains to do. The analogy of State and Individual (the 'large and small letters') must be verified by proving that the Soul has parts corresponding to the classes in the State. This psychological question cannot really be determined without a higher method, i.e. without going beyond psychology to find the metaphysical basis of its distinctions ; but it is for the present settled provisionally in the affirmative, and the definition of Justice in the individual as the harmonious action of the three parts of the soul, is at length obtained.

The continuity of the work so far is obvious, and is § 3. assisted by many minute links, such as (1) the question of the profitableness of justice ; (2) the allusion, in II. 357, to the description of medicine as a mode of money-making in I. 342, 346; (3) the power of doing good to friends (I. 334) and of pleasing the gods (I. 331) is claimed for Injustice in II. 362, 366 ; (4) Justice, according to Polemarchus (I. 333), is ἐν τῷ κοινωνεῖν,—this prepares for the suggestion (II. 372 A) that it is ἐν χρείᾳ τινὶ τῇ πρὸς ἀλλήλους ; (5) the noble 'lie' in III. 414 B recalls the ἐν τοῖς λόγοις ψεῦδος of II. 382, III. 389.

The end of the dialogue (Bb. VIII–X) is also subtly joined to the beginning. The tyrant, set up by Thrasymachus as having the noblest life (B. I), is cast down to the depths of infamy in B. IX, and receives his final sentence in B. X, where the picture of the world below confirms the remark of

Cephalus in I. 330 D.    The question of the profitableness of injustice, whether it escape or not the observation of gods and men, which had already become ridiculous at IV. 445 A, is finally dismissed in B. IX.    B. VIII resumes the conclusion of B. IV.    The avoidance of poverty and wealth, hinted in B. II. 372, and repeated in IV. 421, is elaborately enforced in Bb. VIII–IX ; where also the division of the soul into νοῦς, θυμός, ἐπιθυμία, demonstrated in B. IV, is further developed and illustrated.    This division is once more referred to in B. X, *sub init.*, although not without a reservation in favour of the unity of the soul (X. 612).

§ 4.    But many students of Plato[1] have been struck by the fact that the central and cardinal portion of the Republic— the third act in which the drama culminates—takes the form of a digression,—an ἐκτροπή, as Plato himself describes it[2].    And some have not been contented with the obvious solution that this break in the conversation belongs to Plato's concealment of his art, like the palinode of the Phaedrus, the hiccough of Aristophanes in the Symposium, the casual inroad of Alcibiades in the same dialogue, the objections of Simmias and Cebes in the Phaedo, and other similar expedients.    They have proceeded to remark on the absence of allusions to V–VII in the concluding books, VIII–X, as compared with the frequent and distinct allusions in VIII–X to I–IV, and have further observed that the references to I–IV which occur in the central portion, V–VII, have more the appearance of deliberate quotation than of the subtle continuity which binds together I–IV, or VIII–X, when taken separately.    A. Krohn[3] also dwells on the difference of tone and of philosophical content between V–VII on the one hand and I–IV and VIII–X on the other.

According to Krohn, in those which he regards as the earlier books, I–IV, VIII–X, the work of Socrates, as described in Xenophon's Memorabilia, is continued on the same lines ; the method is that of empirical psychology ; the ruling

---

[1] See K. F. Hermann, *Geschichte und System der platonischen Philosophie,* 1839, pp. 536 foll.

[2] viii. 543 πόθεν δεῦρο ἐξετραπόμεθα ;         [3] *Der Platonische Staat,* &c.

conception is that of φύσις, i.e. of Becoming; the word εἶδος is frequently employed, but (1) is applied only to the virtues and the parts of the Soul, and (2) these εἴδη are not transcendent, but 'innocently immanent [1],' and are merely modes of γένεσις. These books exhibit Plato in the light of a genial optimist, who thinks by a simple effort of construction to purify nature.

But in v–vii Plato is carried off from the conception of Nature, which still rules in the early part of B. v, into a transcendental, metaphysical region. This purely intellectual act begins with contemplating the ideas of Justice, Beauty, Goodness, &c., not now dynamically but statically, and distinguishing in each kind between the one and the many. Thus a step is made beyond the old Socratic opposition of knowledge and ignorance, and room is gained for δόξα, Opinion, as an intermediate faculty. From this point onward Plato advances on his intellectualizing course by leaps and bounds, until the Good is seen radiating from beyond the realm of Being. At each new stage the foregoing position is ignored. In the series νόησις διάνοια πίστις εἰκασία the crudeness of ἐπιστήμη δόξα ἀγνωσία is silently corrected. And in B. vii, according to this writer, who takes but slight reckoning of the great allegory, even the ideas are lost in the transcendent notion of the Absolute, as the supreme end of Dialectic.

In trying to account for the subsequent addition of Bb. v–vii, Krohn avails himself of a suggestion made by F. A. Wolf and repeated by Meineke, that Aristophanes in the Ecclesiazusae (B.C. 391) aimed his ridicule at the communistic scheme of Plato, of which some hint must therefore have been already published. It is probable enough that, when the comedy was brought out, some notion of 'the monstrous regiment of women' was already in the air [2]; but the only ground for supposing a personal reference is by no means firm. The

---

[1] 'Harmlos immanent.'

[2] The idea of a community of wives, such as Herodotus attributes to the Agathyrsi, was already familiar to Euripides. See the fragment of his Protesilaus (655 in Nauck) κοινὸν γὰρ εἶναι χρῆν γυναικεῖον λέχος.

name Aristyllos occurs in the play (l. 647, cp. Plutus, 314 [1]),
and is twisted by Meineke into a diminutive of Aristocles,
which was Plato's birth-name according to Diogenes Laertius
—though if it were so he had changed it before the death of
Socrates, as we know from the Phaedo.   On such premises
Krohn builds the assumption that the 'Socratic' books (I–IV,
VIII–X) were written before B. C. 391, and that after this Plato
re-edited the work with the addition of the ἐκτροπή (V–VII), at
the opening of which he declares his defiance of τὰ τῶν
χαριέντων σκώμματα.   This whole process is supposed to have
been completed before any other of the Platonic dialogues
had been composed.   All the greatest ones—'which alone we
need care to vindicate,' are viewed as more advanced even
than B. VI, and the rest are discarded as unimportant,
having little, if any, philosophical significance.   Dr. E.
Pfleiderer, who more recently reaffirmed Krohn's theory in
a modified form, conceives on the other hand that the shorter
dialogues came out in the interval between the composition
of I–IV, VIII–IX, and of V–VII, in which interval also, at some
uncertain time, B. X was composed.

§ 5.   Krohn's cavils have been answered in detail by Zeller
in the last edition of his *History of Philosophy*, and in a
Latin Monograph by B. Grimmelt (*De Reipublicae Platonis
compositione et unitate:* Berlin, 1887).   But although his
reasonings are inconclusive, his book is noticeable on several
grounds.

I. It recalls attention to many coincidences between the
earlier books of the Republic and the Memorabilia of
Xenophon, and thus accentuates anew the supremacy of
the ethical motive in Plato's life and work.   With equal
acuteness and candour this critic himself supplies the link
which binds the metaphysics of Book VI to the 'innocent'
psychology of Book IV.   He looks on Plato as throughout continuing the endeavour of Socrates, who strove to

---

[1] It also occurs in Attic inscriptions, C. I. 1. 298, n. 169, 38.   This makes
for the reality of the name.   The jest in Ar. Eccl. would have no point
unless Aristyllos were personally repulsive, which his enemies cannot have
said of Plato as a young man.

counteract the disintegrating tendencies of the age. The Platonic ideas were at first merely the result of moral forces recognized by an empiric optimism. By and by, however, they assumed (*a*) a logical and (*b*) a transcendent aspect. In the former stage (*a*) moral conceptions are co-ordinated with mathematical, but in the sequel (*b*) it is found that Plato's main interest throughout has been to establish the indefeasible regulative value of moral truth, and that his guiding principle is one of ethical teleology, which his imperfect knowledge of Nature led him to blend with a vague cosmology.

2. Krohn's thesis and the controversy to which it gave rise have brought into relief some inequalities in the structure of the Republic, which, whether accidental or intentional, are really there. But his argument proves too much for his case. For, if Plato had at any time regarded the education of Books ii and iii as adequate, or had ever been contented with the psychological method of Book iv, instead of setting out from the point reached by Socrates, he would have fallen behind it. No Socratic dialogue, even in Xenophon, is without an appeal to reason, which is conspicuously absent here. Socrates drew a sharp line of distinction between Knowledge and Ignorance, and aimed simply at basing life on an ideal of Knowledge. Plato in these books provides for that which the method of Socrates excludes;—a life grounded on true opinions, which are determined by a rational authority and moulded by education. If instead of taking the dialogue piece-meal after Krohn's fashion, the description of the 'first state' is regarded as an integral portion of a larger whole, it reveals a conception not only in advance of the purely Socratic point of view, but also passing beyond the paradoxical attitude which Plato himself assumed when he raised the question whether virtue could be imparted otherwise than scientifically. Such a positive conception is only rendered possible by the conception of the state considered as a complex whole,—a constructive notion not anticipated in 'Socratism.' This will appear more clearly by and by in studying the relation of the Republic to the Protagoras and Meno. See below, p. 23.

3. The idea of Nature is more pervasive in the Platonic writings than Krohn is willing to admit (see Essay on Diction). The fact is that while pure 'dialectic' remains to the last an unrealized ideal, a fresh appeal to experience is continually made. At the height of the intellectual argument (VI. 506 D, E, VII. 533 E) Socrates will only go where he can take Glaucon with him. That there is some disparity between the ethical and the metaphysical books of the Republic is undeniable ; the attributes of the philosophic nature are not the four cardinal virtues, nor in the series νοῦς διάνοια πίστις εἰκασία is there any recognition of the other series νοῦς θυμὸς ἐπιθυμία. But this independent treatment of different aspects of the truth is quite in the manner of Plato, and it is best to take his own account of the matter, and to say that in the earlier books it was necessary to proceed provisionally, because the true philosophers had not yet been distinguished from the false, nor had the intellectual kingdom been revealed. In passing from the lower to the higher education, and from the mere guardian or soldier to the philosopher-king, he has entered on another region of thought, and is no more compelled to continue the same method than a poet feels bound to continue the same rhythm in passing from a dramatic to a lyrical strain. In Books VIII–X we descend again into the ethico-political region, and the emotional elements (which had no place in the intellectual argument) naturally reappear.

4. Krohn should be accepted as an independent and competent witness to the comparative lateness of the dialectical dialogues. His remarks on the Sophist and Philebus in their relation to the Republic are especially acceptable. For the coincidences between the Philebus and Rep. Book VI, on which Zeller lays so much stress, do not really bear out his conclusion that the Philebus is the earlier writing. It may be argued with at least equal probability, that the longer and more elaborate statement of Plato's theory of pleasure was subsequent to the cursory indication of it. See below, p. 22.

5. Plato himself has noticed the discrepancy between Bb. III and V, with regard to the appointment of the rulers and

had prepared for it by the qualifying expression (III. 414) ὡς ἐν τύπῳ, μὴ δι' ἀκριβείας, εἰρῆσθαι. In the original constitution of the State, before the higher education had been divulged, the elder guardians were made to rule the younger. But now that the rulers are to be trained for dialectic, it is necessary to make the selection while they are still young. It does not follow that they are to rule while very young, for the training is a long one, and they are not to be admitted, even to military commands, until thirty-five; still the first provisional order is superseded by the necessities arising out of the principle that kings shall be philosophers, which has been subsequently introduced.

Precisely the same difficulty is encountered by the founders of the colony from Cnossus in the Sixth Book of the Laws. The Athenian stranger explains to them that the first appointment of the νομοφύλακες and other magistrates cannot possibly conform to the regulations as to selection and training which are to be afterwards in force (Laws VI. 751 c, D). And one of the cautions imposed by this necessity is analogous to that enjoined in Republic, Book III. The men selected to nominate the rulers are to be the eldest as well as the best, so far as possible (εἰς δύναμιν Laws VI. 754 c). This comparison of the two writings places the superficiality of Krohn's objection in a strong light [1].

The unity of the Republic is not that of a syllogistic § 6.

---

[1] The following passage is characteristic both of Krohn's acuteness and of his illogical logic (*Der Plat. Staat*, p. 107, ed. 1876) :—

' Hier wird der grosse Riss des Platonismus sichtbar. Der moralisirende Sokratiker hatte den ersten Entwurf geschrieben, der Metaphysiker fand eine wahrere Wesenheit. Beide treffen jetzt kämpfend auf einander, Beide verleugnen sich nicht. Der Reformer, der die Krankheit seines Volkes heilen will, muss glauben und vertraut der eigenen Kunst: aber mit der Substanz unter verfliessenden Formen besiegelt der Denker seinen Verzicht. Instinktmässig zieht der Eine die Idee auf die Erde, um sie zu gestalten, in bewusster Erkenntniss hebt sie der Andere in ein intelligibles Reich. *Aber dieser Riss des Platonismus ist der Riss, der durch das Leben aller edelen Geister geht. Sie wirken hier mit ihrer besten Kraft und wissen, dass das Hier ein flüchtiges Etwas ist.*'

This is really to say that Plato's philosophy has a body as well as a mind. But if such an antinomy is so deeply inherent in Platonism, why deny that a work in which it is found was written continuously ?

treatise, but partly the unity of a philosophical movement or development and partly of a piece of literary art. Students of the Phaedo, Symposium, Phaedrus, Theaetetus, should be aware that it is Plato's way in the earlier stages of any exposition to hold much strictly in reserve. His method is 'regressive,' as it has been termed, continually passing from a partial or superficial view of the subject in hand, to another which he regards as more complete or more profound; ascending, as he himself would say, from hypothesis to hypothesis in the approach towards absolute truth. Whether the lower hypothesis is refuted, as in the Theaetetus, or discarded by a seemingly capricious impulse, as in the Phaedrus, is merely a question of form. The words of Socrates (Theaet. 187 A) are equally applicable in both cases—ὅρα δὴ νῦν πάλιν ἐξ ἀρχῆς, πάντα τὰ πρόσθεν ἐξαλείψας, εἴ τι μᾶλλον καθορᾷς, ἐπειδὴ ἐνταῦθα προελήλυθας.

In the Republic, as in the Phaedo, the disciples suggest difficulties which provoke the master into disclosing what he has so far kept in the background. The gradual evolution of the thought by this means is not referable to the incoherence of an unformed thinker, but to the most deliberate literary and philosophical design. To imagine Plato as in any single dialogue himself groping tentatively along the path by which he conducts his reader, or like the guide across the ford (Theaet. 200 E) taking his audience with him into depths which he has not explored, is an error no less grave than to suppose with Schleiermacher and others, that the whole body of the dialogues, the work of fifty years, was composed according to a preconcerted plan. It argues a strange insensibility both to the irony and the dialectical economy of Plato, that any one should take literally such expressions as 'whither the argument like a breeze may carry us, on that course we must proceed.' Such words express the spirit of the catechetical mode of exposition; but only a blind simplicity can believe the master serious when he professes not to know the way.

Another general feature of Plato's discourse has not been sufficiently noticed, and it is this:—the most elaborate discussion of the higher aspects of metaphysical or psychological truth does not prevent the recurrence of crude statements essentially inconsistent with the results so gained. Observe, for example, how the mythical doctrine of pre-existence is resumed in the Politicus, notwithstanding the clear dialectic of the Theaetetus and Sophist which has avowedly come between.

The unity of the Republic as a literary masterpiece hardly § 7. needs defence. Each part has its own climax of interest, and, in spite of the intentional breaks and digressions, or rather with their aid, there is a continuous rise and fall,—as in a tragedy,—pervading the whole work.

The *peripeteia* of the drama is made by the revelation of the truth about the philosopher-king, which is disclosed, after being purposely held back by the digression on the laws of War, and by the 'coy excuses' of Socrates, precisely at the middle point of the dialogue. (The culmination of the earlier portion in the definition of Justice had been similarly heightened by ingenious delays.) The breaking of this 'third wave of the τρικυμία' of course overwhelms Glaucon with surprise. That is the rhetorical artifice. But the attentive reader of the preceding books should not be wholly unprepared for the discovery. What else is implied by the identification of ἀρχή with ἐπιστήμη in I. 342, III. 389? or by the true ruler who is unwilling to rule, I. 346, cp. VII. 520? or by the few wise men through whose wisdom the State is wise (IV. 428)? The supremacy of reason is a Socratic principle which could not be absent from any part or aspect of Plato's Commonwealth. A similar outburst of astonishment marks the importance of the discovery that the education of the philosopher is to be carried up to the Idea of Good. That is the culminating point of this central portion, which developes the intellectual and philosophical ideal. But for this surprise also there had been some preparations in the earlier books. The 'Fables' for which rules are given in Bb. II, III, are characterized in 376 E as containing elements of truth. And although this remark is merely dropped by the way, the rules themselves are determined by the motive that when the age of reason comes, the truth may be accepted, because it harmonizes with the légends that were learned in childhood (402 A).  The child so trained will have been made familiar with the elementary forms of goodness (σωφροσύνης καὶ ἀνδρείας καὶ ἐλευθεριό-τητος . . . καὶ ὅσα τούτων ἀδελφά)[1], and may hope therefore to attain to true μουσική.  And while the τύποι θεολογίας are thus a reflexion of the Form of Good, the law of simplicity in education and even the division of labour are associated with the philosophical coception of Abstract Unity.  Lastly, the psychology of B. IV is avowedly provisional—those who would discuss the Soul and virtue adequately must go round by the 'longer way.'  (This thread is explicitly resumed in VI. 503 A.) And the definition of courage, in particular, is limited by the term πολιτική, thus reserving a place for the intellectual courage and fortitude of the philosopher, who regards human life as a little thing and is dauntless and indefatigable in the pursuit of truth.

§ 8.    Those who would break up the Republic have not observed that Bb. V–VII are linked to the preceding book by the image of a 'sea of difficulty.'  The first hint of this is given at IV. 435 C, by the word ἐμπεπτώκαμεν, which is followed up by ταῦτα μόγις διανενεύκαμεν ib. 441 C.  This renders less abrupt the image in V. 453 D (ἄν τέ τις εἰς κολυμβήθραν μικρὰν ἐμπέσῃ ἄν τε εἰς τὸ μέγιστον πέλαγος μέσον, ὅμως γε νεῖ οὐδὲν ἧττον), which gives distinct note of preparation for the continued metaphor (457 B ἐν ὥσπερ κῦμα φῶμεν διαφεύγειν—ὥστε μὴ παντάπασι κατακλυσθῆναι, 472 A μόγις μοι τὼ δύο κύματε ἐκφυγόντι νῦν τὸ μέγιστον καὶ χαλεπώτατον τῆς τρικυμίας ἐπάγεις, 473 C εἰρήσεται δ' οὖν, εἰ καὶ μέλλει γέλωτί τε ἀτεχνῶς ὥσπερ κῦμα ἐκγελῶν καὶ ἀδοξίᾳ κατακλύσειν).  Socrates reverts to the figure implied in IV. 441 C, although the image of a 'swarm of arguments' (V. 450 B) had come between.

§ 9.    One point affecting the structure of the Republic, which requires careful elucidation, is connected with the famous allegory of the cave at the opening of B. VII,—the passage

---

[1] It has been observed that this enumeration comes nearer to the list of philosophic attributes in B. VI than to the Cardinal Virtues.

which suggested the 'idola specus' to the mind of Bacon. At the end of B. VI, the Platonic Socrates had shadowed forth a hierarchy of pure ideas, constituting the supra-sensual kingdom of being and truth, presided over and vitalized by the supreme Form of Good. This is not only a turning point of the Republic, but may be regarded as marking a critical moment in the development of Platonism. The 'Reason of the Best' is said indeed in the Phaedo to be the Atlas of the World, and true causes to be more effectually approached through the examination of language and thought than through external nature; but in that dialogue there is no such clear vision of an ideal unity of knowledge as is here given. In the Phaedrus-myth the forms of Justice and Holiness appear to be raised on lofty pedestals above the rest. And it is shown that to be man at all one must understand general notions abstracted from sense. But there is no well-defined path of ascent from the first or primary generalization of experience to the height of moral vision. Now in the Republic, the conception of such an ascent is formulated in the concluding passage of B. VI, and carried further in B. VII. Plato here anticipates that gradation of mental stages, and that remotion of the Divine from Man, which, as will be presently shown, is increasingly characteristic of the later, or more constructive, phase of his philosophy.

But in passing onwards from the conclusion of B. VI to the allegory of B. VII, the ground is insensibly shifted, as the idealizing impulse gathers strength, so that not only the distinction between πίστις and εἰκασία is dropped (since from the higher point of view the sensible world consists entirely of images)[1], *all* ordinary experience being now merged in εἰκασία,

---

[1] Professor E. Caird writes as follows on this passage :—

'1. I do not think it need cause us any difficulty to find the whole visible world viewed as standing in the same relation to the whole intelligible world as the parts in each do to each other, after we have been told that the former is the "offspring and likeness" of the latter. In fact this gives us three pairs standing to each other as image to reality :

$$1 : 2 :: 2 : 4 :: 3 : 6$$
$$a : b :: c : d :: (a + b) : (c + d). \text{ That is}$$

εἰκασία : πίστις :: διάνοια : νόησις :: τὸ ὁρώμενον : τὸ νοούμενον.

but the actual scientific processes which rank with διάνοια in B. VI are now degraded to the level of ordinary experience. The geometers, the astronomers, the 'empiric' harmonists, are all found guilty of the same error, that of not rising beyond and above sensible things and narrow everyday utilities. They are still tied and bound, still watching the fleeting shadows on the wall of the den.

§ 10.    The passage now to be considered extends from VI. 504 to VII. 519. The difficulty of interpretation is increased by the fact that Plato's exposition here is avowedly imperfect, being (1) relative to the immediate purpose of the dialogue, and (2) figurative from beginning to end.

Much turns on the significance of VI. 511 A, especially the words εἰκόσι δὲ χρωμένην αὐτοῖς τοῖς ὑπὸ τῶν κάτω ἀπεικασθεῖσι. (Cp. VII. 532 C.) That αὐτοῖς here designates not the ideas but merely sensible objects as distinguished from their shadows, is proved by comparing supr. 510 E *αὐτὰ μὲν ταῦτα,*

---

' 2. I suppose the difficulty in the case of the artificial figures lies in this, that it is not real beings whose shadows are seen in the cave, but marionettes, and that therefore the process of rising to true knowledge involves *two* steps : first to turn from the shadows to the marionettes, and then to discover that they are merely artificial figures, and to turn from them to the realities they copy. What Plato would suggest by this is I think, that individual things are not seen as what they are, till we have turned away from their first appearance and tried to define them. Then we find, as Plato shows in the 5th book, that they cannot be defined. They are great or small, good or bad according to the reference in which they are viewed. We thus discover that they are σκευαστά, combinations of elements which have no real unity, but are merely imitations of real things. We are therefore obliged to go up to the intelligible world in order to find real things, first in the sciences under their subordinate principles, and finally in dialectic which sees all things in the light of the highest principle of knowledge and reality ("sees all things in God").

' 3. The sciences are conceived by Plato as starting with principles, which are hypothetical in the sense that they have not been carried back to the *first* principle. He further adds that, when this is the case, science has to help its deductions by employing sensible images : in other words he thinks that, when we do not carry back knowledge to its first principle, we are obliged, in Kantian language, to use the *Anschauung* to supply the defects of the *Begriff*, and to make demonstration possible. This is illustrated by the mathematical use of diagrams, in which we prove universal truths by means of the particular image we set before us.

' I think the principles in question are not merely the principles of mathematics, though it is the type of mathematical science that is present to Plato, and on which he conceives the other sciences to be constructed.'

ἃ πλάττουσί τε καὶ γράφουσιν, ὧν καὶ σκιαὶ καὶ ἐν ὕδασιν εἰκόνες εἰσί, τούτοις μὲν ὡς εἰκόσιν αὖ χρώμενοι, κ.τ.λ.

It follows that the ὑπόθεσις is a scientific proposition, the subject of which is not the sign but the thing signified; while the εἰκών is a sensible object, employed as the symbol of the abstraction which is the subject of such a proposition. The visible square symbolizes the ideal square, whose properties are to be mathematically determined. Διάνοια, then, in B. vi, is the intellectual process, which, starting from hypotheses (of which mathematical assumptions are the clearest example) works out results through the *mediation* of sensible figures, plane (διαγράμματα) or solid (πλάσματα).

This general view is not forgotten in the discussion of the particular sciences. Astronomy, for example, *ought* to be a process of true διάνοια, but the actual astronomers, like the actual geometers, misunderstand the case so far that they think their science has for its object the visible revolutions of the stars, and not the laws of motion which these typify.

The higher aspect of διάνοια remains as a process intermediate between sense and knowledge, but in B. vii is represented by a new image, that of the upward path, rugged and steep, from the cave into the light of day. What meanwhile becomes of the σκευαστά and of the light of the fire? This part of the figure, involving as it does a dualism from which Plato was working himself free, is almost lost sight of in what follows, being only cursorily alluded to as a part of the circumstances of the cave. It is a provisional 'hypothesis,' which Plato discards (ἀναιρεῖ) in pressing onwards and upwards. But in its place this feature also of the allegory must have its own significance, and Socrates himself gives a partial interpretation of it by saying that the light of the fire represents the power of the Sun. There is some confusion, however, even here; for the objects seen by the denizens of the cave are not lights but shadows. What, then, are the things of which our unenlightened consciousness perceives only the shadows? What are the ἀγάλματα σκευαστά, the 'manufactured articles,' which hands unseen exhibit between the prisoners and the artificial (i.e. created) Sun? What else but the realities of γένεσις, Nature as the embodiment of the ideas, the facts of human experience, as they really happen, and not as they seem?

1. Plato is engaged in bringing out a twofold distinction, (1) between Nature and the Ideas, (2) between Appearance and Reality in Nature. This, and not merely the requirement of a fourth term for his analogy, was his motive for separating πίστις from εἰκασία.

2. The ἀγάλματα are not themselves immediately perceived by sense at all. It is only when the individual mind has been freed by Socratic questioning, and turned about, and asked What is it? (τί ἐστι;),—or, in more Platonic language, by a process of διαίρεσις and συναγωγή,—only, in more modern terminology, when some effort is made to distinguish, abstract, and generalize,—that the soul begins to have an inkling of the nature of that world, which was dimly represented to her in crude experience,—of a real finger, of a real square, of the Sun himself as an embodied god, &c. And she learns that these things, however perfect in their kinds (VII. 529 E), have been created after some higher pattern,—in other words, that their being is determined by universal and eternal Laws, and ultimately by the Law of the Best,—τῇ τοῦ ἀγαθοῦ ἰδέᾳ. While not absolute νοητά, they are νοητὰ μετὰ ἀρχῆς (VI. *sub fin.*). It is not improbable that in this part of the allegory there is still some reference to the διάνοια of B. VI as a process intermediate between sense and reason. But the 'manufactured articles' here exhibited by unseen powers correspond, not to the εἰκόνες of the geometers, for example, but to the realities typified by them. Those πλάσματα and διαγράμματα were only shadows and copies of these, which answer more nearly to the subjects of their ὑποθέσεις.

3. In the Timaeus, the true phenomena of nature are attributed to the created gods, who are said to make and set in order the living creatures in whom soul and body are temporarily combined (Tim. 43). Similarly, the παραφέροντες, who are clearly δαίμονες, exhibit the σκευαστά here.

4. The ἀγάλματα or εἴδωλα of the allegory constitute a lower stage of the ideal which in Plato's language is alone the real, not the immediately visible, but the truth of phenomena, the ἐν ἐπὶ πολλῶν ἑκάστων τῶν αἰσθητῶν, the *infima species,* the first intention of the ἐν λογισμῷ ξυναιρούμενον.

Now these realities of γένεσις, τὰ φύσει ξυνεστηκότα, of which the shadows or impressions are presented to the uneducated mind, are not really known until we get above and behind them. Then they are seen to be themselves the images or copies (εἴδωλα) of higher things, and the mind reaches beyond them and lays hold on the primal cause of being and of knowing, the ἰδέα τοῦ ἀγαθοῦ.

May not this notion of a 'lower stage' help to remove the difficulty which is felt in seeking to reconcile the αὐτοκλίνη of B. x with the higher teaching of B. vi? For the purpose of degrading the poets it is not necessary to mount to the ἀνυπόθετον or to the Form of Good. It is enough to have risen from shadows to objects, and from objects to their first abstraction—to the truth of γένεσις. The painted bed is the shadow of the actual bed, which is made after the pattern of the ideal bed. This we are 'disposed' (as Platonists) to say that God has made and set in nature (ἐν τῇ φύσει). But God made that, as he made the world, under the guidance of yet loftier ideals, the ideal of utility, of rest, of stability, of security, of permanence, of symmetry. However this may be, Plato's views of ontology, as seriously held by him at the time of writing the Republic, are to be gathered rather from Bb. vi, vii, than from B. x, where the reference to the doctrine of ideas is merely illustrative.

And it is worth observing that while mathematical truths are put in the forefront amongst the objects of 'hypothetical science,' because they are the most definite and distinct, moral notions are by implication co-ordinated with these. The fact is rendered manifest by the words in 517 E, where the disputants in the den are said to argue περὶ τῶν τοῦ δικαίου σκιῶν ἢ ἀγαλμάτων ὧν αἱ σκιαί, i.e. 'impressions about right, or rules of right,' the latter (τὸ νόμιμον) holding an intermediate place between abstract Justice (αὐτὸ τὸ δίκαιον) and the actual constitutions of states in the world (τὰ ἐν τοῖς ἀνθρώποις νόμιμα). This intermediate position of τὸ νόμιμον as ἄγαλμα τοῦ δικαίου may be compared to the function ascribed to Law in the Politicus. Compare also VI. 501 πρός τε τὸ φύσει δίκαιον καὶ πρὸς ἐκεῖνο αὖ τὸ ἐν τοῖς ἀνθρώποις.

§ 11.    Bb. VIII–X, as already indicated, have less in common with VI–VII than with the earlier portion. It does not follow that they are unconnected with what immediately precedes them: still less that they could be read continuously after B. IV without leaving a deplorable gap. The 'number of the state' in VIII. 546 is from a 'laboratory' of which Bb. I–IV afford no trace. And in contrasting the pleasures of the tyrant with the happiness of the philosopher-king, the account of the higher education is manifestly presupposed. The hope of conforming the individual life

X. 592 B.    to the 'pattern in the sky' precisely answers to that which is left to the actual philosopher of B. VI, who lets the

VI. 496 D.    storm rage past him, and strives to imitate the regular courses of the stars[1]. But the later books have also a special tone and quality of their own. If Bb. VI, VII carry us to a height of intellectual contemplation that is unsurpassed, Bb. VIII, IX are even more impressive in the depth of ethical feeling which they convey. The growing intensity of earnestness, as state after state, man after man, discloses a lower circle or stage of evil, is incomparably grand, and it is expressed with extraordinary wealth and happiness of imagination. The effect is not less different from the serene and smiling optimism of Bb. III, IV, than from the specu-lative abstraction of Bb. VI, VII. And when the return

[1] See Eur. Fr. Inc. 902 (N.) :—

ὄλβιος ὅστις τῆς ἱστορίας
ἔσχε μάθησιν,
μήτε πολιτῶν ἐπὶ πημοσύνην
μήτ' εἰς ἀδίκους πράξεις ὁρμῶν,
ἀλλ' ἀθανάτου καθορῶν φύσεως
κόσμον ἀγήρω, πῇ τε συνέστη
καὶ ὅπῃ καὶ ὅπως.
τοῖς δὲ τοιούτοις οὐδέποτ' αἰσχρῶν
ἔργων μελέτημα προσίζει.

is made, towards the end of B. ix, from the life of the tyrant to that of the king, the philosopher is invested with new majesty. The continuity of this portion (the fourth act of the drama) is assisted by the recurrence of a few great topics, each of which is gradually amplified: (1) Wealth and poverty; (2) the three principles of intellect, anger, desire, corresponding to the ruling, defending, and industrial classes in the State; (3) the necessary and unnecessary desires; (4) the image of the drones, stinging and stingless (i. e. rogues and paupers), leading up to the description of the tyrant's master passion as a great winged drone; (5) the insurrection in the soul (an image which intensely vivifies the analogy between the individual and the State); (6) the relation of the tyrant to the *Demos* represented as that of son to father; (7) the image of the man and beasts within the man—the lion and the serpent and the many-headed brute. The management of these notions and successive images so as to characterize the evolution of ever fresh aspects of social and personal life, is most curious and instructive, even as a literary study [1].

At the beginning of B. x, Socrates reviews his creation § **12**. and finds it good. The point immediately resumed is the exclusion of the poets—which occasioned Plato more compunction than the community of wives; but, in returning to the discussion, he, as usual, takes up new ground, and glances at the conversation which has intervened. Although the allegory of the cave is not distinctly referred to, yet in defining μίμησις it is now permissible to assume the existence of an ideal world, and to speak of the artist as the maker of shadows of images, thrice removed from reality and truth. And, as Socrates says explicitly, the psychological distinctions of Bb. iv, ix, enable us now to affirm that these unrealities appeal to the lower part of the soul, i.e. to emotion and not

---

[1] When tested by statistical evidence, i.e. by the presence or frequency of particular modes of expression, the eighth and ninth Books are found to have as many features in common with Plato's later writings as any other part of the Republic. See Constantin Ritter's *Untersuchungen*, &c., pp. 33-47.

to reason, so rendering more difficult that control of the feelings and that abnegation of pleasure, which has been shown to be of the essence of virtue.

Thus Plato leads us back to the main question:—the intrinsic value of justice, independently of reputation and reward. Socrates claims to have established this; and now begs leave to restore what for the sake of argument had been taken away, the outward happiness attending a good life. And to crown all, he makes known the immortality of the Soul, and the future blessedness of the just: to which is added, as the natural counterpart, the punishment of the wicked [1]—the tyrannical tyrant in chief.

§ 13. Accepting the Republic from the hand of Plato as an artistic whole, we refuse to examine curiously into the exact time when the several parts were written. That the central portion may have been written last is a possibility which we neither affirm nor deny. Such speculations lie beyond the scope of criticism. That on the Republic, with all its comprehensiveness and variety, the author has impressed an unmistakable unity of design, is a proposition which no mature and sober student is likely to dispute.

## II

*The Republic considered in relation to other dialogues of Plato.*

§ 14. From the fulness and range of its contents, and especially from the combination of moral and political with purely intellectual elements in its composition, the Republic has more affinities with other writings of Plato than are to be found elsewhere in any single dialogue.

Gorgias. To the Gorgias it stands in a close and peculiar relation. For the longer writing is in fact an elaborate endeavour to substantiate that supremacy of right, which Socrates so

---

[1] This has been thought inconsistent with III. 386 ff. What Plato there deprecates is the fear of death. Here he is enforcing the fear of sin. Cp. Laws V. 727 D τὰ γὰρ ἐν Ἅιδου πράγματα πάντα κακὰ ἡγουμένης τῆς ψυχῆς εἶναι ὑπείκει καὶ οὐκ ἀντιτείνει, κ.τ.λ. The words in III. 387 C ἴσως εὖ ἔχει πρὸς ἄλλο τι possibly refer to the other aspect of the truth.

eloquently vindicates in refuting Gorgias and Polus. The Gorgias asserts the claims of justice. The Republic reiterates the claim and adds a definition. The counsel of perfection, 'Do right in scorn of consequences,' leaves the disciple of Socrates unsatisfied, until he finds an answer to the question 'What is right?' And this can only be obtained through the study of Man in Society. In the Republic, accordingly, the social environment of the higher life is elaborately set forth; and this constitutes a real and at first sight a very wide distinction between the two dialogues. But the difference appears less when it is considered that Plato's Commonwealth is an ideal projected into the future, and that the philosopher in the Republic, like Socrates in the Gorgias, takes no part in actual politics, but 'stands under the shelter of a wall' and lets the storm of unrighteousness VI. 496 D. rage past him.

In Bb. I–IV of the Republic, the most characteristic positions of the Gorgias are restated and developed further. Thrasymachus may be described as a magnified and more original Polus, and like Polus he is tongue-tied at last, through fear of opinion[1]. Then, in place of the thorough-going cynicism of Callicles, who speaks openly what other men implicitly believe, the brothers Glaucon and Adeimantus give their clear philosophic exposition of the worldly principles from which their generous natures instinctively recoil. The theory, although put differently, is in both dialogues essentially the same,—that Might is Right, and that Justice (as Shakespeare's royal villain says of Conscience)

> 'is but a word that cowards use,
> Devised at first to keep the strong in awe.'

The sophistical paradox is associated in both dialogues with admiration of the tyrant as the one strong man, who by trampling upon so-called rights secures his interest and asserts his power. Adeimantus, however, introduces a new element into the discussion, when he says that the praise of Justice, as commonly enforced, is no less immoral than the

---

[1] I. 352 B ἵνα μὴ τοῖσδε ἀπέχθωμαι.

praise of Injustice,—that prudential morality encourages immorality.

The parallel between the Gorgias and the Republic,—not to touch on many minute coincidences, which are mentioned in the notes to this edition,—extends also to the vision of judgement with which both dialogues alike conclude, and which in the Gorgias, although briefer, is even more vivid and terror-striking than the tale of Er. The description of the tyrant's soul, naked before her judge, contains some hints of the conception of the last state of the tyrannical man, which is elaborated towards the end of the ninth book of the Republic.

Cp. Rep.
I. 349.

The Gorgias also agrees with the Republic in assuming an intellectual or scientific basis for morality (Gorg. 508 A σὺ δὲ πλεονεξίαν οἴει δεῖν ἀσκεῖν· γεωμετρίας γὰρ ἀμελεῖς), and in the rejection of Hedonism.

Which dialogue came first in order of composition? The question is perhaps an idle one, and in the absence of adequate external evidence the answer must necessarily be uncertain. But some grounds may be adduced for the opinion that the Republic was planned after the Gorgias was written. The shorter dialogue has, comparatively speaking, some of the crudeness and also of the freshness of a sketch contrasted with an elaborate picture. The impressive figure of 'Socrates against the world' is softened, in the more finished work, with a halo of ideal optimism. 'The world is not unreasonable, could it but hear reason,' is a note that would have sounded strange in the presence of Callicles. The companion portraits of the Just and Unjust Man are completed, in the Republic, by filling in their imaginary surroundings.

Taking either dialogue as a whole, it may be fairly argued that the assertion, 'A right will is all in all,' which is the upshot of the Gorgias, is naturally previous to the inquiry, 'What is essential rectitude? and how is righteous action possible?'

§ 15.

Philebus.

It has been assumed by Schleiermacher and Zeller that the passages of B. VI, where the claims of Thought and

Pleasure are contrasted (505-509, see also IX. 581-587), pre-
suppose the composition of the Philebus. The coincidence is
obvious, but not less so is the comparative simplicity of the
point of view advanced in the Republic. It is possible that
the principles here briefly stated may have been previously
elaborated. But it is by no means necessary to assume that
it was so. And it is at least equally conceivable that Plato
had arrived at this general conception of the relative worth
of Pleasure, Thought, and the Good, before giving to it the
full and complex expression which the Philebus contains.
If the assertion of Justice is held to precede the definition of Justice, it may be similarly maintained that the
solemn adumbration of the Idea of Good precedes the
laboured attempt to seize this Supreme Form (and, as it
were, 'confine the Interminable'[1]) through metaphysical determinations. But the position of the Philebus in the series
of the Platonic writings is part of the larger question of the
place to be assigned to the other dialectical dialogues, to
which it is manifestly akin. Some observations pertinent to
this subject will be made in the sequel.

The Republic provides an approximate solution of the §16.
uifficulty paradoxically raised in the Protagoras, and imper- Protago-
fectly met in the Meno by the theory of 'inspiration,' viz. ras, Meno.
the question 'How is virtue possible without perfect knowledge?' In the Republic, Science is more strenuously than
ever asserted to be the basis of well-ordered life, but in all
except the Rulers it is unconsciously so. By selecting the
right natures for the reception of Culture, by the reformation
(1) of mental, and (2) of physical education, the predominance
of Virtue is secured even in those not yet capable of Reason,
so that they may ultimately embrace her the more readily,
because they have nothing irrational to unlearn. Thus the
conception of the State affords the means of reconciling an
opposition, which, as we learn from the Protagoras, tended
to hinder, by making it seem impossible, the application of
Philosophy to the bettering of human life. Protagoras professed to benefit his pupils by promoting their attainment of

[1] Milton.

that civic and social excellence which was shared in some degree by all the citizens of a civilized community, and which the primary education of Greek freemen was already calculated to foster, in evolving those seeds of Justice and of mutual respect which had been scattered broadcast at the remote origin of human society. Socrates denies that such a process deserves the name of teaching, or that the virtue thus communicated is really virtue. He makes the seemingly impossible requirement that a science of exact measurement should be applied to human life and action. Now the philosopher of the Republic is in possession of such a science, and he is entrusted with the control of primary education. Thus the unconscious, relative, approximate virtue of the subordinate class, who again compel the obedience of those beneath them, is essentially grounded in philosophy. And the whole State is wise, although the wise amongst its citizens are still the few. The work professed by the Sophist is now undertaken by the Philosopher, with far better assurance of a solid foundation.

§ 17.
Symposium and Phaedrus.
It is more difficult to find the angle (if the figure may be allowed) at which the Republic stands towards those dialogues which symbolize philosophic enthusiasm under the form of Love. There are mystic passages in the Republic also, but in the work as a whole, what may be termed the ecstatic phase of Platonism is greatly toned down and subdued. Whether Plato is here addressing a wider audience, or has now entered on a further stage in the evolution of his thought, is a question by no means easy to determine. The points where some approximation to the spirit of the Phaedrus and Symposium occurs are chiefly two.

III. 403, 404.
Even the earlier culture is not completed without a description of the modest loves of beautiful souls.

VI. 490 A, B.
And in describing the philosophic nature, the love of truth is characterized in words which might have been used by Diotima :—ὅτι πρὸς τὸ ὂν πεφυκὼς εἴη ἁμιλλᾶσθαι ὅ γε ὄντως φιλομαθής, καὶ οὐκ ἐπιμένοι ἐπὶ τοῖς δοξαζομένοις εἶναι πολλοῖς ἑκάστοις, ἀλλ᾽ ἴοι καὶ οὐκ ἀμβλύνοιτο οὐδ᾽ ἀπολήγοι τοῦ ἔρωτος, πρὶν αὐτοῦ ὃ ἔστιν ἑκάστου τῆς φύσεως ἅψασθαι ᾧ προσήκει

ψυχῆς ἐφάπτεσθαι τοῦ τοιούτου· προσήκει δὲ ξυγγενεῖ· ᾧ πλη-
σιάσας καὶ μιγεὶς τῷ ὄντι ὄντως, γεννήσας νοῦν καὶ ἀλήθειαν,
γνοίη τε καὶ ἀληθῶς ζῴη καὶ τρέφοιτο καὶ οὕτω λήγοι ὠδῖνος, πρὶν
δ᾽ οὔ.

Essentially cognate to the same aspect of Platonism are the account of education as a development from within, the rising scale of Being, through sense, opinion, thought, and reason, to the idea of Good, recalling the stages leading to the ocean of Beauty in the Symposium ; the upper air and sunshine of the ἀνυπόθετον in Bb. vi, vii, compared with the outer rim of Heaven in the Phaedrus-myth ; the enthusiastic account of Dialectic, and the wanderings of the soul in B. x. The prayer to Pan and the Nymphs with which the Phaedrus ends, has, of course, many echoes in the Republic. Constantin Ritter, who has examined all the Dialogues by the 'statistical' method introduced by Dittenberger (in *Hermes* xvi, 1881), regards the Phaedrus and Theaetetus as belonging to the same period with the Republic. He is disposed to think that both were written while the Republic was in course of composition, and that the Theaetetus is the earlier of the two. This last opinion may be disputed on the following grounds :—

1. Not to dwell upon the signs of immaturity which some critics (Usener amongst others) have discovered in the Phaedrus, it appears inconceivable that Plato should have expressed the paradoxical preference of oral to written speech, at a time when he was himself actively engaged in preparing a written work so large and important as the Republic.

2. Those who attach any weight to L. Spengel's arguments —and some weight they certainly deserve—are bound to give the Phaedrus the earliest date which a comprehensive view of all the facts will admit. Whether the dialogue is earlier or later than Isocrates' περὶ τῶν σοφιστῶν, there are strong grounds for supposing it to have been written not long after the opening of the Academy.

3. The Theaetetus presents a matured harmony of thought and expression. The gravity of Theodorus, which tempers

the irrepressible playfulness of Socrates, is evidently in keeping with Plato's own deeper mood.

4. The soaring idealism of the Phaedrus, which reappears in the Republic, is likewise modified in the Theaetetus by an approach towards a rational psychology. This point will be further developed by and by.

§ 18.
Phaedo.

The doctrine of immortality (incidentally recognized in the Meno) is expressly maintained in the Phaedo, Phaedrus, and Republic. And while the line of proof is different in all three, the demonstration chosen in the Republic is closely allied to one of those in the Phaedo—that by which it is shown in answer to Simmias that the soul is not a harmony.

Phaedo 93.

X. 611 B.

The words of Socrates, ὅτι μὲν ἀθάνατον ψυχή, κἂν ἄλλαι φανεῖεν ἀποδείξεις, ὡς ἐμοὶ δοκεῖ, may or may not contain an allusion to the Phaedo, or to the Phaedo, Phaedrus, and Symposium in one. But it is at least tolerably clear that the Republic and Phaedo both belong to a stage of Platonism in which the doctrine of ideas had been distinctly formulated, while the logical and metaphysical bearings of the theory had not yet been thought out so clearly as in the period of which the Parmenides marks the opening stage. Coincidences between the Phaedo and Republic are the more significant, as the meditation of death is a different subject-matter from the supreme realization of life in the world.

§ 19.
Theaetetus.

There is a very close approximation both of style and substance between the most serious part of the Theaetetus (173–177) and Rep. VI, VII, although in the dialogue concerning knowledge, as in the Gorgias and Phaedo, the philosopher is described as withdrawn from action and as knowing nothing of his neighbour. In this he corresponds not to the King-philosopher of the Republic, but to the actual philosopher who is 'useless to his State,' who in his contemplation of realities has no time to look down on human affairs (VI. 500), and who seeing mankind replete with lawlessness is content to live apart, if only he can keep his own life pure. The contrast between the philosopher and the lawyer resembles also the description of the awkward plight of him who descends again out of the daylight into the glimmering den (VII. 517). Once

more, the nature of retribution is similarly conceived by
Socrates in Theaet. 177 and by Adeimantus, while the ideal II. 363 E.
pattern of the blessed life is similarly set forth in Theaet. 177,
and in Rep. IX, *sub fin.* Such near agreement at once
of matter and of tone as becomes perceptible on a repeated
reading of these passages, albeit by no means a certain test,
is more decisive than such chronological indications as the
allusion to the battle of Megara (B.C. 394?), and the fact that
Cleomenes, who was at that time king of Sparta, counted
precisely twenty-five generations from Heracles (cp. Theaet.
175 A). These points, however clearly demonstrated, belong
to the time assigned to the imaginary conversation. They
cannot determine the date of its composition (except as giving
a *terminus a quo*). On the other hand the dialectics of the
Theaetetus evince a maturity of psychological reflexion, and
a moderation and firmness of metaphysical handling, which
had scarcely been attained by Plato when he wrote the
Republic. This may of course be a deceptive appearance,
attributable to the fact that in the larger dialogue the mind is
taken off from abstract speculation, and plunged in politics
and popular moralities. But there are considerations which
point the other way, and which incline the balance in favour of
placing the Theaetetus after rather than before the Republic.

1. The manner of approaching the subject through the
criticism of earlier philosophies would seem to mark a distinct
stage in the development of Plato's mind (cp. Soph. 246 ff.).

2. The allusion to the Parmenides seems to mark the Theaet.
Theaetetus as one of the same group with the Parmenides 183 E.
and Sophist. And in the statement of metaphysical ἀπορίαι
the Theaetetus and Parmenides are companion dialogues.

3. The clear conception of Being, not-being, Unity, number, sameness, difference, similarity, diversity, as logical
categories or ideas of relation, which comes out at Theaet.
184, 185, could hardly have been possible, while Plato held the
doctrine of ideas in the crude and undeveloped form which
is still implied in the Republic, and which the Parmenides
for the first time showed to be unsatisfying.

4. The greater subtlety and accuracy of the psychological

distinction between ἐπιστήμη, δόξα, αἴσθησις, as compared with Rep. VI, *sub fin.*, and still more with the end of B. V, is also apparent, though here, too, the difference of subject may have involved disparity of treatment.

§ 20.

*The further consideration of the dialectical dialogues must be postponed, until we have glanced at the Laws.*

As was previously said (p. 22) with reference to the Philebus, the presumption thus raised can neither be substantiated nor set aside without taking into account the other dialectical dialogues, Parmenides, Sophistes, and Politicus. And for reasons which will presently become apparent, the consideration of these dialogues in their relation to the Republic must be postponed to some brief remarks on the great work which in subject-matter as well as in extent comes nearest to the Republic, viz. the Laws. As this dialogue, by those who acknowledge its genuineness, is admitted to be the last of Plato's writings, the contrast which it presents to the Republic is the more instructive, since difference may here be interpreted to imply some change. But the comparison must be made with caution. For two main points have to be borne in mind : (1) that Plato in the Laws is confessedly aiming only at the second best, and (2) that the work is doubly incomplete :—the composition of many portions is unfinished, and the question of Higher Education is expressly reserved, so that, to employ Plato's own metaphor (Laws VI. 752 A), the dialogue is without a head. The attempt to supply this latter defect in the Epinomis (according to a credible tradition, by Philip of Opus, the editor of the Laws) only shows how incapable Plato's immediate successors were of continuing what was most significant in his philosophy. The Platonism that survived the Master in the Old Academy was indeed

Ψυχὴ καὶ εἴδωλον, ἀτὰρ φρένες οὐκ ἔνι πάμπαν.

It may be argued, however, that both these peculiarities are indicative of changes in the philosopher's own mental attitude.

The very notion of a second-best in politics, of an aim worth striving for which yet falls short of the highest, is alien to the spirit of the Republic. Before entertaining such a notion Plato must have come to think that the realization of the Divine ideal was even more distant than in the fifth and

ninth books of the Republic he had declared it to be : that it
was in fact impossible 'for such a creature as man in such
a state as the present.'

Even in the Republic he had acknowledged that the State
of primitive innocence could not last, and his ideal constitution presupposes the inevitableness of war.   But in the Laws
that constitution also, so far as it involved the principle of
communism, is relegated to the reign of Cronos, and is declared to have been suited not for human government, but
only for a theocracy.   The Athenian Stranger finds it necessary to strike into the middle path between two extreme
views : (1) that legislation is futile, seeing that 'time and chance
happen unto all,' and (2) that God governs all things without
the aid of man.   The third or intermediate view is that human
skill, taking advantage of opportunity, may imitate from afar
off the principles of Divine action.   And the opportunity now
prayed for is one less unlikely than the union of philosophy
and sovereignty in the same person.   It is the conjunction
of a 'temperate' sovereign with the wise legislator (Laws iv).
Now such a change from 'optimism' to 'meliorism' cannot
have taken place without a mental struggle.   It must have
cost Plato something, one would imagine, to discover that in
his greatest work he had only been uttering a vain, though
pious, aspiration,—ἄλλως εὐχαῖς ὅμοῖα λέγων.   And of such
a struggle, with the bitterness naturally accompanying it, there
is very distinct evidence in the Politicus ; where there
is also a foreshadowing of the very solution arrived at in
the Laws.

Through a skilful process of generalization and division, § 21.
Socrates Junior has been led by the Eleatic Stranger to Politicus.
define Statesmanship as 'the art of man-herding,'—according
to the figure repeatedly used by Socrates in the Republic.
But on reflexion the image is found unsuitable to the actual
state of the world, in which the work of tending mankind is
shared by many functionaries besides the statesman or ruler.
Not the human governor, but the divine superintendent of
the Golden Age, may be thought to have included all these
functions in his own person.   Our science of politics must

condescend to the actual present world and distinguish more definitely between the art of government and the other modes of managing mankind.

This position is illustrated by the wonderful myth, in which a more serious effort is made, than was attempted in the Republic, to face the problem of the existence of evil. ' God alternately guides the world and lets it go.' There can be no doubt under which dispensation we are living. Amidst this anarchy, of which Zeus is the reputed lord, the only hope of improvement lies in cherishing some faint remembrance of the Divine Order which was once a reality. Occasionally this remembrance comes with exceptional clearness to the mind of the philosopher, who is the only law-giver. Happy is that portion of the human race, that, when he appears, is willing to listen to him, and to obey his precepts. But his time upon the earth is brief, and when he departs, like a physician going into a far country, he leaves a prescription behind him. In his absence, the only feasible rule is the observance of Law, which is better than caprice, though far inferior to the immediate rule of Mind.

§ 22. It is sufficiently manifest how all this leads up to the point from which the Athenian Stranger makes his departure in counselling Cleinias and Megillus ; although in the Politicus there is little as yet of the spirit of compromise, which appears in the Laws,—for example, in the partial adoption of election by lot, notwithstanding the often expressed scorn of Socrates.

Also in many isolated points the Statesman anticipates the Laws. (1) The distinction between oligarchy and democracy is regarded in both as non-essential. Either may be better or worse according as it is administered. And constitutional democracy is far better than unconstitutional oligarchy. (2) The *weaving together* of diverse elements in a State is a notion to which prominence is given in both dialogues ; especially (3) in the provisions concerning marriage. And (4) as the name of Statesman is denied to the actual politicians in the Politicus, so the actual constitutions are contemptuously referred to in the Laws as the ' non-constitutions ' (διὰ τὰς οὐ πολιτείας

ἐκείνας). They are not polities but parties. (5) The conception of an infinite past, by which Plato accounts for the
growth of civilization, appears most distinctly in the Timaeus,
Critias, Politicus and Laws (B. III).

Although the philosopher's practical scope has thus shifted, § **23.**
and numberless minute provisions are expressly made of a
kind which the τρόφιμοι of the Republic were meant to discover for themselves, the reader of the Laws is often reminded
of the leading thoughts of the Republic. Each individual, as
far as possible, is to be not many but one. The definition of
Justice, obtained with so much difficulty, is silently discarded,
but Plato still glances with disfavour on the heretical view
that Justice is conventional, and he still dwells on the phenomenon that self-preservation is the basis of *de facto* govern-
ments upheld by statute. At the same time he points out that
no government is overthrown but by itself. The law of
Charondas, by which the money-lender was left to take the
risk of loss, is spoken of with emphatic approval both in the
Laws and the Republic. The avoidance of the extremes of
wealth and poverty is equally a principle of both. General
rules (τύποι, ἐκμαγεῖα) are laid down, as in the Republic, so also
in the Laws, for the censor of the poets. Early education is
again regarded as an anticipation of Reason. The importance
of *rhythm* in education is more than ever insisted on. The
music is still to be subordinated to the words[1]. And although
the paradoxical view that gymnastic also has a mental purpose
does not expressly reappear (it had already been ignored in
Rep. VII. 521 E), the merely utilitarian conception of physical
training is not the less scornfully rejected. The neglect
of education by Cyrus and Darius is held accountable for
the vices of Cambyses and of Xerxes (cp. Prot., Gorg.). The
supremacy of mind is vehemently asserted. The passions
are in the individual what the populace are in a State.
Yet here also the later phase of Plato's philosophy makes
itself felt, and the conjunction of sense with intellect is
introduced, not merely as the cause of error (Rep. VIII), but 546 B.

---

[1] Laws II. 669.

62 B,C. as the condition of practical wisdom (compare the Philebus).
On the other hand the unity of Virtue (Justice and Temperance especially running up into a single principle), which is
only hinted as a possibility in the Republic, is prescribed
as a main dogma of the Higher Education, which is to be
presided over by the Nocturnal Council.

§ 24.    This Higher Education is spoken of in two passages of
the Laws as a subject reserved for future consideration.

α'. B. VII. 818 (in speaking of the higher arithmetic, geo-
metry and astronomy) ταῦτα δὲ ξύμπαντα οὐχ ὡς ἀκριβείας
ἐχόμενα δεῖ διαπονεῖν τοὺς πολλοὺς ἀλλά τινας ὀλίγους· οὓς δέ,
προϊόντες ἐπὶ τῷ τέλει φράσομεν . . . χαλεπὸν δὲ αὐτὰ προ-
ταξάμενον τούτῳ τῷ τρόπῳ νομοθετεῖν· ἀλλ' εἰς ἄλλον, εἰ δοκεῖ,
χρόνον ἀκριβέστερον ἂν νομοθετησαίμεθα.

β'. B. XII. 969 ἐγὼ δ' ὑμῖν συγκινδυνεύσω τῷ φράζειν τε καὶ
ἐξηγεῖσθαι τά γε δεδογμένα ἐμοὶ περὶ τῆς παιδείας τε καὶ τροφῆς
τῆς νῦν αὖ κεκινημένης τοῖς λόγοις· τὸ μέντοι κινδύνευμα οὐ
σμικρὸν οὐδ' ἑτέροις τισὶ προσφερὲς ἂν εἴη.

The former passage (α') may be compared with Rep. IV.
435 C, where Socrates remarks that for the true account of
the virtues it would be necessary to take the 'longer way'
(which is afterwards identified with dialectic); the latter (β')
is very similar to Rep. VI. 536, 537, where Socrates introduces
the 'Idea of Good.' But, whereas in the Republic, Socrates
at least partially satisfies expectation, the statement promised
by the Athenian Stranger is deferred until a more convenient
season.

The student of the Laws is consequently left in a position
resembling that in which readers of the Republic would have
been, had Books V, VI, VII of that dialogue remained un-
written. He is aware, indeed, that the Nocturnal Council
were to comprehend the single underlying principle which
gives unity to the Virtues, that they would acknowledge
Wisdom to be the guide (cp. Rep. IV. 428) and Temperance
the inseparable condition of them all; that their minds would
have been cleared and strengthened by a *sound* training in
the *necessary* truths of mathematics and astronomy; that the
absolute priority of Mind to Body would be a principle deeply

infixed in their souls. But beyond this we are unable to judge how far the education and nurture which the Stranger advocates, resembled or differed from that developed in Rep. VII, or indeed whether he proposes that the members of the Nocturnal Council of this secondary State should be 'philosophers,' in what Plato at the time of writing conceived to be the highest sense of the word. Like the definition of the Philosopher projected by the Eleatic Stranger, the Athenian Stranger's account of the Highest Education seems never to have been written down by Plato[1].

We can only dimly trace some fragments of his leading thoughts, in the directions for elementary study given in B. VII, the religious principles inculcated in B. X, and some detached sentences towards the end of B. XII.

(1) Mathematics as the Truth of Nature, VII. 818 τίνες οὖν, ὦ ξένε . . . κατὰ φύσιν ἃ λέγεις.

(2) Priority of Mind, x. 887 ff., XII. 966 ff.

(3) Necessary existence of a '*primum mobile*,' x. 894, cp. Phaedr. 245.

(4) Eternal supremacy of the better mind over the worse, x. 897.

The author of the Epinomis has gathered up these scattered threads, but the pattern into which he has woven them is not Plato's, still less are there to be found there the traces of the untrammelled thought and free intelligence, of a mind not enslaved to its own formulae, which are absent from no genuine Platonic writing.

A theory of knowledge and of the object of knowledge is, therefore, not to be looked for in the Laws. Yet the study of dialectic has left its trace, in the pedantic elaboration of method, which marks the earlier and more finished part of the dialogue, and is analogous to the tedious classifications which the Eleatic Stranger in the Politicus remarks on and defends.

---

[1] 'Of a supreme or master science which was to be the coping stone of the rest, few traces appear in the Laws. He seems to have lost faith in it, or perhaps to have realized that the time for such a science had not yet come, and that he was unable to fill up the outline which he had sketched.' Jowett's Plato, vol. v, Laws, Introduction, p. 130.

§ 25.
Consider-
ation of the
Dialectical
dialogues
resumed.

The position of the Politicus, as intermediate between the Republic and the Laws, is sufficiently evident after what has been said. Now the Politicus cannot be far removed from the Sophistes, and the Philebus in style and structure bears evidence of belonging to the same period. The Timaeus is avowedly later than the Republic.

We are therefore not left without data for the difficult inquiry :—Did Plato's theory of knowledge undergo any change after the composition of the Republic? In what direction were his thoughts moving with respect to this, which he himself regarded as the highest subject of study?

The inquiry *is* difficult. For each work of Plato's is a separate whole, in which the parts have reference, not to any previous statement, but to the particular aspect of the Truth to which for the time being the philosopher addressed himself, and in which his mind was wholly absorbed. Even such distinct references as those in the Timaeus and Laws to the Republic, or those in the Theaetetus and Sophistes to the Parmenides[1], do not involve any attempt to adjust the later dialogue to the earlier one. Yet, on a general survey of the group of dialogues above-named, from which the Parmenides and Theaetetus (perhaps even the Euthydemus) cannot altogether be separated, there is observable a greater amount of consistency, as well as of positive content, than, for example, appears in grouping together Protag., Apol., Symp., Phaedr., Phaedo, Gorg. And this general observation may be of use, if, instead of attempting a detailed harmony, or 'peering between the lines' of detached passages for the evidences of a system which is nowhere formulated, we content ourselves with marking the broad outlines, and so endeavouring to follow the main movement of Plato's thought.

The concluding passage of Rep. VI[2] contains a statement of the unity of knowledge, which may be summed up as

---

[1] The reference to the Sophist in Polit. 284 B ὡς ἐν τῷ Σοφιστῇ ('as in dealing with the Sophist'), is not in question here, as the Sophist and Statesman are to all intents and purposes one dialogue.

[2] See above, p. 13.

follows :—'The investigation of Truth under the conditions of human life on earth must start from assumptions based on sensible perception. But that is only the starting-point. The philosophic spirit cannot rest, until the mind's conceptions have been purified by the activity of thought from every sensible mean, and so rising from height to height of abstraction, the thinker may lay hold on the Absolute (τὸ ἀνυπόθετον), whence again descending, he may pass from Form to Form, and end with pure ideas.' Nowhere else had Plato hitherto so clearly asserted the connexion and gradation of the Forms of Being.

But if we ask, what is the nature of the connexion, or of the transition from the higher to the lower forms, the Republic yields no consistent answer.

1. In the fifth book the εἶδος is said to be related to its particulars, as the whole to the parts. Are the higher εἴδη of Book vi thus related to the lower ? Do they form a series of which the extreme terms are *Summum Genus* and *Infima Species* ?

2. The reader of B. x is at once presented with a different conception. The ideal Bed is not a whole of which the actual bed is part, but the Pattern after which it is made. Are the higher ideas related to the lower, as the Perfect to the Imperfect ? The beginning of B. vii and the end of B. ix may lend some colour to this view ; which, however, is inconsistent with the preceding.

3. Once more, in studying the educational discussions of B. vii, in which the general conception of Science is practically applied, we are led upwards from the mind's first perceptions of difference and identity, through the abstract study of number, form and motion, first to the common principles determining all such studies, then to universal principles worked out by Dialectic, and last of all to the primal, ultimate, creative, regulative, alone substantial Form of Good. Are the Ideas, then, Forms of Thought, and are the higher related to the lower as the ideas of the Reason to the categories of the Understanding, and those of the Understanding to those of pure intuition,—to use a Kantian figure ?

§ **26.**    The truth is that Plato had not yet cleared his mind from some confusion on this subject. It may be doubted whether he ever did so completely. Three points of view, which to modern thinkers are obviously distinct, the logical, the cosmological, the psychological, repeatedly cross and recross each other in his writings.

The moment came, however, when he keenly felt the need of solving this and other metaphysical difficulties. It is generally acknowledged that the Parmenides reflects precisely such an intellectual crisis. He could no longer satisfy himself with making a vague metaphysic the imaginary basis of an empirical morality.

The Parmenides.    Plato's thought in the Parmenides is directed towards (1) the theory of general forms and (2) the opposition of the one and many, not with barren contemplation, nor yet with scepticism, but with serious inquiry. At the same time Plato's Dialectic for the first time consciously stands face to face with Eleaticism. Most of the objections afterwards brought by Aristotle against the εἴδη are here raised in the form of ἀπορίαι, which are discussed, but not finally answered. And a tentative effort is made towards a New 'Kritik' of pure truth, through a disjunctive method, which the aged Parmenides recommends as a necessary *propaedeutic*, but which nowhere recurs. The dialogue ends, after the Socratic manner of the Protagoras or the first book of the Republic, with contradiction and the confession of ignorance, but the reader has been carried into higher regions of speculation than in the purely 'Socratic' dialogues.

The Theaetetus again.    In the Theaetetus likewise the Socratic mask of irony is effectively resumed. There is much in it of the playfulness of the Phaedrus or Symposium, but without the wildness. That is sobered down through the presence of the grave Theodorus. We have again, as in the Parmenides, a chain of ἀπορήματα, most subtly reasoned out, but not finally got rid of. Once more comes back the old familiar Socratic ending— 'What knowledge is, I do not know.' But just as the Parmenides breathes the profound conviction, 'No philosophy without ideas, whatever the ideas may prove to be,—nor without the One, however our conception of Unity may have to be modified,' so the Socrates of the Theaetetus will never discourse without assuming the reality of Knowledge, nor will Theaetetus hesitate to affirm that unity and diversity, sameness and difference, number and quantity, are not perceived through any bodily organ ; but the perception of them, however manifestly evoked through sensible impressions, is in each case a direct intuition of the mind. Plato in the Theaetetus is again conscious of Eleatic influence, while he reckons with Heraclitus, Protagoras, and the Cyrenaics,— perhaps also with Antisthenes.

In these two dialogues, then, the philosopher is directly grappling with the chief difficulties which surround his own as well as other theories of Knowing and Being : the Parmenides breaking ground which is afterwards to be renewed, and dealing mainly with questions of Being ; the Theaetetus (in this approaching modern thought) treating the central questions of philosophy chiefly from the subjective side.

Taken together, these writings represent a time of § **27.** strenuous mental effort, when Plato was resolutely bent on going by the 'longer way,' and on fulfilling, even 'through hours of gloom,' the 'tasks in hours of insight willed.' Whatever tedium it may cost him, whatever intellectual fatigue, he is determined to see more clearly and fix more definitely those lines and veins of truth 'according to Nature' of which he has spoken in the Phaedrus. No result of this endeavour is formulated. That is not Plato's way. But as his Socrates says to Theaetetus, βελτιόνων ἔσῃ πλήρης διὰ τὴν νῦν ἐξέτασιν, so the philosophy of this whole group of dialogues (Parm., Theaet., Soph., Polit., Phil., Tim.) has distinctive features which clearly separate them not only from the Phaedo or Symposium, but even from the Phaedrus and the Republic.

1. The first point to notice is the serious criticism of earlier and contemporary philosophies. As Socrates questioned with individuals, so Plato now cross-questions doctrines and methods. He had elsewhere glanced allusively at the Heracliteans, the Pythagoreans, the Cyrenaics the Mega-

rians and others,—he had perhaps satirized Antisthenes ;—
but it is now through the lengthened examination of whole
schools of thought that he at once developes and tests his
own conceptions.    This is a new thing in philosophy, and
argues a great advance in dialectical method.

2.  Plato has had many a fling at the art of controversy
(ἀντιλογική), with its love of cross distinctions (Rep. v. 454),
its confusion of facts with principles (Phaedo 90 B), and all the
array of sophisms which are grouped together for ridicule in
the Euthydemus.    But he has now discovered that in a deeper
sense a cognate error lies at the root of all the intellectual
confusion of the time—that an illogical logic based on
abstract contradictions has been responsible not only for the
vain jangling of Dionysodorus and his fellows, but for the
waste of serious thought over such problems as whether false
opinion is possible, whether an element can be defined,
whether all discussion is not unreal, and other cognate difficulties, which were threatening the very life of philosophy.
This element of contemporary speculation he traces to the
Zenonian logic, in which the profound speculative thought
of Parmenides had been beaten out and misapplied.

3.  Hence comes his endeavour to turn the weapons of the
Megarians against themselves, and to evolve, at least approximately, a theory of predication both in thought and language
which, instead of hindering, may stimulate and aid the healthy
growth of eager minds.    His interest in dialectic is at this
stage more than ever educational.    And this is especially true
of that aspect of it which carries on the work commenced in
the Phaedrus, – the use of Classification.

§ 28.    The 'dichotomies' of the Sophist and Politicus are not to
be taken too seriously.    They afford a method of approach
to the main subject, by which the mind of the youthful hearer
or reader is to be at the same time kept on the alert, and
awakened to the difficulties with which the scientific treatment
of any general question is surrounded.    They remind us of
the description in the Philebus of the charm which the logical
'one and many' had for young Athenians.    They may even
be regarded as bearing some analogy to the arithmetical

puzzles which the Egyptians had invented for the amusement of children. But there are turns and moments of the laborious game where some principle of method is illustrated. These are marked with special emphasis, and by attending to them we learn something of the direction of Plato's own thoughts.

In the Phaedrus the ideal of generalization and division had been left disappointingly vague. The spirit of dialectic seems there to be regarded as its own evidence in determining the outlines of Truth, as an organic whole. In generalizing, the dialectician recognizes the εἶδος of which his soul had once the vision; in dividing, he will 'follow Nature,' hitting the joints, and not hacking the limbs. It is further indicated that 'Nature' has a 'right-hand' and a 'left-hand' segment, —which may be interpreted indifferently as positive and negative, or as good and evil. But in the Sophistes, and even more in the Politicus and the Philebus, while the dialectical method is still upheld, and still subordinated to the free activity of the philosophic mind, the difficulties and hindrances attending on it are more seriously felt. The process is accompanied with much labour, and leads through 'slippery' places. The several definitions of the Sophist, all based on observation and attained through successive excursions, at first seem to have little in common. The synoptic and selective faculty must be called in, to gather from all these the characteristic difference of the creature. And it is at this point (Soph. 233) that the investigation passes from the formal to the real.

In resuming the work of 'carving' to define the statesman the young respondent is warned that he must not cut off too much at once (for fear of 'hacking the limbs'),—whereupon he asks the difficult and important question, 'How is one to know an accidental segment (μέρος) from a true form (εἶδος).' He is further made aware that the process of residues is insufficient for the purposes of science, (since, as was shown in the Sophist, negation also has a positive content), and that before I can know the nature of *this*, I must know something also of what is *not this but akin to this*. Thus dialectic becomes more concrete, no longer turning on the mere perception or intuition of elementary forms, but endeavouring to recognize them as actualized in the complexity of the world. Hence the great value of the argument from example. Nor should the hearer of dialectic ever complain of mere length as tedious, for length and brevity are relative not to each other merely, but to the requirements of investigation and discovery. Thus, as by a side wind, is introduced the principle of τὸ μέτριον, which plays such an important part in the Philebus.

The same increasing consciousness of the intricate developments of real science as opposed to mere logic appears in the well-known passage of the Philebus, 16 foll., where it is shown that the lover of truth must not rest in the mere discovery of a one and many, but pursue his investigation until he ascertains 'how many.' This is not a mere return to Pythagoreanism, but a real advance towards a fuller conception of scientific truth.

§ 29.    There is another aspect of this part of the subject, on which Plato dwells in different ways, but with similar emphasis, in the Parmenides, Sophistes and Politicus. The Sun of Science, as Bacon says, shines equally on the palace and the dunghill. Socrates, replying to Parmenides, is doubtful whether he ought or ought not to assume ideas of dirt and refuse. But he is assured by the philosopher that when the love of knowledge has taken hold of him, as one day it will take hold, he will neglect none of these things. And in like manner his namesake, the Younger Socrates, raises no objection when the Eleatic Stranger affirms that in the eye of Science the vermin-killer is as much a huntsman as the general, or when he reminds him afterwards that, in classification, no preference should be given to what is not ridiculous. And Socrates himself tells Protarchus (Phil. 58 c) that the art of which we are in search is not that which produces the grandest effect, but that which discovers some particle of truth, however seemingly unimportant [1].

These hints of an ideal of science are in entire keeping with the curiously modern description of the intellectual life as 'an

---

[1] Rep. III. 402 B οὔτ᾽ ἐν σμικρῷ οὔτ᾽ ἐν μεγάλῳ ἠτιμάζομεν αὐτά, may seem an anticipation of this, but should rather be compared with supr. II. 369 D, infr. IV. 435 A.

interrogation of all natures with the view of learning from each what it has to contribute from its particular experience towards collective wisdom ' (Politicus, 272 B, c).

If in these dialogues Plato's logical method assumes a more § 30. definitely scientific aspect, his metaphysical theory undergoes modifications of a corresponding kind.

Not only is each ' natural kind '[1] to be regarded as a whole [2], but (as in the scheme foreshadowed in Rep. vi) the several wholes must be known in the light of higher conceptions, and as forming one vast totality. The primary forms or notions of unity, likeness, unlikeness, numerical difference, motion, rest, must be recognized as no less real than the attributes of each several kind. ' Quality' itself is a new abstraction which has to be named. Now this implies, what is not explicitly formulated, the admission of 'ideas' not only of existence, but of relation. Plato nowhere seems distinctly conscious of the difference between a genus and a category [3]. The terms εἶδος and γένος are used by him indifferently for both. But in the dialectical dialogues he dwells more and more on those universal conceptions which are inseparable from knowledge and being. These are the 'birds that fly everywhere about the aviary,' sameness and difference, unity and plurality, number, quantity, motion and rest. And it is in the effort to realize ideas of relation and to understand the relativity of thought that he takes in hand the central problem of Being and Not-Being, affirmation and negation. The reasoning of the Sophistes, based as it is on a critical review of previous philosophies, marks one of the most decisive moments in the history of thought, exploding the prime fallacy, which had its stronghold then in the misapplication of the great conception of Parmenides, and has since haunted many a polemical dispute, the confusion of the *Dictum Simpliciter* with the *Dictum Secundum quid.* When it is once recognized that *omnis negatio est determinatio,* a fatal obstacle is removed out of the way of science.

---

[1] Theaet. 157 ἕκαστον ζῷόν τε καὶ εἶδος.

[2] Ibid. 174 A τῶν ὄντων ἑκάστου ὅλου.

[3] See above, p. 35.

This great advance in Plato's central point of view has sometimes been represented as if Plato had now for the first time introduced Motion amongst the ideas. But the identity of thought and life is of the very essence of Platonism throughout,—witness the proof of immortality in the Phaedrus, and the description of the Idea of Good as the supreme efficient cause in the Republic. It was precisely because Eleaticism made this impossible, by assuming the incommunicability of Being and Becoming, One and Many, that Plato found it necessary to lay hands on 'Father Parmenides,' and to prove the maxim, Τελεωτάτη πάντων λόγων ἐστὶν ἀφάνισις τὸ πᾶν ἀπὸ πάντων ἀποχωρίζειν. That 'love of the Whole' of which he speaks again and again never ceased to be his ruling passion. The more he becomes aware of the variety and intricacy of things, the more he is bent on binding them with the unity of knowledge. But in the speculative region, as in he practical, he loses something of the daring confidence of his earlier essays, and while his vision of mental phenomena becomes clearer, in speaking of the Universe he betakes himself again to Mythology.

Soph.
259 E.

§ 31.    The preceding observations may serve to commend the

Common character-istics of the dialectical dialogues.

view which is here maintained, viz. that the Parmenides, Theaetetus, Sophistes, Politicus, Philebus, in the order named (with the doubtful insertion of the Euthydemus before or after the Theaetetus, as a πάρεργον), form a distinct group or series, and that this series, *taken as a whole*, is subsequent to the great literary effort which terminated with the Republic.

The dialogues thus grouped together have certain characteristics in common.

Condensa-tion and compara-tive dry-ness.

1. The thought expressed in them is far more condensed, and, except in the Theaetetus, is much less richly clothed with imagination and humour, than that expressed in the dialogues which are here supposed to have preceded them.

Altered style.

2. On grounds of style as well as of substance it has been shown that the Politicus holds an intermediate place between the Republic and the Laws [1], and also that the manner of

---

[1] See L. Campbell's edition of the Sophistes and Politicus, 1867. The position therein assigned to the Sophistes, Politicus and Philebus, has

the Sophistes and Philebus has marked affinities to that of the Politicus. It may be added that although the Theaetetus and Parmenides are not throughout written in this later vein, the dialectical passages in both of them indicate an approach to it.

3. In these dialogues there is an increasing clearness and minuteness of psychological analysis and definition. Compare for example the analysis of vision in the Theaetetus with Rep. VII. 525 c, or the description of αἴσθησις, φαντασία, μνήμη, ἀνάμνησις, &c. in the Philebus with the tabular view of νοῦς, διάνοια, πίστις, εἰκασία, in Rep. VI *sub fin.* — Psychological distinctness.

4. Plato is no longer contented with positing the existence of universals, nor even of such a hierarchy of pure ideas as he imagines at the end of Rep. VI. He is now seriously bent on discovering the nature of Knowledge and its object, and of determining the connexion and correlation of ideas. — Epistemology.

5. From the recognition that every εἶδος is a νόημα, through the account of Being, not-being, sameness, difference, &c. as pure categories of perception, and the admission of Otherness as a mode of Being, up to the description of Measure as the Supreme Law, we trace the tendency, which is certainly less perceptible elsewhere in Plato, to define conceptions, which, while still regarded as objective, are essentially forms or modes of mind. The Philebus is rich in such determinations, which sometimes cross each other inconveniently, and even the seven forms of civic life in the Politicus, 289 B (τὸ πρωτογενὲς εἶδος [ = ὕλη], ὄργανον, ἀγγεῖον, ὄχημα, πρόβλημα, παίγνιον, θρέμμα) may be quoted as illustrative of a similar effort after συναγωγή. — Lists of categories.

6. Without admitting that a metaphysical system or consistent body of doctrine ('Plato's later theory of ideas') can be gathered from these dialogues, it is possible to trace in them the development of a metaphysical attitude which differs — Metaphysical attitude.

since been given to these same dialogues on independent grounds by W. Dittenberger (*Hermes*, XVI), M. Schanz (*Hermes*, XXI), and Constantin Ritter (*Untersuchungen* 1888). The convergence of different lines of investigation towards the same result has now reached a point which must surely be acknowledged to be convincing. See *Excursus, infra* pp. 46 ff.

both from that of the Protagoras and of the Republic. The supposed incommunicableness of knowledge and sense, being and becoming, universal and particular, one and many, which had threatened to paralyze philosophy, is felt to have been practically overcome, and the unity and correlation of knowledge and of nature is re-established.

Genesis or Production.

7. That speculative interest in γένεσις,—in the origin and growth of phenomena,—in what modern thinkers call the laws of evolution,—which had been the prime motive of the Ionian physiology, but had on different grounds been discarded both by Parmenides and Socrates,—is now, therefore, once more re-awakened in Plato's mind, and is partially justified by a metaphysic, in which the absolute comprises and sustains the relative, and evil is but a necessary moment in the self-development of Good.

Decline from Optimism.

8. But this speculative advance involves what cannot but be felt as retrogression on the practical side. For by introducing the conception of infinite gradation, it defers, without destroying, the hope of perfectibility :—

οὐ ταῦτα ταύτῃ μοῖρά πω τελεσφόρος
κρᾶναι πέπρωται

is the tone to which the ear of philosophy is now attuned. The distance between Man and God is found to be greater than in the first bright vision of the Ideal it had been conceived to be.

Religious tone.

9. And the spirit of the philosopher becomes less sanguine, but more profoundly religious than before.

Democritus.

10. This phase of Platonism is marked by some obscure but not uncertain indications of a controversial attitude towards Democritus [1].

§ 32.
The Timaeus.

The Timaeus is linked on to the subject of the Republic, but although both dialogues are referred to a time of public festival, they can hardly be viewed as strictly continuous. Socrates had on the previous day expounded to Timaeus, Critias, and Hermocrates his conception of an ideal state, —not, apparently, in the form of a reported conversation.

[1] The latter observations (7, 8, 9, 10) are supported by the following passages of Soph., Polit., Phileb. : viz. Soph. 216, 246-248, 265 (cp. Theaet. 173, 185 D, E) ; Polit. 269-275 (the myth), 278, 301, 302; Phileb. 22, 28, 30, 54, 59 A, 62, 64.

The Higher Education seems to have been cursorily mentioned, and the institution of infanticide must have been suppressed. However this may be, the Timaeus reflects the later phase of Plato's philosophy which has been just described. There is no room here for an exposition of the most difficult, if not, as some still declare it to be, the most important of Plato's dialogues. It must suffice to observe that metaphysical conceptions which are formulated in the Sophistes and Philebus are here applied, e. g. the θατέρου φύσις, and the μικτὴ οὐσία ; that the new conception of matter or extension as γενέσεως τιθήνη is of the same order with the πρωτογενὲς εἶδος of the Politicus, and that the mythological colouring more resembles the myth in that dialogue, than any other of the Platonic myths, although the relation of God to the world is more nobly conceived[1]. Cosmological and Pythagorizing notions are not absent from other dialogues. The Phaedo and Republic are both influenced by them. But a comparison of passages makes it clear that the point of view implied in the Timaeus is different and more developed.

The Timaeus is only the opening page or prelude of the most magnificent prose-poem ever planned by a single mind ; a complete Bible, had it been written, of philosophical imagination. The story of Creation was to have been followed up by the history of the Chosen People, of their wars with the Unbelievers, and of the final triumph of the Good. Here indeed would have been an account of Evolution. But it breaks off before the rebel *armada* had been set in array.

What stayed the hand of the veteran thinker and creator from this fair work ? We can only conjecture. But the Laws afford a possible reply. His practical enthusiasm was inexhaustible. In ages far remote, it might be, the vision of that conflict of the Sons of Light with the material Power of Atlantis might operate for good. But ere then, the day of Hellas might be dim. The states for whose reform he had so cared might all have foundered. The years were closing

---

[1] Compare for example the desperate notion of God relinquishing the helm, with the delegation of the lower works to the demiurgi: Tim. 42 E ὁ μὲν πάντα ταῦτα διατάξας ἔμενεν ἐν τῷ ἑαυτοῦ κατὰ φύσιν ἤθει.

round him, the setting of his life[1] was near at hand.  He had
no longer strength for both efforts.  The speculative and
imaginative powers, perhaps, were ebbing from him.  But
practical earnestness remained.  He would attempt what
still was possible.  And perchance those who had turned a
deaf ear to his ideal strains might listen to suggestions of
reform if pitched in a somewhat lower key.

Some such reflections are naturally suggested by Plato's
sudden descent from the Council Chamber of Zeus, where
the Critias breaks off, to enter on the long and weary labour
of the Laws.

---

# EXCURSUS

*On the position of the Sophistes, Politicus, and Philebus in the
order of the Platonic Dialogues ; and on some characteristics of Plato's latest writings[2].*

§ 1.  It had long since occurred to students of Plato that,
while it appeared antecedently probable that all the shorter
dialogues were previous to the Republic, the Sophistes
in particular implied a philosophical point of view in
advance of the definition of knowledge and opinion at the
end of Republic, Book v.  It seemed possible, however, that
such an opinion might be coloured with some metaphysical
preconception, and in editing the Sophistes I resolved to
verify this observation without having recourse to 'metaphysical aid.'  The objections which Socher had raised
against the genuineness of this and the companion dialogue
had been answered by W. H. Thompson[3], who had defended
both writings as having the general characteristics of Plato's
style.  I felt, however, that the discrepancies to which attention had been called by Socher and Schaarschmidt[4] could not
be thus easily disposed of, and must have some significance.

---

[1] Laws VI. 770 A ἡμεῖς δ' ἐν δυσμαῖς τοῦ βίου.

[2] From a paper read to the Oxford Philological Society in June 1890, by
L. Campbell.

[3] In the Cambridge Philosophical Transactions.

[4] Rheinisches Museum.

Now, as difficulties of a similar kind had been urged with reference to the Laws, it seemed a question worth raising, whether any affinity could be established between these several works, as belonging to one and the same period of Plato's literary activity. For if the Laws were assumed to be genuine on the authority of Aristotle, the genuineness of the other dialogues would be rendered more probable, if their peculiarities were found to approximate to those of a well-authenticated writing. And the difficulty about the Laws would at the same time be lessened. For the authorities which attest their genuineness (to lay no stress on the confessions of the Athenian Stranger) represent them as Plato's latest—or even posthumous—work, and any differences either of manner or of matter between this dialogue and the Republic would be made more intelligible by the discovery of an interval and a period of transition. A step would also have been made towards the solution of the problem stated by Schleiermacher, but not satisfactorily solved by him—nor by Hermann—the order of the dialogues.

The Timaeus and Critias are avowedly subsequent to the Republic. And the right method for testing my hypothesis was, therefore, to ascertain what elements of style and diction, as well as of opinion, were 'common and peculiar' to the Sophist and Statesman with the Timaeus, Critias and Laws : i. e. what special features are shared by the members of this group, which are absent from the other dialogues, or less apparent in them. It was a method of concomitant variations. The result of a somewhat tedious inquiry was to confirm my anticipation, and to include the Philebus also amongst the works which are intermediate between the Republic and the Laws. The only support for this view which I could find in any previous writer, was the opinion expressed by Ueberweg in his *Untersuchungen über die Echtheit und Zeitfolge Platonischen Schriften* [1] (pp. 207–209), but afterwards abandoned by him in deference to the objections of Schaarschmidt.

The argument set forth in my Introductions to the Sophistes and Politicus, possibly through some fault of §2.

[1] Wien, 1861.

exposition[1], seems to have escaped the attention of scholars. And yet, so far as it was sound, it tended to establish a fact of real significance, viz. that the Republic and Laws are separated by a period of great philosophical activity :—an activity which renders more conceivable the discrepancies which have troubled critics of the Laws, and accounts for the supposed anomalies in the intervening dialogues.

The same conclusion is now upheld in Germany on similar, but wholly independent grounds—viz. on a statistical estimate of variations in Plato's use of particles and recurring formulae. In 1881 W. Dittenberger in *Hermes* (vol. xvi, pp. 321–345)[2] called attention to the fact that the formula τί μήν—so familiar to the Platonic student,—is entirely absent from two-thirds of the genuine dialogues. From this point onwards the statistics of Platonic formulae have been pursued by successive inquirers. Dr. Martin Schanz, for example, in vol. xxi of *Hermes* (1886), pointed out a striking variation in the comparative frequency of τῷ ὄντι and ὄντως, the latter being found only in a fraction of the dialogues, while in some of these it has completely ousted τῷ ὄντι[3]. The avoidance of hiatus (noticed by Blass in 1874, *Att. Ber.* ii, p. 426) is another phenomenon of which the varying frequency points to the same result.

The accumulated outcome of seven years of this kind of inquiry is recapitulated by Constantin Ritter in his little book of *Untersuchungen* (Stuttgardt, 1888), in which he has recorded also valuable observations of his own.

Notwithstanding the tendency—which seems to be inseparable from such investigations—to aim at more precise results than the method justifies (of which Dittenberger's inference from the use of τί μάν ; in Epicharmus[4] is an amusing example), yet, when minor uncertainties are discarded, there remains a strong concurrence of evidence in favour of

---

[1] I take this late opportunity of correcting a serious misprint. For 'Critias,' in the tabular view on p. xxxiii of the work in question, read 'Crito.'

[2] *Sprachliche Kriterien für die Chronologie der Platonischen Dialoge.*

[3] Herm. xxi. 439-459, *Zur Entwickelung des Platonischen Stils.*

[4] That Plato brought back τί μήν from his journey to Sicily.

placing the Soph., Polit., Phileb., Tim., Critias, and Laws—
nearly in this order—as latest in a separate group.

When it is considered that the facts thus collected unite
in corroborating the observations published in 1867, it will
probably be admitted that the inference is irresistible, and
that the question of the order has to this extent been solved.

It is therefore worth some pains to examine the significance § 3.
of the phenomenon, the reality of which is now abundantly
demonstrated.

We are really considering an important movement in the
development of Greek prose writing :—the gradual prevalence
over Plato's style of the rhetorical artificiality, which in the
earlier periods he had alternately ridiculed and coquettishly
played with.

And we are met on the threshold by one of those
observations by which the mere collection of instances has to
be checked. Some of the features which we are now taught
to identify with Plato's later manner are already present in
the Phaedrus,—the balanced cadences, the vocabulary enriched from the poets and the earlier literature, the comparative rareness of hiatus, the use of ὄντως for τῷ ὄντι, of δῆλον ὡς
for δῆλον ὅτι, even the Ionic dative plural, all are represented
there. But the most casual reader cannot fail to see that in
the Phaedrus these are but decorations of a sort of carnival
dress that is worn for the occasion only. Plato is caught by
a fascination at which he himself is laughing all the while.
His Socrates is νυμφόληπτος and a strange fluency possesses
him. For Phaedrus' sake he is compelled to phrase his
thoughts poetically,—he speaks in dithyrambs[1]. It would
therefore be rash, as F. Blass long since observed, to argue
from the avoidance of hiatus, for example, to the date of the
Phaedrus. But this dialogue has, notwithstanding, a real
bearing on the subject in hand. For in spite of all his

---

[1] Observe the suggestion of lyrical cadences—

$$- \overset{''}{\phantom{x}} \cup - - - \overset{''}{\phantom{x}} \cup \underline{\phantom{x}} -$$
ἐρρωμένως ῥωσθεῖσ᾽ ἀγωγῇ
$$\cup \overset{''}{\phantom{x}} \cup \ \cup \underline{\phantom{x}} \ \cup \overset{''}{\phantom{x}} \ \cup \ \underline{\phantom{x}} -$$
ἐπωνυμίαν ἔρως ἐκλήθη.

persiflage it is evident that the tricks of style which Plato
there parodied were exercising a powerful charm upon his
mind.   In the Politicus and Laws, where, under the grander
name of ῥητορεία (Polit. 303), the once ridiculed ῥητορική is
admitted to have a legitimate function, the ornate manner
is employed not in humorous irony, but with solemn gravity.
It is therefore reasonable to regard the rhetorical flowers
of the Phaedrus as the early anticipation of a habit which
long afterwards becomes fixed.

§ 4.    The following are some of the peculiarities of language
in which the Sophistes, Politicus and Philebus are found
to approximate to the Laws, and which therefore mark the
transition towards Plato's later style.   It may be well to take
first the particles and formulae, to which Dittenberger and
others have recently directed attention.   For the purpose
of the argument we may for the present neglect those which
(like τί μήν ;) bear only on the relation of the Republic (with
Phaedr., Theaet.) to the earlier dialogues.

γε μήν occurs only twice in Rep., and once in each of the
following :—Euthyd., Symp., Phaedr., Theaet. ; but 6 times
in Soph. (52 pp.)[1], 8 times in Polit. (54 pp.), 7 times in Tim.
(76 pp.), and 25 times in Laws (368 pp.).

περ, added to adverbs and pronominal words :—

|  |  |  |
|---|---|---|
| μέχριπερ | only in | Tim. (4), Critias (1), Laws (16). |
| ὅπῃπερ | „ | Soph., Tim., Laws. |
| ὁπόσοσπερ | „ | Polit., Laws. |
| ὁσαχῆπερ | „ | Tim. 43 E. |

τάχ' ἴσως (combined) only in Soph. (2), Polit. (3), Phil. (3),
Tim. (1),  Laws (11).

σχεδόν without τι, frequent in Aristotle,—a use which first
appears in Euripides[2],—is rare in Plato *except* in Soph. (26),
Polit. (13), Phil. (14), Tim. (9), Criti. (4), Laws (122).

The use of ὄντως is one of many coincidences between
Plato's later style and tragic Greek.   According to Stephanus
(*Thesaurus*) the word appears first in Euripides.   It is used

---

[1] The pages referred to are those of the edition of Stephanus, 1578.

[2] In Soph. Trach. 43 with τι πῆμα following the omission of τι is accidental.

also by Aristophanes in burlesque of tragedy, and by Xenophon in the *Banquet* (which Dittenberger has shown to be not one of his earlier writings). In Plato—

$\tau\hat{\omega}$ ὄντι occurs repeatedly in Lach., Prot., Euthyd., Apol., Euthyphr., Gorg., Symp., In Rep. 42 times, In Soph. once, and hardly ever in Polit., Phileb., Tim., Critias, Laws.

ὄντως occurs not at all in Lach., Charm., Prot., Euthyd., Apol., Crito, Euthyphr., Gorg., Meno, Symp.: but
In Theaet. once.
In Phaedr. 6 times.
In Rep.　　9 „
In Soph.　21 „
In Polit.　11 „
In Phileb. 15 „
In Tim.　　8 „
In Laws　 50 „

τὰ νῦν or τὸ νῦν for νῦν (clearly a tragic form) occurs singly in Charm., Prot., Phaedo, Theaet., Rep., not at all in Lach., Euthyd., Crat., Apol., Crit., Euthyphr., Gorg., Meno, Symp., Phaedr.,—but in Soph. 5 times, Polit. 5 times, Phileb. 9 times, Tim. 7 times, Critias 3 times, and Laws 79 times.

μῶν in questions (also tragic) occurs sporadically in Charm. (2), Euthyd. (3), Phaedo (1), Meno (3), Theaet. (4), Rep. (3): but frequently in Soph. (12), Polit. (8), Phileb. (10), Laws (29). (There are very few questions in Tim., Critias.)

χρεὼν (ἐστί) for χρή occurs *only* in Soph. (1), Polit. (1), Tim. (3), Critias (2), and Laws (57).

The suppression of ὁ μέν &c. in antitheses, and the use of abstract plurals (especially of the dative pl.), as in ἀνυποδησίαις συγγίγνεσθαι (Laws), are also tragic uses which become more frequent in the same group of dialogues.

Another marked difference appears in the preference of the more concentrated εἰς (or κατὰ) δύναμιν for εἰς (or κατὰ) τὸ δυνατόν. This occurs in

| | |
|---|---|
| Euthyd. 1 | Soph. 3 |
| Phaedr. 1 | Phil. 4 |
| Rep. 6 | Tim. 10 |
| | Critias 1 |
| | Laws 63. |

A usage, not tragic but Ionic, which is continued in Aristotle, is the employment of καθάπερ as the equivalent of ὥσπερ.
See Bonitz' *Index Aristotelicus*, s. v. καθάπερ. In the few
instances in which καθάπερ appears in Lach., Euthyd., Crat.,
Gorg., Symp., Theaet., Phaedr., Rep. (6 times), it may
generally be distinguished from ὥσπερ, which occurs in Rep.
212 times.

But in Soph., Polit., Phileb., Tim., Critias, Laws, it occurs
more frequently, and with less discrimination.

ὥσπερ appears in Soph. 9 times, Polit. 16, Phil. 9, Tim. 10,
Critias 2, Laws 24.

καθάπερ appears in Soph. 14 times, Polit. 34, Phil. 27, Tim.
11, Critias 5, Laws 148.

Another Aristotelian use (see Bonitz, s. v. δέ) is that of δέ
for ἀλλά, e. g. in Soph. 248 D, Laws II. 666 E.

The Ionic dative plural form is a point of resemblance
between the Politicus and the Laws,—although, according to
the best MSS., it appears also in a few places of the Phaedrus
and Republic[1].

The three such datives in the Phaedrus have an obvious
rhythmical intention,—240 B ἡδίστοισιν εἶναι ὑπάρχει : 276 B
ἐν ἡμέραισιν ὀκτώ : 278 B ἄλλαισιν ἄλλων ψυχαῖς (where this
form prevents the concurrence of 3 spondees).

In the Republic there are only five genuine instances, for
κενεαγορίαισιν in X, νώτοισιν in V occur in poetical quotations :
and of these five σμικροῖσι and θεοῖσι in B. III occur in a passage
that is much coloured with poetical citation ; μεγάλοισι in B. IX,
in a highly-wrought piece of declamation ; αὐτοῖσι (*bis*) is in
both instances emphatic and not attributive.

But in the Laws—especially in the later books—the use of
such forms has become a confirmed trick of style. It is
extended to participles, and is by no means confined to
words in common use. And of the four examples in the
Politicus, while one (279 E τούτοισι) is doubtful (Bekker reads
τουτοισί), two at least are of the freer kind : 262 A διπλασίοισι,
304 E ἑπομένοισιν. The less rhetorical vein of the Sophistes and

---

[1] See Schneider's Rep. vol. 1, p. 222.

Philebus may account for the absence of such forms in them.

The periphrastic tendency (noticed in the Introduction to Soph. and Polit., p. xxxiv), of which χρεών, πρέπον ἂν εἴη, λέγοις ἄν, δέον ἂν εἴη, διὰ τὸ μετέχον εἶναι (Tim. 47 B)[1], ἡ τοῦ θατέρου φύσις, τὸ τῆς ἀποπλανήσεως, &c., are examples, belongs likewise to the same preference for earfilling and rhythmically balanced expression.

The peculiar diction of these later dialogues is next to be illustrated.    § 5.

In tabulating the Platonic writings so as to bring out the fact that many words were 'common and peculiar' to a certain section of them, it was formerly observed that 'the position of the Phaedrus and Parmenides'—'and,' it should have been added, 'of the Philebus'—was due to exceptional circumstances[2]. This meant that from the nature of the subject matter, and from the mode of treatment intentionally adopted, the vocabulary of the Phaedrus was exceptionally rich, while that of the Parmenides and of the Philebus, in consequence of the dry abstractedness of the discussions in them, was exceptionally poor. It follows that in order to show the bearing of the Phaedrus or of the Philebus upon the present discussion (the Parmenides is not immediately in point), a somewhat closer analysis of either dialogue becomes advisable.

(*a*) The Phaedrus has more than 170 words which occur in no other dialogue—about three for every page in the edition of Stephanus. The Theaetetus, which may be taken as representing Plato's normal style, has 93 words not occurring in other dialogues—or 1½ words for every page of Stephanus. The peculiar words of the Phaedrus are borrowed from all literature, especially poetic literature, whether Epic, Lyric, or Tragic. Such words as γάννυμαι, γλαυκόμματος, γνάθος, ἡνιοχέω, λιγυρός, μελίγηρυς, μετεωροπορέω, μήνιμα, ὁμόζυξ, τελεσιουργός, ὑποβρύχιος, ὑψαύχην, and others which the beauty of Phaedrus draws from the full breast of

---

[1] Cp. Laws ii. 661 B ἀθάνατον εἶναι γενόμενον ὅ τι τάχιστα.
[2] General Introduction to Soph. and Polit. p. xxxiii.

Socrates, are foreign alike to the style of the Republic and the Laws. What then is the specific element of diction which the Phaedrus owns in common with Tim., Critias, Laws? It consists (1) of physiological words, (2) words borrowed from the dialect of tragedy, and (3) words having a religious or mystical significance.

(1) Not Isocrates only, but also 'Hippocrates the Asclepiad' is mentioned with commendation in the Phaedrus[1]. And whatever may be the significance attaching to that circumstance, the following words, connected with physical states or processes, occur in the Phaedrus and Timaeus, and in no other Platonic dialogue :—βρέχω, γαργαλίζω, διαθερμαίνω, διαχωρέω, ἐπιμίγνυμι, ἐρείδω, ἰσχίον, κατακορής, κολλάω, πτερόν, συμφράττω, φάτνη.

If now we include Phaedr., Tim., Critias, Laws, the following words peculiar to this small group are of the same complexion :—ἀκέφαλος (Phaedr., Laws), ἀπορρέω (Phaedr., Tim., Critias, Laws), ἀσήμαντος (Phaedr., Laws), διατρέχω (Phaedr., Laws), ἔκφυσις (Phaedr., Laws), ἐμπλέκω (Phaedr., Laws), εὔροια (Phaedr., Laws; cp. εὔρους, Tim., Laws), προσάντης (Phaedr., Laws), σπάω (Phaedr., Laws), ὑπεραίρω (Phaedr., Laws), ὕψος (Phaedr., Tim., Critias, Laws).

(2) The Phaedrus borrows at least as much from Epic and Lyric sources as from tragedy ; but the poetical words which it adopts in common with Tim., Critias, Laws, are mostly of the tragic, or old Attic, type. For example, ἀηδία (Phaedr., Laws), αἱμύλος (Phaedr., Laws), ἄκαρπος (Phaedr., Tim.), ἄνους (Phaedr., Tim., Laws), ἄπαις (Phaedr., Laws), ἄσιτος (Phaedr., Laws), ἑκασταχοῦ[2] (Phaedr., Critias, Laws), ἐμμανής (Phaedr., Tim., Laws), ἐμπεδόω (Phaedr., Laws), εὐπειθής (Phaedr., Laws), θαλλός (Phaedr., Laws), θήρειος (Phaedr., Tim.), νομή (Phaedr., Tim., Critias, Laws), παμμέγας (Phaedr., Tim.), παράνοια (Phaedr., Laws), πρόνοια (Phaedr., Tim.), συμμιγής (Phaedr., Laws), ταπεινός (Phaedr., Laws), τύμβος (Phaedr., Laws), ᾠδός (Phaedr., Laws).

(3) Words having religious or mystical associations are

---

[1] 270 c.    [2] Thucyd. III. 82.

δαιμονίως (Phaedr., Tim.), ἐνθουσιαστικός (Phaedr., Tim.), ἐποπτεύω (Phaedr., Laws), ὀργιάζω (Phaedr., Laws), ὀρκωμοσία (Phaedr., Critias), συνεύχομαι (Phaedr., Laws).

The Phaedrus, like the Republic, has many words unknown to the earlier literature. The following are peculiar to the Phaedrus :—ἀνήκοος, ἀπειρόκαλος, ἀποπολεμέω, ἀχρώματος, δημωφελής, δικαιωτήριον, δοξόσοφος, ἐνθουσίασις, εὐαπάτητος, ἰσομέτρητος, κακηγορία, λογοδαίδαλος, μετεωρολογία, πολυήκοος, προσπαραγράφω, πτερορρυέω, συγκορυβαντιάω, τερατολόγος, ὑπερουράνιος, ὑψηλόνους, ψιλῶς, ψοφοδεής, ψυχαγωγία.

(*b*) It has been admitted that the proportionate number of 'late words' in the Philebus, i. e. of words common and peculiar to it with the Timaeus, Critias, and Laws, is below that of the Republic, and even of the Phaedo and Symposium. And this fact appears at first sight to contradict the evidence of the more recent statistical inquiry, as well as the other data adduced in 1867. But the anomaly is explained, as already said, by the restricted vocabulary of a dialogue which deals so exclusively as the Philebus does with metaphysical and psychological formulae. In 55 pp. (St.) the Philebus has only 55 peculiar words, i. e. only one for a page, or one-third of the proportion of the Phaedrus. Now of these 55, notwithstanding the prosaic cast of the dialogue, the following are tragic :— ἀναίνομαι, ἀναπολέω, ἄοινος, μισητός, περιβόητος, προχαίρω, χαρμονή, ψευδῶς, while these are Epic— ἀσπαστός, θέρομαι, μισγάγκεια (but cp. Ar. Pl. 953). A good many are late derivatives—ἀπόρημα, δυσχέρασμα, προσδόκημα, στοχασμός, ἀναχώρησις, θεώρησις, στόχασις, φάρμαξις, διδυμότης, δυσαπαλλακτία (or -ξία), εὐδοκιμία, δοξοκαλία, αὐτάρκεια, παιδαριώδης, περατοειδής, νηφαντικός, ξυλουργικός, ἀνοηταίνω. The rest are chiefly new compounds (with ἀνα, ἐν, ἐπι, προσ, συν, ὑπεξ).

If we now examine the group consisting of Soph., Polit., Phil., Tim., Critias, Laws, we shall find that although the contribution of the Philebus to the special vocabulary of this group is not large, it is notwithstanding significant. It contains about

20 tragic words, including ἀμήχανος, ἄμικτος, ἐνδίκως, καίριος, λῴων, πάθη, περιφανής, τέκνον, τέρψις.

50 new compounds, including ἀποσώζω, διαμερίζω, ἐξιάομαι, συγκεφαλαιόομαι.

10 late derivatives, including ἀναισθησία, δοξοσοφία, ἐπιχείρησις, πῆξις, σύστημα, σωμασκία.

And 13 physiological words, amongst others διάκρισις, σύγκρισις, σύγκρασις, σύμμιξις, ὑπομίγνυμι, ὑποδοχή.

The Phaedrus affects ornateness, novelty, and copiousness of diction, and in doing so anticipates some of the peculiarities which became fixed in the later vocabulary. The Philebus on the other hand is below the average of copiousness; and yet, when its characteristic features are examined not by number but by kind, it is found to partake, even in its diction, of the special characteristics which mark the Timaeus, Critias, and Laws.

**§ 6.** (*c*) Every reader of the Laws must have been struck by the frequency of Old Attic and Ionic words and forms. Stallbaum [1], in reply to Zeller, tried to account for this by the nature of the subject and the gravity of phrase belonging naturally to a book on legislation. But the same features are present more or less in all the six dialogues now under review. Dionysius must have had these in mind, when he coupled Plato with Thucydides as having written in the earlier Attic. The familiar observation that the later prose runs more and more into Iambic and Paeonic rhythms might also be largely illustrated from these writings.

Such obvious facts as the use of τέκνον for παιδίον, βλάβος [2] side by side with βλάβη, of κλαυθμονή for ὀλοφυρμός, of τέρψις and χαρμονή side by side with ἡδονή, the preference of full-sounding words like φράζειν, φλαῦρος, the fondness shown for νᾶμα, ἐπιρροή, γεννήτωρ, ἀμαθαίνω, and similar words, are apparent even to the cursory reader. ἡσυχαῖος is preferred to ἡσύχιος, εἵνεκα to ἕνεκα (if we may trust the MSS.), ᾿Απόλλωνα to ᾿Απόλλω. The mannerism of the style appears not only in the use of different forms, but in the frequency of

---

[1] Vol. x, pp. 57 foll.          [2] βλάβος = damage, βλάβη = hurt.

some which occur sparingly elsewhere. Thus manuscript evidence favours πτάσθαι (not πτέσθαι), φευξεῖσθαι (not φεύξεσθαι) in the Laws more than in other parts of Plato [1]. Some inflexions, although true to analogy, are altogether new—such as ἠπιστήθη (1 aor. of ἐπίσταμαι) Laws 686 D. A noticeable peculiarity is the substitution of the common γυμναστής for the specially Attic παιδοτριβής.

The following specimens are taken from a list of 150 tragic, Ionic and Old Attic words, which are found in the Laws and not elsewhere in Plato :—

ἀΐστωρ, ἀκταίνω, ἀρτίπους, βασιλίς, γαμετή, γέννα, δολιχός, ἔρεισμα, θράσος, κλαυθμονή, κλύδων, λύσιμος, νέηλυς, οἰκισμός (Solon), ὁμίλημα, ὄττα, παίδειος, παιδουργία, παπαῖ, πέλανος, πλησιόχωρος (Herodotus), ῥέζω, σφριγάω, τητάομαι, τόλμημα, φορβάς, χόρευμα, χρόνιος.

The following, on the other hand, are amongst the words which appear in the Laws for the first time. Some of these also have an Ionic flavour. Others are obviously recent derivatives and compounds :—

ἀναθόλωσις, ἀπηγόρημα, γλυκυθυμία, γοώδης, διαθετήρ, διαφωνία, δυσκληρέω, ἔνρυθμος, ἐξείλησις, ἐπιτηδειότης, ἑτεροφωνία, εὐθημονέομαι, θρασυξενία, καλλίφωνος, κηπεία, κλεμμάδιος [2], κόσμημα, λοιδόρησις, μακαριότης, μεγαλόνοια, μετακόσμησις, μοναυλία, ὀχεταγωγία, παιδοποίησις, πατρονομέομαι, σκάμμα, σωφρονιστύς, ταπείνωσις, τάφρευμα, φιλοστοργέω, φωνασκέω.

(*d*) There are marked differences of style between the Timaeus and the Laws. The high-wrought concentration, the sustained movement, the strong energy of the shorter dialogue might be effectively contrasted with the leisurely progress, the lengthy diatribes, even the tedious wordiness of a conversation, for which the longest day can hardly have sufficed. Yet the two writings have a large common element, and as compared with the Republic they both exhibit changes pointing the same way. At present we are concerned with the vocabulary. Of 81 words common and peculiar to the

---

[1] Schanz' Plato, vol. XII, p. 18.  [2] Qu. an κλεπτάδιος ?

Timaeus and Critias (considered as one dialogue) with the Laws (Tim. 68, Critias 13), about 40 are tragic, including—

ἀθλέω, ἀπειθής, δυσθυμία, ἐξαίσιος, ἐξορθόω, εὐαγής, εὔψυχος [1], εὐψυχία, ἰσάριθμος, κύτος, κῶλον, μετάστασις, ξενών, παίδευμα, πλημμελῶς, σαλεύω, φράττω.

Of 348 words peculiar to the Timaeus and Critias a certain number may be attributed to the special subject of the Timaeus. But more than 100 (or about one-third) belong to the language of tragedy: for example, αἰνιγμός, ἄση, βασιλείδης, δύσφορος, εὐήμερος, θλίβω, καθαγίζω, κάρτα, κατηρεφής, κεραυνός, κτῆνος, κτυπός, μένος, νοτερός, πεδάω, περιθύμως, σκέπη, στενωπός, συντόμως, σφίγγω, τιμαλφής, τραχηλός, ὑπόστεγος, φλόξ, χειρουργέω, χλόη, ὠχρός.

Of late forms in the Timaeus some of the most remarkable are—

ἀδιάπλαστος, ἔγερσις, ἔγκαυμα, ζύμωσις, θερμαντικός, ἱμαντώδης, κηροειδής, ὀξυήκοος, ὀργανοποιία, παραφορότης, φάντασις (side by side with φαντασία).

(*e*) It remains (under the head of diction) to show that the vocabulary of the Sophist and the Statesman, apart from the special subject matter of either dialogue, has much in common with that which has been found to belong to the Philebus, Timaeus, Critias and Laws.

The vocabulary of the Sophist (52 pp. St.) coincides in 54 instances with that of the Laws.

The Politicus (54 pp. St.) exhibits 72 such coincidences.

Between the Timaeus (with Critias) and Soph. there are 36 coincidences of diction. Between Tim., Critias, and Politicus, 42.

This estimate includes only words which are found in no Platonic dialogue, except those immediately in question.

The number of tragic words found in Soph., Polit. (taken together), and in none of the 'earlier dialogues,' is 116, of which the following are the most remarkable:—ἀγήρως (Polit., Phileb., Tim., Laws), ἀντίσταθμος (Soph.), ἄπλετος (Soph.,

---

[1] In the Laws εὐψυχία has the special sense of 'good mental condition,' but εὔψυχος = ἀνδρεῖος.

Laws), δεσπότις (Polit., Tim., Laws), εὐλαβής (-ῶς) (Soph., Polit., Laws), κρηπίς (Polit., Laws), κρυφαῖος (Soph., Tim.), νωθής (Polit., Tim.), πάλη (Soph., Polit., Laws), πάμπαν (Polit., Tim., Laws), σκέπασμα (Polit., Laws), στέγασμα (Polit., Tim., Critias), στέλλω (Soph., Polit., Laws), συμφυής (Soph., Tim., Laws), σύνδρομος (Polit., Laws), σύντομος (Polit., Critias, Laws), σύντροφος (Polit., Laws), τολμηρός (Soph., Laws), χαῦνος (Soph., Polit., Laws).

In adverting briefly to the less tangible subject of § 7. structure and rhythm, I may refer to the Introductions to the Sophist and Statesman, ed. 1867. A word of reply is due, however, to a friendly objector, who urges that the tone and colouring of these dialogues are dramatically suited to the presence of Timaeus, of the Eleatic friend, and of the Athenian Stranger.

(1) Why should the chief speakers in these six dialogues talk so nearly in the same curious manner?

Compare together, for example, the following places, taken almost at random :—

Soph. 258 D τὴν γὰρ θατέρου φύσιν . . . τὸ μὴ ὄν.
Polit. 284 E, 288 E.
Phileb. 53 B,C σμικρὸν ἄρα καθαρὸν . . . καλλίων γίγνοιτ' ἄν.
Ib. 67 *ad fin.* οἷς πιστεύοντες . . . ἑκάστοτε λόγων.
Tim. 53 B νῦν δ' αὖ τὴν διάταξιν . . . ξυνέψεσθε.
Laws I. 644 D θαῦμα μὲν . . . ξυνεστηκός.
Ib. I. 648 D, E.

And (2) Why, within the limits of the same dialogue, should Socrates, Critias, and Hermogenes adopt the language of Timaeus, or why should Socrates, Theodorus, Theaetetus and the younger Socrates adopt the fashion of their new acquaintance from Magna Graecia? Why should the young Protarchus ape the new-fangled affectations of his teacher? Or how is it that Kleinias and Megillus, although less in-structed, have caught so readily the style of their Athenian companion for the day?

Compare once more—

> Sophist. 217 C (Socrates).
>     ,,    265 D (Theaetetus).
> Polit. 257 B (Theodorus).
> Phileb. 13 B, C (Protarchus).
> Tim. 20 C (Hermocrates).
>     ,,   23 C (Kritias).
>     ,,   29 D (Socrates).
> Laws IV. 713 B (Megillus).
>     ,,   VI. 752 B (Kleinias).

Surely the resemblance of style between the Cretan and Spartan, and of both to their Athenian friend, is closer than that between the several Athenian speakers in the Symposium.

I have tried to show, not only that the six dialogues, Soph., Polit., Phil., Tim., Critias, Laws, are rightly grouped together as the latest, but I have also endeavoured to describe the nature of the change in Plato's manner of writing which this fact involves. The chief characteristics of his later style are the following :—

1. A measured and elaborately balanced gravity of utterance, in which the rhetorical artifices which he had once half affected and half despised are passing into a settled habit of ῥητορεία and conscious impressiveness.

2. The increasing prevalence of certain particles and formulae, adopted partly for euphony, and partly to suit with an archaic and tragic colouring.

3. A range of diction passing far beyond the limits of 'Attic purity,' and reverting in a remarkable degree to the use of the Old Attic and Ionic words. Macaulay speaks of Milton's prose as 'stiff with cloth of gold.' Plato's later style is stiffened with a sort of τραγικὸς λῆρος, or antique embroidery, while the tendency to employ new compounds and derivatives, already active in the Republic, is present here in a more advanced stage.

4. The artificial balancing and interlacing of phrases is carried much further than even in the Phaedrus, Republic and Theaetetus.

§ 8. If we turn from the form to the substance of these six dialogues, we find in them an increasing sense of the remoteness of the ideal, without any diminution of its importance. A deepening religious consciousness is associated with a clearer perception of the distance between man and God, and of the feebleness and dependence of mankind. But the feeling is accompanied with a firm determination to face and cope with the burden and the mystery of the actual world—to provide support for human weakness, alleviations of inevitable misery. The presence of Necessity in the universe and in life is acknowledged, in order that it may be partially overcome.

The change here implied is not one of creed, but of mental attitude, induced, as we may gather from indications that are not obscure, by a large acquaintance with the contemporary world, and by the writer's own experience in wrestling with intellectual and practical difficulties. The effect is traceable (1) in metaphysics, (2) in logic, (3) in psychology, (4) in physics, (5) in politics, (6) in ethics and religion, and (7) in the conception of history.

## (1) METAPHYSICS.

In their metaphysical aspect, these dialogues turn chiefly on a few highly abstract notions, the essential forms of Being, not-being, sameness, difference, motion, rest, limit, finite, infinite:—and these are no longer merely contemplated in their isolated reality, but in their connexion with phenomena and with one another. The method becomes less ontological and more logical. 'The idea of good' is approached not merely through Socratic definitions or figurative adumbration, but through the direct analysis and manipulation of primary conceptions—for example those of measure and symmetry. The five γένη of the Sophist, the description of the ideas in the Politicus as τὰ τῶν πάντων στοιχεῖα, the metaphysical categories, as one may venture to term them, of the Philebus, belong to a more exact mode of philosophizing than had been thought of when the Phaedo was written, and one which was only vaguely anticipated in the Republic as 'the longer way.' The θατέρου φύσις and μικτὴ οὐσία of the Sophist and Philebus are resumed and applied in the Timaeus.—The Laws contain but few references to metaphysical problems. But this is in entire keeping with the remotion of the actual from the ideal; and the attentive student is aware of an ever-growing conviction of the significance of measure and of number, and a fixed belief in the supremacy of Mind. 'Measure' is indeed the first and last word of Plato's metaphysic—the μετρητική of the Protagoras anticipates the μέτρον of the Philebus.

## (2) Logic.

The dialectical achievement in the Sophistes is the pivot of the logical movement. Plato had found that thought was being sacrificed to the instrument of thought, or rather that the instrument was itself endangered. Zeno had 'jammed' the weapon of Parmenides. The Sophist-dialogue brings for the first time into a clear light the nature of predication, of classification, and of proof, and places the science of Logic on a rational footing. The effects of the discussion, which is continued in the Politicus, are apparent in the method of that dialogue, and even in the elaborate distinctions of the Laws. As Mr. Paul Shorey observes in his able papers on the Timaeus, the practical aim of the whole business is 'to obtain a working logic.'

## (3) Psychology.

The dialectical advance accompanies, and indeed occasions, a corresponding progress in psychological analysis—which is especially apparent in the Philebus. It is needless to illustrate this familiar fact. See especially Tim. 42 A, 69 D;

Laws III. 644–646, IV. 770 D (comparing this last passage with Rep. VI *sub init.*).

## (4) Physics.

In all these dialogues, and not in the Timaeus only, there is an unceasing interest in production (γένεσις), and a tendency to look upon things from the point of view of the Universe rather than of Man. See especially the myth in the Politicus, and the mention of prehistoric cataclysms in the Laws :—also Soph. 265 C and Phileb. 59 A, compared with Tim. 59 C, D. The physical conditions of mental states, especially of Sensation, Pleasure and Pain, and of moral evil are more insisted on. The importance of health, and of the care of the body generally, is more fully recognized. The allusions to medicine and gymnastic in the Republic are in strong contrast to those in the Timaeus and Laws. And a great advance in clearness of cosmological conception is implied in the discussion of ἄνω and κάτω in the Timaeus, as compared with the employment of the same notion in the Phaedo and Republic.

## (5) Politics.

In Rep. B. v Plato already acknowledges that it is hard to realize the ideal. Notwithstanding, he is absolutely bent on realizing it. He will not swerve aside in deference to opinion or circumstances, but will wait until circumstances favour, and till opinion shall come round. He is sure that mankind are not unreasonable, could they but hear the truth. Before he wrote the Laws, a varied intercourse with man had dashed his confidence and lessened his hope, but had not impaired his zeal for the improvement of mankind. He is now ready to adapt himself to human weakness and, the higher road having proved impracticable, to seek a *modus vivendi* that may embody as much of righteousness and wisdom as the race will bear. The work is full of the gentleness and consideration of one who lives on

> Till old experience do attain
> To something like prophetic strain.

Now the crisis of this tradition from Optimism to Meliorism
is reflected in a very interesting manner in the Statesman-
dialogue.    Plato has been brought to feel that in his ideal
Republic he had been grasping at the moon.    He had legislated for the age of Cronos during the reverse cycle which
is *said to be* under the government of Zeus.    The dialogue is
instinct with a suppressed bitterness, which time had mel-
lowed when he wrote the Laws.    But the author of the
Politicus is not less keenly bent on finding a practicable way.
The problem he sets before himself is how to bring scientific
thought to bear upon the actual world.    Despairing of spon-
taneous obedience to a perfect will, he has recourse to
legislative enactment, as a second best course, by which men
may be led or driven to imitate from afar off the free movement of Divine Reason.    The art of legislation is compared
to that of weaving (a metaphor which is repeated in the Laws).
And the same stress is laid, as in many passages of the later
dialogue, on the importance of combining, through breeding
and education, the energetic with the gentler elements of
human nature.    The provision of a διάδοχος in Laws VI to
supplement the work of the legislator, is in accordance
with the hint given in the Politicus, and may be contrasted
with the contempt that is showered on ἐπανόρθωσις in
Rep. IV. 426.

The Timaeus, Critias and Hermocrates, had the trilogy
been completed, would have been the outcome of another
mood, but of one also differing from the spirit of the Republic.    In the Republic Plato contents himself with laying down
great principles.    He is confident that, if these are preserved,
the citizens may be trusted to discover the rest.    The opening of the Timaeus makes a deeper plunge into actuality by
raising the almost impossible demand :—How did the citizens
of the ideal state comport themselves in that far-off time
beyond our ken (Rep. VI. 499 D) ?    This question belongs
to the firm resolution to be practical, to realize abstractions
in the concrete, to make the step from οὐσία to γένεσις, which
finds a less confident application in the Politicus and Laws.
The same motive appears in the admission of approximate

knowledge in the Philebus as requisite 'if a man is to be able to find his way home.'

### (6) ETHICS AND RELIGION.

In these last dialogues, more than elsewhere in Plato, we are made conscious, as has been already said, of the distance between Man and God. The imitation of the Divine is still the highest duty, but it is an imitation from very far away. Although the doctrine of metempsychosis is retained, and the belief in immortality is more than once very finely expressed, yet the proud claim to ἀπαθανατισμός the life which is a meditation of death, and even the formation of the inward man after the pattern in the Heavens, are no longer the leading notes of the new strain. The philosopher is less than ever simply bent on saving his own soul. The speakers rather strive after the partial overcoming of evil with good, the infusion of a spirit of generosity, which may leaven the inherent selfishness of men;—the institution of a rule of life which may prevent society from foundering amid the weltering sea of politics. Sympathy with Orphic observances, especially in the abstention from animal food (ἀλλήλων ἐδωδή) is common to the Politicus and Laws.

The human and divine νοῦς are kept apart in the Philebus more emphatically than in Rep. vi; and in the Timaeus the elements of soul which the Creator dispenses to the δημιουργοί for the creation of man are not of pristine purity ἀλλὰ δεύτερα καὶ τρίτα. The faintness which now attends 'the larger hope' is strikingly apparent in the Politicus-myth.

### (7) HISTORY.

Lastly, in these six dialogues (to which the Menexenus may perhaps be added) we find a more distinct anticipation than elsewhere in Plato of two essentially modern ideas, the conception, namely, of a History of Philosophy and of a Philosophy of History.

(*a*) In the Sophistes, philosophical method is for the first time expressly based on criticism (although the step had been partly anticipated in the Parmenides and Theaetetus). The same plan is carried out in parts of the Philebus.

(*b*) The Hermocrates, on the other hand, was to have been an ideal history of human good and evil. And in speculating on the nature and origin of legislation, the Athenian Stranger Laws III finds it advisable to preface his remarks with a recapitulation of the earlier History of Hellas.

# ESSAY II

## ON THE TEXT OF THIS EDITION OF PLATO'S REPUBLIC.

BEKKER'S text of the Republic (1817 to 1823) rests on §1. twelve MSS., which he quotes as A Θ Ξ Π Φ Ṕ K $q$ $t$[1] $v$ m[2] r, all collated by himself; he also mentions the Venetian Codex $t$[3], of which Schanz in editing the smaller dialogues has since made valuable use.

Stallbaum added the Florentine MSS. a b c n x α' β' γ',—and Schneider, besides re-collating $q$ exhaustively, collated Lobcov., Vind. D, Vind. E, Vind. F[4]. To these twenty-four MSS. is now to be added a twenty-fifth, Codex 4, Plutei xxviii, in the Malatestian Library at Cesena, which in the present edition will be quoted as M (Malatestianus). Subsequent editors, especially K. F. Hermann, have relied more exclusively than Bekker did upon the chief MS., Paris A; and Baiter in his preface to the fifth Zurich edition particularizes no other MS. authority.

---

[1] Collated only to p. 441 St.

[2] 'Primo libro caret,' Bekker.

[3] Schneider, Praef. p. xxxi 'Ibidem [Morellius] quartum commemorat non magis a quoquam collatum, absque numero post impressum indicem bibliothecae Marcianae additum, forma maxima sec. xii scriptum, inter alia Platonica civitatem cum scholiis continentem, sed inde a libro tertio usque ad ultimum manu sec. xv exaratum.' It is now numbered App. 4. 1. Schanz has proved that the earlier portion is derived from Paris A.

[4] Schneider's habit of marking all his MSS. anew is a drawback to the otherwise exceptional usefulness of his edition. Bekker's and Stallbaum's marks are here retained, those of Schneider being adopted only for his own MSS. He made little use of Vind. 54, in which the Republic is by a recent hand and copied from Lobcov.

§ 2.    The present text was originally founded on Baiter's edition
of 1881, but in the course of revision has assumed a form
more nearly approaching to that of Hermann.   The select
list of various readings at the bottom of each page has been
for the most part taken from three MSS., A Π M, with
occasional reference to others of those mentioned above.

Paris. A, of the ninth century, has been re-examined
several times since Bekker's edition, notably by K. F.
Hermann, Dübner, and Cobet : also by Baiter, who, however, in his preface to his edition of 1881 still marked
a few readings as uncertain.   In order to clear up these
remaining uncertainties I visited the Paris National Library
in June, 1890, and found that several readings which are
quite clear and unmistakable in Paris. A are still mis-
quoted in the editions[1].   I have therefore now made
a fresh collation of this MS. with the present text, which
had unfortunately been partly printed off before the
opportunity for this collation occurred, and a list of the
corrections which are thus rendered necessary will be found
in the Appendix to this Essay (Appendix I).

Bekker's quotations of Venn. Π Ξ are also not free
from inaccuracy, and Professor C. Castellani, Prefect of the
Library of St. Mark at Venice, has done good service by
providing a complete new collation of these MSS. with
Bekker's text for the purposes of the present edition.   A
list of Bekker's errors and omissions will be found below,
Appendix III.

M. Schanz considers Ven. Π and the MSS. derived
from it (D K q β′ Vind. D), as bearing traces in the
Republic of a tradition independent of Par. A.   And it
may be observed in confirmation of this opinion, that the
erroneous reading λύρα (for αὔρα) in III. 401 C, now shown
to be peculiar to Π, must have arisen from the misreading
of a copy in uncial characters and therefore anterior to A.

A third set of MSS., having some probable readings not

[1] I refer especially to Baiter's Zurich editions since 1881.

distinctly referable to A or Π, are regarded by many recent editors as merely interpolated. To this class of 'bad' MSS. Schanz[1] has consigned the Cesena MS., our M. A full description of this MS., written by Professor Enrico Rostagno, who has collated it for this edition, is given below (Appendix IV).

In Mucciuoli's catalogue of the Malatestian Library it is described as of the twelfth century, and Signor Rostagno, whose judgement is of weight, speaks of it as for the most part written towards the end of that century. The absence of iota subscript from the portion written in the earlier hand, and the constant accentuation of the enclitic τέ, after unaccented syllables, afford some slight confirmation of this view. The portion of the MS. which is by a later hand, is referred to as *M* (*italicé*) in the critical notes to this edition (pp. 308–319).

Other MSS. occasionally referred to in the critical notes are :

> b Laurentianus, 85, 6, containing Books I and II :
> but from II. 358 E πολλάκις τις νοῦν ἔχων in
> a fifteenth century hand. The earlier part,
> ending with περὶ γὰρ τίνος ἂν μᾶλλον was
> formerly quoted as of the twelfth century,
> but according to E. Rostagno belongs to
> the thirteenth.
>
> x Laurentianus, 85, 7, thirteenth century (?).
>
> a Laurentianus, 80, 7, fifteenth century.
>
> γ Laurentianus, 42, thirteenth century (?).
>
> D Parisiensis, 1810, thirteenth century.
>
> K Parisiensis, 1642, fifteenth century.
>
> m Vaticanus, 61, 'bombyc. aut chart.' Bekker.
>
> r Vaticanus, 1029 a b, 'membr. f. max. foliis
> bipartitis,' 2 vols.
>
> Vind. E Vindobonensis, 1, 'chart.'

---

[1] *Studien*, p. 67.

Vind. F  Vindobonensis, 55, fourteenth century.

Vind. D  Vindobonensis, 89, 'chart. f. max.'

  *q*  Monacensis, 237, fifteenth century.

  Ξ  Venetus, 184, fifteenth century.

§ 3. Some further observations on the more important MSS.
are here subjoined [1] :

A *Parisiensis* A : Paris National Library MS. Gr. 1807 :
ninth century. On the left-hand margin, at the end of
the volume, the following note has been written with contractions in reddish ink, and in a cursive hand :—ὠρθώθη
ἡ βίβλος αὕτη ὑπὸ κωνσταντίνου μητροπολίτου ἱεραπόλεως τοῦ
καὶ ὠνησαμένου. If this Hierapolis might be assumed
to be the Metropolis of Phrygia, the question raised by
Mr. T. W. Allen in the *Journal of Philology*, vol. xxi,
as to the *provenance* of the group of MSS. to which A belongs, would be partly answered. But the Bishop is not to
be held responsible for the more serious corrections, which
were probably made by the copyist of the Scholia before
the book was exposed for sale. Indeed, some of the most
trivial annotations, ignorant emendations, and impossible
various readings, bear a suspicious resemblance to the
metropolitan's writing. The question whether the first
diorthotes, who seems to have been a careful person, had
before him any other MS. than that from which the first
hand had copied, is important, but can hardly be resolved.
In point of authority there is in fact hardly any difference
between the first and second hand. It will be observed
that there are several cases in which words omitted in the
text are supplied in the margin, to all appearance by the
second hand. The first hand corrected many slips in the

---

[1] For a complete catalogue of the MSS. of Plato, see Martin Wohlrab's
*Die Platonhandschriften und ihre gegenseitigen Beziehungen*, Leipzig, 1887.
Those left out of account in the present essay are Venetus 187 (closely
related to Ξ) ; Vindobonensis 54, collated in part by Schneider ; Mon. C. =
Monacensis 490 (collated by Schneider in B. vii and part of B. x) ; Mona-
censis 514, Venetus 150, and the fragments ♭ (Bekker) and Palatinus
(Schneider) in the Libraries of Darmstadt and Heidelberg. (On Lobcov.,
Φ, Θ, see below.)

course of writing, and has frequently covered the blank made by erasure with ÷ ÷ ÷ instead of writing again over the same space. Many slight omissions are supplied either by the first or second hand between the lines. Adscript iota is often added by the second hand, sometimes a little above the line (ἄ˙δης) which appears to have been a mode intermediate between adscription and subscription (αι and ᾳ). Many, if not most of the accents have been added after writing,—perhaps by the diorthotes. They are in a different ink, as Cobet observed.

Habits of the MS. to be noticed once for all are:

1. Spelling:—

ποιῶ not ποῶ, υἱός or ὕός more often than ὑός, πορρωτέρωι, ἐγγυτέρωι, &c., σώιζω, θνήισκω, &c. Paragogic ν retained before consonants: οὕτως and οὕτω interchanged.

2. Accentuation:—

a. τέ, ποῦ, τίς (*sic*):—enclitics are constantly thus accented—especially after unaccented syllables.

b. ἄλλό τι, ἤπέρ ἐστιν, &c.

c. γ᾽οῦν (not γοῦν).

d. ὅστισ οὖν, &c. (generally corrected to ὁστισοῦν, &c., by a recent hand).

e. μὴ δὲ μία, &c.

f. ἐπαυτοφώρῳ, καθαυτό, αὐτοδικαιοσύνη, &c.

g. ἀφίῃ, παρίῃ, ξυνίῃ (retained in the text).

h. The accent on μέν, δέ, &c., in antitheses often doubled,—the second accent often added by another hand.

i. A singular practice of distinguishing ἄν = ἐάν, by omitting the accent and writing ἀν. In many cases the accent originally written has been erased.

k. ἔστιν and ἐστίν constantly confused.

l. τᾶλλα, not τἄλλα:—also τῆνδε, τοιᾶνδε, &c.

3. Breathings:—

a. Confusion of αὐτοῦ and αὑτοῦ, αὐτή and αὕτη, &c.

b. ὡσ αὕτως.

c. ἀθρόος, ἄσμενος, ἄττα, ἴκταρ.

4. Abbreviations are very infrequent; the commonest is ◡ for *v*. Possibly, however, some errors, such as ζητεῖ for ζεῖ in IV. 440 C may be due to early compendia.

5. The persons are distinguished with : between the words and a line — in the margin. The punctuation is careful on the whole.

Later hands have busied themselves in various ways :—

1. In changing ω to o, ι to η and vice versa, not always rightly ;—ὠφελία to ὠφελεία.—ἐλλειπῆ remains unchanged.

2. In constantly changing ει of the 2nd per. sing. middle and passive to ηι, η of the plup. 1st per. sing. to ειν, and placing the mark of elision ' over ἐγῷμαι, οὐχ', &c.

3. In changing the division of syllables between lines by erasing a letter at the end of one line and inserting it at the beginning of the next, or vice versa.

4. Marking interrogation by subjoining a comma to the colon between the speeches, thus ⁚.

5. Adding marginal glosses, various readings and initial letters of respondents' names, inserted where a doubt seemed possible.

Π    *Venetus* Π : St. Mark's Library, Venice ; MS. Gr. 185 : twelfth century. It contains the Republic, with the loss of about four leaves, from VI. 507 E to VII. 515 D, and from X. 612 E ἔστι ταῦτα to the end.

The first hand has been but slightly corrected while the MS. was new, but a hand of the fifteenth century has altered many readings, generally in accordance with the tradition which is now represented by Ven. Ξ. Ven. Π supplies some words that are omitted in Par. A, though it agrees with A in other places, where both have to be corrected from a different source.

The following brief description of the MS. is from the hand of Professor Castellani, Prefect of St. Mark's Library at Venice :

'Cod. 185, membr. Saec. XII [1], 348 × 260 millim., ff. 349,

---

[1] Morelli, *Bibl. manuscripta*, p. 109.

quadragenorum versuum. Continet, praeter Timaeum
Locrum, Platonis Euthyphr., Socratis Apol., Crit., Phaed.,
Cratyl., Theaet., Sophist., Politicum, Parmen., Phileb.,
Sympos., Phaedr., Alcib. A et B, Hipparch., Amat.,
Clitoph., Rempublicam. In Republica vero deest finis
libri sexti et initium libri septimi, duo enim folia ibi
abscissa sunt : deest quoque finis libri decimi, qui desinit
in verbis : ὥσπερ καὶ καταρχὰς ὡμολογοῦμεν· ἔστι ταῦτα.
Accedunt nonnulla scholia, partim a manu eadem qua
textus, partim a recentiore exscripta. Emendationes quoque sunt frequentes, eaeque saeculo XV adscribuntur.'

*Cesenas* M : 28. 4, in the Malatestian Library at Cesena : M
twelfth to thirteenth century. This MS. is here selected
as a sufficient representative of the third or inferior class of
MSS. which retain some readings independently of A and Π.
It is older than any of the Florentine MSS.[1], and it has
a close and indisputable affinity to Vaticanus m, the last of
Bekker's MSS. which M. Schanz eliminated in his process
of reducing the apparatus to A and Π. The age of m is not
given, but Bekker's description of it as 'bombyc. aut
chartac.' shows that it has no high claim to antiquity.
This MS., while agreeing in very many points with M, is
much more seriously interpolated, and may be assumed to
represent a later stage of corruption[2]. M therefore holds
a high place in the sub-family m Ξ *v t*, to which the
Florentine MSS. a c γ' may be confidently added. Of this
class Schanz writes as follows :

' So liegt die Schlussfolgerung nahe, dass die Mutterhandschrift von m Ξ *v t* aus dem Parisinus A stammt.
Nicht zu verwundern ist, dass bei der grossen zeitlichen
Entfernung von A die Handschriften m Ξ *v t* Inter-
polationen und Ergänzungen der Lücken, welche A bietet,

---

[1] The older hand of Flor. b, was formerly attributed to the twelfth century.
But E. Rostagno, who has examined both MSS. (M and b) places nearly
a century between them.

[2] See this fact brought out below, pp. 87 ff.

aus der zweiten Klasse erfahren haben. So kommt es, dass mehrmals A mit seinen Weglassungen allein dasteht [1].'

§ 4. Whether or not the Cesena MS. is the 'Mutterhandschrift' in question, it will be presently shown to belong to the same sub-family, and to be much purer than m, while it is older by two centuries than Ξ *v t*, and little younger, if at all, than Π, the head MS. of the 'second class,' above referred to. Schanz's reasoning in the passage quoted is thus invalidated in so far as changes are accounted for by long lapse of time, and while every assumption in a matter of this kind may be regarded as provisional, we are in the meantime justified in regarding M as a third witness agreeing in some things with A, in others supporting Π, and also giving independent testimony for some readings which have hitherto depended on the inferior evidence of Ven. Ξ, Mon. *q*, Vind. E, or Flor. a c x *a' γ'*. This opinion rests upon the following grounds :

A M *versus* Π　　I. It is admitted that M agrees with A in many points where Π diverges from both.

|  | A M | Π |
|---|---|---|
| I. 328 D | °ἀλλ' ἡμεῖς—ἰέναι | *om.* |
| „ D | νεανίαις | νεανίσκοις |
| „ D | †χαίρω | χαίρω γε |
| 330 A | °πάνυ τι—ἐπιεικὴς | *om.* |
| 342 B | °ἢ οὔτε αὐτῆς | *om.* |
| 343 A | χρῆν | χρὴ |
| 346 E | °ἀλλ', ὅπερ—παρα-σκευάζει | *om.* |
| II. 358 E | †τί ὄν τε | τί οἷόν τε |
| 365 C | °ἀλάθειαν | ἀλήθειαν |
| 366 A | †*om.* | αὖ μέγα δύνανται |
| 367 A | °ξύνοικος ἦ | ξυνοικοίη |
| 372 C | °σύκων | συκῶν |
| 373 A | *om.* | καὶ τὴν ποικιλίαν |

---

[1] Hermes xii. p. 181 (Berlin, 1877).

| A M | Π |
|---|---|
| II. 377 E °κακῶς τῷ | κακῶ οὐσίαν τῷ |
| 379 A *om.* | ἐάν τε ἐν μέλεσιν |
| 381 A *om.* | καὶ ἀμφιέσματα |
| 382 E *om.* | οὔτε κατὰ φαντασίας |
| 383 B °παιῶν᾽ | παιὼν |
| III. 389 D †κολάσεως Α: κολά- σαι ὡς Μ | κολάσει ὡς |
| 394 D °ἐγώ—γὰρ δὴ | *om.* |
| 401 C °αὔρα | λύρα |
| 402 C οἰόμεθα | οἰώμεθα |
| 403 B °δόξει | δόξῃ |
| 404 D °ἐν τῷ | ἐν τῇ |
| 405 C °λυγιζόμενος | λογιζόμενος |
| 407 B °μὲν | μὲν γὰρ |
| 408 C ὀρθότατα | ὀρθότατά γε |
| 411 D †γενομένου | γενομένου |
| 414 E °δημιουργουμένη | δημιουργουμένου |
| 416 C παρασκευάσασθαι | παρεσκευάσθαι |
| IV. 421 A °ἔχουσιν | ἔχωσιν |
| 423 B αὐξομένη | αὐξανομένη |
| 425 C τὰ ἀγοραῖα | τάδε τὰ ἀγοραῖα |
| 427 E μὴ οὐ βοηθεῖν | μὴ βοηθεῖν |
| 429 A °εὑρῆσθαι | εἰρῆσθαι |
| 437 C †ἐρῶντος (corr. from ἐρωτῶντος Α) | ἐρωτῶντος |
| „ D ἢ οὐ Α (corr.): ἢ οὖ Μ | που (που Α² mg. corr.) |
| 438 C δὴ δεῖ | δεῖ |
| 443 B †τελευταῖον | τέλεον (et Α² mg.) |
| V. 451 B φόνου καὶ καθαρὸν | φόνου καθαρὸν |
| 460 D τιτθαῖς | τίτθαις |
| 461 C °τούτων | τῶν τοιούτων |
| 462 C °κομιδῇ μὲν οὖν— κατὰ ταὐτὰ (Μ *om.* πόλει) | *om.* |
| 463 B °οἱ δ᾽ | *om.* |

|  | A M | Π |
|---|---|---|
| v. 464 E | °ἀνάγκην | ἀνάγκη |
| 465 C | °παιδοτροφίαι A<br>παιδοτροφία M | παιδοτρόφω |
| 466 B | °φαμὲν | ἔφαμεν |
| 468 C | °μηδενὶ | καὶ μηδενὶ |
| 469 A | °ἀνθρώπων—θεοῦ | om. |
| 470 A | φοβησόμεθα | φοβηθησόμεθα |
| 472 B | τόδε χρὴ | χρὴ τόδε |
| „ C | °τελέως | om. |
| „ D | °ἀποδεῖξαι | ἐπιδεῖξαι |
| 478 B | °φαμέν | ἔφαμεν |
| „ C | °φανότερον | φανερώτερον |
| „ D | °ἐντὸς | ἑνὸς |
| 479 C | °ᾧ (ὦ M) | ὡς |
| 479 C D | °μὴ εἶναι—μᾶλλον | om. |
| VI. 487 C | †ταύτην | ταύτῃ |
| 488 A | χαλεπὸν πάθος | χαλεπὸν τὸ πάθος |
| 490 D | †τοὺς | τοὺς μὲν |
| „ D | τῆς διαβολῆς | τῆς ἤδη διαβολῆς |
| 504 B | ἄλλη | ἀλλ' ἡ |
| „ C | ἀπολείπων | ἀπολειπὼν |
| 505 A | ᾖ | ᾖ καὶ |
| 506 B | τελέως | παντελῶς |
| 507 B | °ἔστι ταῦτα | om. |
| VII. 522 C | ποῖον | τὸ ποῖον |
| 529 C | †ἐξ ὑπτίας μὲν | ἐξ ὑπτίας νέων |
| 533 A | μοι | ἐμοὶ |
| „ B | ἢ πρὸς θεραπείαν | ἢ καὶ πρὸς θεραπείαν |
| 536 A | τὰ τοιαῦτα σκοπεῖν | πάντη τὰ τοιαῦτα σκοπεῖν |
| 538 C | °πρὸς τοὺς ἁπτομένους | προσαπτομένους |
| 540 B | °κοσμεῖν | κατακοσμεῖν |
| „ E | δέκ' ἐτῶν | δεκετῶν |
| VIII. 543 B | °ὦν | ὡς |
| „ C | °διεληλυθὼς | διελήλυθας |
| 544 C | καὶ ἡ πασῶν | καὶ πασῶν |

| | | A M | Π |
|---|---|---|---|
| VIII. | 547 E | τοιούτους | τοὺς τοιούτους |
| | 554 B | °τοῦ χοροῦ | τοῦ χρόνου |
| | 556 A | οὔτε γ᾽ | καὶ οὔτε γ᾽ |
| | 559 C | °τὸν τῶν | τὸν |
| | 560 B | °ὑποτρεφόμεναι | ὑποστρεφόμεναι |
| | „ E | °εὐπαιδευσίαν | ἀπαιδευσίαν |
| | 561 A | τὴν τῶν | εἰς τὴν τῶν |
| | „ A | °μάλα | μάλιστα |
| | 562 B | προύθεντο | προύθετο |
| | „ B | ἀπώλλυ | ἀπόλλυ |
| | „ D | αὐτῆς | αὐτοῦ |
| | 564 A | καὶ ἐν πολιτείαις | καὶ δὴ καὶ ἐν πολιτείαις |
| | „ E | σμικρὰ | σμικρὸν |
| | 569 C | °πῦρ δούλων | πῦρ δοῦλον |
| IX. | 571 C | καὶ τίνας | τίνας |
| | 572 A | °ἐᾷ | ἐὰν |
| | „ A | ἐλθὸν | ἐλθὼν |
| | „ D | ἕκαστον | ἑκάστων· |
| | 573 A | ὅταν | ὅταν δὴ |
| | „ A | αἱ ἄλλαι | καὶ αἱ ἄλλαι |
| | „ D | °διακυβερνᾷ | διακυβερνῶ |
| | 574 C | °πάνυ γε | οὐ πάνυ γε |
| | 578 E | ἢ πλείω | ἢ καὶ πλείω |
| | 579 C | καρποῦται ἀνὴρ | καρποῦται ὁ ἀνὴρ |
| | 581 A | °ἀεὶ ὅλον | δεῖ ὅλον |
| | 584 B | τοῦτο | τούτῳ |
| X. | 597 B | ἢ τῇ φύσει | ἢ ἐν τῇ φύσει |
| | 598 B | °πόρρω ἄρα που | πόρρω που ἄρα που |
| | 600 D | ἐπιστατήσωσι τῆς παιδείας | τῆς παιδείας ἐπιστατήσωσι |
| | 601 A | †ἐν τοῖς τοιούτοις | ἑτέροις τοιούτοις |
| | „ E | °ὑπηρετήσει | ὑπηρέτης εἶ |
| | 602 A | °πάνυ γε—ἐπιστήμην | *om.* |
| | „ D | καὶ αἱ ἄλλαι | καὶ ἄλλαι |
| | 603 E | †ψυχῆς | τύχης |

| A M | | Π |
|---|---|---|
| X. 604 D | ἰατρικὴν θρηνῳδίαν | ἰατρικὴν καὶ θρηνῳδίαν |
| 606 A | °εἰ ἐκείνῃ | ἐκείνῃ |
| „ C | °αἰσχύνοιο | αἰσχύνοις |
| „ C | °ἂν εἴης | ἀνείης |
| 610 E | °ἐσκήνηται | ἐσκήνωται |
| 611 D | κεκλάσθαι | ἐκκεκλάσθαι |

The fifty-five places which are marked with ° in the foregoing list afford ample evidence that the main text of M is independent of Π. But for the purpose of testing the relationship between M and A, these passages may be neglected, for they merely show that both MSS. agree so far in a sound tradition. What is correct in both comes from the archetype and does not prove any closer affinity.

In one place, IV. 437 D, M is free from the suspicion of error which attends the reading of A. In another, III. 389 D, the reading of M is intermediate, and accounts for the corruption of Π. It remains then to consider those places in which A and M agree in readings (1) erroneous or (2) doubtful.

(1) In the twelve places, which are here marked with an obelus †, the two MSS. are clearly following the same mistaken original. But it is still an open question whether the later is derived from the earlier, or whether they are both derivatives from an older copy in which these errors were already to be found. Such changes as those in III. 411 D (from γενομένου to γενομένου), VI. 487 C (from ταύτηι to ταύτην), X. 603 E (from ψυχῆς to τύχης), may have occurred at an early stage of the tradition.

In IV. 437 C A hesitates between two readings, the first hand having written ἐρωτῶντος, and the diorthotes having corrected this to ἐρῶντος, which is the reading of M. This being so, it is not a little remarkable that in II. 383 B, M gives ἐνδυτεῖσθαι, the reading of A[1], but *not* of the diorthotes, who has changed it to ἐνδατεῖσθαι. The reading μὲν for νέων (529 C) is so widely spread that it may be assumed to be an early corruption, and νέων is by no means certain.

There remains τί ὄν τε (II. 358 E), a mistaken reading, but one into which an early copyist might easily have fallen, and ἐν τοῖς for ἑτέροις (X. 601 A), which forms part of a phrase supplied in the margin by the diorthotes of A, and therefore not with certainty attributable to the MS. from which A was copied.

(2) So much for the erroneous agreement of M with A. There remain fifty-one places which may be considered doubtful. In most of these the reading of Π has been rejected by recent editors in deference to the authority of A. If they are right in this, the same argument recurs :— A and M agree in following the archetype, which proves nothing as to their special affinity. Where all three MSS. are in error, as in X. 604 D, Π shows a further stage of corruption, and the error is not one which commenced with A. For it is presupposed in Π, which *ex hypothesi* is independent of the A tradition. In IV. 437 D there is a reading which appears significant. A seems originally to have read που, the reading of Π. An early corrector changed this to ἢ οὗ, and wrote που in the margin. M has ἢ οὗ, and ἢ οὗ is the true reading. In IX. 576 D, on the other hand, the true reading ἀρετῇ is absent from A Π M, but is given as a variant by A² in the margin. If M were copied from A, the scribe would surely have availed himself of this. With regard to the omissions not marked with °, viz. II. 373 A, 379 A, 381 A, 382 E, it may be reasonably argued that Π is right, although not demonstrably so, for the words supplied are not necessary to the sense. But the error, if so be, is one which may have occurred at any period. Even in the few cases, such as III. 408 C, V. 451 B, VI. 488 A, VIII.564 A, where it may be thought that the advantage is on the side of Π, this would indicate affinity between A and M, but would not prove the derivation of the later from the earlier MS.

When all is said, the amount of agreement here exhibited

proves a close relationship between A and M, but does not necessitate the inference of direct derivation.

§ 5.  II. What then is to be inferred from the places in which M agrees with Π while differing from A?

In the following list A = A + A², that is the places are discounted in which the reading of Π M is anticipated by an early corrector of A.

|  |  | A | Π M |
|---|---|---|---|
| A *versus* Π M | I. 330 C | ἤπερ | °ἤπερ |
|  | 332 C | ἔφη ὦ πρὸς | ἔφη πρὸς |
|  | 339 B | καὶ δίκαιον φῇς | °δίκαιον φῇς |
|  | 342 A | δεῖ αἰεὶ | °δεῖ |
|  | 344 E | οὐδέ τι | οὐδὲ |
|  | 345 C? | πιαίνειν c. γρ. ποι- μαίνειν | °ποιμαίνειν |
|  | 347 C | δεῖ δὲ | °δεῖ δὴ |
|  | 349 B | πλεῖον | πλέον |
|  | 352 D | ὥστ' ἐμοὶ | °ὥς γέ μοι |
|  | II. 358 A | *om.* | °ἀδικία δ' ἐπαινεῖται |
|  | „ E | πλέονι | πλέον |
|  | 359 C | ἐπαυτοφώρῳ | ἐπ' αὐτοφώρῳ |
|  | „ C | νόμῳ δὲ βίᾳ | νόμῳ δὲ καὶ βίᾳ |
|  | „ D | μυθολογοῦσι | °ἃ μυθολογοῦσι |
|  | „ D | ἄλλο μὲν | °ἄλλο μὲν ἔχειν |
|  | 360 E | τί οὖν | τίς οὖν |
|  | 364 D | λιστοὶ δὲ στρεπτοί τε | °στρεπτοὶ δέ τε |
|  | „ D | *om.* | τε καὶ δικαιοσύνη |
|  | 366 A | ἀζήμιοι | ἀζήμιοι μόνον |
|  | 374 B | οἰκοδόμον, ἵνα— γίγνοιτο | οἰκοδόμον ἀλλὰ σκυτοτόμον, ἵνα—γίγνοιτο Π oἰκοδόμον ἵνα — γίγνοιτο, ἀλλὰ σκυτοτόμον Μ |
|  | „ C | σκυτοτόμων | σκυτοτομῶν |
|  | 378 D | τοιαῦτα μᾶλλον | °τοιαῦτα λεκτέα μᾶλλον |
|  | III. 387 C | ὑπὸ | °ὑπὲρ |
|  | 390 A | νεανικεύματα | ˙νεανι(σκ)εύματα |

|  | A | ΠΜ |
|---|---|---|
| III. 392 A | περιορίζομεν οἷς | °πέρι ὁριζομένοις |
| 395 C | ἵνα ἐκ τῆς μιμήσεως | °ἵνα μὴ ἐκ τῆς μιμήσεως |
| 396 D | ἑαυτοῦ | °ἑαυτὸν |
| 398 A | τε εἰς | τ' ἂν εἰς |
| 399 C | ἀποβαίνοντα | °τὰ ἀποβαίνοντα |
| 401 C | ἀνεμόμενοι | °νεμόμενοι |
| 402 D | διότι | °δὴ ὅ τι |
| 404 A | τε καὶ ἀνάγκη | °τε ἀνάγκη |
| IV. 421 D | διαφέρει | °διαφθείρει |
| 431 A | τὸν | °τὸ |
| 432 C | φράσεις | °φράσῃς |
| 433 E | τοῦτο | °τούτου |
| 434 C | ὧδε λέγωμεν | °ὧδε λέγομεν |
| 435 B | ἑαυτῇ | °αὐτῇ |
| 439 D | ἕτερον | °ἑταῖρον |
| 440 E | εἶδος | °τι εἶδος |
| 443 A | μὲν καὶ | °μὴν καὶ |
| „ D | *om.* | °αὐτὸν αὑτοῦ . . . ἑαυτῷ |
| V. 450 A | ταὐτὰ | °ταῦτα |
| „ C | πειρῶ ἂν | πειρῶ οὖν |
| 451 B | λέγειν δὲ | °λέγειν δὴ |
| 453 E | ὁμολογοῦμεν | ὁμολογοῦμεν Π<br>°ὡμολογοῦμεν Μ |
| 466 A | φύλακας ποιοῦμεν | °φύλακας ποιοῖμεν |
| 469 E | βαλόντος | βάλλοντος |
| VI. 491 C | πάντως | °παντὸς |
| 496 C | τῷ δικαίῳ | τῶν δικαίων |
| „ D | ἀποστάς | ὑποστάς |
| 497 B | ἐκπίπτειν | ἐκπίπτει |
| 498 B | φιλοσοφίᾳ | φιλοσοφίαν |
| 502 B | ἔσθ' ὅστις | ἔσθ' ὅτις |
| 504 D | *om.* | °ἢ γυμναζομένῳ· ἤ, ὃ νῦν δὴ<br>ἐλέγομεν, τοῦ μεγίστου τε |
| VII. 516 E | ὅτι οὗτος | °ὁ τοιοῦτος |
| 518 D | δεῖ . μηχανήσασθαι | °διαμηχανήσασθαι |

|  | | A | Π M |
|---|---|---|---|
| VII. | 521 B | οἱ περὶ | °οἱ περὶ |
|  | 526 D | προσιὸν | °προϊὸν (*M*) |
|  | 527 C | καὶ δὴ καὶ πρὸς | καὶ δὴ πρὸς |
|  | 528 D | μετὰ ταύτην | μετ᾽ αὐτὴν (so Bekker) |
|  | 534 D | πάντα ταῦτα | ταῦτα πάντα |
|  | 537 E | καλὸν | °κακὸν |
| VIII. | 552 D | τί οὖν ; | °δῆλον ἔφη : τί οὖν ; |
|  | 558 B | ἅπαντ᾽ αὐτὰ | ἅπαντα ταῦτα |
|  | 561 A | τὸ μὲν | °τότε μὲν |
|  | 567 B | ὑπεξαίρειν | °ὑπεξαιρεῖν |
| IX. | 582 D | οὕτως | °οὗτος |
|  | 584 D | ἀλλ᾽ ὡς | °ἄλλως |
|  | 585 C | ἀληθείας καὶ αὖ τὸ | °ἀληθείας καὶ αὐτὸ |
| X. | 597 E | τραγῳδοποιός | τραγῳδιοποιός |
|  | 601 D | ἦν ἂν | °πρὸς ἦν ἂν |
|  | 602 B | τὸ δὲ δὴ | τὸ δὴ |

§ 6.   Schanz's theory would assume that in these places M has been emended from a MS. of the family of Π. Is this assumption probable? Let us first consider the places where omissions are supplied or words added :—

II. 358 A, 359 C, D (*bis*), 364 D, 366 A, 374 B, 378 D ; III. 395 C, 398 A ; IV. 443 D ; VI. 504 D ; VIII. 552 A.

Of these II. 358 A, 359 D *bis*, 378 D, 395 C ; IV. 443 D ; VI. 504 D ; VIII. 552 A (eight in all) are probably genuine readings, and in that case need not be accounted for by derivation from Π, while they certainly point to a source independent of A. But if they are not genuine, the supposition that they are borrowed by M from Π is weakened by the fact that the not less plausible additions in II. 366 A, 373 A, 379 A, 381 A, 382 E, have not been similarly borrowed. (*See* above, pp. 74, 75.)

The interpolations in II. 366 A μόνον and 374 B ἀλλὰ σκυτοτόμον must indeed be due either to Π or to an ancestor of Π, it is impossible to say how far removed. But the different position of the words ἀλλὰ σκυτοτόμον in the two MSS., makes against the supposition that they came directly from Π to M. And it is not impossible that they are genuine: see below, p. 112.

Two passages, V. 453 E and VI. 485 A ὡμολογήσθω, in which the reading of M is offered as an alternative in Π, ὁμολογείσθω<sup>ω η</sup> M, ὡμολογήσθω<sup>ὁ εἰ</sup> Π, rather point to the conclusion that M's text, here differing from A, is independent also of Π, since Π is here corrected from the archetype of M. The omission of λιστοὶ δὲ in II. 364 D is clearly right, and is not likely to have been derived from Π, supposing M to have been copied from a derivative of A. The interpolation of μόνον (perhaps corrupted from an earlier μέν) in II. 366 A, and the insertion of ἀλλὰ σκυτοτόμον at different points in 374 B, are wholly insufficient grounds on which to establish any connexion between M and Π. They rather point to a source anterior to both, which may or may not be earlier than A. If the forty-seven readings marked with ° in the foregoing list, or any of them, are genuine, the common source of Π and M represents a tradition independent of A. Besides retaining the words which A omits, in particular the forty letters in VI. 504 D, that source in all probability gave ποιμαίνειν (I. 345 C), πλέον (349 B), στρεπτοὶ δέ τε (II. 364 D), ἀζήμιοι †μόνον (366 A), ἀλλὰ σκυτοτόμον in mg. (374 B), μήν (IV. 443 A), ὡμολογοῦμεν (V. 453 E), ὁμολογείσθω (VI. 485 A), παντός (491 D), τῶν δικαίων (496 C), ὑπηρεσίαν †φιλοσοφίαν (498 B), ἔσθ' †ὅ τις (502 B), μετ' αὐτήν (VII. 528 D).

The amount of variation and corruption which is here implied, may easily have come into existence long before the ninth century. The certainty of corruption after all is limited to the three places here marked with †.

III. So far a presumption has been raised, (1) that M, while closely related to A, is not necessarily derived from it ; (2) that where A and M differ, the difference need not be accounted for by the correction of M through Π. This

A Π *versus* M

view has still to be confirmed by considering the passages in which M differs from A and Π.

§ **7.**    1. M upholds the following sixteen correct readings which have hitherto rested on weak MS. authority, as they are ignored both by A and Π :

I. 330 B ποῖ' M K x $v$ Vind. F    ποῖ A Π

347 A ὧν M b c a a' γ' t    ᾧ A    οὗ Π

„  E πότερον ἀληθεστέρως M x $v$ Vind. F    πότερον ὡς ἀληθεστέρως A Π

III. 402 B καὶ εἰκόνας M Ξ q x $v$ β'    καὶ εἰ εἰκόνας A Π

406 D μακρὰν M Ξ x    μικρὰν A Π

IV. 425 D δικῶν λήξεως M Φ q K $v$ a' β'    δικῶν λήξεις A Π

„  D τὸ παράπαν M K a c    τὸ πάμπαν A Π

441 C ἑνὸς ἑκάστου M Ξ q ꞅ x    ἑνὶ ἑκάστου A Π

V. 462 B ξυνδῇ M Ξ x q ꞅ K $v$    ξυνδεῖ A Π

472 A λόγον λέγειν τε M Ξ a c x    λέγειν λόγον τε A Π

VI. 492 E ἐξαιρῶμεν M Fic.    ἐξαίρωμεν A Π

VIII. 564 E βλίσειε M m a c x γ'    βλίσσειεν A    βλίσσειν Π pr.

IX. 574 D ἐπιλίπῃ M Ξ ꞅ m    ἐπιλείπῃ A    ἐπιλείπει Π

X. 607 E ἀπολελογήσθω M Ξ q c    ἀπολελογίσθω A Π

611 C θεατέον M m a c a' γ' (διαθεατέον Ξ) διαθετέον A Π

N.B.—The reading ᾧ καὶ ἐφ' οὗ, V. 479 C, in which M agrees with a c x a' γ' m $v$ Vind. D, E, F, Athen., now proves to be the reading of Par. A.

And in X. 606 E ἄξιος, for which Π used to be the single early witness, is now supported by A Π M.

2. In the following places, M, while differing from A[1] Π, is anticipated by a corrector of A, though not in every case by the diorthotes :

| A Π | M A$^c$ |
|---|---|
| III. 411 C γεγένηται | γεγένηνται |
| 415 C σίδηρος φύλαξ | σιδηροῦς φύλαξ |
| IV. 424 B ἐπιφρονέουσιν | ἐπιφρονέουσ' |
| 430 E φαίνονται | λέγοντες |
| V. 471 A οὐ πολέμιοι | ὡς οὐ πολέμιοι |
| 474 D ἐπαινεθήσεται | ἐπαινεῖται |

| A Π | M Aᶜ |
|---|---|
| VI. 486 C ἀνόητα | ἀνόνητα |
| 505 B εἰδέναι | εἶναι |
| VII. 525 D δύο ὡς | ὡς (M) |
| 537 E ἐμπίπλαται | ἐμπίμπλανται Aᶜ |
| | ἐμπίπλανται M |
| VIII. 548 B οὐ φανερῶς | φανερῶς |
| 549 A τισιν | τις |
| 557 A φόβων | φόβον |
| IX. 582 C σοφὸς | ὁ σοφὸς |
| 584 B ἔφην δ᾽ | ἔφην |
| X. 613 E ὅρα | ὅρα εἰ |

It will perhaps be said that in these passages the copyist of M or its original had before him the emended text of A; but if so, why in other instances should he have preferred the first hand to the corrector? See Book I. 351 C, II. 383 B, VII. 524 D (M), X. 612 B. The argument is not a strong one, but it at least suggests the alternative possibility, that, in the preceding instances, A may have been corrected from an ancestor of M. And it is observable in this connexion, that while alternative readings occur frequently on the margin of M, in the places here referred to the readings of A¹ do not appear at all.

3. The following readings, for which M is the oldest witness, are improbable or doubtful:

| A Π | M |
|---|---|
| I. 332 E ἐν τῷ | *om.* |
| 340 A αὐτὸς γὰρ Θρασύμαχος | αὐτὸς Θρασύμαχος |
| II. 365 B παρασκευασαμένῳ | παρεσκευασμένῳ |
| 370 B πρᾶξιν | πράξει |
| III. 403 B αὕτη ἡ ἡδονή | αὐτὴν ἡδονή (η and ν confused) |
| V. 475 B τιμᾶσθαι | τιμῶνται |
| VI. 495 A ὅταν | ὃς ἂν |
| 496 A πάνσμικρον A, πᾶν σμικρὸν Π | πάνυ σμικρὸν |

| A Π | M |
|---|---|
| VI. 496 C γενόμενοι | γευόμενοι |
| 499 E ἀλλοίαν | ἀλλ' οἵαν |
| VIII. 546 C τῇ, προμήκη | τῇ προμήκει |
| X. 598 D πάσσοφος | πᾶν σοφὸς |
| 607 C δία σοφῶν A<br>διὰ σοφῶν Π | διασοφῶν |
| 612 A ἀπελυσάμεθα | ἀπεδυσάμεθα |

§ 8.　　4. The evidence so far has tended to show (1) that M in a few passages confirms the genuineness of a text which is otherwise supported only by late MSS. (2) That while thus to some extent independent both of A and Π, it agrees very closely with A and still more closely with the text from which A has been corrected. (3) That it notwithstanding diverges from that text in more than seventy places, where it stands in agreement with Π. (4) That it is not sufficiently removed from Π in point of time to make it probable that in these places it has been altered through contamination with derivatives of Π.

It remains to support the position that, of the inferior MSS., M may be safely taken as the most competent witness. Schanz, in the article already referred to, Hermes XII. p. 181, concludes a careful examination of the MSS. which he regards as derivatives of A by stating that Vat. m is the only one about which for some time he hesitated in forming this conclusion ; or rather, he takes Ξ m *v t* as a sub-family of which m is the oldest representative. The relation of M to m (whose age is uncertain) is therefore now to be exemplified.

M and m　　M is (1) closely related to m, and (2) it is far more free from corruption. Both points may be illustrated from a passage taken almost at random, viz. III. 390 B — V. 465 A.

(1) Close agreement of M m :

| M m | A &c. |
|---|---|
| III. 390 B ἢ βία | ἢ Δία |
| 392 A οἷς οἵους | οἵους |
| 394 D ἴσως δὲ καὶ | ἴσως, ἦν δ' ἐγώ· ἴσως δὲ καὶ |
| 398 C ποῖα ἄττα δοκεῖ | ποῖ' ἄττα δεῖ |
| 403 A ὕβρις | ὕβρει |
| 415 C σιδηροῦς (et A') | σίδηρος |
| IV. 420 E ἐπικλίναντες | κατακλίναντες |
| 425 D περὶξ συμβολαίων | περὶ ξυμβολαίων |
| 428 C ἔφη | ἔχοι |
| V. 457 B ἐπὶ γυμναῖς ταῖς γυναιξὶ (so quoted by Eusebius and Theodoret)[1] | ἐπὶ γυμναῖς γυναιξὶ |
| 461 A θύσας | φύσας |
| 465 A πρὸς πρεσβύτερον | πρεσβύτερον |

In particular these MSS. show coincidences of a minute kind in the elision of final vowels, and this although M frequently avoids elision (e. g. II. 361 C ἀλλὰ ἤτω, III. 408 C εἰ δὲ αἰσχροκερδής, X. 614 B κομισθεὶς δὲ οἴκαδε). The following are a few out of many such coincidences:

| | |
|---|---|
| II. 357 C τί δ' ὃ αὐτό τε | IV. 423 E μᾶλλον δ' ἀντὶ |
| 374 E οἶμαι ἔγωγ', ἦ δ' ὅς | V. 477 E εἰς τοῦτ', ἔφη |
| III. 390 C οὐ μὰ τὸν Δί', ἦ δ' ὅς | VIII. 569 A νὴ Δί', ἦ δ' ὅς |
| 399 D τί δ' αὐλοποιοὺς | |

(2) The following list of corruptions of M and m within the same limits, viz. in V. 466–480, may serve to substantiate the second assertion, that M is considerably less corrupt than m:

| M | m |
|---|---|
| 466 A εὔδαιμον *om.* pr. (perhaps rightly?) | |
| A καὶ ἀμείνων *om.* pr. | |
| | B ποι for πη (Ξ) |
| B μηδ' ἀρκέσῃ | B μηδ' ἀρκέσῃ (Ξ) |

---

[1] The agreement of M m in this place with the quotations of the Fathers, affords an additional argument for the independence of the M tradition.

| M | m |
|---|---|
| 466 | C τῷ ὄντι *om.* |
| | D εἰ for ἦ |
| | E τῶν *om.* |
| 467 | B δή που for εἴ που (Ξ) |
| | C οὐκ for καὶ οὐκ Π |
| C διαφέρειν | C διαφέρειν |
| 468 | A αὐτὸν for αὐτῶν (ɪ Ξ) |
| | A γεωργῶν for γεωργόν |
| B χρῆναι *om.* (perhaps rightly?) | |
| | C τἀριστεῖον (τὸ ἀρ. Ξ) |
| | D διηνεκέεσι (Ξ) |
| 469 | A εὐδαιμόνων (ɪ) |
| C οὖν after ἂν erased | C οὖν after ἂν *om.* (Ξ) |
| | C ἢ οὐκ ἢ for ἢ οὐ (Ξ) |
| | D δὲ δὴ for δὲ |
| E μέλλη for μέλη (Ξ) σκυλεύσεις } E διακωλύσεις } | σκυλεύσεις } E διακωλύσεις } |
| 470 A καὶ τμήσεως for τμήσεως | A καὶ τμήσεως for τμήσεως |
| | B μὲν *om.* |
| | B οὖν *om.* (Ξ) |
| | B οὐδέ for οὐδέν |
| | D ὡμολογουμένη for ὁμολογουμένη |
| E καὶ (before σφόδρα) *om.* | E καὶ (before σφόδρα) *om.* |
| 471 A ὡς οὐ for οὐ | A ὡς οὐ for οὐ |
| | B ἐθέλουσι for ἐθελήσουσι |
| | C ταῦτά γε (Ξ) |
| | C μνησθήσεται |
| D μάχοιτο τὸ | D μάχοιτο τὸ |
| D στρατεύοιτο pr. for συστρατεύοιτο | D στρατεύοιτο for συστρατεύοιτο |
| | E ἡ (before πολιτεία) *om.* |

| M | m |
|---|---|
| 472 A συγγιγνώσκει | A συγγιγνώσκει |
| | A καὶ ἴσως for ἴσως (Ξ) |
| A λέγεις for λέγῃς (sic A¹) | |
| B γίγνεται for γίγνεσθαι | B γίγνεται for γίγνεσθαι (Ξ) |
| | B ζητοῦντι for ζητοῦντες |
| C οἱ νῦν for ἡμῖν | |
| D ἐκείνης <sup>οι</sup> | |
| D ἱκανῶς misplaced | |
| | D ἢ for εἴη •(Ξ) |
| E δυνατόν τ' ἂν sed in rasura, for δυνατώτατ' ἂν | |
| 473 A οὕτως *om.* pr. | |
| B ἂν before ἀγαπῴην *om.* (r Ξ) | |
| E λέγειν *om.* pr. (probably right ?) | |
| E εὐδοκιμήσειεν for εὐδαιμονήσειεν (but mg. γρ. εὐδαιμονήσειεν) | E εὐδοκιμήσειεν (Ξ pr.) |
| | E οὐ *om.* |
| 474 | A γυμνοῦν for γυμνοὺς |
| | A τὸ for τῷ |
| | B σοὶ for σὺ (before οὕτω) |
| | B λέγοντας for λέγοντες |
| D ἐπαινεῖται for ἐπαινεθήσεται (given as an alternative by A²) | D ἐπαινεῖται for ἐπαινεθήσεται |
| 475 A φιλοτίμως | A φιλοτίμως |
| B τούτου *om.* pr. | |
| D πολὺ pr. for πολλοὶ | D πολὺ for πολλοὶ |
| | D ὅς δ' for ὥς γ' |
| | E τοὺς for τοῦτο |
| | E αὐτῷ for αὐτὸ |

|        | M | m |
|--------|---|---|
| 475 E | ἄλλων pr. for ἄλλον | E ἄλλων for ἄλλον |
| 476 C | ὃ for ᾧ | C ὃ for ᾧ |
| D | τι before αὐτὸ *om.* pr. | |
| | | D καὶ before οὔτε *om.* |
| D | χαλεπήνῃ (Ξ) | |
| 477 A | πλειοναχῇ | A πλειοναχῇ |
| B | ἐπὶ τῷ μὴ ὄντι | |
| C | τι *om.* pr. after γένος | C δὴ for τι |
| | | C βλέπων for ἀποβλέπων |
| | | (Ξ) |
| D | ἐκάλεσαν | |
| D | ἐπὶ τὸ αὐτὸ τεταμένην (τ) | |
| 479 A | οὐδαμοῦ for οὐδαμῇ | A οὐδαμοῦ for οὐδαμῇ |
| A | καὶ . . . ἄδικον *om.* pr. | A καὶ . . . ἄδικον *om.* |
| E | ἀλλὰ for ἀλλ' οὐ | E ἀλλὰ for ἀλλ' οὐ |
| 480 A | τινὰς for καλὰς | A τινὰς for καλὰς |
| A | τὸ ἓν for τὸ ὂν | |

It will be seen at once that the errors of m are not only more numerous, but more grave. And it is also noticeable that of the variants which belong to the M tradition one, λέγεις 472 A, agrees with the first hand of A, another, ἐπαινεῖται 474 D, was acknowledged by the diorthotes (or an early corrector) of A, while some of the variants in which M stands alone, e. g. the omissions in 466 A, 468 B, 473 E, and χαλεπήνῃ (476 D) in which Ξ agrees, are defensible readings. There remain thirty-six errors in M to fifty-seven in m.

m    The character of Vat. m sufficiently appears from what has been already said. Vat. m is referred to in this edition only where in consequence of the lacuna in VI and VII the direct evidence of M is not available.

§ 9. τ    Vat. Θ (Vaticanus 266), which was highly valued by Stallbaum, is shown by M. Schanz to be derived from Ven. t as far as III. 389 D, and in the remainder of the

Republic from Π. It is said to be the second volume of Vat. Δ, which is in close agreement with the Bodleian MS. It has now and then a peculiar reading, but where it has any pretentions to independence it generally agrees with Vat. r, which on the whole seems to have a higher claim. The Raudnitz MS. (Schneider's Lobcovicianus), is of the same family, which with rare exceptions comes into use only where there is a lacuna in Π. It may be mentioned incidentally, though it is a matter of slight consequence, that the corrector of M and the writers of the supplementary leaves (*M*) are frequently in agreement with r. This MS. (with Lob. Θ Vind. E) supplies at least one indisputable reading I. 354 B ἐγώ μοι (Α Π ἐγῶμαι).

Here and elsewhere it is uncertain whether an obviously correct reading, appearing only in a comparatively late MS., is derived from earlier tradition or from Byzantine conjecture. Critics have been fond of adopting this last supposition ; the rashness of which, however, becomes evident, when it is considered that the reading ἐπαινεῖται V. 474 D, formerly supposed peculiar to some of the later MSS., has now been found in a text of the twelfth century, and is given as an alternative by the diorthotes of Par. A. Be that as it may, no text of the Republic can be constituted aright without placing some reliance on late MSS. Par. K for example, like Par. D, is in the main a derivative к from Π : but, besides agreeing in special points with *q*, it has here and there a singular reading, which it would be unwise to neglect, and one at least, which although clearly interpolated is demonstrably early, and cannot possibly be due to conjecture (Schneider vainly argues against this position). In IX. 580 D, the reading of K (fifteenth century) λογιστικὸν ἐπιθυμητικὸν θυμικὸν is manifestly anterior to the readings of A τὸ λογιστικὸν, and Π λογιστικὸν, and helps to account for them. This being so, it deserves consideration whether the reading πολλοῖς in X. 615 B, though only a correction of πολλοὶ in Par. D, may not be D

the original of the impossible reading πολλοὶ in Par. A, for
which Ξ gives πολλῶν, the received reading.   It is on the
whole most probable that the copyists or correctors of
the fifteenth century MSS. from which the first printed
editions were chiefly taken, paid more respect to earlier
MSS. than to the conjectures of their contemporaries.
Conjecture has of course played a certain part in the interpolation of texts, but MS. conjecture is generally traceable
to some mis-writing having introduced obscurity which the
scribe has instinctively sought to remove.   This process
began early and was never discontinued.   It has aggravated
corruption, but, except in the removal of the simplest clerical
errors, can seldom be credited with the restoration of an
original text.

§ 10. Ξ    The MS. Venetus Ξ, 184, of the M family (closely related
to A), was written in the fifteenth century by a scholar,
Johannes Rhosus, for the learned Cardinal Bessarion, who
like the Bishop of Hierapolis, amused himself with corrections of the text.   The following is Signor Castellani's
description of it.

'Cod. 184, membr. Saec. XV, 433 × 280 millim., foll. 494,
quinquagenorum versuum.   Continet post Introductionem
Alcinoi in Lectionem Platonis, Platonis Dialogos omnes,
praeter Eryxiam, quibus subjungitur Timaei Locri De
Anima Mundi : Plutarchi De Animae procreatione.   In
calce primi folii r. legitur : Κτῆμα Βεσσαρίωνος καρδηναλέως τοῦ
τῶν Τούσκλου, et in calce ejusdem primi folii v. : Platonis
omnia opera : Liber pulcherrimus et correctissimus Bessa-
rionis Cardinalis Tuscularis.   Codex, litteris aureis picturis-
que exornatus, totus exaratus est manu Joannis Rhosi,
qui addidit in marginibus Scholia locupletissima nitidis
etsi minutis characteribus exscripta.   Accedunt emendationes complures partim ab eodem Rhoso, partim ab ipso
Bessarione recensitae.'

Venetus Ξ is of some historical interest, as it appears to

have been a chief source of the *editio princeps*, the Aldine Plato of 1513. In more than thirty-six places where Ξ differs from A Π M, the Aldine follows this MS.:—even in some passages where the Basle editions and Stephanus give a different reading. These coincidences include two lacunae :

VII. 533 E ἀλλ' . . . ἐν ψυχῇ *om.* Ξ Ald. Steph. (where the reading of Ξ is unnoticed by Bekker) ;

X. 604 D ἰατρικῇ τὴν *om.* Ξ Ald. Steph. :

and such distinctive readings as

II. 359 E δακτύλιον φέρειν ὄν

367 D ἀδικίαν ὃ βλάπτει

VIII. 544 E ῥεύσαντα

562 B ἀπόλλυσιν (again unnoticed by Bekker).

Places where Aldus agrees with Ξ against Steph. are :

II. 360 E διαισθάνεσθαι Ξ (διεσθάνεσθαι Ald.) : διαισθάνεται Steph.

IV. 433 C ὑποληφθὲν Ξ Ald. (and A¹) : ὑπολειφθὲν Steph.

IX. 587 E ἥδιστον Ξ (not quoted by Bekker) Ald. : ἥδιον Steph.

X. 607 D ἀπολογησαμένη Ξ Ald. (and A¹) : ἀπολογησομένη Steph.

620 C περιοῦσαν Ξ Ald. : περιιοῦσαν Steph.

These facts are enough to raise a strong presumption. But Aldus was not tied to one MS. For in II. 358 E he read τί τε ὂν τυγχάνει with Flor. b, in 377 E κακῶς οὐσίας with the same MS., and in VIII. 560 A ἐπιστρεφόμεναι with q D K (a correction of ὑποστρεφόμεναι the reading of Π).

In II. 363 B he may have corrected ἀδικίας, the reading of Ξ, to εὐδικίας by referring to the Odyssey.

Ξ still remains the chief or sole authority for the reading of several places which have gone wrong in A Π M. It is enough to point to—

I. 331 D ἔφην ἐγώ . . . ἔφη ἐγώ A Π M

III. 407 C τινὰς . . . τινὸς A Π M

IV. 434 E ἐκεῖνο . . . ἐκεῖ A Π M

440 E τοῦ λογιστικοῦ . . . τὸ λογιστικὸν A Π M

IV. 440 E καὶ τούτου . . . καὶ τοῦτο Α Π Μ

442 C ὑπὸ τοῦ λόγου . . . ὑπὸ τῶν λόγων Α Π Μ

,, E τοῦτο αὐτὸν . . . τοῦτον αὐτὸν Α Π Μ (τοῦτον αὐτὸ cj. Schneider)

444 B τῷ τοῦ . . . τοῦ δ᾽ αὖ δουλεύειν Α Π Μ

V. 465 A ἄλλως . . . ἄλλος Α Π Μ

VII. 534 A ὅσων . . . ὅσον Α Π Μ

VIII. 544 C διαφέρουσα . . . διαφεύγουσα Α Π Μ

557 E ἄρχειν καὶ δικάζειν . . . ἄρχῃς καὶ δικάζῃς Α Π Μ (δικάζεις Π pr.)

IX. 590 E βούλεται Ξᶜ(x υ Iambl. Stob.) . . . βουλεύεται ΑΠΜ

X. 604 C αἱρεῖ (Ξ q) . . . ἐρεῖ Α Μ (ἔρρει Π)

611 C διαθεατέον . . . διαθετέον Α Π : θεατέον Μ

614 A ἑκάτερος Ξ corr. . . . ἑκάτερον Α Μ (lacuna in Π)

615 B πολλῶν . . . πολλοὶ Α Μ (πολλοῖς D corr.)

See also VII. 532 D διέλθωμεν, now supported by M.

On the important fact of the occasional agreement of Ξ with the papyrus fragment of the Phaedo, see below, p. 98.

x     Flor. x is another MS. without which the apparatus criticus would be imperfect. It is of the M family, but has been corrected from other sources. See especially VIII. 549 A δούλοις τις ἂν.

§ II. q    Flor. β′ is also a 'learned' MS. (Laurent. 80. 19) with which q (Munich 237, fifteenth century) constantly agrees. The date of β′ being uncertain, it is hard to say which is derived from its fellow, but as q has been collated not only by Bekker, but after him by Schneider in the most complete manner, it has been thought safer to refer to q. Bekker's high estimate of this MS. is on the whole justified, although Hermann has rightly rejected many of its readings in deference to the authority of Par. A. The two MSS. q β′ represent a recension based on the Π tradition, partly preserved also in Paris. D K, in which the defects of that tradition have been somewhat boldly supplemented with interpolations which the examination of other MSS. enables us to detect.

For example :

I. 333 E φυλάξασθαι καὶ μὴ **παθεῖν**

II. 358 E τί οἴονται

360 B περιθεῖτο *om.*

364 E μετά τινων ἑορτῶν τε καὶ θυσιῶν (for διὰ θυσιῶν)

365 C πρόθυρα μὲν **γὰρ**

366 D ὡρμήθη (et Par. K pr.)

„ E αὐτὸ δ' ἑκάτερον *om.* pr.

368 C φαύλου

381 D βίον δώροις (supplying an object for ἀγείρουσαν)

IV. 437 D ἢ ποτοῦ (conflatum ex ἢ οὐ et που)

V. 450 D καλῶς εἶχε παραμυθεῖσθαι

„ E οὐ φαύλων (for φίλων)

459 B δεῖ ἄκρων (for δεῖ ἄκρων εἶναι)

475 B οὗ ἄν τινα (for ὃν ἄν τινος)

„ D ἐπιθέουσι (for περιθέουσι)

476 B ὑπ' αὐτὸ τὸ καλὸν

VI. 501 C ὅτε (for ὅτι)

502 B καὶ πῶς and γενόμενος *om.*

VII. 529 C ἐν θαλάττῃ ἢ ἐν γῇ (for ἐν γῇ ἢ ἐν θαλάττῃ)

VIII. 544 E ῥίψαντα *q* corr. (ῥήψαντα *q* pr.)

545 E μὴ τραγικῶς *q*, μὴ inter versus (with ὡς δὲ σπουδῇ following)

548 A περὶ ταὐτοῦ for περὶ ταῦτα

553 C μετὰ for κατὰ

IX. 575 A τῶν αὐτοῦ for τῶν αὐτῶν

X. 595 C τούτων *om.*

619 C σκέψαιτο

This recension, however, remains responsible for some true readings which it would be unsafe to assume to be conjectural.

See for example :

| *q* | A Π M |
|---|---|
| II. 365 D οὐδ' ἡμῖν μελητέον | καὶ ἡμῖν μελητέον |
| 370 A ῥᾷον | ῥᾴδιον |
| III. 397 A μᾶλλον μιμήσεται | μᾶλλον διηγήσεται |

| | | $q$ | A Π M |
|---|---|---|---|
| III. | 414 E | δεῖ | δὴ |
| IV. | 429 C | γεγονυίας | γεγονυῖαν |
| | 444 C | τὸ δίκαια | τὰ δίκαια |
| V. | 454 D | καὶ ἰατρικὸν | καὶ ἰατρικὴν |
| VI. | 500 A | ἢ οὐκ ἐὰν | ἢ καὶ ἐὰν |
| VII. | 529 B | νοήσει | νοήσειν (M) |
| | 537 D | τούτους | τούτοις |
| VIII. | 553 C | τὸ ἐπιθυμητικόν | τὸν ἐπιθυμητικόν |
| | 559 B | ἦ τε μὴ παῦσαι | ἦ τε παῦσαι |
| | 567 E | τί δὲ | τίς δὲ |
| IX. | 585 A | ὥσπερ δὲ | ὥσπερ |
| X. | 604 B | δύο τινὲ | δύο |
| | „ B | φαμὲν ἐν | φαμὲν |
| | „ D | πρὸς τῷ | πρὸς τὸ |
| | 610 D | τούτου | τοῦ |
| | „ D | διὰ τοῦτο | διὰ τούτου |
| | 617 B | τρίτον | τὸν τρίτον A M |

The interpolations, or would-be emendations, of $q$ and $q$ corr., so far weaken the authority of this MS. as to render it an unsafe guide (for which reason several possible readings adopted by Bekker and Stallbaum have been rejected). And in accepting the readings above-mentioned, it may remain an open question whether they are conjectural or not. This question, which has been already touched upon, will be more fully considered below.

Glosses of MSS.　　The principal MSS. of the Republic may accordingly be classified as follows :

1. A b $a'$ $\gamma'$
2. (1) Π D $q*$ $\beta'*$ K* : (2) r Φ Θ : (3) Vind. D E F
3. M Ξ* m a c x* $t$ $v$

Ven. t and Flor. n are not referred to.

* Those marked with the asterisk are emended MSS., i. e. they admit readings derived from various sources and sometimes conjectural.

### Textual Errors and Emendations.

The discovery of fragments of classical texts in Egypt § 12. on papyrus rolls, some of which are known to have been written before the Christian era, has brought out some unexpected results. 1. The texts so far deciphered, where they differ from our MSS. of the ninth and tenth centuries, differ almost always for the worse. 2. For the most part they confirm the received tradition. 3. Very rarely, and then only in minute particulars, have they confirmed the conjectural emendations of modern scholars. 4. On the other hand, they do occasionally support the authority of readings which have hitherto rested on the evidence of some late MS.

These remarks may be illustrated from the long fragment of the Phaedo discovered by Mr. Flinders Petrie and published by Professor Mahaffy. See an article by the present writer in the *Classical Review* for October and December, 1891, pp. 363–365, and 454–457.

1. The papyrus, besides several patent errors of slight importance, exhibits at least two striking variants, ἀνδραποδώδη for εὐήθη in 68 E, and ὧι δὲ αὐτὴ προσέχει for ὃ δὲ αὐτὴ ὁρᾶι in 83 B. In the former case the scribe being familiar with the text has awkwardly anticipated a point which is presently to be made (viz. in 69 B); cp. Theaet. 158 C where for ὅτῳ χρή the Bodleian MS. gives ὅτῳ χρόνῳ χρή, anticipating the mention of the *time* which occurs eight lines lower down. See also in the same dialogue 149 C where ἀτόποις is written in the Bodleian MS. for ἀτόκοις with ἀτοπώτατος half a page higher up. A somewhat similar instance occurs in Rep. V. 469 E in the v. r. διασκυλεύσεις for διακωλύσεις with σκυλεύειν occurring, as a prominent notion, in the same passage. In the latter of the two cases in the Phaedo, 83 B, a prosaic and somewhat late mode of expression is substituted for the simple and vivid language of Plato.

2. The only matter of any consequence in which the papyrus tends to invalidate the existing text is in 81 D, the passage about apparitions. Here our MSS. appear to have omitted a phrase which in the papyrus is unfortunately illegible. This *lacuna* has never been suspected by any scholar.

3. In the space which the papyrus covers there are nineteen places where modern scholars have proposed emendations, all of which have appeared to Schanz deserving of mention in his critical notes. Only one of these is confirmed by the papyrus. This is the rejection of the words ἕνεκά φασιν in 83 E, which was proposed at one time by K. F. Hermann but afterwards withdrawn by him.

4. On comparing the readings of the papyrus with the existing *apparatus criticus*, they are found, in eight instances at least, to be in agreement with Ξ and the corrector of Π, both of the fifteenth century, and with no other MS. of Plato. These readings, then, which have hitherto been referred to the fifteenth century A. D., are found to have existed already in the third century B. C.

The same lessons, of caution in conjecture, and of trust in the persistence of tradition, have been taught by other similar discoveries. Among the papyri published in Mr. Kenyon's *Classical Texts* (1891) is one containing a great part of the third 'Letter of Demosthenes,' on which F. Blass has written an instructive monograph in Fleckeisen's *Jahrbuch für Klassischen Philologie* for 1892, pp. 33–44. He observes :—

(1) That in eleven pages of Reiske's edition, the papyrus gives sixty new readings which are clearly right.

(2) That twelve of these had been anticipated by conjecture, but except the proper name Εὐθύδικον for Εὔδικον (Blass' own emendation) only in matters of light moment (such as ἀγνώμοσι for ἀγνῶσι, τιν' for τήν, γενέσθαι for γενήσεσθαι).

(3) Out of nineteen places in which Blass had admitted

conjectures into the text, nine only agree with the papyrus.

(4) On the other hand the papyrus supports the principle of not relying exclusively on one MS. in constituting a text. The readings of the later MSS. are in some instances confirmed.

Blass remarks that in another part of Demosthenes the proportion of successful conjecture might prove larger; but he adds that the reverse might be the case, *as in the passage of the Phaedo.*—(The emendation of an 'Epistle' is easier, because the language is less highly wrought; the orations would be copied with greater care, and they exist in more MSS. of the highest class.)

The observation of such facts is the best corrective for § 13. the extravagances to which textual criticism has been always liable; proceeding, as it does, at one time by the wholesale excision of supposed 'accretions,' at another by the detection of 'lacunae,' now relying on close resemblances of written characters, now on the hypothesis of the frequent substitution of glosses for the words which they explain. Each of these methods has a show of scientific precision, but, when indiscriminately applied, involves rash and unwarranted generalization from scattered instances. Palaeography, in particular, has supplied the textual critic with an armoury of weapons, in which as Bacon would have said 'opinio copiae causa est inopiae'; the *ductus literarum* often drawing the mind away insensibly from the context, which is the principal thing. The other main requirement, familiarity with the individual author, is also apt to be forgotten, and an attempt is made to emend Plato on the same principles which have proved applicable to Demosthenes or Isocrates. No MS. is without errors: but the most recent discoveries have tended to show that the preservation of ancient texts of the greatest authors has on the whole been extraordinarily successful. It is hardly paradoxical to say that all interpolation comes by way of emendation, and that to ' emend ' is mostly to interpolate. The various modes of so-called ' scientific ' emendation are liable to one and the same fallacy, that of assuming, because a thing is known to have happened sometimes, that it must have happened indefinitely often.    Whereas the available evidence tends to show, that the changes in MSS. between the tenth and fifteenth centuries were greater in the most important texts than in the ten centuries preceding.

§ 14.    In the multiplication of MSS. at the revival of learning, all copies must have diverged from very few centres ; since the remnants of the Classics which had found their way from Constantinople to Western Europe were enshrined in the comparatively small number of MSS. which had been rescued by the men who prized them.    But in the earlier periods, those who (whether at Alexandria or at Constantinople) were preparing a copy that should be valued as authentic, had a choice of almost countless apographa of high repute at their disposal; and if the scribe followed too closely his immediate archetype, or himself fell prone into some error, the *diorthotes* who revised his work, in many cases the same person who wrote out the scholia, was able to correct the first hand and add alternative readings by the comparison of other texts, thus increasing the solid value of the recension.    Under such conditions corruption would not proceed in an increasing ratio.    At the same time this process has aggravated the difficulty of tracing the affiliation of MSS., readings belonging to different families having continually crossed each other, thus causing a mixture of traditions.    The question remains, whether amongst the manifold corruptions of the fifteenth century, some grains of genuine tradition may not be preserved, having descended by some fortunate accident from the text or margin of some MS. which was then extant and has since been lost.    There is a balance of probabilities here. On the one hand such MSS. must have been few and far between, but on the other hand the feebleness of conjecture at best, and especially in the infancy of criticism, makes it antecedently improbable that Rhosus or Cardinal Bessarion, for example, should have hit, by mere intuition, on readings which had been lost for sixteen centuries. Between the time of the occupation of Constantinople by the Latins and its destruction by the Turks, notwithstanding the decline of learning, many copies even of classical works must have still existed which perished in the final conflagration. The example of Vat. r shows that Plato was sometimes written in two volumes. Is it likely that Arethas, the deacon of Patrae, would procure, or that Constantine, the Metropolitan of Hierapolis, would purchase, an incomplete book? If otherwise, there must have existed, perhaps for centuries, a second volume of 𝔄 (the Bodleian MS.) and a first volume corresponding to A, and on the margin of these correctors of the tenth century probably wrote many various readings from other recensions. This belief is justified by the instances in which the Petrie papyrus supports Ξ and the corrector of Π against the Bodleian. And the inference here indicated bears a striking analogy to Messrs. Hort and Westcott's conclusion respecting certain 'cursive' MSS. of the New Testament, which together with variations due 'to ordinary degeneracy of transmission,' contain others which 'supply important documentary evidence. They are virtually copies of minute fragments of lost MSS.' Introduction, pp. 144, 145; § 197.

*Textual Errors.*

1. *Simple Clerical Errors.*   § 15.

(*a*) The mere mistaking between forms of letters is a less frequent cause of error than is often supposed, and almost always the mistaken letter has suggested some familiar word. For example:—

a for ω: ἀφελείας for ὠφελείας Π, III. 398 B.

o for ε: προσῆκον for προσῆκεν (?) A (προσῆκεν is the reading of Stobaeus), IV. 442 B.

η for ν : Confusion of η and ν. ζῶν for ζώη A¹, I. 344 E :
κακονοίας for κακοηθείας Π, III. 401 A : αὐτὴν
for αὕτη ἡ M, III. 403 B.

ν for ι : τῶν δικαίων for τῷ δικαίῳ Π M, VI. 496 C.

ν and υ : γενόμενοι for γενόμενοι M, VI. 496 C.

λ for α : λύρα for αὔρα Π, III. 401 C : ἀπολλύειν for ἀπολαύειν A², x. 606 B.

δ for λ : ἀπεδυσάμεθα for ἀπελυσάμεθα M, X. 612 A.

τ for γ : Confusion of τε and γε passim ; πλήττοντος for
πληγέντος A, X. 604 C (this confirms the
correction of V. 472 A) : ἠτεῖσθε for ἡγεῖσθε A,
X. 612 C.

τ and ψ : τύχης and ψυχῆς, II. 366 C, X. 603 E.

Compendia—The signs for καί and ὡς have perhaps been
confused in V. 471 A, where the v. r. ὡς οὐ πολέμιοι (A mg. M)
perhaps stands for καὶ οὐ πολέμιοι [1].

(*b*) More frequently the sound has been mistaken, as
between ο, ω and ου ; between η and ε ; between ε and αι ;
between η and οι ; between ει and η and ι ; between ν and οι ;
π for φ : πάνυ for φάναι M pr., x. 610 C ; αβ for αυ : ἀπολαβὼν
for ἀπολαύων IX. 572 D (A M) ; ἀπολαβεῖν for ἀπολαύειν X.
606 B, an error shared by A Π M ; cp. VIII. 544 C, where
διαφεύγουσα for διαφέρουσα (A Π M) is attributed by Schneider
to a similar cause, the burring pronunciation of γ ; and
lastly,. but only in late MSS., between ευς and εψ, e.g.
ῥεύσαντα for ῥέψαντα (Ξ) VIII. 544 E. (Similarly οφ for αυ :
ἐκκοφθήσεται for ἐκκαυθήσεται M, II. 361 E.)

(*c*) Letters added or omitted.

α. Letters *added* : ἀνεμόμενοι for νεμόμενοι A, III. 401 C :
διαστάσεις for διατάσεις A, III. 407 C : ζητεῖ for ζεῖ A Π M,
IV. 440 C : διατεταγμένους for διατεταμένους A pr., V. 474 A
(ξυντεταγμένως A¹, VI. 499 A) : παραγενόμενοι for παραγόμενοι A,

---

[1] It is less apparent what ᷂ the sign for ἥλιον, first written, then
marked with dots and then erased, in Π after τιμήν in II. 359 C can have
meant. Perhaps it originated in dittographia of ἥν.

VI. 487 B : ὑποστρεφόμεναι for ὑποτρεφόμεναι Π (corr. to ἐπιστρ. in q D K), VIII. 560 A : προσεστὼς for προεστὼς A, VIII. 565 E : so perhaps ἐπηινέγκαμεν A¹, X. 612 B : ἰδίᾳ λαβόντες (ἰδία Aᶜ) Aᶜ Ξ, X. 615 E.

*Dittographia or repetition.* Not only single letters but words and even whole phrases are accidentally repeated, and in a MS. like Π, which has been little emended, this fault is more perceptible. Thus in IX. 561 B the words μέρη . . . ἐκπεσόντων were written over again in this MS., and there are many other examples of the same mistake.

β. More commonly letters and syllables are *omitted*, where the word thus formed is in some way possible: cp. Theaet. 185 D ὀργανίδιον for ὄργανον ἴδιον Bodleian MS.: IV. 421 D διαφέρει for διαφθείρει A : V. 461 B φήσομεν for ἀφήσομεν A: IX. 574 D δίκας for δικαίας Π M: X. 611 C διαθετέον for διαθεατέον A Π.

Many such errors have been corrected by the first or second hand in Par. A ; for example, in VIII. 548 D, the first hand wrote οἶμεν, which is corrected by the second hand to οἶμαι μὲν. A similar mistake remained uncorrected in all MSS. and editions in VIII. 554 B καὶ ἔτι(μα) μάλιστα until Schneider's conjecture. See also corrections of the third epistle of Demosthenes mentioned above (p. 98) as confirmed by Mr. Kenyon's papyrus.

A single letter is often put for the double, and vice versa, especially in the case of λ, ρ, ν : thus μέλει and μέλλει are often confused ; II. 375 B ἐνενόηκα Π for ἐννενόηκα: III. 401 A ἀρυθμία is written for ἀρρυθμία, and there is a doubt between βαλάντιον and βαλλάντιον A, VIII. 552 D : μελιτουργὸς and μελιττουργὸς A, VIII. 564 C.

One of two similar syllables is very apt to be lost; e.g. ὂν after the neuter adjective. See especially VIII. 564 C ἐκτέτμησθον for ἐκτετμήσεσθον A: X. 600 D ὀνεῖναι for ὀνινάναι A.

*Homoeoteleuton.* In the MSS. of the Republic there are many instances of omission due to the recurrence of the same word or syllable, the eye of the scribe having reverted to the wrong place. Venetus Π, which had not the benefit of correction until three centuries after it was written, supplies seventeen examples of this fault, of which the following seven occur in Book I:—328 D δεῦρο ἰέναι [ἀλλ' ἡμεῖς ... δεῦρο ἰέναι]: 330 A ὁ ἐπιεικὴς [πάνυ τι ῥᾳδίως ... ὁ μὴ ἐπιεικὴς]: 335 B εἰς τὴν τῶν ἵππων [εἰς τὴν τῶν ἵππων ... εἰς τὴν τῶν ἵππων]. A clear example in A is III. 400 A εἴποιμι [ποῖα δὲ ποίου βίου μι]. See also II. 379 B, 380 E. So in M, II. 377 C ὃν δ' ἂν μή, ἀποκριτέον is omitted after ἐγκριτέον [1]. And in Lobcov. VIII. 550 A καὶ αὖ ... ὁρῶν *om.*

Another cause of such omission is the dropping of a line or more than one line. Thus, in I. 335 C ἀμούσους ... ἱππικῇ (forty-two letters) *om.* Π : II. 367 C φρονεῖν ... γόνιμα τῇ (forty-three letters) *om.* Π : III. 400 B ἄλλον τροχαῖον ... βραχύτητας (thirty-nine letters) *om.* Π : 410 C ὅσοι ἂν ... σκληρότητος, καὶ (seventy-five letters or two lines) *om.* Π. Two very striking examples occur in X. 607 A ὕ[μνους θεοῖς καὶ ἐγκώμια τοῖς ἀγαθοῖς ποιήσεως παραδε]κτέον (forty-five letters) *om.* Π, leaving the vox nihili ὑκτέον, which is changed in *q* D K to ἐκτέον : and 616 C εἶ[ναι ... ὑποζώμα]τα *om.* (forty-eight letters) D K in absence of Π, which has a lacuna here : εἶτα remained unsuspected, as a good Greek word.

For similar omissions in A[1] see II. 376 D, IV. 443 D, VI. 493 D, VII. 528 B, X. 601 A, B, 609 B.

(*d*) Division of words.

α. As the words were not divided in the earliest MSS., some confusion has arisen in consequence, e.g. in IV. 442 B, where the best MSS. give φυλάττοι τὴν for φυλαττοίτην (corrupted to φυλάττοι· τῷ in Ξ St.), III. 403 B, where A wrote νομοθέτης εἷς for νομοθετήσεις and X. 620 B ὡσαύτως εἰκός. τὴν MSS. for ὡσαύτως. εἰκοστὴν.

β. Conversely, words are unduly run together; as in III. 415 C φυλάξῃ for φύλαξ ἦ Ξ : VI. 496 B ἀνέλθοι for ἂν ἔλθοι A : IX. 577 B ἀνοφθείη for ἂν ὀφθείη A.

---

[1] The termination of γίγνονται in VIII. 563 C possibly hides such an omission, e.g. ⟨σεμνύνονται⟩.

(*e*) Transposition of words or letters ; often corrected by the scribe :—

α. Of letters, as in VII. 538 D καταλάβῃ (for καταβάλῃ) A : IV. 437 D ἐν ὀλίγῳ (for ἑνὶ λόγῳ) MSS. : IX. 571 D ἐν ὀλίγῳ (for ἑνὶ λόγῳ) seems to have been the reading of A[1].

β. A new word is made by transposition of two letters in III. 400 A where for εἴποιμι Π reads ἐπίοιμι. Cp. VII. 530 C ἀρχῆς του (for ἀχρήστου) A[1]. Words are transposed in III. 412 D εἰ μὴ δὲ M. For inversion without such marks see III. 404 D δοκεῖ ταῦτα (for ταῦτα δοκεῖ) M.

It may be remarked generally with reference to the preceding examples that the scribe often misunderstood the meaning, but he generally knew a Greek word when he saw it or fancied that he saw it.

## 2. *Errors due to mental association.*

(*a*) False construction. By a kind of spurious attraction § 16. the case of a noun or pronoun is altered to what the immediate context suggests. This is most frequent in late MSS., but occurs even in A, e. g. III. 391 D ἄλλου θεοῦ παῖδα for ἄλλον θ. π. : VII. 529 E διαφέροντος (sc. γραφέως) for διαφερόντως. (The similar mistakes in I. 338 E τίθεται . . τοὺς νόμους ἑκάστῃ ἡ ἀρχὴ, for ἑκάστῃ ἡ ἀ. and VII. 521 E γυμναστικὴ . . μουσικὴ for γυμναστικῇ, &c., have not been transmitted, having probably been obliterated through the disuse of the ι adscript in the twelfth century.) VIII. 550 E γυναῖκες αὐτῷ (sc. τῷ νόμῳ) for γυναῖκες αὐτῶν A : VIII. 561 B ἑαυτῷ ἐνδῷ for ἑαυτὸν ἐνδῷ A. Prepositions are also confused, e. g. ὑπὸ for ἀπό, ὑπὸ for ὑπέρ, περὶ for παρά.

(*b*) Confusion of tenses and moods. There is often a doubt between the perfect and aorist, I. 330 E ἠδίκηκεν A[2], present and aor. subj. VII. 538 D ἐξελέγχῃ A, aor. and future middle V. 474 A ἐργασαμένους for ἐργασομένους A pr. Π ; X. 607 D ἀπολογησαμένη changed to ἀπολογησομένη (A) ; As the feeling for the moods grew weaker, subjunctive and

optative were confused through itacism : I. 333 D δέοι (A)
for δέῃ. Also indicative with optative or subjunctive, e. g.
II. 376 A πεπόνθει (with οι above) for πεπόνθῃ M ; V. 450 D δοκοῖ Ξ, δοκεῖ Π,
for δοκῇ. The omission of ἄν, when favoured by other
causes of error, may often be thus accounted for, e. g.
I. 353 A ἀμπέλου, for ἂν ἀμπέλου, A Π M.

(*c*) A word of frequent recurrence is apt to be substituted
for the word in the text, I. 352 C δικαίους A¹ for δὴ καὶ
οὖς : II. 365 A ἐπισπόμενοι for ἐπιπτόμενοι q D K ; IX. 579 C
τὸυτῷ A¹ for ἑαυτῷ. In IV. 437 C where ἐρωτῶντος is
wrongly changed to ἐρῶντος, some Platonic ἔρως must have
been haunting the mind of the corrector. By a converse
error in II. 375 B ἀλλοτρίοις is written for ἄλλοις. So in
Theaet. 148 C ἀκριβῶν for ἄκρων Bodl. pr., IV. 440 C ζητεῖ
for ζεῖ, VIII. 568 E συμπολῖται for συμπόται.

(*d*) Again, the context suggests the wrong word in place
of the right one : e. g. V. 469 E where an early corrector of
M proposes διασκυλεύσεις for διακωλύσεις. In VI. 510 D M
reads εἰρημένοις for ὁρωμένοις which seemed to contradict εἴδεσι; VI. 510 B confusion of μιμηθεῖσιν A and τμηθεῖσιν M and
VI. 511 A τετμημένοις A¹ for τετιμημένοις A² ; X. 606 C μιμήσῃς
for μὴ μισῇς Π, where μίμησις is in question. So in Polit.
279 A παραδειγματείαν for πραγματείαν, where παράδειγμα is
the subject under discussion. Other associations, possibly
from the reminiscence of a different part of Plato, give rise
to various readings, for example V. 458 E γυμνοῦσθαι for
μίγνυσθαι A M, cp. Laws VI. 772 A.

§ 17.    (*e*) Logical confusions, especially between affirmative
and negative, positive and privative, are peculiarly frequent
in the text of Plato. There are more than fifty instances
of this form of error in the Republic ; mostly, however,
amongst the later MSS.

α. The following examples of the omission of the negative
are the most important, and in some of these the earliest
MSS. are involved. II. 365 D οὐδ᾽ ἡμῖν μελητέον q, καὶ ἡμῖν

μελητέον Α¹ ; III. 395 C ἵνα μὴ Π Μ, ἵνα Α ; IV. 429 C ἢ οὐ τοῦτο ἀνδρείαν καλεῖς; οὐ omitted by Π and ten other MSS.; V. 454 B τὸ μὴ τὴν αὐτὴν Ξ, τὸ τὴν αὐτὴν Α Π Μ ; 455 E γυμναστικὴ δ᾽ ἄρα οὔ Α, καὶ γυμναστικὴ, ἢ δ᾽ ἄρα οὐ Ξ ; VI. 511 C ἱκανῶς μὲν οὔ Ξ, ἱκ. μ. οὖν Α ; VII. 537 E καλὸν Α, κακὸν Π Μ ; VIII. 548 B οὐ φανερῶς Α pr. Π, οὐ erased in Α and omitted in Μ ; 559 B ἢ τε παῦσαι most MSS., for ἢ τε μὴ παῦσαι q ; IX. 574 C οὐ πάνυ Π, πάνυ Α.

β. In the following cases a negative is wrongly added : I. 330 B οὖ τοι ἕνεκα Π b (οὗτοι Π), οὗτοι Α Μ ; 336 E οἴου, μὴ οἴου q K ; IV. 437 D ἢ οὔ, ἢ οὐ Α ; V. 451 A ὥστε εὖ με παραμυθεῖ Α Π Μ, ὥστε οὐκ εὖ q ; VII. 526 E ὃ δεῖ, οὐ δεῖ Α¹.

It is doubtful whether the following belongs to α or β :— VI. 500 A ἢ καὶ ἐὰν οὕτω Α Π Μ, ἢ οὐκ ἐὰν οὕτω q. See note.

γ. Positive and privative are confused in II. 363 A τῷ δικαίῳ most MSS. for τῷ ἀδίκῳ (q); 363 B ἀδικίας for εὐδικίας Ξ ; VIII. 560 E ἀπαιδευσίαν for εὐπαιδευσίαν Π.

The following list of similar errors in inferior MSS. might possibly be augmented.

(1) Negative omitted :

| | | |
|---|---|---|
| I. 352 C οὐ γὰρ ἂν ἀπείχοντο | ἢ γὰρ ἂν Μ (ἢ t) | |
| II. 373 E οὔτι σμικρῷ | ὄντι σμικρῷ r | |
| III. 388 D καὶ μὴ καταγελῷεν | καὶ δὴ καταγελῷεν r | |
| 398 D τοῦ μὴ ᾀδομένου | τοῦ ἡμῖν ᾀδομένου q | |
| IV. 421 E πῶς δ᾽ οὔ | πῶς δὴ Φ | |
| 428 C οὐκ ἄρα | καὶ ἄρα q | |
| 429 C ἢ οὐ τοῦτο | ἢ τοῦτο Π r | |
| V. 462 C τό τε ἐμὸν καὶ τὸ οὐκ ἐμὸν | τό τε ἐμὸν καὶ τὸ ἐμὸν Π | |
| 479 E ἆρ᾽ οὐ γιγνώσκειν | ἆρ᾽ οὖν q corr. ἆρα Ξ | |
| „ E ἀλλ᾽ οὐ δοξάζειν | ἀλλὰ δοξάζειν Μ | |
| VI. 484 B πλανώμενοι οὐ φιλό-σοφοι | πλανώμενοι οἱ φιλόσοφοι r | |
| 489 A οἱ φιλόσοφοι οὐ τιμῶνται | οἱ φιλόσοφοι τιμῶνται Μ | |

| | | |
|---|---|---|
| VI. | 500 C μὴ μιμεῖσθαι | μιμεῖσθαι M |
| | 504 E μὴ μεγίστας | μεγίστας M |
| | 511 D ἀλλ' οὐ νοῦν | ἀλλ' οὖν Ξ |
| VII. | 521 A πλούσιοι, οὐ χρυσίου | πλούσιοι χρυσίου Π r |
| | 527 E οὐχ ὁρῶσιν | ὁρῶσιν M |
| | „ E ἢ οὐ πρὸς οὐδετέρους | ἢ πρὸς οὐδετέρους *M* |
| | 530 A τί δ' οὐ μέλλει | τί δὲ μέλλει r |
| IX. | 585 D πῶς γὰρ οὔ ; | πῶς γάρ ; q Vind. E F |
| X. | 608 A ὡς οὐ σπουδαστέον | ὡς σπουδαστέον D K |
| | „ D τὸ οὐ χαλεπὸν | τὸ χαλεπὸν q |

## (2) Negative added:

| | | |
|---|---|---|
| I. | 330 C καὶ κατὰ τὴν χρείαν | καὶ οὐ κατὰ τὴν χρείαν *t v* |
| II. | 377 A πρότερον δ' ἐν τοῖς ψευδέσιν | πρότερον δ' οὐ τοῖς ψευδέσιν m |
| III. | 388 C εἰ δ' οὖν θεούς | εἰ δ' οὐ θεούς r |
| | 393 C φήσομεν· τί γάρ ; | φήσομεν· τί γὰρ οὔ ; Ξ |
| | 398 E σὺ γὰρ μουσικός | οὐ γὰρ μουσικός *t* |
| | 416 C εἰ μέλλουσι τὸ μέγιστον | μὴ μέλλουσι τὸ μέγιστον M |
| | „ D εἰ τοιόνδε τινὰ τρόπον | οὐ τοιόνδε τινὰ τρόπον r |
| IV. | 426 A καὶ μὴν οὗτοί γε | καὶ μὴν οὔ τοί γε q corr. |
| | „ E χαριέστατοι οἱ τοιοῦτοι | χαριέστατοι οὐ τοιοῦτοι m |
| | 431 B καὶ ἀκόλαστον | καὶ οὐκ ἀκόλαστον r |
| | 435 B γενῶν ἀλλ' ἄττα πάθη | γενῶν καὶ οὐ κατ' ἀλλ' ἄττα πάθη Ξ corr. |
| | 438 A ἀλλὰ χρηστοῦ σίτου | καὶ οὐ χρηστοῦ σίτου Φ |
| V. | 452 E καὶ καλοῦ αὖ σπουδάζει | καὶ οὐ καλοῦ αὖ σπουδάζει q β' |
| | 478 B ἆρ' οὖν τὸ μὴ ὂν δοξάζει | ἆρ' οὐκ οὖν τὸ μὴ δοξάζει m |
| VI. | 484 C ἢ οὖν δοκοῦσί τι | ἢ οὖν οὐ δοκοῦσί τι q β' |
| | 492 C οἰχήσεσθαι | οὐκ οἰχήσεσθαι r |
| | 503 C ἀλλ' οἱ τοιοῦτοι | ἀλλ' οὐ τοιοῦτοι r |
| VIII. | 562 D ἆρ' οὐκ ἀνάγκη | οὐκ ἆρ' οὐκ ἀνάγκη Π |
| | 564 E χρηματιζομένων που πάντων | χρηματιζομένων που οὐ πάντων q |

IX. 581 D νομίζειν πρὸς          νομίζειν οὐδὲν πρὸς Ξ M
                                                      corr.

„   585 E καὶ βεβαίως          καὶ οὐ βεβαίως ṛ M corr.

In several of the above instances, other causes may be assigned ; but it is manifest that in most of them 'logical confusion' has been at work. In some also we may perhaps trace the effect of bias; a sort of pedantic euphemism having stolen into the mind of the scribe.

### 3. *Complex errors.*                                    § 18.

In several of the preceding examples, two or more of the causes specified are combined, for example in μιμήσῃς for μὴ μισῇς there is itacism and false association assisting the wrong division of words ; but still more confusion arises where an initial error of the simpler kind leads to the interpolation of a letter or syllable on the part of a corrector, who in the attempt to retrieve matters goes far to make them irretrievable.  For example, in III. 403 B, where for νομοθετήσεις following ἔοικε the first hand of A wrote νομοθέτης εἶς, an early corrector supposing the ν to belong to ἔοικεν, and ο to be the article, supplied the apparently missing syllable νο (ἔοικεν ὁ νομοθέτης εἶς)[1].  Similarly the reading of the Bodleian MS. in Theaet. 152 E ἐξαίσιοι σοφοὶ for ἐξῆς οἱ σοφοὶ may be thus accounted for : an early hand wrote ε for η ; this was again changed through similarity of sound to αι, making ἐξαίσοι, which a later scribe assumed to be mis-written for ἐξαίσιοι.

In X. 604 C ἐρεῖ (A) having been written for αἱρεῖ was again changed to ἔρρει (Π), ὅπῃ ὁ λόγος ἔρρει = 'which way reason moves.'  In X. 610 E several MSS. including M ṛ have expanded ζωτικῷ to ζῶντι κακῷ by some similar process.  In V. 468 B τί δέ; δεξιωθῆναι, the second δε has been regarded as dittographia, and ἐξιωθῆναι has con-

---

[1] See also III. 401 C, where νεμόμενοι was changed first to ἀνεμόμενοι then to ἀνιμώμενοι ('drawing up'), and III. 391 E οἱ ζηνὸς ἐγγύς, ὧν where οἱ having been dropped ζηνὸς ἐγγὺς ὤν became the reading of A : VI. 499 A προσώπου for τρόπου A M (this may be due to a compendium).

sequently been changed to ἐξιαθῆναι. In VI. 498 B ὑπηρεσίαν φιλοσοφίᾳ A, ὑπηρεσίαν φιλοσοφίαν Π, ὑπηρεσίᾳ φιλοσοφίαν M r. In VIII. 556 D παραχθεὶς having been
accidentally written for παραταχθεὶς in some MSS. of the
Π tradition (D K q) (supr. 1 (c)), the scribe of β′ has changed
this to ταραχθεὶς. See also the curious variant I. 342 B M mg.
ἢ ὡς ἡ σφαῖρα for ἔωσπερ ἂν. In VIII. 568 D πωλουμένων, having
been written πωλομένων, was altered first to πολομένων then
to ἀπολομένων, with supposed reference to the proscription
of the tyrant's enemies, and was further changed, with
a view to the nearer context, into ἀποδομένων, by a corrector
who was aware of the frequent interchange between λ and δ.

§ 19.　　4. *Accretions.*

Few errors of this description can be detected with any
confidence in the older MSS. The supposed redundancies
which recent scholars have excised on the ground of their
omission in Par. A (II. 358 A, &c., see above), more probably
belong to the class of omissions through homoeoteleuton.
Now that the words in II. 366 A αὖ μέγα δύνανται prove to be
extant in the first hand of Π, the argument in favour of
this view is considerably strengthened. In the Byzantine
period scholars contented themselves with adding here and
there a single word such as (I. 329 C) γὰρ and (II. 359 C) καὶ.
But towards the fifteenth century, as it became fashionable
to discourse on Plato, attempts were made here and there to
supply real or apparent defects in the tradition by explanatory phrases, which in several instances found their way
into the text of that period. In I. 341 D, q adds, after ἄλλο,
οὗ προσδεῖται, ἢ ἐξαρκεῖ ἑκάστη αὐτὴ ἑαυτῇ ; in II. 371 A for οἷα
καὶ ὅσα ἐκείνοις ὧν ἂν δέωνται, q reads οἷα καὶ ὅσα ἐκείνοις
ἄξουσιν, οἳ μεταδώσουσιν ὧν ἂν δέωνται. In III. 407 E for
οἱ παῖδες αὐτοῦ, ὅτι τοιοῦτος ἦν the correctors of Π M introduce
δεικνύοιεν with or without ἂν before ὅτι, and in this they are
followed by most of the later MSS., one of which, however,
v, has ποιοῦσιν (to be construed with δῆλον) instead. In
VII. 529 B (after συμμεμυκὼς) q adds τούτων τι μανθάνῃ ἐὰν

δ' ἄνω που κεχηνὼς ὁτιοῦν—a conflation of interpolated texts. VII. 532 C Ξ adds ἐνταῦθα δὲ πρὸς φαντάσματα after φ. θεῖα. In X. 616 A the case appears more complicated. Here A reads ὧν ἕνεκά τε καὶ εἰς ὅ τι τὸν Τάρταρον ἐμπεσούμενοι ἄγοιντο. A sense may be obtained by excising τὸν Τάρταρον as a gloss—'the causes wherefore and the place whereinto they were to be thrown.' But it has been more commonly assumed that εἰς ὅ τι has arisen by simple transposition from ὅτι εἰς. Adopting this view, and feeling still unsatisfied, the correctors of M Ξ and the scribe of x supplied the phrase ταῦτα ὑπομένοιεν before καὶ. In the passage immediately succeeding this, there is a cognate difficulty. The words τὸν φόβον which seem genuine but are dropped in A have been preserved by M and Ξ, while the words μὴ γένοιτο ἑκάστῳ τὸ φθέγμα appear to have been lost in the archetype of M, which gives for them the inferior substitute εἰ μυκήσαιτο (legendum μυκήσοιτο) τὸ στόμιον. Here a marginal gloss or scholium seems to have taken the place of the original text.

See also II. 368 E where v and Vind. F read πρῶτον ἐν τῷ μείζονι ζητήσωμεν ἐν ταῖς πόλεσι. A similar process may be traced at a somewhat earlier stage in III. 388 E, where, the verb having been lost through the simple error of writing ἔφην for ἐφῆι, a recent hand in Par. A adds κατέχοιτο after ἰσχυρῷ, while the r subfamily and q adopt the different expedient of reading γέλωτι ἁλῷ, following the suggestion of a scholar whose note has been preserved on the margin of Vind. D, ἐμοὶ δοκεῖ ἁλῶ προσθεῖναι.

The only manifest accretions in Par. A besides IX. 580 D τὸ λογιστικόν, spoken of elsewhere, are (1) VII. 525 E the addition of δύο to δεινούς :—it is an early interpolation, for it is shared by Π, and is difficult to account for ;—possibly the scribe of some early MS. had begun to write δεινούς over again, and on discovering his mistake had proceeded without erasing the superfluous letters: and (2) II. 364 D λιστοὶ δὲ στρεπτοί τε a gloss in the text. In IX. 581 E a gloss ἡδονῆς has supplanted ἀληθινῆς, which would seem to have been the original reading.   In Π, at II. 377 E, a singular reading κακῶ οὐσίαν (sic) for κακῶς has obtained a place. A cognate reading κακῶς οὐσίας was adopted by Aldus from some other MS., probably Flor. b.    This interpolation may have arisen from an early dittographia of the letters ος.   Some doubtful cases remain to be considered. In V. 459 E the word ἔσονται Ξ Fic. proves to be absent from all the chief MSS. including A.   It is harmless but can well be spared.   In the Cesena MS., M, some words are omitted, which could be dispensed with, but for the authority of A.   In I. 335 D βλάπτειν ἔργον, ἔργον *om.* M pr. (Some MSS. read ἔργον βλάπτειν, changing the order.)

In I. 346 D ἡ τοῦ μισθοῦ λῆψις *om.* M pr.: λῆψις is marked as doubtful in A.

In V. 466 A τοῦτο εὔδαιμον πλάττοιμεν, εὔδαιμον *om.* M.

In V. 468 B δοκεῖ σοι χρῆναι, χρῆναι *om.* M.

In V. 475 B παντὸς τοῦ εἴδους τούτου, τούτου *om.* M pr.

Of the phrases omitted by A which recent editors have bracketed or cancelled, only three are really open to suspicion, II. 382 E οὔτε κατὰ φαντασίας : 378 C καὶ ποικιλτέον and 379 A ἐάν τε ἐν μέλεσιν : and considering the grounds on which the other phrases are retained it would be illogical to reject them [1].

The confusing interpolation in IV. 444 B τοῦ δ' αὖ δουλεύειν (A Π M) has probably arisen from dittographia.   Some other words which have been rejected as accretions may possibly be right after all.   Thus in II. 374 A ἱκανοὶ διαμάχεσθαι is the reading of Π, and ib. B the words ἀλλὰ σκυτοτόμον occur in the text both of Π and M, although

---

[1] The slightest external evidence would justify the rejection of VI. 504 E ἄξιον τὸ διανόημα, suspected by Schleiermacher.   But with the testimony of all the MSS. in its favour, it would be rash to cancel either this, or the troublesome εἰς βραχύ . . . γιγνόμενον in III. 400 B.   The word ἄξιον in VI. 496 A is inconvenient, but the reading of Π (ἄξιον ὡς) suggests that, instead of cancelling it, we should read ἀξίως.   In II. 376 D the words ἵνα μὴ ἐῶμεν . . . διεξιῶμεν (om. A pr.) could be dispensed with.

differently placed (in Π before, in M after the clause ἵνα ... γίγνοιτο). They probably existed as a various reading on the margin of some copy from which M is derived, and may therefore be due to earlier tradition. As an explanatory gloss they seem unnecessary, and they may have been originally dropped after οἰκοδόμον through homoeoteleuton. If genuine they might be accounted for by the wish of Socrates emphatically to impress the principle of the division of labour on Glaucon's mind. In IX. 572 A καὶ αἰσθάνεσθαι could well be spared, and confuses the sense. A troublesome obscurity, perhaps due to an accretion, occurs in VII. 533 E ἀλλ' ὃ ἂν μόνον δηλοῖ πρὸς τὴν ἕξιν σαφηνείᾳ ὃ λέγει (λέγειν M, λέγεις A²) ἐν ψυχῇ. It might be justifiable to follow Ξ Steph. in omitting these words altogether[1]. Of single words which have been suspected, in V. 468 C καὶ μηδενὶ, καὶ proves to be absent in A, and now rests on the sole authority of Π. The progressive corruption of the later MSS. may be illustrated from the Darmstadt Fragment Ϸ, in which several passages, instead of being copied, are briefly paraphrased, as if from memory. The interpolations in Theaet. 156 C, 190 C may be compared with some of the above.

### Textual Emendations.

Mistakes occurred in the earliest MSS.; and the attempt § 20. to rectify them immediately followed, not always with success. In one of the oldest and best papyrus fragments, that of Iliad XXIII and XXIV, lately published by Mr. Kenyon, the habit of correction, by writing between the lines, and putting a dot over a superfluous letter, is already begun. If nothing but Π in its original condition had come down to us, or even if we depended solely on A as at first written, before it was revised, whether by the first or second hand, not to mention other early correctors, no human ingenuity

---

[1] Perhaps also in v. 477 B the words κατὰ τὴν δύναμιν ἐκατέρα τὴν αὐτῆς, which are likewise omitted in Ξ, and are variously read in other MSS.

could have brought the text of Plato to its present state.
Even if the lacunae were suspected, they could not have
been filled.    Modern criticism could at best have provided some such stop-gaps as were adopted by scribes and
diorthotae of the Renaissance, in the absence of the best
tradition.    On the other hand, it cannot be assumed that
in every case where the text of A has been preferred,
a contrary decision might not be justified by the discovery
of some earlier authority.    In several instances, where the
evidence of A had been misinterpreted through the silence
of Bekker, it now proves that its witness goes the other
way, and turns the scale in favour of a rejected reading ;
e. g. in III. 391 C ὥρμησαν not ὥρμησεν : in VI. 496 C τῷ δικαίῳ
not τῶν δικαίων : X. 6c6 E ἄξιος not ἄξιον is the reading of
A.    The later MSS. exhibit an increase both of corruption
and of attempted emendation ; but we have seen reason to
believe that in the few instances in which the readings of
these MSS. are alone to be relied on, it is quite possible
that by some happy accident they have preserved an
earlier tradition.

The simplification of the *apparatus criticus* by the
supposed affiliation of all the MSS. to one, is sometimes
alleged to justify the license of conjecture.    But the argument is fallacious.    For the comparison of independent
traditions is a firmer ground on which to base conjecture
than a breakdown in the evidence of a single document.
There are few places in the Republic, however, about
which any serious doubt remains.    Those most intimately
acquainted with the text are the least inclined to emend it
conjecturally.    Schneider, the most accurate of critical
editors, and the author of the certain emendation in VIII.
554 B ἐτίμα μάλιστα for ἔτι μάλιστα, was even extreme in his
conservatism.    He defended places which are indefensible,
and where the remedy when once suggested cannot admit
of doubt.    For example, in Book I. 352 E he maintains
φαμὲν with the MSS. against φαῖμεν, the reading of

Stephanus, Ast, Bekker and Stallbaum. In IV. 445 B he defends ἀποκνητέον, in VI. 494 B ἐν πᾶσιν against ἐν παισὶν, and in VI. 497 D argues with great subtlety, but doubtful success, against Bekker's emendation, οὐ πάντων ῥᾷστον for οὐ πάντως ῥᾷστον. He only adopted στραγγευομένῳ (V. 472 A) on finding it anticipated by an early corrector of Vind F., and to the last refused to treat τὸ λογιστικὸν (IX. 580 D) as a gloss in the text, on the insufficient ground that Par. K is manifestly derived from Ven. Π. He was also willing to retain δικῶν λήξεις in IV. 425 D, with the transposition of the words into a different order which he found in Vat. Θ.

Passages still open to suspicion, where no convincing §　21. remedy seems to be attainable are :—

II. 358 E οἷόν τε καὶ ὅθεν γέγονε. The reading of Aldus and the editions before Bekker τί τε ὂν τυγχάνει καὶ ὅθεν γέγονε has very weak manuscript authority ; being confined so far as we know to Flor. b, which in this passage and what follows it, is in a very late hand. The expression is therefore probably a conjectural expansion of the same kind with the addition of δεικνύοιεν ἄν in III. 407 E. τί ὄν τε is the reading of A M Ξ ; but gives a poor sense, requiring τί ὂν γέγονε to be joined. The reading of Π τί οἷόν τε καὶ ὅθεν γέγονε, taking οἷόν τε in two words, may be explained ' what, and of what nature, and from whence, justice has arisen.' The choice lies between this and the simpler reading of Flor. x οἷόν τε καὶ ὅθεν γέγονε, ' The nature and origin of justice.' The slight obscurity of this may be defended by supposing Plato to remember that he is speaking of the γένεσις not of the οὐσία of justice. But after all it is quite possible that τί ὄντε is a mis-writing for τί ἐστί. Bekker adopted τί οἴονται and wrote γεγονέναι.

II. 359 C τῷ [Γύγου] τοῦ Λυδοῦ προγόνῳ. There is clearly something wrong here ; but the emendation is doubtful : see note in loco.

III. 387 C φρίττειν δὴ ποιεῖ ὡς οἴεται (ὡς οἷόν τε q). Neither of these readings is satisfactory, and conjecture is at fault.

IV. 439 E ποτὲ ἀκούσας τι πιστεύω τούτῳ. For various suggested interpretations of this passage, see note in loco. Perhaps it is one of those in which a negative has been omitted (see above p. 107). π. ἀ. τι οὐ πιστεύω τ., 'I once heard a story told which *prevents* me from accepting that.' But the emendation remains uncertain.

VII. 533 E ὃ ἂν μόνον δηλοῖ πρὸς τὴν ἕξιν σαφηνείᾳ λέγεῖ ἐν ψυχῇ. The whole is omitted in Ξ and may possibly be an accretion. For an attempt to treat the text as it stands in the MSS., see note in loco.

VIII. 562 B τοῦτο δ᾽ ἦν ὑπέρπλουτος. The compound substantive is anomalous, and the attempts at emendation are hitherto unsuccessful. For the grounds of the conjecture τοῦτο δ᾽ ἦν *που πλοῦτος, see the notes.

VIII. 567 E τί δέ; (or τίς δὲ) αὐτόθεν (τοὺς δὲ Steph.).

VIII. 568 D ἀποδομένων. Reasons are given above, p. 110, for the conjecture *πωλουμένων.

IX. 581 E τῆς ἡδονῆς οὐ πάνυ πόρρω. See above (pp. 111, 112) for the conjecture τῆς ἀληθινῆς : but certainty is unattainable in a passage which has to be emended in more places than one. The difficulty in IX. 585 C εἰ δὲ ἀληθείας κ.τ.λ. may be due to some want of logical precision in Plato, but Madvig's theory of a lacuna must also be considered.

IX. 590 D οἰκεῖον ἔχοντος. Here again the grammatical inaccuracy may be due to Plato, but one cannot exclude the supposition that there is some corruption in the text arising from the words ἔχοντος ἐν αὐτῷ preceding. Madvig's οἰκεῖον ἐνόντος may be right.

X. 603 C μή τι ἄλλο ᾖ. Ast very probably conjectured μή τι ἄλλο ἦν.

X. 615 C for αὐτόχειρας Ast conjectured αὐτόχειρος or αὐτοχειρίας. Once more, in X. 616 A. the passage considered above, p. 111, it is difficult to arrive at a perfectly definite conclusion.

The following are the places, twenty-nine in all, in which § **22.** the present text relies on conjecture :—

| Steph. | MSS. |
|---|---|
| I. 330 B τουτοισί Bekker | τούτοισιν |
| 336 E οἷου γε σὺ Bekker | οἷου τε σὺ |
| 341 B ὃν νῦν Benedictus | ὃ νῦν (o in erasure A) |
| 352 E φαῖμεν Stephanus | φαμὲν |
| II. 361 C ἴτω Neukirch | ἤτω (but η from ι ? A) |
| III. 392 B ζητοῦμεν Hermann | ἐζητοῦμεν |
| 401 E χαίρων καὶ δυσχεραίνων τὰ μὲν καλὰ ἐπαινοῖ καὶ Vermehren | δυσχεραίνων τὰ μὲν καλὰ ἐπαινοῖ καὶ χαίρων καὶ (χαίρων καὶ om. q) |
| 410 C ἀμφοτέρα Schneider | ἀμφότερα |
| IV. 431 C ἐν παισὶ H. Wolf | ἐν πᾶσι |
| 437 B ἂν ἀλλήλοις Baiter | ἀλλήλοις |
| D ἑνὶ λόγῳ Cornarius | ἐν ὀλίγῳ, cp. IX. 571 D |
| 440 C διὰ τοῦ (bis) L. Campbell | διὰ τὸ |
| 443 B ἄλλο . Ἔτι τι Hermann | ἄλλο ἔτι . Τί |
| 445 B ἀποκμητέον Bekker | ἀποκνητέον |
| V. 465 B δέος δὲ τοῦ Madvig | δέος δὲ τὸ |
| VI. 492 C ποίαν Cobet | ποίαν ἂν |
| 493 B ἑκάστας G. van Prinsterer | ἕκαστος (ἑκάστοις, ἑκάστοτε) |
| 494 B παισὶν Geer | πᾶσιν |
| 497 D πάντων Bekker | πάντως |
| 499 B κατηκόῳ Schleiermacher | κατήκοοι |
| 505 B κεκτήμεθα Bekker | κεκτήμεθα |
| VIII. 551 C ἧστινος Ast | ἤ τινος |
| 554 B ἐστήσατο καὶ ἐτίμα μάλιστα. Εὖ Schneider | ἐστήσατο. Καὶ ἔτι μάλιστα εὖ |
| 556 E παρ' οὐδὲν Baiter | (γὰρ) οὐδὲν |

| Steph. | | MSS. |
|---|---|---|
| IX. 581 D τί οἰώμεθα Graser | | ποιώμεθα |
| 585 C τοῦ (*bis*) Madvig | | *om.* |
| 590 A τὸ δεινόν , ἐκεῖνο | | τὸ δεινὸν ἐκεῖνο |
| Schneider | | |
| X. 600 D ὀνινάναι Ast | | ὀνεῖναι or ὀνίναι |
| 606 C ὅτι, ἂν Schneider | | ὅτι ἂν |

The following rest only on slight manuscript authority:—
II. 363 A τῷ ἀδίκῳ *q* x and Muretus cj. : III. 388 E ἐφῆ
Vind. D mg. (ἔφην A) and Hermann cj. : V. 472 A στραγγευο-
μένῳ Vind. F. corr. and C. Orelli cj. (στρατευομένῳ cett.).

A few others depend on citations of ancient writers:—
II. 361 C τῶν ἀπ', Euseb. Theodoret (τῶν ὑπ' MSS.) : V. 461 B
ἀφήσομεν, Euseb. Theodoret (φήσομεν MSS.) : VII. 540 C
ξυναναιρῇ Aristides (ξυναιρῇ MSS. except Vind. E which
has ξυνανέρῃ) : IX. 589 D ἐμοί Stobaeus (μοι MSS.).

§ 23.    The most important conjectures on the text of the
Republic in recent years have been those of Cobet, Madvig,
W. H. Thompson, and Ingram Bywater (see Baiter's Preface). Still more recently Mr. Herbert Richards has contributed many ingenious suggestions in the *C. R.* for 1893.
It may be not unprofitable to examine at some length the
most considerable of the fifty-seven emendations of the
Republic proposed by Cobet in *Variae Lectiones*, ed. II,
pp. 526–535. We shall best obey his favorite precept νᾶφε
καὶ μέμνασ' ἀπιστεῖν by not yielding blindly to his authority.

To begin, then, with those passages in which he appeals
to the authority of the chief MS.

X. 612 B ἐπηνέκαμεν for ἐπηνέγκαμεν. The former is really
the reading intended in Paris. A, where the η has ι adscript
and there is a dot over the γ (sic ἐπηινέγκαμεν), which is
thus marked by the diorthotes as superfluous. In Politicus
307 A, where ἐπηνέκαμεν is the best reading, the Bodleian
gives ἐπηνέγκαμεν, and in both passages there is a variant
ἐπηνέσαμεν. And although ἐπηνέγκαμεν in the Republic

admits of a possible meaning, the pointed reference in ἐπηνέκαμεν (or ἐπηνέσαμεν?) to II. 367 D τοῦτ' οὖν αὐτὸ ἐπαίνεσον δικαιοσύνης . . . μ' ους σε καὶ δόξας πάρες ἄλλοις ἐπαινεῖν— is the more probable, as the context shows that Plato has that passage distinctly before him. Cobet failed to remark, however, that, if ἐπηνέκαμεν is right the perfect is used together with the aorist ἀπελυσάμεθα. So that ἐπηνέσαμεν, the reading of Par. K, should perhaps in strictness be preferred; and it may be still argued in favour of ἐπηνέγκαμεν that notwithstanding the reference to II. 367 D this need not involve the repetition of the same words.

VI. 503 B διεσπασμένα for διεσπασμένη. Here the critic has been less fortunate: διεσπασμένη is the reading of Paris. A (not διεσπασμένα as he supposed). It is also (*subaudiendo ἡ φύσις*) the more idiomatic reading. The variant διεσπασμένα is due to the tendency, noted elsewhere by Cobet himself, to adapt terminations to the nearest word. See above, p. 105.

The remaining passages may be taken in their order of sequence.

I. 343 B *διακεῖσθαι for διανοεῖσθαι (so Faesi). If there were any evidence for διακεῖσθαι the word might be accepted. But the familiar truth that κεῖσθαι is an equivalent for the perfect passive of τίθημι is not a sufficient proof that διανοεῖσθαί πως πρός τινα is bad Greek.

II. 362 B ξυμβάλλειν for ξυμβάλλειν, κοινωνεῖν. The exact equivalence of these two words is not proved by the fact that Socrates in I. 333 A leads Polemarchus by gentle transition from *contracts* to *partnerships*. The use of both words here recalls the preceding conversation more effectually.

II. 376 A οὐδὲ ἕν for οὐδὲν δέ. Cobet's suggestion is very ingenious, and may be right, but the reading of the inferior MSS. οὐδὲν δή is at least equally plausible.

III. 411 A *καταντλεῖν (so Van Heusde) for καταυλεῖν καὶ καταχεῖν. καταυλεῖν sc. αὐτοῦ or τῆς ψυχῆς. Cobet's assumption that the construction must be καταυλεῖν τῆς ψυχῆς τὰς ἀρμονίας is wholly gratuitous. The words καὶ καταχεῖν κ.τ.λ. are an expansion of the notion of καταυλεῖν. The idea underlying many of these suggestions, that Attic Greek loves parsimony in expression, is peculiarly inapplicable to the language of Plato.

III. 412 E ἐπιλανθανόμενοι to be omitted ? There is some awkwardness in the introduction of the word in this place, considering what follows in 413 B κλαπέντας . . . τοὺς ἐπιλανθανομένους, but Plato has elsewhere admitted similar tautology and verbal inconsistency.

V. 452 E ἄλλον τινὰ σκοπὸν προστησάμενος for πρὸς ἄλλον τινὰ σκοπὸν στησάμενος. An ingenious but doubtful way of correcting a doubtful text. Ib. ἡ φύσις ἡ θήλεια for φύσις ἡ ἀνθρωπίνη ἡ θήλεια. Cobet seems to have forgotten the reference to the lower animals in 451 D, E.

V. 477 E θήσομεν for οἴσομεν. This seems to be a genuine conjecture, although anticipated by Θ Φ r (see Bekker and Schneider) and also by the corrector of M. Cobet's logic sometimes coincides with that of the later scribes. οἴσομεν is really unobjectionable. Ficinus has *dicemus* (φήσομεν ?).

VI. 491 B ⌊εἰ τελέως μέλλοι φιλόσοφος γενέσθαι⌋, 'verba soloece concepta sententiam onerant et impediunt.' The imputed solecism is really a Platonic idiom. To get rid of all such *impedimenta*, many pages would have to be re-written.

VI. 496 C ἢ γάρ πού τινι [ἄλλῳ] ἢ οὐδενί. 'Attic parsimony' is again assumed ; but the passages quoted are not exactly in point, and it is Plato's manner in employing an idiom to adapt it to the immediate context.

VII. 521 C οὐσίαν ἐπάνοδος for οὖσαν ἐπάνοδον. Cobet's emendation, εἰς ἀληθινὴν τοῦ ὄντος οὐσίαν ἐπάνοδος still leaves the expression cumbrous, and περιαγωγή . . . εἰς . . . ἐπάνοδον is in close agreement with the description in 515 C–E.

VII. 527 E οὐδὲ πρὸς ἑτέρους for οὐ πρὸς οὐδετέρους. Neat, but not certain.

VII. 528 C *μεγαλαυχούμενοι for μεγαλοφρονούμενοι. Cobet

objects to μεγαλοφρονεῖν as a late Greek word and to the use of the middle, but many compounds and singular uses of the middle voice occur for the first time in Plato.

VII. 538 C προσποιουμένων for ποιουμένων. For similar uses of ποιεῖσθαι see note in loco.

VIII. 555 A and IX. 576 C [ὁμοιότητι]. The argument from parsimony is again misplaced, and the same gloss is not very likely to have crept into the text in both places. In the latter passage the word had been previously cancelled by Ast and Badham.

X. 615 C ἀπογενομένων for γενομένων. The suggestion is ingenious but unnecessary. Not birth, but death, is the pervading notion of the passage, and is therefore more easily understood. Not ' those who *died* immediately' (on birth) ' but those ' (whose death occurred) ' as soon as they were *born.*'

X. 618 A διὰ τέλους for διατελεῖς. The adverbial phrase διὰ τέλους would require a *participle* such as κατεχομένας, which the adjective dispenses with. Cobet proceeds on the assumption that the Athenians always expressed the same thing in the same way. The same fallacy underlies his emendation in VIII. 565 C of ἕνα γέ τινα for ἕνα τινά.

Some of Madvig's suggestions, in spite of their acuteness, § 24. are decidedly wanting in good taste. For example, his proposal to change φαντάσματα θεῖα VII. 532 C to φαντάσματα ἄδεια is almost ludicrous, and reminds one of modern Greek. Not much happier is his suggestion of χωλαί for πολλαί in V. 473 D supported by referring to VII. 535 D. The two passages stand in no relation to each other, and the abrupt introduction of the metaphorical word is foreign to the manner of Plato. Such hariolations as these tend to disable a critic's judgement, and to cast suspicion on other proposals of his which are at first sight more plausible. The most ingenious of Madvig's suggestions are in VIII. 546 D δεύτερά τε for δεύτερον δὲ τά, and X. 608 A ἀσόμεθα for αἰσθό-μεθα, but in the latter case it appears more probable that the corrupt αἰσθόμεθα has taken the place of some expression answering to the ὥσπερ clause, such as ἀφεξόμεθα. In X. 606 C there is much to be said for his conjecture ἂν κατεῖχες for αὖ κατεῖχες.

W. H. Thompson, in IX. 585 A, with great plausibility conjectured πρὸς λύπην οὕτω τὸ ἄλυπον for πρὸς τὸ ἄλυπον οὕτω λύπην, but see note in loco. Another very probable suggestion which he does not seem to have communicated to Baiter, is in VIII. 545 B ἀλλ' ἤ for ἄλλο· ἤ. For other conjectures of the same critic, see notes on VIII. 563 D, 567 D, and IX. 573 C.

Charles Badham is responsible for a conjecture which Cobet approved, and Baiter received into his text, VIII. 560 D δι' ὤτων for ἰδιωτῶν. Reasons against adopting this and in support of ἰδιωτῶν are given in the commentary to this edition. He also proposed to cancel μισθωτοί in IV. 419 A.

Prof. Bywater's chief suggestion is V. 476 A ἀλλ' ἄλλων for ἀλλήλων in a passage where needless difficulty has been felt. See note in loco. In VI. 504 A Orelli's ἄθλοις for ἄλλοις would be convincing, if ἆθλος had been a usual word in Plato, but he uses it only in the Timaeus and Laws.

In VII. 532 B, C Nägelsbach's ἔτι ἀδυναμία for ἐπ' ἀδυναμίᾳ is exceedingly plausible and is supported by the quotation of Iamblichus. But it hardly bears examination ; see note in loco. Even if the absence of ἤ may be excused, the construction with the infinitive, instead of ἡ ἀδυναμία τοῦ βλέπειν, is hardly Greek. In Theaet. 156 A, where δύναμιν ἔχον is construed with the infinitive, probably the closest parallel, the case is altered by the presence of the participle. For δύναμιν ἔχειν = δύνασθαι.

Of Mr. Richards' conjectures on I–V, the most persuasive are :—

III. 407 E Δῆλον, ἔφη, ὅτι τοιοῦτος ἦν· καὶ οἱ παῖδες αὐτοῦ οὐχ ὁρᾷς ὅτι κ.τ.λ. It would be quite as easy, however, to cancel ὅτι . . . ἦν as an 'accretion'; and in either case the received reading gives a preferable rhythm.

IV. 430 E κρείττω δὴ αὐτοῦ *ἀποφαίνοντες κ.τ.λ.

433 D καὶ δούλῳ καὶ ἐλευθέρῳ ⟨καὶ γεωργῷ⟩ καὶ δημιουργῷ.

444 C *αὐτὰ μὲν οὖν ταῦτα (so Stob.). Probably right.

V. 457 C *ἄγε δή, ἴδω for λέγε δή, ἴδω. This is better than Cobet's *φέρε δή. But neither is required. See Goodwin, *M. and T.* 257.

462 C ἐπὶ τῷ αὐτῷ for ἐπὶ τὸ αὐτό. This is possibly right.

468 A λέγ', ἔφη, ποῖα δή for λέγ', ἔφη, ποῖ' ἄν. If the text is corrupt, this is the most likely way of emending it.

On Muretus' conjecture in II. 364 C, ᾄδοντες for διδόντες, see note in loco.

The present editor has suggested the following con- § 25. jectural changes, which he has not, however, ventured to introduce into the text :—

II. 358 E τί *ἐστι καὶ ὅθεν γέγονε

III. 387 C φρίττειν δὴ ποιεῖ ὡς *ἐτεά

IV. 439 E ἀκούσας τι *οὐ πιστεύω

442 E τοῦτον *αὐτό for τοῦτο αὐτόν (τοῦτον Α Π Μ)

V. 471 A ὄντες, *καὶ οὐ πολέμιοι (ὡς οὐ π. Α mg. Μ)

479 D *ὡμολογήσαμεν (for ὡμολογήκαμεν)

VI. 496 A φρονήσεως *ἀξίως ἀληθινῆς ἐχόμενον (ἄξιον Α : ἄξιον ὡς Π)

500 A ἢ οὐκ (sic q) . . . ἀλλοίαν *τε φήσεις . . . ;

VII. 518 D ἐγγύς τι *τείνειν τῶν τοῦ σώματος

VIII. 562 B τοῦτο δ' ἦν *που πλοῦτος for τοῦτο δ' ἦν ὑπέρπλουτος

563 C οἷαίπερ αἱ δέσποιναι γίγνονται, ⟨σεμνύνονταί⟩ τε δὴ καὶ ἵπποι καὶ ὄνοι

568 D τὰ τῶν *πωλουμένων for τὰ τῶν ἀποδομένων

IX. 581 E τῆς *ἀληθινῆς οὐ πάνυ πόρρω; for ʽτῆς ἡδονῆς, οὐ π. π.

IX. 585 C καὶ *ἀληθοῦς for καὶ ἀληθείας

X. 610 A ὀρθότατά γ᾽ for ὀρθότατα

And the following readings, mostly of inferior authority, are recommended for further consideration :—

I. 333 E δεινὸς φυλάξασθαι [καὶ] μὴ παθεῖν q

  335 D βλάπτειν (omitting ἔργον) M

  340 A αὐτὸς θρασύμαχος (omitting γάρ) M

  346 D ἡ τοῦ μισθοῦ λῆψις *om.* M

II. 358 E πλέον δὲ κακῷ Π M

  367 A ἕκαστος ἄριστος φύλαξ Π

  370 B ἐπ᾽ ἄλλου ἔργου πράξει M

  374 B μήτε οἰκοδόμον, ἀλλὰ σκυτοτόμον Π

III. 409 D καὶ τοῖς ἄλλοις M

IV. 435 D ἄλλη γὰρ a Galen.

  436 A τούτων ἕκαστα q corr.

  442 B προσῆκεν q Stobaeus

  444 C αὐτὰ μὲν οὖν Stob. et cj. H. Richards 1893

V. 459 E ἔσονται *om.* A Π M

  468 B χρῆναι *om.* M

VI. 489 B τἀληθῆ λέγει D

  497 B ἀλλότριον εἶδος Ξ

  499 B παραβάλῃ Ξ

  509 D οὐρανοῦ Ξ

  510 B μιμηθεῖσιν A Proclus

VII. 522 A πρὸς τοιοῦτόν τι ἄγον (γρ.) Π mg.

  525 A ταὐτὸν πέπονθε τοῦτο Π

  528 C κωλυόμενα Ξ pr.

  532 E τίνες αἱ ὁδοί r

VIII. 554 D ἐνευρήσεις A² Π M

IX. 587 E καταπεφώρακας r Ξ corr. v

X. 601 B αὐτὰ ἐφ᾽ αὑτῶν γενόμενα A²

  ,, C ἐφ᾽ ἡμίσεως q

  603 B καὶ ἡ κατὰ τὴν ἀκοήν q

  607 D ἀπολογησαμένη r (et forsitan A pr )

  612 C ᾐτεῖσθε A

  615 B πολλοῖς D corr.

It may not be out of place to quote an example of the §26. manner in which a scholar of the sixteenth century approached the task of emendation :—

'Enimvero quum in plerisque locis fidem eorundem librorum a me frustra implorari viderem, alii autem non suppeterent, ad coniecturas, tanquam ad δεύτερον πλοῦν, me convertere necesse habui. Sed quum intelligerem quàm periculose sint coniecturae, et quàm fallaciter plerunque suis coniecturis adblandiantur, ex ingenio meo profectas emendationes non in ipsum recepi contextum (ut antea etiam cum vulgo appellavi) sed partim margini adscripsi, partim Annotationibus reservavi, ubi earum rationem etiam reddere daretur. . . .

'Quinetiam contingebat interdum ut quantumvis pectus concuterem (non foecundum illud quidem, sed nec omnino, quorundam iudicio, infoecundum) nihil quicquam ex eo egrederetur, antequam loci in quibus haerebam excusi essent: simulatque autem iam excusos relegerem, ex eo illorum emendatio velut sponte sua prodire videretur. Ex eorum numero duos mihi nunc suggerit memoria: quorum unus habet, ἵνα μὴ μεμφῇς, alter δ' ἕξειν: horum enim emendationem assequi coniectura non potueram antequam paginae in quibus erant, excusae essent: at quum operae meae penso suo manum extremam imponerent, ego superveniens, perinde ac si longè quàm antea perspicacior factus essem, pro [μὴ] μεμφῇς quidem [μή] με φθῇς [1] [Polit. 266 E] : pro δ' ἕξειν autem, δείξειν scribendum esse, primo ferè aspectu animadverti.'

'*Henricus Stephanus lectori* :' Preface to Plato ed. 1578.

Plato is one of a select number of Greek authors whose text is known to us as it existed in the ninth century A.D. The Byzantine MSS. of that period were not only carefully written, but carefully revised; with the aid, as there is good

---

[1] This conjecture is partly confirmed by Bodl. Vat. Δ reading μήτ' ἔφθης.

reason to think, of other MSS. besides the one immediately
in hand.   Some of the errors in these early copies have still
to be corrected by the help of later ones, into which, as it
now appears, some grains from a yet earlier tradition have
in some way filtered down.   There remains little scope for
conjecture.   Such achievements of intuition as Schneider's
ἐτίμα μάλιστα and Orelli's στραγγευομένῳ remain isolated
instances of success.   Plato's language is so highly wrought,
so various, and so full of unexpected turns, that the task of
emending him is like that of emending poetry.   In a so-
called epistle of Demosthenes there is more room for
‘ certain conjecture ’ than in a whole tragedy of Aeschylus
or Sophocles, where the most brilliant suggestions, such as
Conington's λέοντος ἶνιν or Jebb's λυτήριον λώφημα, are still
open to doubt ;  or in one of those plays of Euripides, where
the judgement is sufficiently perplexed by the discrepancies
of thirteenth century MSS. without having recourse to vain
*hariolatio*.   The thesis might be maintained, however,
that the more a text requires emendation (either from bad
copying, or from the use of technical terms, as in the
musical or mathematical writers, or from obscurity or
singularity of style), the less possible it is to emend it.   Take,
for example, the portion of the Oresteia which is lost in the
Medicean MS., or again the Supplices of Aeschylus, which
is manifestly corrupt in the Medicean MS. without having
any other independent MS. authority.   Conjecture has been
active, with but little of agreement in the result.   In the
case of Pindar, although we have no MS. earlier than the
twelfth century, those we have seem to give evidence of
a constant and authentic tradition.   The difficulty is at its
height in the later part of the Bacchae, 755 ff., where there
is only one MS. and that of an inferior description : or
again in the case of such an author as Marcus Aurelius,
where the critic has to choose between late MSS. and
a printed text founded on an earlier MS. now lost.

It would be unsafe to argue from the analogy of Latin

authors ; the great variety of style and dialect in Greek of all periods involving ever fresh uncertainty [1]. Lucretius or Catullus may be emended with more probability than Aeschylus or the fragments of Alcman. Different literatures admit of different treatment. Bentley in his proposals for a text of the New Testament says expressly that he is well aware that conjecture can have no place in the sacred text. This may have been intended to soothe orthodox apprehensions, but it at least involves an admission of the precariousness of conjecture [2].

The invention of so-called Canons of Criticism introduces an appearance of scientific precision, which is really fallacious. The rule of the more difficult reading, 'Potior lectio difficilior,' may often prove misleading. The balance is in favour of the less common word, if equally in point : e. g. ψέγει for λέγει. But when an absurd reading has once found its way into an approved text, the conservatism of tradition will often maintain it for centuries against common sense. The true reading meanwhile may have passed down through weaker channels, and may be supported, though less authoritatively, by independent evidence. For example, in IV. 442 B ὧν οὐ προσῆκόν αὐτῷ γένει, προσῆκον is the harder reading, and is supported by the better MSS. ; but the change from ε to ο might be made early, and once made would remain in one line of tradition, and the easier reading προσῆκεν, having the support of Stobaeus, would

§ 27.

---

[1] Yet it is not to be overlooked that here also the unwisdom of employing one manuscript authority exclusively has been clearly shown. See Prof. Ellis' 'Praefatio' to his *Noctes Manilianae* (Clarendon Press, 1891) :—' Gemblacensis Codex . . . ueterrimus ille quidem, utpote saec. XI scriptus, et integerrimus est omnium ; ita tamen, ut si absit Vossianus is secundus Iacobi, cui scriba suus annum 1470 in fine addidit, uera manus poetae relicta sit in incerto, idque plurifariam.' The same scholar adds his testimony to the general fact—' antiquos codices ita praestare recentibus ut his tamen supersederi nequeat.'

[2] It is also a strong instance of the general fact that the more reverently an author is handled the fewer are the conjectures which find their way into his text.

seem to be traditional in *q*.   It should be remarked,
however, that the best MS. of Stobaeus is, according to
Gaisford, of the fourteenth century.

Nor is the 'ductus literarum' in every instance a safe
guide.   Many other causes beside the forms of letters have
been at work, as we have seen above, and the only effect
of an apparently simple change may be to 'skin and film
the ulcerous place.'    Who could have supposed that
between the syllables of ἐκτέον, the reading of D K in
x. 607 A, there lurked a lacuna of forty-three letters?    Or
what palaeographer could have corrected χρησμὸν λέγοντας
in Solon fr. 36, l. 9, to χρείους φυγόντας, which the Ath. Pol.
now proves to be the true reading?    What critic could have
guessed it?    Or, if he had, who could have assured us that
he was right?—The errors of printed books present only
a distant analogy to those of classical MSS., which in the
great authors, have often been more carefully revised.    Yet
even here conjecture has proved of little avail.    Of innu-
merable emendations of Shakespeare by far the greater
number have been rejected by recent editors, and very few
have the certainty of Johnson's 'no more, but *e'en* a woman,
—(Foll. '*in*')—*Ant. and Cleo.* iv. 15, l. 73.   Who shall emend
with certainty 1 *Henry IV*, Act iv. 1, ll. 98, 99 'All plumed
like estridges that with the wind | Baited like eagles having
lately bathed,' or supply the 'missing word' in Sonnet 146
'Poor soul, the centre of my sinful earth, ... by these rebel
powers that thee array'? or in *Hamlet* iv. 1, ll. 40, 41
'And what's untimely done ... | Whose whisper o'er the
world's diameter,' &c.   Or, to take a more modern instance,
what but documentary evidence can determine between 'an
unbodied joy' and 'an embodied joy' in Shelley's *Skylark*?

Yet it must be admitted that Shelley's text affords some
examples of conjectural emendation subsequently corroborated by documentary evidence.   The subtle criticism
of W. M. Rossetti suggested several corrections of the
printed text which examination of the MSS. has since

confirmed [1]. *Julian and Maddalo* (vol. ii. p. 324, l. 18) 'and *even* at this hour :' *ever* cj. Rossetti and so Shelley's MS. *Letter to Maria Gisborne* (vol. iii. p. 48, l. 1) ' or those in *philosophic* councils met :' *philanthropic* cj. Rossetti [2] and so Shelley's MS. *Hellas* (vol. ii. p. 145, l. 20) ' The caves of the Icarian isles *Hold* each to the other in loud mockery :' *Told* cj. Rossetti and so the MS., and also a list of errata in Shelley's handwriting.

I understand also that in Chaucer five conjectural readings of Tyrwhitt's have been found in the Ellesmere MS. which is supposed to have been unknown to him. But his examination of MSS. may have been more minute than appears on the surface of his edition. Have all the twenty-four MSS. mentioned by him been identified and thoroughly collated ?

The history of classical texts presents few such examples. In Soph. Philoctetes 29 Lambinus suggested κτύπος for τύπος, and this was afterwards found in the Laurentian MS., and as a marginal variant in Γ. In Phil. 689 Auratus suggested κλύων for κλύζων, and this has also received some MS. confirmation. The correction of errors in the third epistle of Demosthenes, confirmed by the British Museum Papyrus as noted above, is perhaps the most striking example hitherto of such success.

Of Platonic editors probably Heindorf and Schneider have come nearest—Schleiermacher and K. F. Hermann being not far behind. Two conjectures of Schleiermacher though turning on a very slight change of letters are of distinguished merit :—in Rep. VI. 499 B κατηκόῳ for κατήκοοι and Protag. 328 C ὀνῆσαι for νοῆσαι. C. Orelli's στραγγευομένῳ for στρατευομένῳ (V. 472 A) confirmed by Vind. F corr. is the best example in the Republic [3]. It is also rather a striking

---

[1] I quote the earlier readings from ed. 1847 (reprint of Mrs. Shelley's edition).

[2] 'The epithet " philosophic " does not appear specially apposite ; should it be " theosophic " or " philanthropic "?' W. M. Rossetti, note to vol. ii. p. 245 of his edition, 1870.

[3] For several instances in which conjecture has coincided with MS.

fact that τὴν τῷ δικαίῳ βοήθειαν, which Schneider adopted from Vind. F pr. in place of τ. τῶν δικαίων β. in VI. 496 D, now proves to be the reading of Par. A.

In some cases, where all the MSS. are at fault, the true reading has been found in a quotation by some ancient writer, as Galen, Athenaeus, Stobaeus, and the Fathers Eusebius and Theodoretus. A doubt may arise, where the consent of the oldest MSS. is opposed to the reading of some inferior MS. supported by such quotation. When the author who gives the quotation is preserved in MSS. say of the tenth century, the evidence is nearly balanced,— the only remaining uncertainty being that which attends upon all quotations. The commentary of Proclus also supplies some evidence; but the Scholia to Plato, for the most part, throw but little light upon his text. They are full of Neo-platonic fancies, and few of them can be referred to the Alexandrian time. This is the more unfortunate, because, as a general rule, the best emendations have been those to which scholars have been led by some discrepancy between the explanation of a scholiast and the traditional text. The best emendation of a Sophoclean passage is Boeckh's φονώσαισιν for φονίαισιν in Ant. 117, founded on the scholion ταῖς τῶν φονῶν ἐρώσαις λόγχαις. Another, almost equally good, without such help, is ἀνῇ (Auratus and Pierson), in Phil. 639, confirmed by the gloss in L, παρῇ.

Were the corruptions and interpolations of the text of the Republic as numerous as recent scholars have imagined, the difference of meaning involved would be still infinitesimal. Some feature of an image might be obscured, or some idiomatic phrase enfeebled, but Plato's philosophy would remain uninjured. That is not a reason for careless treatment, but it is a consideration deserving to be set against the natural bias which minute and long-continued attention to the details of criticism is apt to produce.

evidence (in Euthyphr. Apol.) see Wohlrab *Platonhandschriften*, &c., p. 651.

The fashion of Greek orthography has changed somewhat since this text was printed. Exact scholars, whose eyes are accustomed to recent classical editions, will miss θνῄσκει, σῴζω, ποεῖν, μείξας, ὑεῖς, and other forms, which inscriptions show to have been usual in Attica from about 400 B.C. The new-old spelling is hardly yet finally established, and a text which is *arrière* in this respect may perhaps have some compensating advantages for those who in their school days were familiar with the former practice ; to whom ὑὸς μαίας μάλα γενναίας τε καὶ βλοσυρᾶς (Theaet. 149 A) still presents an awkward ambiguity, and who are for the moment puzzled when, in perusing a Latin treatise on Greek races, they come across the familiar patronymic, 'Jones.' The retention of φιλόνεικος, φιλονεικεῖν, φιλονεικία (against φιλόνικος, &c.) deserves a more serious defence. (See an elaborate note on the point in Leopold Schmidt's *Ethik der alten Griechen*[1].) There is no doubt that Greeks in Plato's time and afterwards associated the word with νίκη. But Greek etymological fancies are hardly solid ground to rest upon ; and the derivation from νεῖκος appears more probable: cp. φιλαπεχθήμων. The accentuation of ἀφίῃ (VII. 520 A) is indefensible. But I have followed the MSS. and editions. No scholar has yet suggested the adoption of the ι adscript in our ordinary texts. But this, together with the abolition of capitals and the recasting of our type in imitation of the earliest uncials, may follow in time.

[1] Vol. i. p. 386.

# APPENDIX I.

## COLLATION OF THE PRESENT TEXT WITH PARIS A (1807).

THE purpose of these pages is to supplement and partly to correct the list of various readings subjoined to the Text of this edition. Where my collation agrees substantially with Baiter's report, I give my own observation without any distinctive mark. An asterisk is placed against items believed to be new. And where these tend either to confirm or to alter the text as it stands, the reading of A is printed in larger type. It will be observed that in six places the new collation turns the scale against readings formerly adopted: III. 391 C ὥρμησαν not ὥρμησεν : IV. 428 D τελέους not τελέως : VI. 496 C τῷ δικαίῳ not τῶν δικαίων : 503 B διεσπασμένη not διεσπασμένα : X. 606 E ἄξιος not ἄξιον : 607 D ἀπολογησαμένη not ἀπολογησομένη.

L. C.

For the List of Errata in Text, see the last page of this volume. And for general peculiarities of Paris A, neglected here, see above, p. 70.

| | Page. | Line. | Steph. p. | Text. | Par. A |
|---|---|---|---|---|---|
| Rep. I. | 2 | 30 | | Critical note on l. 6 | γρ. ἐν |
| | 3 | 15 | 328 D | ὡς παρὰ φίλους τε | in mg.: *om.* pr. |
| | | 24 | E | αὐτὸ | αὐτὸς A² |
| | 5 | 2 | 329 E | σου | σόυ (corr. rec.) |
| | 6 | 2 | 330 C | αὐτῶν | αὐτῶν (et sic saepius) |
| * | | 23 | E | ἠδίκηκεν | ἠδίκηκεν A² |
| | 9 | 13 | 332 C | τί οἴει; ἔφη | The persons were at first divided with : after ἔφη. This was afterwards erased |
| | | 23 | D | τίσι | τισίν (sic saepius) |
| | 11 | 21 | 333 C | τί | τι (et saepius) |
| | | 31 | D | δέῃ | δέοι |
| *12 | | 18 | 333 E | φυλάξασθαι, καὶ λαθεῖν | φυλάξασθαι καὶ λαθεῖν (sic) |

| Page. | Line. | Steph. p. | Text. | Par. A |
|---|---|---|---|---|
| *12 | 29 | | Cr. n. 12 | οὐκ ἂν οὖν in mg. m. vet. Rep. I. The ν of ἂν partly eaten away |
| 15 | 22 | 335 C | ἄρα | ἄρα pr. |
| 18 | 17 | 337 A | ἀνεκάγχασε | ἀνεκάγ \| χασε in two lines, but a recent hand has erased γ and written κ at the beginning of the next line |
| 19 | 30 | E | ἀποκρίναιτο | ἀποκρίναιτο : ναι is written over an erasure of two letters |
| 21 | 15 | 338 E | ἑκάστη | ἑκάστηι (ι adscript) |
| *23 | 9 | 339 E | οὑτωσὶ δίκαιον εἶναι ποιεῖν τοὐναντίον ἤ | οὑτωσὶ δίκαιον εἶναι ποιεῖν τοὐναντίον, ἢ (sic) |
| 25 | 4 | 341 A | ἄρχων ἐστὶ | ἄρχων ἔστι pr. |
| | 9 | | εἶεν | Corrected by a recent hand to εἶέν and so constantly elsewhere |
| * | 31 | | Cr. n. 20 | ὃ is written over an erasure in A |
| 26 | 18 | D | ἔστι τι | ἔστίν τι (et saepius) |
| | 30 | 342 A | αὐτὴ | αὖ . . pr., αὐτὴ corr. |
| 27 | 7 | B | σκέψεται | σκέψεται (ται in erasure) |
| | 12 | | αὐτὴ | αὕτη |
| | 31 | | Cr. n. 4 | δεῖ αἰεὶ A |
| *31 | 10 | 344 E | ζῴη | ζων pr. : corr. p. m. |
| 32 | 12 | 345 D | μέλει | μέλλει pr. |
| | 31 | | Cr. n. 7 | ποιμαίνειν A² mg. |
| *34 | 3 | 346 D | λῆψις | Χῆψις |
| | 7 | | ἑκάστη | ἑκάστη (η in erasure) |
| 35 | 4 | 347 A | ξυνίης | ξυνιεῖς |
| 36 | 8 | E | ἔγωγε, ἔφη | ἔγωγ᾽ ἔ φη (sic) |
| | 13 | 348 A | πείθωμεν | πείθοιμεν pr. |
| | 17 | | αὖ | corr. from ἂν by p. m. |
| 37 | 30 | | Cr. n. 20, 21 | ut videtur A ; viz. — : σὺ δὲ . . . λέγειν : |
| *39 | 31 | | Cr. n. 19 ὁ δὲ μὴ | ὁ δὲ, μὴ A² |

| | Page. | Line. | Steph. p. | Text. | Par. A |
|---|---|---|---|---|---|
| Rep. I. | 41 | 19 & 31 | 350 C | ὁ δὴ Θρ. | ὁ δὲ Θρ. |
| | 42 | 5 | 350 E | ἐᾷς | ἐᾷσ. . followed by an erasure |
| | | 31 | | Cr. n. 14 | The breathing of εἴπερ has absorbed the sign ˉ for ν |
| | 43 | 5 & 31 | 351 C | εὖ γε σὺ ποιῶν | εὖ γε σοι ποιῶν: pr. (as if there were a change of persons) |
| | | | | Cr. n. 5 | γρ. σὺ A² mg. |
| | * | 28 | E | οὐδὲν ἧττον | οὐδὲν with ἧττον in mg. by A² |
| | 44 | 1 | | τοιάνδε τινὰ | τοιᾶνδέ τινα (et alibi) |
| | * | 24 | 352 C | δὴ καὶ οὕς | δικαίους pr. |
| | *45 | 7 & 30 | D | ὡς ἐμοὶ | ὥστέμοι corr. to ὡσ ἐμοὶ by A² |
| | 47 | 31 | | Cr. n. 6 | πραξαισ̊ A² |
| | 48 | 10 | 354 A | Βενδιδείοις | Βενδιδίοις |
| Rep. II. | *49 | 21 | 357 C | εἶπον | εἶπον (o in erasure) |
| | *50 | 3 | | φαῖμεν | φαῖμεν (ι from μ) |
| | 52 | 31 | | Cr. n. 24 | μυθολογοῦσιν A |
| | 53 | 14 | 360 B | τῶν παρὰ τὸν βα-σιλέα | *om.*: supplied in mg. by A² |
| | | 27 | C | καίτοι | καί το pr.    καί τὸ A² |
| | 54 | 7 | D | ἀνοητότατος | Corrected to ἀνοητοτάτοις |
| | *55 | 13 | 361 C | ἴτω | ἤτω : but η from ι p. m. |
| | 57 | 13 | 363 A | ἀπ' αὐτῆς | ὑπ' αὐτῆς pr. |
| | *59 | 17 | 364 D | ἀνάντη | καὶ τραχεῖαν added in mg. by A² |
| | 60 | 9 | 365 A | ἐπιπτόμενοι | Changed to ἐφιπτάμενοι by m. rec. with καὶ ἐπιπτώμενοι in mg. |
| | 62 | 14 | 366 D | ὡς δέ | ὡ°δὲ (sic) A¹ or A²? |
| | | 19 | | εἰπεῖν | εἶπεν corr. to εἰπεῖν by A¹ or A² |
| | 63 | 19 | 367 C | ἀλλὰ τὸ δοκεῖν | *om.*: supplied in mg. by A² |
| | | 23 | | μὲν | *om.*: inserted above the line by A² |

| Page. | Line. | Steph. p. | Text. | Par. A | |
|-------|-------|-----------|-------|--------|--|
| *64 | 5 | 367 D | κελεύεις | κελεύοις : ι in erasure (it never was κελεύεις) | Rep. II. |
| | 24 | 368 B | χρήσωμαι | Changed to χρήσομαι by A² | |
| | 29 | | Cr. n. 2 | The words γρ. ἀποδεχοίμην are by A² | |
| 68 | 25 | 370 D | χαλκῆς | χαλκεῖς : ει by A² in space of two or more letters | |
| | 31 | | εἶς ἕν | So corrected by A² | |
| 69 | 15 | E | κενὸς | κ . ε . νὸς (ε in space of four letters) | |
| 71 | 11 | 371 E | ηὔξηται ἡ πόλις | ηὔξηται ͞η πόλις (sic) | |
| | 20 | 372 A | διαιτήσονται | διαιτήσωνται pr. | |
| *72 | 29 | E | εἰ δ' αὖ . . . ἀποκωλύει | Point erased after βούλεσθε and οὐδὲν ἀποκωλύει marked off with :...: as Glaucon's by A² | |
| | 31 | | Cr. n. 11 | σύκων (sic) is the reading of A | |
| *73 | 29 | | Cr. n. 2 | κλῖναί is the reading of A | |
| 74 | 9 | 373 D | ἐκείνοις | ἐκείνης pr. | |
| | 19 | E | καὶ ἰδίᾳ καὶ δημοσίᾳ | om. : add. in mg. A² | |
| 78 | 19 | 376 A | προπεπονθώς | προ -:- πεπονθὼς corr. to προ-:-πεπονθὸς by A² | |
| 79 | 7 | C | φιλόσοφον | om. pr. : add. in mg. A² | |
| | 18 | D | ἵνα μὴ . . . διεξίωμεν | In mg. (διεξιῶμεν primitus) by A² | |
| *84 | 10 | 379 B | μὴ βλάπτει . . . ὃ δέ γε | om. : supplied in mg. by A² | |
| *86 | 27 | 380 E | καὶ κινεῖται . . . σιτίων τε | om. : supplied in mg. by A² | |
| *89 | 15 | 382 B | ἐψεῦσθαι καὶ | First omitted and then supplied by A¹ | |
| 90 | 27 | E | οὔθ' ὕπαρ οὔτ' ὄναρ | ὕπαρ corr. to ὕπαρ by A² ͞οὔθ' οὐδ' ὄναρ | |
| *91 | 25 | | Cr. n. 2 | γόητας ὄντας is the reading of A | |
| | | | ,, | αὐτῆς is the correction of A² | |

| | Page. | Line. | Steph. p. | Text. | Par. A |
|---|---|---|---|---|---|
| Rep. II. | *91 | 27 | | Cr. n. 12 | παιῶν' (with M Ξ) ηι |
| Rep. III. | 95 | 18 | 388 B | ἀμφοτέρῃσι | ἀμφοτέραισι A² : no mark of quotation here |
| | 96 | 8 | D | σχολῇ | σχόλῃι with gloss, ἀντὶ τοῦ οὐδαμῶς |
| | | 19 | E | ἰσχυρῷ | A recent hand has added κατέχοιτο in mg. |
| | 97 | 12 | 389 C | τοιούτους | om. : add. in mg. A² |
| | | 18 | | τις | τῆς |
| | | 21 | | ἂν | ἂν = ἐὰν without accent here and elsewhere, e.g. 411 C |
| | *99 | 5 | 390 B | ὡς μόνος ... ἐπι-θυμίαν | Marked off with :...: as a separate speech |
| | | 19 | D | ἠνίπαπε | ἠνείπαπε |
| | 100 | 7 | 391 A | δι' | δὴ with accent over erasure : perhaps δὴ |
| | *101 | 1 | C | ὥρμησαν | ὥρμησαν |
| | | 2 | D | ἄλλον | ἄλλου (sic) |
| | | 17 | E | *οἱ Ζηνὸς ἐγγύς, ὧν | Ζηνὸς ἐγγὺς ὧν |
| | 109 | 9 | 396 C | αὐτὸς | αὐτὸς pr. |
| | *110 | 4 | 397 A | δὴ ἐλέγομεν | διελέγομεν pr. |
| | * | 5 | | βρ ας τε | βροντάς γε |
| | | 31 | | | For 3 in cr. n. read 5 |
| | | | | Cr. n. 18 | σμικραὶ A² : σμικρὰ A |
| | 113 | 10 | 398 E | συντονολυδιστὶ | συντονο'λυδιστὶ A² |
| | | 21 & 31 | | αἵτινες | αυτινες pr. : αἵτινες A² : αὖ τινες in mg. m. vet. |
| | * | 30 | | Cr. n. 7 | οὐ γὰρ οὖν is the reading of A |
| | *115 | 23 | 400 A | εἴποιμι· ποῖα δὲ ποίου βίου μιμή-ματα | εἴποι μιμήματα |
| | 117 | 13 | 401 A | ἀρρυθμία | ἀρυθμία A : ἀρρυθμία A² |
| | *118 | 29 | | Cr. n. 6 | αὔρα is the reading of A |
| | 121 | 3 | 403 B | ὡς ἔοικε, νομοθετή-σεις | ὡς ἔοικενο \| μοθετὴς εἶς A ὡς ἔοικενόνο \| μοθετὴς εἶς A² |
| | 123 | 3 | 404 B | ἐπὶ στρατείας | ἐπὶ στρατιᾶς |

| Page. | Line. | Steph. p. | Text. | Par. A | |
|-------|-------|-----------|-------|--------|---|
| 127 | 11 | 407 B | τῷ μὴ μελετῶντι, ἢ νοσοτροφία | τῷ μὴ μελετῶντι ἡ νοσοτρο- φία | Rep. III. |
| | 22 | C | ἀεὶ | αἰεὶ | |
| | 28 | | Cr. n. 15–17 | Et A Socrati tribuit cum : . . . : et — in mg. | |
| 129 | 3 | 408 B | τραγῳδιοποιοί | τραγῳδοποιοί (A on the whole favours τραγῳδιο- ποιός) | |
| | 28 | E | ῇ | ἡ (sic pr.: ῇ rec.) | |
| * | 31 | | ῇ | ηι pr. : ῇ corr. p. m. | |
| 134 | 3 | 411 C | κομιδῇ | ( . . . ) κομιδῇ | |
| | 4 | | γυμναστικῇ | γυμναστικῇ A² | |
| | 21 | E | ἀρρυθμίας | ἀρυθμίας pr. : ἀρρυθμίας A² | |
| | 22 | | ἀχαριστίας | ἀχαριστίας A² | |
| | 24 | | ἐπὶ δὴ | ἐπειδὴ | |
| * | 31 | | Cr. n. 13 | **οὔτε ζητήματος** is the reading of A | |
| 142 | 22 | 416 D | ἐπαροῖ | ἐπάρῃ | |
| 151 | 24 | 424 B | ἐπιφρονέουσιν | ἐπιφρονέουσιν (sic) A² | Rep. IV. |
| 152 | 31 | | Cr. n. 7 | αὐτὴ A | |
| 153 | 30 | | Cr. n. 18 | ὃν A (non inter versus) | |
| 154 | 24 | 426 A | ὑγιεῖς | ὑγιής | |
| 155 | 1 | B | αὐτὸν | αὐτῶν A² | |
| | 24 | D | ἔγωγ', ἔφη, | ἔγωγ', ἔφη : (sic) | |
| 157 | 29 | 428 A | ἐκεῖνο | ἐκεῖνο A² | |
| 159 | 5 | D | ἑαυτῆς | αὐτῆς | |
| * | 10 | | τελέους | **τελέους** (not τελέως) is the reading of A | |
| 160 | 23 | 429 C | παρήγγειλεν | παρήγγειλλεν | |
| 163 | 7 | 430 E | λέγοντες | φαίνονταί (sic) cum γρ. λέγοντες A² | |
| 165 | 23 | 432 B | τοῦτό ἐστιν | τοῦτ' ἐστὶν | |
| *167 | 21 | 433 C | ὑπολειφθὲν | ὑπολ(η)φθὲν pr. ? | |
| * | 31 | | Cr. n. 26 | ἡ ὁμοδοξία (ἡ not *om.*) | |
| 168 | 18 | E | τούτου | τοῦτο | |
| | 30 | | Cr. n. 13 | γρ. εἰ σαυτῷ mg. | |
| *169 | 27 | 434 D | ἄλλῃ | ἄλλη pr. | |

| | Page. | Line. | Steph. p. | Text. | Par. A |
|---|---|---|---|---|---|
| Rep. IV. | *170 | 4 & 29 | 434 D | ἐκεῖνο | ἐκεῖ is the reading of A ; so that for ἐκεῖνο we are thrown back on Ξ D q |
| | 172 | 22 | 436 B | ὥστ᾽ ἐάν που | ὥστε ἄν που |
| | 174 | 21 | 437 C | ἐρωτῶντος | ἐρῶ(τῶ)ντος |
| | 175 | 6 | D | ἐστὶ δίψα ἀρά γε | — ἐστὶ : δίψα : ἀράγε |
| | | 29 | | Cr. n. 5 | ἢ οὐ γρ. που (it was at first που γρ. η ου) |
| | *179 | 9 | 439 E | τι †πιστεύω | τι, πιστεύω (sic) |
| | 183 | 19 | 442 B | τούτω | τούτω· (letter erased) |
| | 184 | 29 | 443 A | οὐδέν ἀν | οὐδὲν ἀν |
| | 185 | 19 & 32 | B | τέλεον | τελευταῖον γρ. τέλεον mg. |
| | *186 | 31 | | Cr. n. 16 | ἢ περὶ τὰ ἴδια with Π Μ |
| Rep. V. | 191 | 7 | 449 A | ἔφη | om. |
| | *193 | 29 | | Cr. n. 5 | μέτρον is the reading of A |
| | *195 | 24 | 451 E | καὶ διδακτέον | καὶ om. pr. |
| | | 31 | | Cr. n. 23 | καὶ τοῖς A |
| | 200 | 2 | 454 C | καὶ τὴν | om.: add. in mg. A² |
| * | | 4 | D | μόνον | μόνον ᵒⁿ A² |
| | | 5 | | ἰατρικὸν μὲν καὶ ἰατρικὸν | ἰατρικὸν (ἰατρικῶν pr.) μὲν καὶ ἰατρικὴν |
| | 201 | 10 & 31 | 455 B | τὸν μὲν | τὸ μὲν pr. τὸν μὲν A² |
| | 202 | 24 | 456 A | ἢ | om. |
| | | | | ἰσχυροτέρα | ἰσχυροτέρα ᵒ A² |
| | 204 | 28 | 457 B | γυμναζομέναις | γυναζομέναις |
| | | 29 | | ἀτελῆ | γρ. ἅτε δὴ A² mg. |
| | 207 | 29 | 459 A | παιδοποιίαις | παιδοποιίαι (ι adscript) |
| | 208 | 16 | B | ἢ | ἢ |
| | *209 | 17 & 31 | E | νομοθετητέαι ἔσονται | νομοθετητέαι (omitting ἔσονται) |
| | 211 | 7 | 460 E | εἰκοσιέτιδος | εἰκοσιετίδος pr. |
| | | 8 | | τετταρακονταέτιδος | τετταρακονταετίδος pr. |
| * | | 18 & 30 | 461 A | φύς, ἃς ἐφ᾽ ἑκάστοις | φύσας. ἃς ἑκάστοις : γρ. ἐφ᾽ έ. A² mg. |
| | | 31 | | Cr. n. 27 | φήσομεν A (no corr.) |
| | *212 | 30 | | Cr. n. 8 | μὴ δέ γ᾽ ἐν (sic) A² |
| | 213 | 1 | E | ἐπομένη | ἐπομένηι |
| | | 2 | | βελτίστη | βελτίστηι |

| Page. | Line. | Steph. p. | Text. | Par. A | |
|---|---|---|---|---|---|
| 213 | 15 | 462 B | ξυνδῇ | ξυνδεῖ | Rep. V. |
| *218 | 26 | 465 A | ἄλλως | ἄλλος : (ἄλλως Ξ q) | |
| 223 | 24 | 468 A | ποῖ ἄν | ποῖ ἄν | |
| 224 | 10 | B | τί δέ ; δεξιωθῆναι | τί δαὶ δ᾽ ἐξιωθῆναι cum γρ.<br>(mg.) τί δὲ ἐξιαθῆναι: A² | |
| * | 16 & 31 | C | καὶ μηδενὶ | μηδενὶ (καὶ om.) | |
| 229 | 28 | 471 C | αὕτη | om. add. in mg. A² | |
| 231 | 1 | 472 B | γ᾽ | om. add. A² | |
| | 16 | D | μοῖραν | μοῖραν ἂν pr. (ἂν erased) | |
| 233 | 11 | 473 D | βασιλῆς | βασιλεῖς (ει over erasure<br>of three letters) | |
| * | 22 | E | ἄλλῃ | ἄλλη | |
| 236 | 31 | Cr. n. 26 | | Delete (?) : μαθητικοὺς A² | |
| 237 | 22 | 476 B | που | ποι | |
| *243 | 31 | Cr. n. 25 | | ᾧ (ὦι, sic, not ὦν) | |
| 246 | 10 | 484 B | ἑξῆς | ἑξῆς : ἐξ ἀρχῆς A² mg. | Rep. VI. |
| 250 | 19 | 486 C | πλέως | πόλεως ? pr. | |
| | 30 | | Cr. n. 22 | γρ. ἀνόνητα A² mg. | |
| *251 | 31 | | Cr. n. 1 | μὴν (not μὴ) | |
| 252 | 29 | | Cr. n. 1 | παραγόμενοι A² mg. | |
| 253 | 27 | 488 C | ἀποκτιννύντας | ἀποκτιννύντας (ιννύ in era-<br>sure) : κτεινό A² mg. | |
| | 31 | | Cr. n. 8 | γρ. πλῆθος A² mg. | |
| 260 | 10 | 492 D | φήσειν | φησιν pr. | |
| *262 | 7 | 493 D | εἴτε δὴ . . . ὁμιλῇ | om. pr. add. in mg. A² | |
| *263 | 23 | 494 D | ἐξαρεῖν | ἐξαιρεῖν | |
| | 28 | | κτήσει | κτίσει pr. | |
| 265 | 13 | 495 D | εἰργμῶν | εἰργμῶν A² | |
| 266 | 11 | 496 A | ἦν δ᾽ ἐγώ | ἔφη ἦν δ᾽ ἐγώ | |
| * | 18 | B | ἂν ἔλθοι | ἀνέλθοι | |
| *267 | 1 & 30 | C | τῷ δικαίῳ | τῷ δικαίῳ | |
| 269 | 3 | 497 E | δεῖ | δὴ pr. | |
| 270 | 13 | 498 E | πολὺ | πολὺ A² | |
| | | | τοιαῦτ᾽ ἄττα ῥήματα | γρ. τοιαυτὶ ῥήματα A² mg. | |
| | 22 | 499 A | ἐπήκοοι | ἐπήκοι (sic) | |
| * | 23 | | ξυντεταμένως | ξυντεταγμένως pr.(γ erased) | |
| | | | τρόπου | πρόσώπου γρ. τρόπου A²<br>mg. | |

| | Page. | Line. | Steph. p. | Text. | Par. A |
|---|---|---|---|---|---|
| Rep. VI. | *270 | 31 | | Cr. n. 22 | οἴων A² |
| | *273 | 4 | 500 C | ἀγάμενος | ἀγάμενος (sic) |
| | * | 18 & 22 | E | χαλεπανοῦσι | χαλεπαινοῦσι pr. |
| | 275 | 20 & 30 | 502 A | τις | τίς |
| | **277 | 11 & 23 | 503 A, B | παρακαλυπτομένου . . . διεσπασμένη | **παρακαλυπτομένου** and **διεσπασμένη** are the readings of A |
| | 280 | 32 | | Cr. n. 26 | εἰ δέναι (sic) A² |
| | *284 | 4 | 507 A | κομίσασθε | κομίσασθαι pr. : κομίσασθε with θαι in mg. A² |
| | | 16 | B | αὐτὸ δὴ καλὸν | αὐτοδηκαλὸν (sic) |
| Rep. VII. | 293 | 3 | 514 A | ἰδὲ | ἴδε pr. |
| | | 7 | B | εἴς τε τὸ πρόσθεν | εἴς τε πρόσθεν pr. : εἴς τε πρόσθεν A² |
| | | 12 | | ἰδὲ | ἴδε |
| | 295 | 4 | 515 D | μᾶλλόν τι | μᾶλλόν (sic) |
| | *300 | 28 | | Cr. n. 1 | τούτου is the reading of A |
| | | 31 | | Cr. n. 14 | χρήσιμόν τε A |
| | 304 | 28 | 521 E | γυμναστικῇ . . . μουσικῇ | γυμναστικὴ . . . μουσικὴ |
| | 311 | 28 & 31 | 525 E | ὡς | δύο ὡς (A¹ or ²) |
| | 312 | 28 | 526 C | ἂν εὔροις | ἀνεύροις |
| | 313 | 20 | E | ὃ δεῖ | οὐ δεῖ pr. : οὗ δεῖ A² |
| | 314 | 30 | | Cr. n. 13 | γρ. εὐομολόγητον A² mg. |
| | 316 | 8 | 528 B | τε | om. pr. : supr. lin. add. A² |
| | * | 10 | | οὐκ ἂν . . . μεγαλοφρονούμενοι | om. pr. : in mg. add. A² |
| | *317 | 22 | 529 B | ἴσως . . . εὐηθικῶς | : ἴσως . . . εὐηθικῶς : A¹ or ² (i. e. given to Glaucon) |
| | * | 29 | | Cr. n. 19 | η pr. : ῇ A² |
| | *319 | 30 | | Cr. n. 16 | ἐξ ἀχρήστου A² |
| | *320 | 25 | 531 B | φθεγγομένων | **φθεγγόμένων** (sic) A² |
| | 321 | 6 | C | ἀνίασιν | ἀνιᾶσιν pr. |
| | | 31 | | Cr. n. 27 | οἱ μὴ |
| | 322 | 6 | 532 A | αὐτὰ τὰ ἄστρα | αὐτὰ ἄστρα |
| | | 12 | B | τῷ τοῦ | τῷ pr. : τῷ A² |
| | 324 | 4 | 533 B | ἅπασαι | ἅπασα |
| | *325 | 31 | | Cr. n. 25 | **φήσεις** (not οὐδὲν φήσεις) |

| Page. | Line. | Steph. p. | Text. | Par. A | |
|---|---|---|---|---|---|
| 326 | 1 | 534 D | ἐπικαταδαρθάνειν | ἐπικαταδαρθανεῖν ? pr. | Rep. VII. |
| *327 | 30 | | Cr. n. 11 | πάντῃ (not πάντα) | |
| 329 | 25 | 537 A | ἐφ' ὁ | ἐφ' ᾧ corr. | |
| 331 | 20 | 538 A | χρόνῳ, ᾦ | χρόνῳ pr. : χρόνῳ A² | |
| * | 30 | | Cr. n. 9 | ἐμπίμπλανται A² | |
| 332 | 4 | B | αἰσθόμενον | αἰσθόμενος pr. : αἰσθόμενος A² | |
| | 26 | D | ἐξελέγχῃ | ἐξελέγχῃ | |
| 334 | 9 | 539 C | μιμήσεται | γρ. μεμνήσεται A² mg. | |
| 335 | 21 | 540 C | ἀπείργασαι | ἀπείγασαι pr. : ἀπείγασαι m. vet. | |
| 337 | 17 | 543 C | εἰς | om. pr. : add. A² | Rep. VIII. |
| | 21 | | Cr. n. 20 | ἀλλά γ' (not ἀλλά γε) | |
| 339 | 14 | 544 D | ἠθῶν τῶν | ἠθῶν pr. : ἠθῶν A² | |
| | 21 | E | ἤδη | δη pr. : δη A² | |
| 341 | 26, 27 | 546 C | ἑκατὸν (bis) | ἕκαστον (bis) pr. | |
| * | 30 | • | Cr. n. 25 | παρέχεται (not παρέχηται) is the reading of A | |
| 342 | 19 | 547 A | φήσομεν | φήσωμεν | |
| | 25 | B | τῷ γένει | τῷ γένει pr. : τῷ γένεε A² | |
| | 27 | | ἀργυροῦν | ἀργύρεον : ἀργύρεον A² | |
| * | 28 | | πενομένῳ ... πλου-σίῳ | πενομένων ... πλουσίων pr. (ν erased, bis) | |
| 344 | 5 | 548 A | οἱ τοιοῦτοι | οἱ οὗτοι pr. : οἱ οὗτοι A² | |
| *345 | 8 | D | οἶμαι μέν | οἶμεν pr. : οἶ μὲν A² | |
| * | 15 & 31 | 549 A | τις ἂν | τισ . . with space for two letters, but what was first written is uncertain | |
| 347 | 30 | | Cr. n. 10 | καὶ αὐτοὺς rec. (not A) | |
| 348 | 2 | 550 C | τοιαύτην | om. pr. : add. in mg. A² | |
| | 18 | E | γυναῖκες αὐτῶν | γυναῖκες αὐτῷ | |
| 349 | 13 | 551 B | ἢ οὐσία | ἡ οὐσία | |
| 350 | 12 & 30 | 551 D | ἀλλὰ μὴν οὐδὲ τόδε | ἀλλὰ μὴν ǀ οὐδε pr. : καὶ μὴν οὐδὲ ǀ τόδε corr. rec. (οὐδὲ being written in the right-hand margin) | |

| | Page. | Line. | Steph. p. | Text. | Par. A |
|---|---|---|---|---|---|
| Rep. VIII. | 351 | 29 & 31 | 552 D | βαλλαντιατόμοι | βαλαντιατόμοι pr. : βαλλαν-τιοτόμοι A² |
| | 354 | 30 | | Cr. n. 22 | **:** καὶ ἔτι μάλιστα \| εὖ (two lines) |
| | 355 | 31 | | Cr. n. 14 | ἐν / εὑρήσεις A² |
| | 356 | 6 | 555 A | μὴ κατὰ | μὴ / κατὰ (sic) |
| | 358 | 26 | 556 E | ἔξωθεν | Written over an erasure of seven or eight letters |
| | 359 | 1 | | ἐπαγομένων . . . συμμαχίαν | *om.* pr. : add. in mg. A² |
| | *360 | 25 & 30 | 557 E | καὶ ἄρχειν | καὶ ἀρχῆς A : καὶ ἄρχῃς A² |
| | 362 | 12 | 558 D | εἶμεν | εἶμεν A² |
| | | 30 | | Cr. n. (for 12 read 13) | δικαίως ἀναγκαῖαι |
| | * | | | Cr. n. (for 22 read 9 and 22) | ἀναγκαίους (not ἀναγκαίας) is the reading of A |
| | 363 | 8 | 559 B | ἢ τοιούτων | ἢ τοιούτων |
| | 364 | 9 | E | ἔφη | *om.* : in mg. add. A² |
| | | 10 | | μετέβαλλε | μετέβαλλε A² (α ει) |
| | 366 | 6 | 561 A | πῶς | **:** πῶς **:** as a separate speech |
| | | 17 | B | ἑαυτὸν ἐνδῷ | ἑαυτῷ ἐνδῷ |
| | 367 | 5 | D | ἀργῶν καὶ | ἀργῶν . . . καὶ (erasure of eight letters) |
| | 372 | 30 | | Cr. n. 7 | μελιττουργὸν A corr. |
| | *375 | 4 | 565 E | προεστώς | προσεστὼς is the reading of A |
| | 377 | 6 | 567 A | πρὸς τῷ | πρὸς τὸ pr. |
| | *378 | 8 | D | ἀνάγκῃ | ἀνάγκη |
| | 380 | 12 | 568 D | ἀποδομένων | ἀποδομένων (λ) |
| | * | 17 | E | ἦν | ἔφην pr. |
| Rep. IX. | 382 | 21 | | Cr. n. 12 | ἐγκαλῶ A (not ἐν καλῷ) |
| | 383 | 22 | 572 A | του | *om.* pr. : supplied by first hand at end of line |
| | | | | καὶ | κα in erasure |
| | *386 | 18 | D | σὺ | .σὺ· (sic) |
| | *389 | 25 | 575 C | ἴκταρ | ἴκταρ |
| | 391 | 23 | 576 D | ἀρετῇ | ἆρα ἡ **:** γρ. ἀρετῇ in mg. A² |

| Page. | Line. | Steph. p. | Text. | Par. A | |
|-------|-------|-----------|-------|--------|---|
| 391 | 31 | | Cr. n. (23 not 20) | ἆρα ἡ A | Rep. IX. |
| *392 | 18 | 577 B | ἂν ὀφθείη | ἀνοφθείη | |
| *394 | 5 & 30 | 578 A | ὀδυρμοὺς δὲ | ὀδυρμούς τε is the reading of A | |
| *395 | 1 & 30 | C | ἢ | ῃ pr. : corr. m. vet. | |
| 396 | 14 | 579 B | εἴη | εἰ εἴη (sic) | |
| | 27 | C | ἑαυτῷ | ταυτῷ pr. | |
| *398 | 29 | | Cr. n. 5 | κρῖνε A (not κρῖναι) | |
| | 30 | | Cr. n. 27 | τὸ λογιστικὸν δέξεται A¹ or ² ι | |
| *399 | 17 | 581 A | φαῖμεν | φαμεν (sic) | |
| 400 | 31 | | Cr. n. 16 | ὑποκείμενον A | |
| *401 | 6 & 28 | D | νομίζειν | (sic : no οὐδὲν) | |
| | 8 & 31 | E | τῆς †ἡδονῆς | 'τῆς ἡδονῆς (sic) | |
| | 29 | | Cr. n. 6 | Dele A² after οὐδὲν | |
| *402 | 13 & 29 | 582 C | τιμὴ μέν | τί μὴν (sic) A | |
| | 15 | | καὶ ὁ σοφὸς | καὶ σοφὸς pr. : καὶ σοφὸς A² | |
| *403 | 21 | 583 A | ὢν . . . βίον | ὢν pr. : βίοὐ (sic) | |
| 404 | 9 | C | λύπην | πην pr. : πην A² | |
| 407 | 11 & 30 | 584 E | κάτω | κάτα pr. : κάτω corr. A¹ or ² | |
| | 25 | 585 A | πεῖνα | πείνη pr. : πείνη A² | |
| 408 | 17 | C | τοῦ μηδέποτε | μηδέποτε (om. τοῦ) MSS. Ast corr. | |
| 409 | 4 & 31 | 585 D | ψυχῆς | τῆς ψυχῆς (sic) | |
| 410 | 31 | | Cr. n. 24 | ἐξηγῆται A² | |
| 411 | 13 | 587 A | ἐξεργάζοιτο | ἐξεργάζοι pr. : ἐξεργάζοι A² | |
| 412 | 2 | B | νόθαιν | νόθοιν (but οι in erasure) | |
| 414 | 30 | 589 A | ἐκείνων | ἐκείνω pr. : ἐκείνω A² | |
| 417 | 13 | 590 D | ἐν αὑτῷ | ἐν αὑτῷ A² | |
| | 18 | | ἐν αὐτῷ | ἐν αὐτῷ | |
| | 25 | E | ἐν αὐτοῖς | ἐν αὐτοῖς | |
| 418 | 22 | 591 C | ἄλλ' | ἄλλα | |
| | 26 | | ζήσει | ζω . . . pr. : ζώιη corr. rec. | |
| 419 | 11 | E | αὑτῷ | ἑαυτῷ A² | |
| * | 13 | | πλῆθος | πλήθους pr. | |

| | Page. | Line. | Steph. p. | Text. | Par. |
|---|---|---|---|---|---|
| Rep. X. | *422 | 31 | | Cr. n. 23 | add. ' but the accent is by a recent hand' (κλῖναι infr. 597 B) |
| | *423 | 11 | 596 c | τάχα | τάχα (the accent and χ in erasure) |
| | *424 | 13 | E | φαινομένην γε | φαινομένην pr. : φαινομένην˙γε A² |
| | *428 | 11 | 599 A | μιμηθησόμενον | μηθησόμενον pr. : μ̇ι̇μηθησόμενον A² |
| | *429 | 16–18 & 30 | E | οὔκουν . . . ὁμήρου | The mark for the change of persons (—:) is before οὔκουν, not before ἀλλὰ (Not ' praescriptum est σω.') |
| | 430 | 27 & 31 | 600 D | *ὀνινάναι | ὀνῖναι A² |
| | 43 | 15 | 601 A | αὐτὸν . . . ἑτέροις | om. pr. : add. in mg. A², with ἐν τοῖς for ἑτέροις |
| | | 18 | B | ἐν μέτρῳ . . . λέγεσθαι | om. pr. : add. in mg. A² |
| | 434 | 11 | 602 c | τῶν | τὸ A² |
| | | 21 | D | αὕτη | αὐτὴ |
| | 438 | 7 | 604 c | ὅ τε δεῖ | ὅτι δεῖ |
| * | | 18 & 31 | | ἰατρικῇ | ἰατρικῇ . A² (letter erased) |
| | 439 | 4 | E | αὐτὸ | om. pr. : add. in mg. A² |
| | | 11 & 31 | 605 A | τε | γε˙ (γ in erasure) |
| *440 | | 31 | | Cr. n. 27 | εἰ ἐκείνη (εἰ not omitted) |
| | 441 | 14 | 606 B | ἀπολαύειν | ἀπολαύειν A² |
| | | 30 | | Cr. n. 22 | μὴ μισῇς (μὴ corr. from μι) |
| | *442 | 14 | E | ἄξιος | ἄξιος (not ἄξιον) is the reading of A |
| | 443 | 4 | 607 B | ποιητικῇ | ποιητικῇμιμ A² |
| * | | 32 | | Cr. n. 19 | ἀπολογησαμένη (sic legendum) corrected by erasure to ἀπολογησομένη |
| | 445 | 5 | 608 D | οὐχ | om. pr. : add. in mg. A² |
| | | 24 | E | ἔγωγ', ἔφη | ἔγωγε τοῦτό γ' ἔφη A² |
| | 446 | 16 | 609 B | ψυχῇ ἆρα . . . ἃ νῦν | om. pr. : add. in mg. A² |

| Page. | Line. | Steph. p. | Text. | Par. A |
|---|---|---|---|---|
| 448 | 22 | 610 D | φανεῖται | φαίνεται is given as an alternative by A¹ or ²   Rep. X. |
| 452 | 3 | 612 D | ἃ | Inserted after κτωμένη by A² |
| | 7 | E | αἰτεῖ | αἰτῇ (sic) |
| | 15 | | γε | $\overset{γ}{τε}$ |
| 454 | 1 | 613 E | λέγων | γρ. λέγοντα A² mg. |
| | 25 & 32 | 614 B | ἐπειδή οὐ | **ἐπειδὴ οὗ** A : ἐπειδὴ οὖν A² |
| 455 | 10 | D | θεᾶσθαι | θε · ᾶ · σθαι (ᾶ in space of three letters) |
| | 18 | E | ἀπιούσας | $\overset{ἐ}{ἀπιούσας}$ A² |
| 456 | 1 | 615 A | ὅσους | · · οὑς (two letters erased) |
| 457 | 14 | 616 A | τοῦτον | $τοῦ\overset{ω}{τ}ον$ A² (o in erasure)— primitus scriptum τουτων |
| * | 24 | B | προσφερῇ | προσφερῇ $\overset{ές}{}$ A² |
| 460 | 7 | 617 E | συνέσται | συνεστε pr. ? |
| | 11 | | ἒ δὲ | ἔδει A² |
| | 27 | 618 B | ὑγιείαις | ὑγείαις pr. |
| 462 | 6 | 619 B | νῷ | om. pr. : supra lineam add. A² |
| 465 | 5 | 621 B | ἔωθεν | γρ. ἄνωθεν A² mg. |
| | 6 | | ἤδη | om. pr., then add. at end of line |
| | 17 | D | χιλιέτει | χιλιετει pr. : χιλίετι A² |

# APPENDIX II.

## Errors of the First Hand in Par. A.

N.B.—To avoid undue length some slight clerical errors such as οὔ τοι for οὖ τοι (I. 330 B), ἤπερ for ἦπερ (ibid. C), ἢ πῶς for ἦ πῶς (ib. 337 C), ἡγεῖται for ἡγῆται (V. 479 A), πάντως for παντὸς (VI. 491 C)—although sometimes confusing enough—are omitted in the following list.

A², for the sake of simplicity, is here made to include, together with readings of the Diorthotes, some corrections by A¹, and some by other early hands, and only manifest errors are admitted.

It will be observed (1) that only thirty-three out of 170 errors of the first hand (about $\frac{1}{5}$) are corrected by A²; (2) that the correction in forty-one places is due to Π as the earliest witness, in fourteen places to M pr. m., in twenty-five places to Ξ, and in twenty-four places to q. Of the remainder x is responsible for three corrections, Vind. D for one, Vind. F for three, and ʀ for one; three rest on the testimonies of ancient writers[1], and nineteen are conjectural.

| Errors of **A** p.m. | Corrected to | By |
|---|---|---|
| I. 331 D ἔφη ἐγώ | ἔφην ἐγώ | Ξ |
| 333 D δέοι | δέῃ | Π M |
| ,, E οὐκοῦν | οὐκ ἂν οὖν | A² mg. |
| 336 E οἴου τε σὺ | οἴου γε σὺ | Bekker (οἷόν γε Ξ) |
| 339 B καὶ αὐτὸς | καὶ αὐτὸ | A² |
| 342 A δεῖ αἰεὶ | δεῖ | Π M |
| 345 C πιαίνειν | ποιμαίνειν | A² mg. |
| 346 A οἷοι | οἷον | A² |
| ,, B ξυμφέρον | ξυμφέρειν | q |
| 347 A ὧι | ὧν | M |
| ,, C δεῖ δὲ | δεῖ δὴ | Π M |
| ,, E πότερον ὡς | πότερον | M |
| 348 E ῥᾶιον | ῥᾴδιον | x |
| 351 A ἔφη | ἔφην | q |
| ,, C σοι | σὺ | A² |
| ,, D διαφέρωμεν | διαφέρωμαι | Π |

To these perhaps two more should be added :—

IV. 442 B προσῆκεν Stobaeus.

444 C αὐτὰ μὲν οὖν Stobaeus.

| Errors of A p.m. | Corrected to | By |
|---|---|---|
| I. 352 E φαμὲν | φαῖμεν | Steph. |
| 354 B ἐγῶμαι | ἐγώ μοι | r |
| II. 360 E ἑαυτῷ | ἑαυτοῦ | Π Μ |
| 361 C ὑπ' αὐτῆς | ἀπ' αὐτῆς | Eusebius |
| 363 A τῷ δικαίῳ | τῷ ἀδίκῳ | q |
| 364 D λιστοὶ δὲ στρεπτοίτε | στρεπτοὶ δέ τε | Π Μ |
| 365 D καὶ ἡμῖν | οὐδ' ἡμῖν | q |
| 366 A αἱ τελεταὶ | αἱ τελεταὶ αὖ μέγα δύνανται | Π |
| ,, D ὧδε | ὡς δὲ | A² |
| 367 D ἀποσχοίμην | ἀνασχοίμην | Ξ |
| 370 A ῥάδιον | ῥᾷον | q |
| ,, E εἴη | ἴῃ | q |
| 375 B ἀλλοτρίοις | ἄλλοις | q |
| 376 D γίγνεται· | γίγνεται; ἵνα μὴ . . . διεξίωμεν. | A² |
| 378 B δοκῶ | δοκεῖ | X |
| ,, C μᾶλλον | λεκτέα μᾶλλον | Π Μ |
| 383 B τοῖς αὐτοῖς | τοῖς αὐτῆς | A² |
| ,, B ἐνδυτεῖσθαι | ἐνδατεῖσθαι | A² |
| III. 387 C ὡς οἴεται | ὡς οἷόν τε ? | q |
| ,, C ὑπὸ | ὑπὲρ | Π Μ |
| ,, E ἄρα | ἄρ' ἂν | Π Μ |
| 388 E ἔφην | ἐφῇ | Vind. D mg. |
| 389 C τῆς | τις | A² |
| ,, D κολάσεως | κολάσει ὡς | Π |
| 391 D τιν' ἄλλου | τιν' ἄλλον | Π |
| ,, E ζηνὸς ἐγγύς, ὧν | οἱ ζηνὸς ἐγγύς, ὧν | Bekker (ὧν some MSS.) |
| 395 A μιμήματά τε | μιμήματε | q |
| ,, C ἵνα | ἵνα μὴ | Π Μ |
| 396 D ἑαυτοῦ | ἑαυτὸν | Π Μ |
| 397 B σμικρὰ | σμικραὶ | A² |
| 400 A εἴποι μιμήματα | εἴποιμ· ποῖα δὲ ποίου βίου μιμήματα | M |
| 401 C ἀνεμόμενοι | νεμόμενοι | Π Μ |
| 402 B καὶ εἰ εἰκόνας | καὶ εἰκόνας | M |
| ,, D διότι | δὴ ὅ τι | Π Μ |
| 404 A τε καὶ ἀνάγκη | τε ἀνάγκη | Π Μ |

| Errors of A p.m. | Corrected to | By |
|---|---|---|
| III. 406 D μικρὰν | μακρὰν | M |
| 407 C κεφαλῆς τινὸς | κεφαλῆς τινὰς | Ξ *q* |
| 411 D γενομένου | γενόμενον | *q* |
| ., E εἶπερ εργον | εἰ πάρεργον | Π |
| 414 E δὴ | δεῖ | *q* |
| IV. 421 D διαφέρει | διαφθείρει | Π M |
| 425 D λήξεις | λήξεως | M |
| 430 E φαίνονται | λέγοντες | A² mg. |
| 431 C ἐν πᾶσι | ἐν παισὶ | H. Wolf |
| 434 D ἐκεῖ | ἐκεῖνο | Ξ |
| 436 A τὸ περὶ | ὃ περὶ | Ξ *q* |
| 437 D ἐν ὀλίγῳ | ἑνὶ λόγῳ | Cornarius |
| 439 B ὥσπερ θηρίου | ὥσπερ θηρίον | Ξ |
| ,, D ἡδονῶν ἕτερον | ἡδονῶν ἑταῖρον | Π M |
| 440 C ζητεῖ | ζεῖ | Ξ |
| ,, E τὸ λογιστικὸν | τοῦ λογιστικοῦ | Ξ |
| 441 C ἐν ἑνὶ ἑκάστου | ἐν ἑνὸς ἑκάστου | M |
| ,, D καὶ ἀνδρείαν | ἀνδρείαν | Ξ |
| 442 C τῶν λόγων | τοῦ λόγου | Ξ |
| ,, E τοῦτον αὐτὸν | τοῦτο αὐτὸν | Ξ (τοῦτον αὐτὸ cj. L. C.) |
| 443 A ἐκτὸς ὢν | ἐκτὸς ἂν | A² |
| ,, B τελευταῖον | τέλεον | A² mg. |
| ,, D περὶ ἑαυτῶν | περὶ ἑαυτὸν | Π M |
| ,, D αὐτὸν καὶ | αὐτὸν αὑτοῦ καὶ κοσμήσαντα καὶ φίλον γενόμενον ἑαυτῷ καὶ | Π M |
| 444 B τοῦ δ' αὖ δουλεύειν ἀρχικοῦ γένους ὄντι | τῷ τοῦ ἀρχικοῦ γένους ὄντι | Ξ |
| ,, C τὰ δίκαια | τὸ δίκαια | *q* |
| 445 B ἀποκνητέον | ἀποκμητέον | Bekker |
| V. 450 C πειρῶ ἂν | πειρῶ οὖν | Π M (πειρῶ δὴ cj. Baiter) |
| 451 B ἅ ποτε | ἃ τότε | Ξ |
| 454 B τὴν αὐτὴν | μὴ τὴν αὐτὴν | Ξ |
| ,, D ἰατρικὸν μὲν καὶ ἰατρικὴν | ἰατρικὸν μὲν καὶ ἰατρικὸν | *q* |

| Errors of A p.m. | Corrected to | By |
|---|---|---|
| V. 455 B τὸ μέν | τὸν μέν | A² |
| 458 E γυμνοῦσθαι | μίγνυσθαι | Π |
| 460 D προθυμούμεθα | προὐθέμεθα | x Stob. |
| 461 A φύσας· ἃς ἑκάστοις | φύς, ἃς ἐφ' ἑκάστοις | Ξ (γρ. ἐφ' ἑ. A²) |
| „ B φήσομεν | ἀφήσομεν | Eusebius |
| „ D ἐκείνου | ἐκεῖνα | Ξ |
| 467 E διδαξομένους | διδαξαμένους | q (corr.) |
| 472 A στρατευομένῳ | στραγγευομένῳ | Vind. F (corr.) |
| „ A λέγειν λόγον | λόγον λέγειν | M |
| „ D ἐκείνης | ἐκείνοις | M Ξ (corr.) |
| 477 A οὐκοῦν ἐπὶ | οὐκοῦν ἐπεὶ ἐπὶ | Hermann (οὐκοῦν εἰ ἐπὶ q) |
| „ B κατὰ τὴν αὐτὴν δύναμιν | κατὰ τὴν δύναμιν | Vind. F |
| VI. 486 C ἀνόητα | ἀνόνητα | A² |
| 487 B παραγενόμενοι | παραγόμενοι | A² |
| „ C ταύτην | ταύτῃ | Π |
| 493 B ἐφ' οἷς ἕκαστος | ἐφ' οἷς ἑκάστας | Prinsterer (ἃς ἐφ' ἑκάστοις q) |
| „ D εἴτε δὴ . . . ὁμιλῇ *om.* | add. | A² |
| 494 B πᾶσιν | παισὶν | Geer |
| 495 A ἄρα | ὁρᾷς | Π M |
| 499 B κατήκοοι | κατηκόῳ | Schleierm. |
| „ D αὐτὴ ἡ Μοῦσα | αὕτη ἡ Μοῦσα | Π |
| 501 A διενεγκεῖν | διενέγκοιεν | q |
| 504 D ἢ γυμναζομένῳ . . . μεγίστου τε *om.* | add. | Π M |
| 511 A τετμημένοις | τετιμημένοις | A² |
| VII. 516 E ὅτι οὗτος | ὁ τοιοῦτος · | Π M |
| 525 E δύο ὡς | ὡς | A² |
| 529 B νοήσειν | νοήσει | q |
| „ C μὲν | νέων | Π |
| 530 C ἐξ ἀρχῆς του | ἐξ ἀχρήστου | A² |
| 533 E σαφηνείᾳ λέγει | σαφηνείᾳ ὃ λέγει ? | q |
| 537 E καλὸν | κακὸν | Π M |
| 538 D καταλάβῃ | καταβάλῃ | M (corr.) Ξ |
| 540 B φιλοσοφίαν | φιλοσοφίᾳ | A² |
| VIII. 544 C καὶ ἡ πασῶν | καὶ πασῶν | Π |

| Errors of A p.m. | Corrected to | By |
|---|---|---|
| VIII. 544 C διαφεύγουσα | διαφέρουσα | Ξ |
| 546 D ἡμῖν | ὑμῖν | Π Μ |
| 549 A τισιν | τις ἂν | Χ |
| 551 C ἤ τινος | ἧστινος | Ast |
| „ D οὐδὲ καλόν | οὐδὲ τόδε καλόν | A² |
| 553 B ἢ τὴν ἄλλην | ἤ τινα ἄλλην | Μ |
| „ C τὸν ἐπιθυμητικόν | τὸ ἐπιθυμητικόν | q |
| 554 B καὶ ἔτι μάλιστα | καὶ ἐτίμα μάλιστα | Schneider |
| 556 E εἰσι γὰρ οὐδὲν | εἰσι παρ' οὐδὲν | Baiter |
| 557 E ἐπιθυμῇ | ἐπιθυμῆς | q |
| „ E ἄρχῃς καὶ δικάζῃς | ἄρχειν καὶ δικάζειν | Ξ |
| 562 B ἦν ὑπερπλοῦτος | ἦν *που πλοῦτος | L. Campbell |
| 567 E τίς δὲ αὐτόθεν | τί δέ; αὐτόθεν | q |
| 568 D τιμὴ ἡ | τιμή | Π |
| „ D τὰ τῶν ἀποδομένων | τὰ τῶν πωλουμένων | L. Campbell |
| „ E ἑτέρους | ἑταίρους | Π Μ |
| 569 A ὑπὸ | ἀπὸ | q |
| IX. 571 B ἐγκαλῶ | ἐν καλῷ | Μ |
| „ D ἐν ὀλίγῳ ? | ἑνὶ λόγῳ | A² |
| 572 D ἀπολαβὼν | ἀπολαύων | Π |
| 573 B ἐπαισχυνόμενος | ἐπαισχυνομένας | Π |
| 576 D ἆρα ἡ | ἀρετῇ | A² mg. |
| 580 D δεῖ δὲ | δὲ δεῖ | Μ (corr.) Ξ |
| „ D τὸ λογιστικὸν δέ-ξεται | δέξεται | Ξ |
| 581 D ποιώμεθα | τί οἰώμεθα | Graser |
| „ E τῆς ἡδονῆς | τῆς ἀληθινῆς | L. Campbell |
| 582 C τί μὴν | τιμὴ μὲν | Θ (corr.) v |
| 584 B ἔφην δ' ἐγώ | ἔφην ἐγώ | A² |
| „ E κάτα | κάτω | A² |
| 585 D τῆς ψυχῆς | ψυχῆς | A² |
| 590 E βουλεύεται | βούλεται | Χ (Ξ corr.) |
| 591 B ἔπι | ἔτι | A² |
| „ C ζω . . . | ζήσει | Μ |
| X. 600 D ὀνεῖναι | ὀνινάναι | Ast |
| 601 A αὐτὸν . . . ἑτέροις om. | add. | A² (ἐν τοῖς for ἑτέροις) Π |
| „ B ἐν μέτρῳ . . . λέ-γεσθαι om. | add. | A² |

| Errors of A p.m. | Corrected to | By |
|---|---|---|
| x. 603 B ἢ κατὰ | ἢ καὶ κατὰ | A² |
| ,, E ψυχῆς | τύχης | Π |
| 604 C ἐρεῖ | αἱρεῖ | Ξ |
| ,, C πλήγοντος | πληγέντος | Π |
| ,, D ἰατρικὴν θρηνῳδίαν | ἰατρικῇ θρηνῳδίαν | q |
| 607 B ἀπολελογίσθω | ἀπολελογήσθω | M |
| 608 A αἰσθόμεθα | εἰσόμεθα ? | q |
| 609 B ψυχῇ ἄρα ... ἃ νῦν om. | add. | A² |
| 610 A ὀρθότατ' ἂν | ὀρθότατά γ' | L. Campbell |
| 61 C διαθετέον | διαθεατέον | Ξ (θεατέον M) |
| 612 B ἐπηινέγκαμεν | ἐπηινέκαμεν (sic) | A² |
| ,, D ἐπειδὴ ἦν τοίνυν κεκριμέναι εἰσίν, ἐγὼ | ἐπειδὴ τοίνυν, ἦν δ' ἐγώ, κεκριμέναι εἰσί | A² mg. |
| 613 E ὅρα | ὅρα εἰ | A² |
| 614 A ἑκάτερον | ἑκάτερος | Ξ (corr.) |
| 615 B πολλοὶ | πολλῶν | Ξ (πολλοῖς D corr.) |
| 616 A εἰς ὅ τι τὸν τάρταρον | ὅτι εἰς τὸν τάρταρον | Ξ |
| 617 B τὸν τρίτον | τρίτον | q |
| 620 B ὡσαύτως εἰκός. τὴν | ὡσαύτως· εἰκοστὴν | Vind. F Plutarch |

# APPENDIX III.

## CORRECTION OF ERRORS AND OMISSIONS IN BEKKER'S COLLATION OF Π AND Ξ. BY C. CASTELLANI.

| Steph. | Bekker (1823) | | Venetus Π |
|---|---|---|---|
| Rep. p. | p. | l. | |
| I. 330 B | 9, | 7 | οὗτοι (not οὗτοι) |
| 335 B | 19, | 6–8 | ἀλλ᾽ οὐ ἢ εἰς τὴν τῶν ἵππων ἀρετήν; (omitting εἰς τὴν τῶν ἵππων. ἆρ᾽ οὖν . . . εἰς τὴν τῶν ἵππων) |
| 336 E | 22, | 6 | εἰ γάρ τι |
| 340 E | 30, | 14 | ἀκριβολογεῖ |
| ,, E | ,, | ,, | καὶ ὁ ἄρχων ἥμαρτε om. |
| 342 A | 33, | 1–3 | καὶ τῇ . . . σκέψεται (not omitted) |
| ,, B | ,, | 3 | ἢ οὔτε αὐτῆς om. |
| 343 B | 35, | 6 | ἢ ὡς ἀληθῶς |
| ,, E | 36, | 10 | τοῖς τε οἰκείοις |
| 350 D | 49, | 9 | ἡμῖν placed after κείσθω |
| 351 A | 50, | 9 | τῇδ᾽ ἐπισκέψασθαι |
| ,, D | 51, | 7 | καὶ μίση |
| 352 D | 53, | 4 | ὅτι om. |
| 353 B | 54, | 9–11 | ἔστιν ἔργον; Ναί. (omitting ἔστιν. ἆρ᾽ οὖν . . . ἦν τι ἔργον;) |
| II. 358 B | 59, | 7 | ἐάν σοι ταῦτα δοκῇ |
| 364 D | 70, | 19 | στρεπτοὶ δέ τε καὶ |
| 366 A | 73, | 11 | αὖ μέγα δύνανται καὶ οἱ |
| 370 C | 81, | 6 | ἐν κατὰ (not ἐν ἢ κατὰ) |
| 371 E | 84, | 1 | ἔχουσιν |
| 372 D | 85, | 11 | σπουδίουσι (not σπουδιοῦσι) |
| 374 A | 88, | 6 | ἱκανοὶ διαμάχεσθαι |
| 380 A | 99, | 10 | ἰαμβία (not ἰάμβια) |
| III. 387 B | 109, | 12 | ἀλείβαντας |
| 397 C | 128, | 5 | καὶ σφόδρα |
| 399 D | 132, | 9 | παραδέξει |
| 400 C | 134, | 4 | ἔγωγε om. |
| 404 A | 141, | 2 | στρατίαις |

| Steph. | Bekker (1823) | | Venetus Π |
|---|---|---|---|
| Rep. p. | p. | l. | |
| III. 405 D | 144, | 1 | ὡς οἶμαι *om.* |
| 408 D | 149, | 2 | οὐχ ὁμοιοῦν πρᾶγμα |
| 411 D | 154, | 6 | οὔτε ζητήματος |
| 413 E | 158, | 13 | ἔν τε (not ἐάν τε) |
| IV. 422 C | 170, | 10 | τοῦτο ποιοῖ |
| „ E | 171, | 11 | ἢ (not ᾖ) |
| 423 B | 172, | 6 | μέχρι οὗ |
| „ C | „ | 16 | αὐτὸν (not αὐτῶν) |
| 425 A | 175, | 8 | κείνοις |
| 428 A | 180, | 18 | τὰ omitted |
| 429 A | 182, | 16 | ἦν (not ἦν καὶ) |
| 435 A | 194, | 3 | βεβαιωσόμεθα |
| 440 B | 203, | 22 | μὴ δεῖν |
| 441 D | 206, | 18 | ἕκαστον τῶν ἐν αὐτῷ |
| 442 A | 207, | 11 | οὐκ αὐτὰ (not οὐκ αὖ τὰ) |
| 444 C | 211, | 15 | τὸ ἄδικα πράττειν |
| „ C | „ | 16 | αὐτὰ (not αὖ τὰ) |
| V. 451 A | 219, | 3 | παραμυθεῖ |
| 452 C | 221, | 15 | πρῶτοι |
| 467 D | 250, | 3 | παραδόξων |
| 468 C | 251, | 9 | καὶ μηδενὶ |
| 477 B | 268, | 2 | κατὰ τὴν αὐτὴν δύναμιν |
| 478 C | 270, | 9 | οὐδέτερα (not οὐδετέρα) |
| VI. 484 A | 274, | 2 | μακροῦ τινὸς |
| 489 D | 284, | 17 | ἀληθὲς (not τἀληθὲς) |
| 492 A | 288, | 18 | σπαρεῖσά τε καὶ φυτευθεῖσα |
| 493 C | 291, | 16 | ἢ οὖν τι τούτου δοκῇ διαφέρειν ὁ τὴν |
| 494 E | 294, | 1 | δὲ πρὸς |
| 496 A | 296, | 10 | πᾶν σμικρὸν |
| „ B | „ | 17 | ἂν ἔλθοι |
| 501 C | 306, | 6 | σωφρονοῦσιν |
| 503 D | 309, | 19 | χρήσαιτο |
| 506 B | 315, | 1 | τὸ δ᾽ αὑτοῦ |
| 507 E | 317, | 20 | Π should not be cited here, as (by Bekker's own showing) this part of the Republic is wanting in Π |
| VII. 516 E | 330, | 15 | θᾶκον |
| 518 E | 334, | 5 | ἔθεσι καὶ (*om.* τε) |

| Steph. | Bekker (1823) | | Venetus Π |
|---|---|---|---|
| Rep. p. | p. | l. | |
| VII. 518 E | 334, | 9 | χρήσιμόν τε καὶ |
| 519 A | ,, | 12 | ταῦτα |
| 524 C | 344, | 17 | ἐρέσθαι |
| 526 D | 348, | 19 | ἐν αὐταῖς τε ταῖς |
| ,, E | ,, | 21 | λογισμὸν |
| 529 B | 353, | 16 | τῶν αἰσθητῶν ἐπιχειρῇ μανθάνειν |
| 539 D | 372, | 17 | ἔτι διπλάσια ἢ τότε |
| 540 D | 374, | 9 | ἄλλῃ ἢ εἴρηται |
| ,, E | ,, | 16 | διασκευωρίσωνται |
| 541 A | ,, | 20 | οἱ γονεῖς |
| VIII. 543 D | 377, | 12 | τὸν ἐκείνῃ ὅμοιον ... ἄνδρα repeated by first hand |
| 544 A | ,, | 16 | ἀνομοίους (not αὖ ὁμοίους) |
| 547 B | 383, | 6 | γένει |
| ,, B | ,, | 8 | αὖ τὸ (not αὐτὸ) |
| ., D | 384, | 5 | κατεσκευάσθαι |
| ,, E | ,, | 9 | κεκτημένην |
| 558 C | 403, | 11 | ταῦτά τε δὴ |
| 559 A | 404, | 16 | ἀναγκαίως |
| 560 A | 406, | 9 | τὸν (not τὸ) |
| 562 C | 410, | 18 | διὰ ταῦτα ἐν μόνῃ ταύτῃ |
| 566 B | 418, | 4 | πολλοθρύλητον (sic) |
| ,, E | 419, | 5 | καὶ before ἰδίᾳ omitted |
| 567 E | 421, | 4 | τίς δε αὐτόθεν |
| IX. 571 B | 425, | 8 | ἐγκαλῶ |
| 581 D | 445, | 1 | εἴ τι αὐτῶν |
| X. 597 E | 471, | 12 | τὸν μὲν δὴ |
| 598 C | 472, | 15 | περὶ τοῦ |
| ,, D | ,, | 20 | πᾶς σοφὸς |
| 602 A | 479, | 13 | περὶ ὧν ἂν ποιῇ |
| 603 C | 482, | 3 | ἡ μιμητικὴ βιαίους ἢ |
| 604 E | 484, | 17 | αὐτὸ om. |
| ,, E | ,, | ,, | μιμουμένου |
| 607 C | 489, | 20 | κηλεῖ |
| 611 A | 496, | 11 | ἐλάττονος |

N.B.—Some of the above corrections have been anticipated by Stallbaum and others; see Schneider's Preface, p. xxxi. The general result is to raise somewhat the character of Π and also to establish more clearly its affinity to the later MSS. D K *q* β′.                                    L. C.

| Steph. | Bekker (1823) | | Venetus Ξ |
|---|---|---|---|
| Rep. p. | p. | l. | |
| I. 350 A | 48, | 8 | ἀλλ' ἴσθι |
| ,, B | ,, | 10 | ἴσως (not ἴσθι) |
| II. 358 B | 59, | 1 | ἐάν σοι ταῦτα δοκῇ |
| 364 A | 69, | 13 | τε καὶ δικαιοσύνη *om.* |
| 376 C | 92, | 15 | δεῖ not δεῖν |
| ,, C | ,, | 16 | δὴ (not δεῖ) after φιλόσοφος |
| ,, C | ,, | 19 | ὑπάρχη not ὑπάρχῃ |
| III. 387 B | 109, | 12 | ἀλείβαντας |
| 389 B | 112, | 16 | θεοῖσι |
| 390 D | 15, | 14 | μὲν (for μὲν δὴ) |
| 391 C | 116, | 19 | νοσήματε (sic) |
| 400 B | 133, | 13 | Δάμωνος |
| 413 C | 157, | 18 | ὡς ποιητέον τοῦτο |
| 415 B | 160, | 19 | ἀργυροῦν καὶ ἐξ ἀργυροῦ |
| ,, C | 161, | 10 | φυλάξῃ |
| IV. 425 A | 175, | 7 | παίζειν παῖδες |
| 426 E | 178, | 19 | τέμνουσι (sic) |
| 429 C | 183, | 14 | εἶναι τινὰ (sic) |
| 434 A | 192, | 10 | δοκεῖ μέγα βλάψαι |
| 437 E | 199, | 3 | προσῇ (sic) |
| 440 B | 204, | 1 | αἴσθεσθαι |
| 444 C | 211, | 15 | τὸ ἄδικα πράττειν |
| 445 D | 213, | 21 | λέγε, ἔφην, τίνες |
| V. 464 C | 244, | 3 | μὴ διασπᾶν τὴν πόλιν |
| ,, C | ,, | 4 | οὐ τὸ αὐτὸ |
| 469 C | 253, | 12 | οὐ ἢ (sic) |
| 474 B | 262, | 6 | παρέχει |
| ,, C | ,, | 15 | ἀμηγέπη (sic) |
| 477 B | | | κατὰ . . . αὐτῆς *om.* |
| VI. 484 A | 274, | 2 | μακροῦ τινὸς |
| 492 B | 289, | 5 | πότε δέ (sic pr.) |
| 498 A | 300, | 2 | μεγάλα ἡγοῦνται |
| 502 C | 307, | 20 | ἐλέγομεν |
| 520 C | 336, | 19 | ὑμῖν (not ἡμῖν) |
| 533 C | 361, | 9 | μόνη |
| ,, E | ,, | 20,21 | ἀλλ' . . . ἐν ψυχῇ *om.* |
| 537 D | 368, | 16 | καὶ τοῖς ἄλλοις |

| Steph. | Bekker (1823) | | Venetus Ξ |
|---|---|---|---|
| Rep. p. | p. | l | |
| VII. 520 B | 336, | 19 | ὑμῖν τε αὐτοῖς |
| 527 C | 350, | 6 | εἶπες ^ας |
| VIII. 557 B | 401, | 13 | ἕκαστος ἂν κατασκευὴν |
| ,, B | ,, | 4 | ἑκάστῳ ἀρέσκοι |
| 561 D | 409, | 12 | ἔπεστι ^ν |
| 563 C | 412, | 18 | ἐν ταύτη (sic) |
| 564 A | 414, | 12 | πλείστη καὶ (*om.* τε) |
| IX. 577 A | 436, | 8 | ἐκπλήττηται |
| 581 C | 444, | 19 | θέλεις |
| 585 C | 452, | 9 | κρῖνε |
| 587 E | 457, | 4 | ἥδιστον |
| X. 597 E | 471, | 10 | τοῦτ᾽ ἄρα |
| ,, | ,, | ,, | μιμητίς |
| 600 A | 475, | 11 | Ἀναχάρσιδος |
| 601 A | 477, | 6 | περὶ σκυτοτομίας (*om.* τῆς) |
| 602 A | 479, | 13 | περὶ ὧν ἂν ποιῇ |
| ,, D | 480, | 20 | ἢ καὶ στῆσαν |
| 603 B | 481, | 17 | τὴν ὄψιν μόνον |
| 604 C | 484, | 5 | πλήττοντος |
| 612 D | 499, | 11 | ἐγὼ πάλιν |
| 620 B | 513, | 16 | ἔχθρᾳ (not ἔχθραι) |

# APPENDIX IV.

[By E. Rostagno.]

## De Cod. 4 Plutei xxviii, qui Caesenae in Bibl. Malatestiana asservatur.

Codex est bombycinus, exeunte saeculo xii maiore ex parte, ut videtur, exaratus, foliis 418, versibus plerumque quadragenis, aut singulis et quadragenis. Ad formam voluminis quod attinet, hanc ita sum mensus: o, 228-40 × o, 339–41. Complectitur autem 52 quaterniones, qui octonis foliis constant, praeter quaternionem 40 [μ'], cui unum deficit: in textu tamen nulla lacuna hic deprehenditur. Singulorum quaternionum seriem numeri, graecis literis exarati, atque in infimo ultimae paginae margine rubro charactere depicti, repraesentant. Postremo quaternio 49 [μθ'], quamquam unius paginae lacuna laborat (vide sis Πολιτειῶν ς', p. 510 d) nihilo minus octo foliis et ipse constat.

Notandum interim est, in hisce 52 quaternionibus haud contineri tria ff., quibus volumen incipit, quaeque seorsim ab illis in vol. collocata sunt.

Insunt praeterea in ipso voluminis ingressu duo ff. membranacea, interioris integumenti locum obtinentia (ut vulgo dicunt 'fogli di guardia'), binis columnis exarata, saeculoque circiter xiv conscripta. De re theologica in illis agitur, ut textus quidem docere nos videtur. Hinc, speciminis ergo, quae sequuntur exscripsi:

'Quia [?] in superioribus consideramus qualiter deus sit secundum se ipsum, restat considerandum qualiter sit in cogitatione nostra, id est, quomodo cogitetur a creaturis. Circa hoc quaeruntur xiii. Primo utrum aliquis intellectus creatus possit essentiam dei videre. Secundo utrum dei essentia videatur ab intellectu per animi [?] speciem creatam. Tertio utrum oculo corporeo dei essentia possit videri.' Et q. s.

Provenisse hae duae paginae videntur ex eodem libro atque opere, e quo nonnulla alia folia avulsa sunt, ut interioris integumenti locum,

ut ita dicam, obtinerent in codd. qui sunt 3 Plut. xxviii [1], Cod. 2
Plut. xxviii [2]; Cod. 5 Plut. xxviii [3]; Cod. 3 Plut. xxvii [4].

In fine autem codicis una pagina bombycina locum interioris
integumenti obtinet.

Primo aspectu codex bifariam dividi posse videtur: altera enim
pars voluminis e charta dente, ut dicunt, polita constat, altera
($4^r$–$171^v$) e charta obsoleta, minus levigata, ut bibulam eam prope
dicas. Ex quo fit, ut in hac priore parte folia $12^r$–$43^v$ et $113^r$–$171^v$,
cum atramenti sucum, ut ita dicam, charta elicuisset, nigrescentem
speciem prae se ferant. Alterius autem partis paginae charactere
ad rubrum vergente plerumque sunt exaratae.

Quod ad manus, ut dicunt, attinet, duas in primis scripturas
codex, de quo agitur, exhibet: altera, satis quidem elegans atque
nitida, qua maior operis pars exarata est, minutis characteribus
constat, nitidis atque subrubentibus; altera autem incompta,
deflexis characteribus, saepius nigricantibus, impolitis crassioribus-
que constans, duorum scriptorum imperitiorem manum redolet. Ut
de duobus hisce scriptoribus, seu mavis, duabus hisce manibus
nonnulla subiciam, hoc arbitror animadversione dignum in primis
esse, duas scilicet has scripturas per alternas vices saepius ita
continuari, ut altera alteram vel in mediis paginis plerumque sub-
sequatur: quod nimirum ut in promptu esset, paginas describendas
curavi, incompta—ut in superioribus dixi—scriptura crassioreque
charactere exaratas, et duas manus illas redolentes. Hinc lucu-
lenter patebit dimidiam ferme paginam saepius altera manu con-
scriptam esse, quam paulo sequioris aevi esse merito dicas.

Altera manu igitur haec ff. exarata sunt:

| | | | |
|---|---|---|---|
| Altera pars f. | $88^r$. | Folium | $122^v$. |
| Inferior ,, ,, | $99^r$. | ,, | $123^v$. |
| ,, ,, ,, | $112^r$. | ,, | $124^v$. |
| Folium | $116^r$, $116^v$. | ,, | $125^v$. |
| ,, | $118^r$. | ,, | $126^v$. |
| ,, | $119^v$. | ,, | $128^r$. |
| ,, | $120^v$. | ,, | $129^r$. |
| ,, | $121^v$. | ,, | $130^r$. |

[1] Cod. 3 Plut. xxviii duo ff. exhibet, ut in voluminis principio, ita in fine:
alterum folium autem cum codicis ligneo integumento compactum est.

[2] Cod. 2 Plut. xxviii duo ff. exhibet in principio, quorum alterum cum
ligneo codicis integumento compactum est.

[3] Cod. 5 Plut. xxviii duo ff. exhibet in fine.

[4] Cod. 3 Plut. xxvii duo ff. exhibet in principio.

| | | | |
|---|---|---|---|
| Folium | 131$^v$. | Maior pars folii | 168$^v$. |
| ,, | 132$^v$. | ,, ,, ,, | 169$^r$. |
| ,, | 135$^r$. | Folium | 170$^v$. |
| ,, | 136$^r$. | Inferior pars folii | 171$^r$. |
| ,, | 137$^v$. | Folium | 171$^v$. |
| ,, | 139$^v$. | ,, | 172$^v$. |
| ,, | 140$^v$. | ,, | 174$^r$, 174$^v$. |
| ,, | 141$^v$. | ,, | 175$^v$. |
| ,, | 142$^v$. | ,, | 177$^v$. |
| ,, | 144$^v$. | ,, | 179$^r$. |
| ,, | 145$^v$. | ,, | 180$^r$. |
| ,, | 147$^r$. | ,, | 181$^v$. |
| ,, | 148$^r$. | ,, | 184$^r$. |
| ,, | 149$^v$. | ,, | 186$^r$. |
| ,, | 151$^r$. | ,, | 188$^r$. |
| ,, | 152$^r$. | ,, | 190$^r$. |
| ,, | 153$^r$. | ,, | 191$^r$. |
| ,, | 154$^r$. | ,, | 192$^r$. |
| Maior pars folii | 155$^r$. | ,, | 200$^r$. |
| Folium | 156$^r$. | ,, | 202$^r$. |
| ,, | 157$^r$. | Altera pars folii | 207$^v$. |
| ,, | 158$^v$. | Folium | 208$^v$. |
| ,, | 160$^v$. | ,, | 210$^r$. |
| ,, | 161$^v$. | ,, | 211$^r$. |
| ,, | 163$^r$. | Altera pars folii | 211$^v$. |
| ,, | 166$^v$. | | |

Altera autem manu haec ff. sunt conscripta :

| | | | |
|---|---|---|---|
| Folium | 214$^r$. | Folium | 246$^r$. |
| ,, | 215$^r$. | ,, | 247$^v$. |
| ,, | 216$^v$. | ,, | 248$^v$. |
| ,, | 217$^v$. | ,, | 249$^v$. |
| ,, | 231$^v$. | ,, | 256$^v$. |
| ,, | 232$^v$. | ,, | 260$^v$. |
| ,, | 233$^v$. | ,, | 265$^v$. |
| ,, | 235$^r$. | ,, | 272$^r$. |
| ,, | 236$^r$. | ,, | 275$^v$. |
| ,, | 237$^r$. | ,, | 277$^r$. |
| ,, | 242$^v$. | ,, | 279$^v$. |
| ,, | 243$^v$. | ,, | 283$^r$. |
| ,, | 245$^r$. | ,, | 293$^v$. |

Folium 295ʳ.
„ 298ᵛ.
Folium 341ᵛ inde e verbis
" τοῦτο δὲ δὴ νοεῖ αὐτῷ, τοῖς
μὲν ἐχθροῖς βλάβην ὀφείλεσθαι
κ.τ.λ." (cf. Πολιτ. αʹ, p. 335 E).
Folium 344ʳ inde e verbis
" πάντα τούτων τἀναντία ὑπάρχει.
λέγω γὰρ ὅνπερ νῦν κ.τ.λ." (cf. sis
Πολιτ. αʹ, p. 343 E sqq.).

Folium 344ᵛ.
„ 357ʳ.
„ 371ᵛ.
„ 375ʳ.
Folium 379ʳ inde e verbis
" ἔχθρα στάσις κέκληται, ἐπὶ δὲ
τῇ τοῦ ἀλλοτρίου πόλεμος κ.τ.λ."
(cf. Πολιτ. εʹ, p. 470 B).
Folium 379ᵛ.

Folium 393 (sc. 393ʳ, 393ᵛ) erectioribus litteris atque rotundis exaratum est. In hac autem parte τῆς Πολιτείας literam ι subscriptam reperimus, quam nusquam in decem libris codex exhibet.

Folium 392 (sc. 392ʳ, 392ᵛ) deflexo maioreque charactere est exaratum, eodem nimirum atque folia 1, 2ʳ, quae εἰσαγωγὴν τοῦ ἀλβίνου complectuntur. F. 392 autem ceteris glutino connexum est.

Pag. 198ʳ et alteram partem pag. 199ʳ diversa manus conscripsisse videtur. Postremo ff. 12–35 nigricante scriptura quae ceteris insignia sunt gravique et crasso charactere: paulo sequiori aevo haec diversaque manu exarata videntur.

Ad scholia quod attinet, quibus marginalibus codex est adspersus, duabus diversis manibus conscripta ea esse constat; pars enim scriptura nitidissima, alia contra inelegante ac recentiore exarata sunt. Quod autem ad Πολιτείας decem libros spectat, tres manus deprehendi hic possunt: nonnulla enim multo recentior manus notavit, characteribus minutis nexibusque plerumque implicitis.

Horum schol. speciminis loco quae sequuntur ita exscripsi, ut signum quod est * recentioribus apposuerim.

Πολιτ. αʹ. 328 D extr.   ὡς εὖ ἴσθι ὅτι ἔμοιγε κ.τ.λ.] σημείωσαι λόγων
                                                    ἡδοναὶ

„        329 A.   παλαιὰν παρανομίαν] περὶ " ἀεὶ κολοιὸς ποτὶ κολοιὸν
                                                    ἰζάνει"

„        330 D.   σημ. τοῦ ἰουστίνου τὸν λόγον

„        337 A.   ὑπὸ ὑμῶν τῶν δεινῶν] δεινῶν*

„ βʹ,  359 D.   ἰστορία τοῦ γύγου

„        372 B.   κριθῶν ἄλφιτα ＼／πέψαντες
                    πυρῶν ἄλευρα ／＼μάξαντες

„        372 C extr.   καὶ τραγήματά που] τραγήματα

„        „   E.   τρυφῶσαν πόλιν

„        „   E extr.   ἀληθινὴ καὶ ὑγίης πόλις

Πολιτ. β', 372 E extr.  φλεγμαίνουσα πόλις

,,    378 B.  θεῶν οἱ πρῶτοι τὲ καὶ μέγιστοι] σημ. τίνας πρώτους
                          καὶ μεγίστους θεῶν λέγει*

,,    ,, D extr.  ὑπόνοια*

,,    379 B.  πρῶτος τύπος θεολογίας, ὅτι οὐκ αἴτιος τῶν κακῶν ὁ
                θεός

,,    ,, C.  πολὺ ἐλάττω τἀγαθὰ τῶν κακῶν*

,,    380 D.  δεύτερος τύπος θεολογίας, ὅτι ὁ θεὸς ἀμετάβλητος :⌒

,,    382 A init.  τρίτος τύπος θεολογίας, ὅτι ἀληθὴς ὁ θεός

,,    ,, B.  ἡ ἐν τῇ ψυχῇ ἄγνοια] τὸ ψεῦδος ἐν τῇ ψυχῇ
                πρῶτον*

,, γ', 388 C.  μέγιστος θεῶν ὁ Ζεύς

,,    392 C.  τὰ μὲν δὴ λόγων κ.τ.λ.] λόγων, λέξεως*

,,    394 D.  ἐνταῦθα σαφέως δηλοῖται τί τὸ "λόγων" τί τὸ
                "λέξεως" σημαίνει*

,,    398 E.  μιξολυδιστὶ καὶ } θρηνώδεις*
                συντονολυδιστὶ }

,,    ,, E extr.  ἰαστὶ καὶ } μαλακαὶ*
                λυδιστὶ }

,,    399 A.  δωριστὶ καὶ } ἀνδρώδεις*
                φρυγιστὶ }

,,    ,, D.  σημ. ὀνόματα ὀργάνων ꞏꞏꞏꞏꞏꞏῶν*

,,    400 B.  οἶμαι δέ με ἀκηκοέναι, κ.τ.λ.] ῥύθμων ὀνόματα*

,,    ,, E.  τί εὐήθεια

,,    402 E.  περὶ τῶν ἀγόνων ꞏꞏꞏꞏꞏꞏ*

,,    403 E.  τῶνδε τῶν ἀσκητῶν] ἀσκηταί*

,,    404 A.  κομψοτέρας δή τινος κ.τ.λ.] τίς στρατιωτῶν ἄσκησις

,,    ,, B.  ἀκροσφαλὴς εἰς ὑγίειαν*

,,    ,, B.  ἑστιᾶ*

,,    ,, E.  ἀπεικάζοντες*

,,    405 D.  φύσας τε καὶ κατάρρους] φύσῃ | κάταρρος*

,,    406 A.  ἐπιξυσθέντα*

,,    ,, A.  ὅτι τῇ παιδαγωγικῇ κ.τ.λ.] ἡ νῦν ἰατρικὴ, παιδαγωγικὴ
                τῶν νοσημάτων

Et alia multa id genus.

,,    416 D.  κοινὸν βίον καὶ εὐτελῆ τοῖς φύλαξι βιωτέον

,, δ', 421 D.  πλοῦτος καὶ πενία διαφθείρει τοὺς δημιουργούς

,,    ,, E extr.  βλαβεραὶ τῇ πόλει πλοῦτος καὶ πενία

,,    436 B.  Δῆλον ὅτι ταὐτὸν τἀναντία κ.τ.λ.] σημ. τὴν πρό-
                τασιν ταύτην

,, ε', 470 B extr.  σημ. τί διαφέρει πόλεμος στάσεως

Πολιτ. ε΄, 477 Β.  ἐπ᾽ ἄλλῳ ἐπιστήμη, κατὰ κ.τ.λ.] ἴσως οὕτω δεῖ
γράφεσθαι. ναί . . κατὰ τὴν αὐτὴν δύναμιν
ἢ κατ᾽ ἄλλην καὶ ἄλλην δύναμιν ἑκατέρα
τῆς αὐτῆς οὕτως

„  ϛ΄, 499 C extr.  ἄπειρὸς (sic) ὁ παρεληλυθὼς χρόνος

„  ζ΄, 518 D extr.  αἱ μὲν τοίνυν ἄλλαι ἀρεταὶ κ.τ.λ.] αἱ μὲν ἀρεταὶ
κτηταὶ, ἡ δὲ φρόνησις ἔμφυτος τῇ ψυχῇ*

„  534 E.  θριγκὸς τοῖς μαθήμασιν ἡ διαλεκτική*

„  η΄, 545 C extr.  πῶς ἐστι ἐξ ἀριστοκρατίας τιμοκρατία*

„  θ΄, 580 B.  βασιλικὸν, τιμοκρατικὸν, ὀλιγαρχικὸν, δημοκρατικὸν,
καὶ τυραννικόν*

„  ι΄, 608 D.  σημ. ὅτι ἀθάνατος ἡ ψυχή*

„  611 A.  σημ. ὅτι ἀεί ἐστιν ἡ ψυχὴ καὶ οὐ μεταβάλλεται*

„  „ D extr.  σημ. ὅτι συγγενὴς ἡ ψυχὴ τῷ θεῷ*

„  615 B.  σημ. ὅτι δεκαπλασίους ἀποδίδονται τιμωρίαι (sic)*

„  617 C.  σημ. περὶ τῶν μοιρῶν*

„  621 A.  εἰς τὸ τῆς Λήθης πεδίον] σημ. περὶ τοῦ ποταμοῦ τοῦ
τῆς Λήθης

De scholiis hactenus.

Iam vero paucis absolvam de iis quae codex complectitur:
in quibus recensendis editione Lipsiensi usus sum Hermanni
MD.CCC.LXIV (voll. 6).

F. 1ʳ.  Rubris literis et maioribus legitur : " εἰσαγωγὴ εἰς τὴν τοῦ
Πλάτωνος βίβλον ἀλβίνου πρόλογος."

Incipit " ὅτι τῷ μέλλοντι ἐντεύξεσθαι τοῖς Πλάτωνος διαλόγοις,
προσήκει πρότερον ἐπίστασθαι αὐτὸ τοῦτο τί ποτέ ἐστιν ὁ
διάλογος."

Desinit (f. 2ʳ): " καὶ ὅπως αὐτοῖς καὶ ὄντινα τρόπον προσφέρεσθαι
κακουργοῦσι περὶ τοὺς λόγους."

„  2ᵛ.  vacuum est scriptura.  Tum occurrit tabula, rubris literis
exarata, quae titulos ac seriem scriptorum repraesentat.
Haec est inscriptio eius :

„  3ʳ.  διαλόγων Πλάτωνος ἀκριβὴς πίναξ.

„  4ʳ.  Sequitur deinde : " βίος Πλάτωνος συγγραφεὶς παρὰ λαερτίου
Διογένους (haec autem rubris literis leguntur)."

Incipit " Πλάτων ἀρίστωνος καὶ περικτιόνης ἢ πωτώνης ἀθηναῖος
κ.τ.λ."

Desinit (f. 11ᵛ): " τὰ μὲν περὶ πλάτωνος τοσαῦτα ἦν ἐς τὸ δυνατὸν
ἡμῖν συναγαγεῖν φιλοπόνως διειλήσασι τὰ λεγόμενα περὶ τἀν-
δρός." | τέλος τοῦ πλάτωνος βίου.

A pag. 12ʳ incipiunt Platonis opera, et quidem hoc ordine[1]:

F. 12ʳ. εὐθύφρων ἢ περὶ ὁσίου :—
„ 16ᵛ. σωκράτους ἀπολογία.
„ 24ʳ. κρίτων ἢ περὶ πρακτοῦ.
„ 28ʳ. φαίδων ἢ περὶ ψυχῆς.
„ 49ʳ. κρατύλος ἢ περὶ ὀνομάτων ὀρθότητος.
„ 63ʳ. θεαίτητος ἢ περὶ ἐπιστήμης.
„ 82ᵛ. σοφιστὴς ἢ περὶ τοῦ ὄντος.
„ 97ᵛ. πολιτικὸς ἢ περὶ βασιλείας.
„ 114ʳ. παρμενίδης ἢ περὶ ἰδεῶν.
„ 126ᵛ. φίληβος ἢ περὶ ἡδονῆς.
„ 143ʳ. συμπόσιον ἢ περὶ ἔρωτος.
„ 158ᵛ. φαῖδρος ἢ περὶ καλοῦ.
„ 174ʳ. ἀλκιβιάδης ἢ περὶ φύσεως ἀνθρώπου.
„ 183ʳ. ἀλκιβιάδης β΄ ἢ περὶ προσευχῆς.
„ 187ʳ. ἵππαρχος ἢ φιλοκερδής.
„ 189ʳ. ἐρασταὶ ἢ περὶ φιλοσοφίας.
„ 191ᵛ. θεάγης ἢ περὶ σοφίας.
„ 194ᵛ. χαρμίδης ἢ περὶ σωφροσύνης.
„ 202ʳ. λάχης ἢ περὶ ἀνδρίας.
„ 209ᵛ. λύσις ἢ περὶ φιλίας.
„ 215ʳ. εὐθύδημος ἢ ἐριστικός.
„ 216ʳ. πρωταγόρας ἢ σοφισταί.
„ 242ʳ. γοργίας ἢ περὶ ῥητορικῆς.
„ 266ʳ. μένων ἢ περὶ ἀρετῆς.
„ 274ʳ. ἱππίας μείζων ἢ περὶ τοῦ καλοῦ.
„ 282ʳ. ἱππίας ἐλάττων ἢ περὶ τοῦ καλοῦ.
„ 286ʳ. ἴων ἢ περὶ ἰλιάδος.
„ 289ᵛ. μενέξενος ἢ ἐπιτάφιος.
„ 294ʳ. περὶ δικαίου. πλάτωνος νοθευόμενοι α΄.
„ 295ʳ. περὶ ἀρετῆς.
„ 296ᵛ. δημόδοκος ἢ περὶ τοῦ ξυμβουλεύεσθαι.
„ 298ᵛ. σίσυφος ἢ περὶ τοῦ βουλεύεσθαι.
„ 300ʳ. ἀλκυὼν ἢ περὶ μεταμορφώσεως.
„ 301ʳ. ἐρυξίας ἢ περὶ πλούτου· ἐν ἄλλῳ ἐρασίστρατος.
„ 306ʳ. ἀξίοχος ἢ περὶ θανάτου.
„ 308ᵛ. τέλος τῶν νοθευομένων.
„    „ κλειτοφῶν ἢ προτρεπτικός.
„ 310ʳ. τίμαιος ὁ μικρός (Incipit : " Τίμαιος ὁ Λοκρὸς τάδ᾽ ἔφα ")

[1] Tituli omnes rubris maioribusque literis constant.

F. 313ʳ. τίμαιος ἢ περὶ φύσεως.

„ 332ʳ. κριτίας ἢ ἀτλαντικός.

„ 336ʳ. μίνως.

„ 338ᵛ. πυθαγόρου σαμίοιο ἔπη τάδ' ἔνεστι τὰ χρυσᾶ:⁓(cf. Cod. 9
Plut. 85, Bibl. Laurentianae, pag. 3ʳ).

Incipiunt haec carmina :

ἀθανάτους μὲν πρῶτα θεούς, νόμω ὡς διάκειται
τούς τε καταχθονίους σέβε δαίμονας ἔννομα ῥέζων κ.τ.λ.

Desinit ibid. : " ἔσσεαι ἀθάνατος θεὸς ἄμβροτος οὐκέτι θνητός :⁓

Demum f. 339ʳ " πλάτωνος πολιτεῖαι :⁓

Reliquum vol. hic dialogos complectitur, qui f. 418ᵛ
desinit.

In infimo margine pag. 418ᵛ literis evanidis legitur : ' opr̄a
Platonis. dialogi nr̄o 50.'

In dialogis huiusce codicis nomina τῶν προσώπων desunt : locus
vero est relictus ad literas saltem eorum initiales ponendas.

Codex demum, de quo hactenus actum est, elegantiorem perpoliti
operis speciem quondam prae se tulisse videtur. Oblita enim auro
folia circum iam fuere : ad hoc lignea integumenta, corio contecta
candentis ferri stigmate perbelle impresso, clavis vel bullis aeneis
etiamnunc sunt transfixa.

# ESSAY III.

## *ON PLATO'S USE OF LANGUAGE.*

—◆◆—

### PART I.

#### *On Style and Syntax.*

THE purpose of the following pages is to bring into
a general view some forms of expression and tendencies of
grammatical construction, which, although not confined to
Plato, more frequently occur in him than in other Greek
writers.  In treating of his writings, principally from
a grammatical point of view. it will be difficult, if not
impossible, to separate absolutely between questions of
syntax and questions of style ; since in the Platonic dialogue,
syntactical peculiarities have often a rhetorical motive.
Whilst the subject is treated generally, the Republic, as
the work immediately in hand, will furnish most of the
examples; but reference will occasionally be made to other
parts of Plato, and, now and again, to various Greek
writers.  A distinction will be maintained between those
dialogues which represent the earlier or middle style of
Plato (e. g. the Symposium, Phaedrus, &c.) and those
which reflect his later manner (e. g. the Politicus, Philebus,
Laws, &c.) [1].

[1] Explanation of references: 'Digest, §   ,' refers to the digest of
Platonic idioms in James Riddell's edition of the Apology; Oxford,
1877.  ' M. and T., §   ,' refers to Professor W. W. Goodwin's *Syntax of the
Moods and Tenses of the Greek Verb*; London, 1889.

## I. STYLE.

§ **I.**   Plato has not one style but several.  No great prose writer has command of an instrument so varied, or an equal power of adapting modes of expression to moods of thought and imagination [1].  Without breaking harmony, he passes often from extreme simplicity to the extreme of complexity, according to the subject handled and the spirit in which he is approaching it.

The ground may be cleared by distinguishing between, (1) simple narration, (2) ornate narration, (3) passages of moral elevation, (4) question and answer, and (5) continuous dialectic.

(1) *Simple statement or narration.*—The narrative passages which introduce the dialogues or are interspersed in them are in many places perfectly limpid and clear. Hardly less so is the language in which Plato often clothes his fictitious tales (Egyptian or Phoenician), using a series of short sentences connected with the ingenuous *naïveté* of the λέξις εἰρομένη.  The simplicity of the language often strikingly contrasts with the incredibility of the myth, as, for example, where Protagoras describes the creation of man, or where the Judgement of the Dead is reported by Socrates in the Gorgias, or in Republic X.  Plato's simpler style, as Littré has remarked, bears some affinity to that of the genuine writings of Hippocrates.

(2) *Ornate narration.*— But there are other mythical discourses in which the language becomes more elevated and at the same time more complex, such as the account of the Soul's Migrations in the Phaedrus, the description of subterranean and supramundane regions in the Phaedo, or of the allegorical cavern in the seventh book of the Republic.  Here the sentences are longer, and are complicated with explanations, illustrations, maxims, reflexions, and incidental statements, free play being given to fancy,

---

[1]  See Phaedr. 277 c παναρμονίους λόγους.

while the effort to surround the marvellous with an air of naturalness and credibility is still maintained.

(3) *Passages of moral elevation.*— Distinct from both these narrative modes is the sustained eloquence of such passages as the discourse of Diotima (Symp. 211 D ff.), the reflections of Socrates addressed to Theodorus on the happiness of the philosophic life (Theaet. 172 D–177 C), or the description of the misery of the tyrant in Rep. IX (579 and 591–592); also, to notice some of Plato's later works, the creation of the world in the Timaeus (29–30) ; the summing up of religious duties in the Laws (V. 726 ff.) ; or again, in the same dialogue the remarks on the commerce of the sexes (VIII. 835 D ff.), and on the sin of Atheism (X. 887 C–888 D). In these notwithstanding occasional exuberances, there is uninterrupted harmony and continuity. But there is an entire absence of formality, and only an approach to that rhetorical smoothness and concinnity which Plato well knew how to assume, as is shown by the speech of Agathon in the Symposium.

(4) *Question and answer.*—As in tragedy στιχομυθία is followed by ῥῆσις, so in Plato the pervading dialectic is at one time broken up, at another continuous and concentrated. Socrates everywhere begins with questions, but often (as is explicitly stated in the Gorgias and the Protagoras) he finds it necessary to take the argument into his own hands. In the questioning stage the logical steps are sometimes so numerous and so minute as to seem little more than verbal ; sometimes, as in the conversation with Polemarchus (Rep. I. 331 D–336 A), they have a sophistical effect, and, as Adeimantus complains (Rep. VI. 487 B, C), lead the respondent unawares to a paradoxical conclusion. In the Republic, while dramatic effect is nowhere relinquished, the use of question and answer, after the contention with Thrasymachus in Book I, is retained more in form than in substance. But in laying afresh the foundations of the doctrine of Ideas, Socrates

again becomes minutely dialectical (Rep. V. 476 ff., VII. 523 ff.—cp. X. 608 E).

(5) *Continuous dialectic.*—In departing from the strictly catechetical method, the style becomes in one way more condensed, and in another more expansive ; more condensed, because Socrates does not wait so often for the respondent to come up with him, more expansive, because, as he flows along in talk, illustrations multiply. It is to be observed also that the more constructive method of the Republic is assisted by the choice of the respondents, Adeimantus and Glaucon, who, although they are more life-like than the Aristoteles of the Parmenides and have many picturesque differences of character which are dramatically maintained, are, on the whole, predisposed to follow the lead of Socrates (V. 474 A), and are carried for the most part unresistingly by the full stream of Platonic discourse. And, as they are made to stand for the objectors, the adversary is often found more amenable to reason than would be the case if he were present in person (VI. 502 E, cp. Soph. 217 D, 246 D, Parm. 136 B, Theaet. 146 B, 162 B).

§ 2.     These remarks lead up to the general question : What relation is there between Plato's use of language and the form in which his works are cast ?

Consisting of argument embodied in fiction, his writings fall under conditions both of exactness and inexactness which are peculiar to them [1]. His style is consequently distinguished on the one hand (1) by conversational liveliness and freedom, and on the other (2) by dialectical precision.

[1] The following passage from Antony Trollope's autobiography shows the consciousness of a modern writer as to the conditions of written dialogue :—' The novel-writer in constructing his dialogue must so steer between absolute accuracy of language—which would give to his conversation an air of pedantry—and the slovenly inaccuracy of ordinary talkers, —which, if closely followed, would offend by an appearance of grimace,— as to produce upon the ear of his readers a sense of reality. If he be quite real, he will seem to attempt to be funny. If he be quite correct, he will seem to be unreal.'

(1) Thought and expression in Plato are in continual movement. Inchoate conceptions grow while being put into words. Illustrations are amplified until they threaten to supplant the original statement, on which they also react. Qualifications are perpetually inserted : abstractions are unexpectedly personified. The more *vivid* of two possible constructions is constantly preferred. Attention is kept on the alert by small dramatic surprises, as when Adeimantus suddenly remembers the ideal state in connexion with the philosopher who is in need of a city, VI. 497 C, or when Glaucon, who thinks that in the tyrannical man he has discovered the most miserable of human beings, is told of one who is yet more miserable, IX. 578 B. Interrogations, adjurations, apostrophes, are abruptly interposed. Crises of the argument are marked by increased liveliness, as when Socrates turns to his respondent with ὦ θαυμάσιε, or when he delights in exaggerating the audacious image of the laughing wave, V. 473 C. At one time, that which is imagined is treated as real, at another, Socrates returns to sad realities, with an outburst of emotion, VII. 536 C. From irony, he sometimes passes to direct seriousness, or with humorous gravity calls attention to some familiar fact, IX. 578 D. And beneath the ebb and flow of outward inconsistencies there is produced a deep impression of advance and growth. (See esp. III. 412 C, VII. 535 ff.)

Closely connected with this ever-fresh vivacity, indeed another aspect of it, is the obvious freedom from restraint. Plato's sentences are less tied down than those of other writers, even in Greek, to a predetermined form. Constructions are often found to shift through the interposition of some afterthought. Corrections, explanations, restrictions, digressions, break the regularity of grammar and occasion either a new construction or a pleonastic resumption of the previous statement, very often both. One protasis has more than one apodosis and *vice versa*. The meaning is followed at the expense of concord (as in the agreement of neuter with feminine, or singular with plural) or, conversely, the nearer construction is chosen at the expense of the meaning. The grammatical order of words is modified by emphasis and by the desire of euphony. Verbs and participles are absorbed by the neighbourhood of kindred words. Not only cases but tenses and moods are employed κατὰ σύνεσιν. The language is at one time more explicit, at another more elliptical than would be allowable in a treatise or set speech. Lastly, the tendency which is common in Greek, wherever there are long sentences, to make the construction of the later clauses independent of the main construction, is peculiarly common in the long sentences of Plato.

But through all this licence, which the grammarian is apt to censure for irregularity, the hand of the creative artist is clearly discernible. Plato is not, like Thucydides, continually struggling with a medium of expression which he has imperfectly mastered ; but the medium itself is one which has not yet attained to perfect lucidity. He moulds contemporary language to his purpose with the greatest skill. But the formal correctness of Isocrates would ill have suited him. It would be unnatural in ' dear Glaucon ' though it is natural enough in Polus to ' speak like a book.' When this is once acknowledged, the meaning is almost always clear, although the combination of subtlety with laxity does sometimes lead to ambiguity. The conversational tone, however, is sometimes fused with rhetoric, and invites comparison with the orators. For sustained force, directness, and rapidity, no style is equal to that of Demosthenes. But the oratorical style of Plato contrasts favourably with the monotonous equability of Isocrates, the plain seriousness of Andocides, and the simple passionateness of Lysias. In ornate passages, Plato often betrays familiarity with poetry; but in his middle period, to which the Republic belongs, epic and lyric elements are more distinctly present than echoes of tragedy. His language coincides, in some points, with that of comedy, but this will become more apparent in considering his vocabulary. (See Part II : *Platonic Diction.*) Tragic phrases become more frequent in his later writings, especially the Laws.

(2) While the dialogue of Plato has a conversational, and § 3. sometimes a rhetorical, it also has a dialectical cast. This gives rise to some refinements of construction, and also to an occasional complexity appearing chiefly in two specific ways, (*a*) coordination, (*b*) remote connexion.

(*a*) *Coordination.*— The disjunctive question, or negation, in which two statements are bound together under a single negative, or interrogative—signifying that they cannot or should not both be true at once—a form of sentence peculiarly Greek, attains a high degree of complexity in Plato. See below, VIII.

(*b*) *Remote connexion.*—In Plato, as sometimes in tragedy, the formula of assent or dissent, instead of referring merely to the concluding words of the question, often reverts to the very beginning of a long speech, implying in the respondent a remarkable power of continuous attention (below, X). Similarly, the whole work is bound together with links of allusion to what has preceded, and preparations for what is to come, demanding a sustained interest far surpassing that of ordinary conversation.

## 2. SYNTAX.

### *A Chapter in Grammar.*

It follows from what has been said that the sentence in § 4. Plato, when looked at from a grammatical point of view, presents exceptional features both of irregularity and also of regularity, the ordinary structure being modified at once by conversational freedom, and by the effort to be precise and clear. This general statement will now be illustrated by a series of quotations from the Republic and other dialogues under the following heads : —

I. Tenses, Moods, and Voices of the Verb.

II. Cases and numbers of Nouns.

III. Article and Pronoun.

IV. Adverbs and Prepositions.

V. Particles and Conjunctions.

VI. Ellipse and Pleonasm.

VII. Apposition.

VIII. Coordination of Sentences.

IX. Deferred apodosis : (Digression and Resumption).

X. Remote Reference.

XI. Imperfect Constructions.

XII. Changes of Construction.

XIII. Rhetorical figures.

XIV. Order of words.

XV. Grammatical irregularities considered in relation to the text.

### I. The Verb.

§ 5.   1. TENSES.

(*a*) The ‘*aorist* of the immediate past,’ referring to what has just been said or felt, though less common than in tragedy, is not infrequent in Plato.

I. 348 E ἀλλὰ τόδε ἐθαύμασα, κ.τ.λ. ‘But this surprises me’ (in what has just been said).

(*b*) The ‘*gnomic aorist*,’ stating a general fact, often occurs, especially in describing mental phenomena.

VII. 523 D οὐδαμοῦ γὰρ ἡ ὄψις αὐτῇ ἅμα ἐσήμηνε τὸν δάκτυλον τοὐναντίον ἢ δάκτυλον εἶναι. ‘Sight nowhere tells her that the finger is the opposite of a finger.’

*Obs.* 1.—In general statements Plato often passes from the *present* to the *aorist* and *vice versa*.

I. 338 D, E τίθεται δέ γε τοὺς νόμους ἑκάστη ἡ ἀρχή . . . θέμεναι δὲ ἀπέφηναν, κ.τ.λ.

VIII. 551 A φιλοχρήματοι . . . ἐγένοντο, καὶ τὸν μὲν πλούσιον ἐπαινοῦσι . . . τότε δὴ νόμον τίθενται, κ.τ.λ.

*Obs.* 2.—The *imperfect* is used in correlation with this as with the ordinary (preterite) aorist.

VII. 524 C μέγα μὴν καὶ ὄψις καὶ σμικρὸν ἑώρα . . . διὰ δὲ τὴν τούτου σαφήνειαν μέγα αὖ καὶ σμικρὸν ἡ νόησις ἠναγκάσθη ἰδεῖν.

VIII. 547 B εἰλκέτην . . . ἠγέτην . . . ὡμολόγησαν.

IX. 572 D **κατέστη** εἰς μέσον ἀμφοῖν τοῖν τρόποιν, καὶ μετρίως δή, ὡς ᾤετο, ἑκάστων ἀπολαύων οὔτε ἀνελεύθερον οὔτε παράνομον βίον **ζῇ.**

*Obs.* 3.—The aorist infinitive without ἄν is used in assured antici_ pation.

v. 457 D οἶμαι . . . πλείστην ἀμφισβήτησιν γενέσθαι.　(So the MSS.) See Goodwin, *M. and T.,* § 127.

Of course ἄν might easily drop out before ἀμφ.

(*c*) The imperfect tense of εἰμί has two special uses in Plato and in other philosophical writers :

*a.* In reference to what has been previously said or assumed—

III. 406 E ὅτι ἦν τι αὐτῷ ἔργον. 'Because as we suggested (405 C) he has something to do.'

IX. 587 C ἐν μέσῳ γὰρ αὐτῶν ὁ δημοτικὸς ἦν.

So (according to Ast's conjecture) in X. 603 C μή τι ἄλλο *ἦν (MSS. ᾖ) παρὰ ταῦτα. Cp. ib. D ἐστασία(ε . . . εἶχεν.

*β.* In stating the result of an enquiry, because what a thing is found to be at the end of search, that it *was* before the search began.

IV. 428 A δῆλον γὰρ ὅτι οὐκ ἄλλο ἔτι ἦν ἢ τὸ ὑπολειφθέν. 'It was all along nothing else.'

IV. 436 B, C ἐάν που εὑρίσκωμεν ἐν αὐτοῖς ταῦτα γιγνόμενα, εἰσόμεθα ὅτι οὐ ταὐτὸν ἦν ἀλλὰ πλείω. 'They were all the while more than one.'

VI. 497 C τότε δηλώσει ὅτι τοῦτο μὲν τῷ ὄντι θεῖον ἦν. 'This was from the beginning undoubtedly divine.'

(*d*) The *perfect* sometimes signifies a fixed habit (cp. Monro's *Homeric Grammar,* p. 28).

VII. 521 E γυμναστικὴ μέν που περὶ γιγνόμενον καὶ ἀπολλύμενον **τετεύτακε**—'is constantly employed.'

VII. 533 B αἱ μὲν ἄλλαι πᾶσαι τέχναι . . . πρὸς θεραπείαν . . . ἅπασαι **τετράφαται**—'apply themselves continually.'

So in VI. 511 A εἰκόσι δὲ χρωμένην αὐτοῖς τοῖς ὑπὸ τῶν κάτω

ἀπεικασθεῖσι καὶ ἐκείνοις πρὸς ἐκεῖνα ὡς ἐναργέσι **δεδοξασμένοις τε καὶ τετιμημένοις**—'usually esteemed and held in honour.'

### § 6.　2. MOODS.

(*a*) *Conjunctive.*—The familiar combination of the ' deliberative subjunctive ' with βούλει, βούλεσθε, occurs in

II. 372 E εἰ δ' αὖ βούλεσθε . . . θεωρήσωμεν, οὐδὲν ἀποκωλύει. This was misunderstood by the diorthotes of Paris. A. See E. on Text, p. 135.

IX. 577 B βούλει . . . προσποιησώμεθα, κ.τ.λ., and elsewhere.

*Obs.*—In such expressions as τί λέγομεν; πῶς λέγομεν; the MSS. often leave it doubtful whether τί λέγωμεν; &c. should not be read.

(*b*) *Optative.*—Plato's optatives are sometimes a little difficult to explain, depending rather on the drift of the sentence than on grammatical rule. The following are the chief places in the Republic requiring special treatment.

I. 337 E πῶς . . . ἄν τις ἀποκρίναιτο πρῶτον μὲν μὴ εἰδὼς . . . ἔπειτα, εἴ τι καὶ οἴεται περὶ τούτων, ἀπειρημένον αὐτῷ εἴη . . . ;

The condition implied in the participial clause μὴ εἰδώς becomes explicit as the sentence proceeds, and is expressed as if εἰ μὴ εἰδείη had followed πῶς ἄν τις ἀποκρίναιτο. Cp. Protag. 327 D εἰ δέοι αὐτὸν κρίνεσθαι πρὸς ἀνθρώπους, οἷς μήτε παιδεία ἐστὶ μήτε δικαστήρια, . . . ἀλλ' εἶεν ἄγριοί τινες.

Here the condition introduced in εἰ δέοι regains its force towards the end of the sentence, which is continued as if the whole from οἷς downwards were a single relative clause (e.g. οἳ μὴ ἔχουσιν or ἔχοιεν, κ.τ.λ.). See Xen. Symp. VIII. 17.

I. 352 E τί δέ ; ἀκούσαις ἄλλῳ ἢ ὠσίν ;

II. 360 B οὐδεὶς ἂν γένοιτο, ὡς **δόξειεν**, οὕτως ἀδαμάντινος, ὃς ἂν μείνειεν, κ.τ.λ.

The clause ὡς δόξειεν, although not conditional, seems to fall under Goodwin's law of assimilation (*M. and T.*, §§ 558, 531). But it is to be observed also that the whole of Glaucon's speech proceeds on the assumption that he is putting the case of another (359 B ὡς ὁ λόγος: 361 E μὴ ἐμὲ οἷον λέγειν), and the mood is affected by the sense of indirect discourse. Cp. IV. 420 C ἐναληλιμμένοι εἶεν.

II. 361 C ἄδηλον οὖν εἴτε τοῦ δικαίου εἴτε τῶν δωρεῶν . . . ἔνεκα τοιοῦτος εἴη. Glaucon's reasoning is hypothetical, though he tries to treat his supposition as a matter of fact. The language therefore wavers between the indicative and optative : i. e. εἴτε . . . εἴη is brought in, as if εἰ δόξει . . . ἔσονται . . . ἄδηλον had been εἰ δοκοίη . . . εἶεν ἂν . . . ἄδηλον ἂν εἴη.

II. 382 D, E ἀλλὰ δεδιὼς τοὺς ἐχθροὺς ψεύδοιτο; In both these cases the construction is continued from a preceding sentence having the optative with ἄν. In the former some editors insert ἄν, and it may possibly have dropped out before ἄλλῳ.

III. 403 B νομοθετήσεις . . . οὕτως ὁμιλεῖν πρὸς ὅν τις σπουδάζοι. 'In Attic Greek an optative in the relative clause sometimes depends on a verb of *obligation* . . . with an infinitive. . . . E. g.

Ἀλλ' ὃν πόλις στήσειε, τοῦδε χρὴ κλύειν,

Soph. Ant. 666.' Goodwin, *M. and T.*, § 555.

III. 410 B, C οἱ καθιστάντες μουσικῇ καὶ γυμναστικῇ παιδεύειν οὐχ οὗ ἕνεκά τινες οἴονται καθιστᾶσιν, ἵνα τῇ μὲν τὸ σῶμα θεραπεύοιντο τῇ δὲ τὴν ψυχήν.

Madvig would read καθίστασαν. But this accords ill with κινδυνεύουσιν following. And for the tense cp. VIII. 566 B ἐξευρίσκουσιν. The indirect discourse here depends on a general statement, which, as Riddell would say, 'belongs to all time' (*Digest*, § 74), or as Goodwin puts it (*M. and T.*, § 323) 'implies a reference to the past as well as the present.' He quotes Dem. XII. 11 τοῦτον ἔχει τὸν τρόπον ὁ νόμος, ἵνα μηδὲ πεισθῆναι μηδ' ἐξαπατηθῆναι γένοιτ' ἐπὶ τῷ δήμῳ.

IV. 428 C, D ἔστι τις ἐπιστήμη ἐν τῇ ἄρτι ὑφ' ἡμῶν οἰκισθείσῃ . . . ᾗ . . . βουλεύεται . . . ὅντινα τρόπον . . . πρὸς τὰς ἄλλας πόλεις ἄριστα ὁμιλοῖ.

Here 'a reference to the past' is implied in the words ἐν τῇ ἄρτι οἰκισθείσῃ. Or the reference to time is altogether vague. Hence in the indirect discourse ὁμιλοῖ. not ὁμιλῇ.

VI. 490 A ἆρ' οὖν δὴ οὐ μετρίως ἀπολογησόμεθα ὅτι πρὸς τὸ ὂν πεφυκὼς εἴη ἀμιλλᾶσθαι ὅ γε ὄντως φιλομαθής, κ.τ.λ. 'Shall we not make a reasonable defence in saying (what we have already indicated),' &c. There is an implied reference to the definition of the philosopher in Bk. V sub fin. This is Professor Goodwin's ingenious explanation of the difficulty, which others have met by conjecturing ἀπελογησάμεθα or ἀπελογισάμεθα,—neither of which is justified by the context: for V. 474 B ff. is neither, strictly speaking, an 'apology' nor a 'reckoning.' (*M. and T.*, § 676.)

(*c*) The imperfect *indicative* in the apodosis of an unreal supposition is made more vivid by the absence of ἄν (*M. and T.*, § 431).

V. 450 D, E πιστεύοντος μὲν γὰρ ἐμοῦ ἐμοὶ εἰδέναι ἃ λέγω, καλῶς εἶχεν ἡ παραμυθία. 'Had I been confident in my knowledge of the things I say, your comfort were indeed welcome.'

(*d*) *Imperative.* The third person imperative has a special use in dialectic, viz. in stating or admitting a postulate or assumption.

VIII. 553 A ἀπειργάσθω δή, κ.τ.λ. 'I may assume that our description of oligarchy is complete.'

§ 7.    (*e*) *Infinitive.* The construction of an infinitive can sometimes be gathered only imperfectly from the context :—

V. 467 C τοῦτο μὲν ἄρα ὑπαρκτέον, θεωροὺς πολέμου τοὺς παῖδας ποιεῖν, προσμηχανᾶσθαι δ' αὐτοῖς ἀσφάλειαν, καὶ καλῶς ἕξει· ἦ γάρ;

προσμηχανᾶσθαι is governed by the notion of obligation (δεῖ or χρή) implied in ὑπαρκτέον, and the construction is assisted by the inf. ποιεῖν coming between. This point will be further illustrated in considering *imperfect constructions* (below, XI).

*Epexegetic uses* of the infinitive : α. following an adjective :—

I. 330 C χαλεποὶ οὖν καὶ ξυγγενέσθαι εἰσίν. 'Troublesome to converse with.'

VII. 537 B ἀδύνατός τι ἄλλο πρᾶξαι. 'Incapable of (admitting) any other employment.'

*Obs.*—In the difficult place I. 333 E καὶ λαθεῖν οὗτος δεινότατος ἐμποιῆσαι, unless something is wrong with the text, there is a double construction of this kind:—'most clever to implant,' 'most clever to escape notice (in implanting).' Schneider's emendation ἐμποιήσας saves the grammar at the expense of natural emphasis.

β. In apposition with a noun:

VII. 531 C ἀλλ' οὐκ εἰς προβλήματα ἀνίασιν, ἐπισκοπεῖν, κ.τ.λ.

VIII. 566 B τὸ δὴ τυραννικὸν αἴτημα . . . ἐξευρίσκουσιν, αἰτεῖν, κ.τ.λ.

The *infinitive,* instead of the participle as elsewhere, sometimes follows φαίνεσθαι:

IV. 432 D φαίνεται πρὸ ποδῶν ἡμῖν ἐξ ἀρχῆς κυλινδεῖσθαι. 'It has manifestly been rolling (ἐκυλινδεῖτο) at our feet all the while.'

(*f*) The *participle.* In expanding his sentences Plato § 8. makes continual use of participial expressions.

1. For pleonastic (or epexegetic) uses see especially III. 397 C ἢ τῷ ἑτέρῳ τούτων ἐπιτυγχάνουσιν . . . ἢ τῷ ἑτέρῳ ἢ ἐξ ἀμφοτέρων τινὶ ξυγκεραννύντες. 'They hit on one or other of these modes, or on a third, which they compound out of both.'

VI. 494 E τί οἰόμεθα δράσειν . . . οὐ πᾶν μὲν ἔργον, πᾶν δ' ἔπος λέγοντάς τε καὶ πράττοντας;

VII. 527 A ὡς γὰρ . . . πράξεως ἕνεκα πάντας τοὺς λόγους ποιούμενοι λέγουσι τετραγωνίζειν τε καὶ παρατείνειν καὶ προστιθέναι καὶ πάντα οὕτω φθεγγόμενοι.

A more doubtful instance is VI. 496 A οὐδὲν γνήσιον οὐδὲ φρονήσεως ἄξιον ἀληθινῆς ἐχόμενον, where the awkwardness may be obviated by reading ἀξίως (ἄξιον ὡς Ven. Π).

2. *Alternation of participle with infinitive.* In Plato's long sentences the participle sometimes alternates with the infinitive:

VI. 488 B ff. (in the allegory of the mutinous crew)

στασιάζοντας . . . φάσκοντας μηδὲ διδακτὸν εἶναι, ἀλλὰ καὶ τὸν λέγοντα ὡς διδακτὸν ἑτοίμους κατατέμνειν, αὐτοὺς δὲ αὐτῷ ἀεὶ τῷ ναυκλήρῳ περικεχύσθαι, κ.τ.λ.

The infinitive περικεχύσθαι may have been occasioned, but is not grammatically accounted for, by κατατέμνειν coming between. This point will be more fully illustrated below, under Changes of Construction.

*Obs.*—As the use of the participle with the article after the preposition instead of the infinitive is doubtfully admitted by some editors in several passages of Thucydides (I. 2, § 5; IV. 63, § 1; V. 7, § 2; VI. 84, § 10: VIII. 105, § 2), it may be worth observing that in Rep. I. 346 B διὰ τὸ ξυμφέρειν the best MSS. have διὰ τὸ ξυμφέρον. Cp. Phileb. 58 c, Laws VIII. 831 E.

3. The participle passive, mostly neuter, denoting a mode of action or existence, occurs in VIII. 561 A ἐκ τοῦ ἐν ἀναγκαίοις ἐπιθυμίαις τρεφομένου : X. 596 D (τρόπος) ταχὺ δημιουργούμενος, 'a manner in which it is easy to produce the effect :' cp. Theaet. 184 C τὸ δὲ εὐχερὲς . . . καὶ μὴ . . . ἐξεταζόμενον, 'an easy-going method, without strict examination.'

4. The accusative and participle, with or without ὡς, have the effect of a reported statement. With ὡς : I. 345 E ὡς οὐχὶ αὐτοῖσιν ὠφελίαν ἐσομένην, 'implying that they would not profit thereby.' II. 383 A ὡς μήτε αὐτοὺς γόητας ὄντας κ.τ.λ., 'conveying the impression that the Gods themselves are not impostors.' III. 390 A, B τί δέ; ποιεῖν . . . δοκεῖ σοι ἐπιτήδειον εἶναι . . . ἀκούειν νέῳ . . . ἢ Δία . . . ὡς . . . ἐπιλανθανόμενον, 'do you think it fitting that a young man should hear such a poetical description, or that he should hear Zeus described as forgetting,' &c. VI. 511 D ὡς . . . τὴν διάνοιαν οὖσαν. VIII. 560 D ὡς ἀγροικίαν . . . οὖσαν. Cp. Phaedrus 245 A πεισθεὶς ὡς . . . ἐσόμενος. Without ὡς : VI. 511 A νοητὸν μὲν τὸ εἶδος ἔλεγον, ὑποθέσεσι δ' ἀναγκαζομένην ψυχὴν χρῆσθαι περὶ τὴν ζήτησιν αὐτοῦ, 'I spoke of this kind as intellectual, but (said) that the mind was compelled to use hypothesis in investigating it.'

*Obs.* I.—In X. 604 B the transition from the genitive to the accusative ὡς οὔτε δήλου ὄντος ... οὔτε ... προβαῖνον is occasioned by the impersonal verb.

*Obs.* 2.—The subject of an infinitive or participle following a verb is accusative even when the same with the main subject, if this happens to be considered in two aspects. x. 621 B ἰδεῖν ... αὐτὸν ... κείμενον ἐπὶ τῇ πυρᾷ. 'He saw that he himself was lying.' The previous narrative referred to the disembodied soul.

*Obs.* 3.—The idiomatic use of the aorist participle with γε in a reply = 'Let me first,' &c. (Phaedr. 228 D δείξας γε πρῶτον, ὦ φιλότης, κ.τ.λ.) occurs in vi. 507 A διομολογησάμενός γ', ἔφην, κ.τ.λ. 'Not until I have come to a clear understanding.' Cp. i. 338 c ἐὰν μάθω γε πρῶτον with similar ellipse.

For a slightly different idiom with the present participle, see viii. 554 A αὐχμηρός γέ τις ... ὤν, 'Ay, because he is a shabby fellow,' and the note in loco.

*Obs.* 4.—The gerundive in -τέον is construed with the accusative: iii. 400 D ταῦτά γε λόγῳ ἀκολουθητέον.

So also in v. 467 E διδαξαμένους ... ἀκτέον, 'we must have them taught and bring them,' where see note, and cp. Tim. 88 B, C τὸν δὴ μαθηματικὸν ... καὶ τὴν τοῦ σώματος ἀποδοτέον κίνησιν, 'the hard student must give his body corresponding exercise.'

*Obs.* 5.—The subordination of participle to participle is very frequent :

viii. 555 E ἐνιέντες ἀργύριον τιτρώσκοντες. 'Stinging by inserting money.'

N.B.—A little-noticed idiom, occurring also in Herodotus and Thucydides, is the use of the aorist participle referring to a time subsequent to that of the principal verb. Parm. 127 D τὸν ... γενόμενον (= ὃς ὕστερον τούτων ἐγένετο). Goodwin, *M. and T.*, § 152.

## 3. VOICES.
§ 9.

(*a*) *Active.*

α. Impersonal. X. 604 B ὡς οὔτε δήλου ὄντος ... οὔτε εἰς τὸ πρόσθεν οὐδὲν προβαῖνον τῷ χαλεπῶς φέροντι.

IX. 580 D δέξεται, sc. τὸ πρᾶγμα (Theaet. 200 E δείξειν αὐτό. Phaedo 73 B σαφέστατα κατηγορεῖ).

β. With a neuter subject, which signifies some condition, aspect, or attitude of mind.

IV. 442 E εἴ τι ἡμῶν ἔτι ἐν τῇ ψυχῇ ἀμφισβητεῖ. 'If there be

any objection lurking in our mind.' More often in the
participle (cp. Thucydides).

IV. 439 B τοῦ διψῶντος καὶ ἄγοντος ... ἐπὶ τὸ πιεῖν. ' The
appetite of thirst, that drags him to the act of drinking.'

γ. Intransitive with cognate subject.

V. 463 D αὗται ... ἢ ἄλλαι φῆμαι ... ὑμνήσουσιν ...; ' are
not these and none but these the strains that will resound
in song ? '

(*b*) *Passive.*— Verbs not strictly transitive acquire a
passive voice.

α. With the cognate accusative of the active for implied
subject.

VI. 490 A τοῖς νῦν δοκουμένοις.   Cp. X. 612 D δοκεῖσθαι.

β. With the remote object of the active for subject.

I. 336 E, 337 A ἡμᾶς ... ὑπὸ ὑμῶν ... χαλεπαίνεσθαι (=ὑμᾶς
χαλεπαίνειν ἡμῖν).

X. 602 A συνεῖναι τῷ εἰδότι καὶ ἐπιτάττεσθαι (sc. ὑπὸ τοῦ
εἰδότος, i.e. τὸν εἰδότα ἐπιτάττειν αὐτῷ).

This use, of which πιστεύεσθαί τι, 'to be entrusted with
anything,' is the most familiar example, is extended in the
later dialogues to ἐπιχειρεῖσθαι (Tim. 53 B ὅτε ... ἐπεχειρεῖτο
κοσμεῖσθαι τὸ πᾶν), διακονεῖσθαι (Laws VI. 763 A), δυστυχεῖσθαι,
ἀσεβεῖσθαι (Laws IX. 877 E ὅταν οὖν τις ἅμα δυστυχηθῇ καὶ
ἀσεβηθῇ τῶν οἴκων, ' when some habitation has received the
taint of misfortune and of crime '), νομοθετεῖσθαι, ' to be
legislated for ' (Laws XI. 925 E, 926 A, where the passive
ἐπιτάττεσθαι again occurs).

Cp. πλεονεκτεῖσθαι in Xen. Mem. III. 5, § 2 πλεονεκτούμενοι
ὑπὸ Θηβαίων.

γ. Passive impersonal.

VII. 530 C ὡς νῦν ἀστρονομεῖται, ' as Astronomy is now
pursued.'

§ 10.   (*c*) *Middle.*

α. The Middle Voice in Plato has still frequently a subtle
force—accentuating some relation in which the action stands
to the agent.

I. 344 E βίου διαγωγήν, ᾗ ἂν **διαγόμενος**, ' conducting his own life.'

I. 349 E ἁρμοττόμενος λύραν, 'tuning a lyre for himself to play upon.'

III. 405 B τὸ πολὺ τοῦ βίου . . . κατατρίβηται, 'wastes the greater part of his life.'

*Obs.*—The distinction of τιθέναι and τίθεσθαι, 'to institute and to adopt a law,' is well discussed by Mr. Postgate in *Journ. of Phil.* xv. 29 (1886). See a good example of this in Laws VII. 820 E τοὺς θέντας ἡμᾶς ἢ καὶ τοὺς θεμένους ὑμᾶς.

β. On the other hand, the voice is sometimes varied almost capriciously.

VI. 484 D μηδὲν . . . ἐλλείποντας . . . μὴ ἐλλείποιντο : cp. Laws IX. 853 C **νομοθετούμενοι** . . . ἐνομοθέτουν : XI. 913 B ἀνελών . . . **ἀνελόμενος**.

γ. A vague reference to self is implied in what has been called the subjective middle voice, of which παρέχομαι, ἀποδείκνυμαι, περιφέρομαι are instances. παρέχεσθαι, for example, is ' to furnish from one's own resources,' or ' to produce by one's own inherent power.'

IV. 421 D ὄργανά γε μὴ ἔχων **παρέχεσθαι**, IV. 443 B ταύτην τὴν δύναμιν, ᾗ τοὺς τοιούτους ἄνδρας τε **παρέχεται** καὶ πόλεις : cp. Phaedr. 240 C ἡ . . . χρόνου ἰσότης . . . φιλίαν **παρέχεται**.

δ. The reciprocal use appears most prominently in ὁμολογεῖσθαι, ' to agree together.'

IV. 436 C ἔτι τοίνυν ἀκριβέστερον **ὁμολογησώμεθα** : VIII. 544 A **ὁμολογησάμενοι** τὸν ἄριστον καὶ τὸν κάκιστον ἄνδρα.

This is sometimes emphasized with reference to λόγος by the addition of the reflexive pronoun.

V. 457 C τὸν λόγον αὐτὸν αὑτῷ **ὁμολογεῖσθαι** : cp. Phaedr. 265 D τὸ αὐτὸ αὑτῷ **ὁμολογούμενον**.

ε. A special use of the middle voice, combined with the construction noted above (the accusative as subject of the verbal in -τέον), gives the most probable solution of the difficulty in V. 467 E καὶ **διδαξαμένους** ἱππεύειν, 'and when they (the guardians) have had them (the young people) taught to ride.' See above, p. 179, *Obs.* 4.

*Obs.*—When the above cases are considered such an isolated use of the middle voice as μεγαλοφρονούμενοι in VII. 528 c appears less remarkable. Another rare use of the middle, VII. 535 B ποῖα δὴ διαστέλλει; 'what distinction do you propose to yourself?' is supported by Aristotle, Pol. II. 8, § 17 μικρὰ περὶ αὐτοῦ διαστείλασθαι βέλτιον. For a similar use of the middle voice in connexion with the dialectical process cp. Phaedo 101 E ἅμα δὲ οὐκ ἂν φύροιο . . . περί τε τῆς ἀρχῆς διαλεγόμενος καὶ τῶν ἐξ ἐκείνης ὡρμημένων.

## II.  The Noun Substantive.

§ II.    1. CASES.

### (a) *Nominative and Accusative.*

α. The preference for the nominative, where the subject is identical with that of the principal verb, extends to instances where the clause is headed by ὥστε, πρίν, or even by a preposition. This is quite regular, but the point is sometimes overlooked.

I. 345 D ἐπεὶ τά γε αὐτῆς ὥστ᾽ εἶναι **βελτίστη**, ἱκανῶς δήπου ἐκπεπόρισται (βελτίστη agrees with the subject of ἐκπεπόρισται, which is perfect *middle* = 'she has provided for herself').

III. 402 A πρὶν λόγον **δυνατὸς** εἶναι λαβεῖν : VI. 501 A πρὶν . . . **αὐτοὶ** ποιῆσαι.

III. 416 C εἰ μέλλουσι τὸ μέγιστον ἔχειν πρὸς τὸ **ἥμεροι** εἶναι.

V. 454 A διὰ τὸ μὴ δύνασθαι . . . **διαιρούμενοι,** κ.τ.λ.

VII. 526 B εἴς γε τὸ **ὀξύτεροι** αὐτοὶ αὑτῶν γίγνεσθαι.

Laws X. 885 D βελτίους ἢ . . . παρατρέπεσθαι **κηλούμενοι.**

(Cp. Xen. Hell. VII. 5, § 5 εἴ τινες δὴ πόλεις διὰ τὸ **σμικραί** τε εἶναι καὶ ἐν μέσαις ταύταις οἰκεῖν ἠναγκάζοντο.)

*Obs.*—The accusative occurs in a similar connexion V. 457 B φῶμεν . . . λέγοντες, ὥστε . . . **τιθέντας.**

β. In the absence of a definite construction, the accusative is the case usually preferred, and the case sometimes reverts to the accusative, although the construction has been previously in the dative (as in the familiar instance,

Sophocles, Electra 479 ὕπεστί μοι θράσος | ἀδυπνόων κλύουσαν | ἀρτίως ὀνειράτων). See note on VIII. 559 B.

γ. It has sometimes been assumed (*Digest*, § 11) that all substantives apparently out of construction are accusatives in apposition. This point will be treated more fully below under Changes of Construction. Meanwhile, it is enough to adduce as an instance of the nominativus pendens VII. 532 B ἣ δέ γε ... λύσις τε ... καὶ μεταστροφή, κ.τ.λ., where, as the sentence proceeds, the nominative is changed to an accusative in C ταύτην ... τὴν δύναμιν.

A good example of the accusative in apposition is II. 365 C πρόθυρα μὲν καὶ σχῆμα, κ.τ.λ.

This idiom is peculiarly frequent in the Timaeus. A common form of it in most dialogues is ἄλλο τι ἤ ... (Gorg. 470 B, &c.), a special case of the familiar idiom of which Theaet. 195 E ἃ μηδὲν ἄλλο ἢ διανοεῖταί τις is an example. Cp. Rep. IV. 420 A οὐδὲν ἄλλο ἢ φρουροῦντες. For ἄλλο τι without ἤ following see below, under Apposition.

Under this heading, whether as nominative or accusative, may be brought the abrupt exclamations in VIII. 557 E τὸ δὲ μηδεμίαν ἀνάγκην ... εἶναι ἄρχειν, κ.τ.λ. : VIII. 563 B τὸ δέ γε ... ἔσχατον ... τῆς ἐλευθερίας τοῦ πλήθους.

δ. An adverbial accusative is sometimes abruptly introduced.

IV. 436 D ὡς οὐ ... τὰ τοιαῦτα τότε μενόντων.

V. 460 B εἴτε ἀνδρῶν εἴτε γυναικῶν εἴτε ἀμφότερα.

VI. 492 B ὑπερβαλλόντως ἑκάτερα.

So in such expressions as Symp. 204 C τί τῶν καλῶν ἐστιν ὁ Ἔρως ;

ε. The cognate accusative (or accusative of the internal object,—too common to be noticed here) has its correlative in the cognate *subject* of the passive voice. This use is especially frequent in the participial form (see above, p. 178, 3), and in the adverbial accusative of the verbal noun ; VI. 510 B τοῖς τότε τμηθεῖσιν (if the reading is sound).

ζ. The accusative, equally with the dative, accompanies

the verbal in -τέον, IV. 421 B, 424 C: for dative see III. 413 C, V. 468 A πῶς ἐκτέον σοι τοὺς στρατιώτας, where the accusative would have given another (i. e. an active) meaning to ἐκτέον. Cp. Tim. 88 C τὸν δὴ μαθηματικόν . . . τὴν τοῦ σώματος ἀποδο-τέον κίνησιν. So in V. 467 E, see above, p. 179, *Obs.* 4.

§ 12.   (*b*) *Genitive.*—The genitive, like the accusative, some-times stands in a loose construction with what follows, the construction being afterwards, in some cases, made more definite.

V. 463 B ἔχεις οὖν εἰπεῖν τῶν ἀρχόντων, κ.τ.λ.

V. 470 A τί δέ ; γῆς τε τμήσεως τῆς Ἑλληνικῆς καὶ οἰκιῶν ἐμπρή-σεως ποῖόν τί σοι δράσουσιν οἱ στρατιῶται πρὸς τοὺς πολεμίους ;

Cp. Symp. 221 C τῶν μὲν ἄλλων ἐπιτηδευμάτων τάχ' ἄν τις . . . εἴποι when περί follows, but in construction with another word.

See also—

II. 375 E οἶσθα γάρ που τῶν γενναίων κυνῶν, ὅτι τοῦτο φύσει αὐτῶν τὸ ἦθος (where αὐτῶν supplies the link).

IX. 571 B ἐνίων μὲν ἀνθρώπων ἢ . . . ἀπαλλάττεσθαι ἢ ὀλίγαι λείπεσθαι . . . τῶν δὲ . . . καὶ πλείους. ' In the case of some men,' &c., where ἐνίων might be construed with ἀπαλλάττεσθαι, but the context shows this not to be the construction.

Special uses of the genitive are—

a. ' *Consisting in*' (*Digest*, § 24).

IV. 433 D ἡ τοῦ . . . τὰ αὑτοῦ πράττειν δύναμις.

β. *Objective* = πρός with acc.

II. 359 A ξυνθήκας αὐτῶν. 'Contracts with one another.'

III. 391 C ὑπερηφανίαν θεῶν τε καὶ ἀνθρώπων. ' Haughtiness towards gods and men.'

VIII. 566 E ἡσυχία ἐκείνων, 'he has tranquillity in regard to them.'

A doubtful instance is VIII. 558 A ἡ πραότης ἐνίων τῶν δικασ-θέντων, κ.τ.λ. (see note in loc.). See also IX. 573 D ὧν ἂν Ἔρως, κ.τ.λ. ' Whatever things are the objects of the passion,' &c. (Prof. Jowett construed the genitive with τὰ τῆς ψυχῆς ἅπαντα, 'of whatsoever men love masters the whole soul.')

γ. *Partitive.*

X. 615 D ἐθεασάμεθα . . . καὶ τοῦτο τῶν δεινῶν θεαμάτων, 'this was amongst the terrible sights we beheld.'

VI. 496 C τούτων δὴ τῶν ὀλίγων οἱ γενόμενοι.  Cp. Laws VI. 754 D οἱ δὲ δὴ γενόμενοι τῶν ἑπτὰ καὶ τριάκοντα.

δ. ' *Requiring.*'

III. 414 C πεῖσαι δὲ συχνῆς πειθοῦς, 'but much persuasion is required to convince men of its truth.'

X. 615 A πολλοῦ χρόνου διηγήσασθαι.

Cp. Phaedr. 246 A οἷον μέν ἐστι, πάντῃ πάντως θείας εἶναι καὶ μακρᾶς διηγήσεως, ᾧ δὲ ἔοικεν, ἀνθρωπίνης τε καὶ ἐλάττονος : Parm. 135 B ἀνδρὸς πάνυ μὲν εὐφυοῦς τοῦ δυνησομένου μαθεῖν : Laws V. 730 A πολλῆς οὖν εὐλαβείας, κ.τ.λ.

ε. ' *In respect of.*'

II. 365 A ὡς . . . ἔχουσι τιμῆς, 'how they are disposed to regard them.'

VII. 518 B εὐδαιμονίσειεν ἂν τοῦ πάθους τε καὶ βίου : VII. 531 D τοῦ προοιμίου.

IX. 571 D ὅταν . . . ὑγιεινῶς τις ἔχῃ αὐτὸς αὑτοῦ (' in comparison with himself ') καὶ σωφρόνως.

This does not occur with other adverbs than those in ὡς. Cp. Xen. Hell. V. 4, § 25 ἀπολυτικῶς αὐτοῦ εἶχον, and Hdt. VII. 188, 3 τοῖσι οὕτω εἶχε ὅρμου.

The genitive in ejaculations is closely allied to this :— VI. 509 C Ἄπολλον, ἔφη, δαιμονίας ὑπερβολῆς.

So perhaps IX. 576 D εὐδαιμονίας . . . καὶ ἀθλιότητος ὡσαύτως . . . κρίνεις : cp. Laws I. 646 D τῆς . . . διατριβῆς . . . διανοητέον.

Phaedo 99 B πολλὴ ἂν καὶ μακρὰ ῥᾳθυμία εἴη τοῦ λόγου.

*Obs.*—Double and even triple genitives are not uncommon, the second being sometimes epexegetic of the first, as in VII. 534 B τὸν λόγον ἑκάστου . . . τῆς οὐσίας.

For other examples see—

VII. 525 C ῥᾳστώνης τε μεταστροφῆς, κ.τ.λ.

  „  537 C εἰς σύνοψιν οἰκειότητος ἀλλήλων τῶν μαθημάτων καὶ τῆς τοῦ ὄντος φύσεως. (Cp. Soph. 254 C κοινωνίας ἀλλήλων πῶς ἔχει δυνάμεως.)

VIII. 544 D ἀνθρώπων εἴδη . . . τρόπων.

  „  560 B δι' ἀνεπιστημοσύνην τροφῆς πατρός.

§ 13.    *c. Dative.*

a. The dative of the person interested has an extended use in Plato.

I. 334 E πονηροὶ γὰρ αὐτοῖς εἰσίν. 'For their friends are bad.'

I. 335 E τοῦτο δὲ δὴ νοεῖ αὐτῷ. ' And this expression means, as employed by him.'

I. 343 A ὅς γε αὐτῇ οὐδὲ πρόβατα οὐδὲ ποιμένα γιγνώσκεις. ' Since she leaves you in ignorance of the difference between shepherd and sheep.'

III.   394 C εἴ μοι μανθάνεις. ' If I take you with me ' (where some would read εἴ μου μ.).

III. 415 B ὅ τι αὐτοῖς τούτων ἐν ταῖς ψυχαῖς παραμέμικται. 'What alloy they find in the souls of their young charges.'

V. 451 D εἰ ἡμῖν πρέπει ἢ οὔ. ' Whether we find it suitable or not, for our purpose.'

V. 462 A ἆρα . . . εἰς μὲν τὸ τοῦ ἀγαθοῦ ἴχνος ἡμῖν ἁρμόττει. ' Whether we find that our proposals fit into the lines of good.'

VIII. 549 C, D ἀχθομένης, ὅτι οὐ τῶν ἀρχόντων αὐτῇ ὁ ἀνήρ ἐστιν. ' Aggrieved to find that her husband is not in the government.'

In X. 602 E, with a participle (τούτῳ δὲ . . . μετρήσαντι, κ.τ.λ.), it has nearly the force of an absolute clause, i.e. ' when this faculty of measurement has done its work, it finds after all,' &c.   See note in loco.

*Obs.* 1.—It may be worth observing that the dative so used (except when amplified as in the last instance) is seldom or never emphatic.

*Obs.* 2.—The dative of reference, in combination with a participle, often introduces a concomitant circumstance or condition, as in the familiar phrase ἐν δεξιᾷ εἰσιόντι &c.—

V. 451 C κατ' ἐκείνην τὴν ὁρμὴν ἰοῦσιν.

VI. 484 A μέλλοντι.

IX. 589 C σκοπουμένῳ.

β. The dative of manner may be added to another dative without any feeling of confusion.

II. 359 C νόμῳ δὲ **βίᾳ** παράγεται ἐπὶ τὴν τοῦ ἴσου τιμήν. 'But is forcibly diverted by law and custom into a respect for equality.'

VIII. 552 E οὓς ἐπιμελείᾳ **βίᾳ** κατέχουσιν αἱ ἀρχαί. It is added pleonastically in VIII. 555 A, IX. 576 C ὁμοιότητι, and it is sometimes expanded by an additional word.

IX. 575 C πονηρίᾳ τε καὶ ἀθλιότητι **πόλεως**. It has the effect of an absolute clause in IX. 578 C τῷ τοιούτῳ λόγῳ, also perhaps in IX. 579 C τοῖς τοιούτοις κακοῖς. The reading has been questioned in both passages, see notes in locis, but cp. X. 598 D ὑπολαμβάνειν δεῖ τῷ τοιούτῳ, κ.τ.λ.

γ. In VI. 490 A παρὰ δόξαν τοῖς νῦν δοκουμένοις, the dative follows a prepositional phrase as if it were an adjective, e g. ἐναντίον, and in 496 C τὴν τῷ δικαίῳ βοήθειαν it is construed with a verbal noun. So in later dialogues, Tim. 23 C φθορὰν ὕδασιν, Laws III. 698 B ἡ Περσῶν ἐπίθεσις τοῖς Ἕλλησιν.

δ. The dative of the measure of excess occurs in the remarkable expression in VI. 507 E οὐ σμικρᾷ . . . ἰδέᾳ, 'by the measure of no unimportant nature,' and has been applied to the interpretation of IX. 579 C cited above.

*Obs.*—The Ionic form of the dative plural in σι(ν) according to the best MSS. occurs only in Phaedr. Rep. Polit. Tim. Laws. In the Phaedrus and Republic, however, it is merely an occasional ornament, whereas in the Laws it is of constant recurrence. (F. Blass finds examples in the earlier orators.) Of the five [1] examples occurring in the Republic (I. 345 E; III. 388 D, 389 B; VIII. 560 E, 564 C), two are of the definitive pronoun I. 345 E, VIII. 564 C αὐτοῖσι (very emphatic in both cases); two of familiar adjectives III. 388 D σμικροῖσι, VIII. 560 E μεγάλοισι and one of θεός, III. 389 B, in a passage coloured by frequent quotations from Homer. All these are of the second declension (κενεαγορίαισι in X. 607 B, like νώτοισιν in V. 468 D, is in a poetical quotation, and should not be counted). In the Laws according to C. Ritter, op. cit., there are eighty-five instances of the form, which here extends, although more sparingly, to feminines of the first declension. The four instances in the Politicus include the participle ἑπομένοισιν (304 E).

[1] C. Ritter (*Untersuchungen*, &c.) mentions six; but he seems to include the quotation in X. 607 B.

§ 14. 2. NUMBER OF NOUNS.

(*a*) The plural of an abstract word is often used to express its exemplification in the concrete. This happens especially when other words in the sentence are in the plural.

II. 364 C κακίας πέρι εὐπετείας διδόντες. 'Offering easy occasions for vice.'

II. 373 D ἰατρῶν ἐν χρείαις. 'In frequent need of the physician.'

V. 449 A περί τε πόλεων διοικήσεις.

VIII. 547 D γεωργιῶν ἀπέχεσθαι τὸ προπολεμοῦν αὐτῆς. 'That its military class abstains from agricultural employments.'

X. 611 C δικαιοσύνας τε καὶ ἀδικίας. 'Its various modes of justice and injustice.'

(*b*) In X. 618 A, B πενίας ... πτωχείας ... πλούτοις καὶ πενίαις the plurals serve to emphasize the variety and complexity of human conditions. Cp. Tim. 65 C τραχύτησί τε καὶ λειότησιν : Laws V. 733 B σφοδρότησιν ἰσότησί τε, 734 A πυκνότησιν.

(*c*) The plural is used with the meaning of the singular to express either admiration or scorn. Cp. Symp. 218 B, Theaet. 169 B.

Rep. III. 387 B Κωκυτούς, κ.τ.λ.

III. 391 B ἕλξεις ... σφαγάς ... (D) ἁρπαγάς.

VI. 495 A πλοῦτοί τε καὶ πᾶσα ἡ τοιαύτη παρασκευή.

VIII. 553 C τιάρας τε καὶ στρεπτοὺς καὶ ἀκινάκας.

(*d*) The plural of abstract verbals and other adjectives is often preferred to the singular.

II. 375 D ταῦτα δὲ ἀδυνάτοις ἔοικε.

III. 387 B ἀποβλητέα.

VI. 498 A μεγάλα ἡγοῦνται.

(*e*) The singular neuter is often used in a collective sense.

IV. 442 B τὸ δὲ προπολεμοῦν.

IX. 577 C σμικρόν γέ τι τοῦτο.

For the combination of neuter with masculine or feminine see below, Imperfect Constructions.

### III. Article and Pronoun.

1. THE ARTICLE is sometimes—  § 15.

(*a*) *Correlative*, i.e. it marks each of two correlative words.

I. 338 D, E τίθεται . . . τοὺς νόμους ἑκάστη ἡ ἀρχή (where it may also be regarded as distributive (*b*)).

V. 455 D κρατεῖται ἐν ἅπασιν . . . τὸ γένος τοῦ γένους. '*The one* sex is beaten by *the other.*'

(*b*) Sometimes *distributive*—

VII. 540 B ὅταν δὲ τὸ μέρος ἥκῃ. 'When the turn of each arrives.'

(*c*) The article of *reference* in οἱ ἄλλοι, οἱ πολλοί, is to be distinguished from the common use of these phrases.

V. 453 E τὰς δὲ ἄλλας φύσεις. 'These natures which have been described as different.'

X. 596 A θῶμεν . . . ὅ τι βούλει τῶν πολλῶν. 'Let us put the case of any one you will of things which exist in plurality.'

(*d*) In the idiomatic use with a future participle the article often resumes an indefinite pronoun—

I. 342 A δεῖ τινὸς τέχνης τῆς . . . σκεψομένης.

I. 348 B δικαστῶν τινῶν τῶν διακρινούντων.

(*e*) For the 'deictic' use with a personal or reflexive pronoun, see Theaet. 166 A τὸν ἐμέ, Phaedr. 258 A.

*Obs.* 1.—The article is sometimes repeated merely for emphasis—

I. 334 E τὸν δοκοῦντά τε . . . καὶ τὸν ὄντα χρηστόν.

*Obs.* 2.—The article is omitted—

(1) With common nouns used as proper names, as λιμήν, ἀγορά, &c. (for the harbour, market-place, &c. of the town where the scene is laid).

Theaet. 142 A οὐ γὰρ ἦ κατὰ πόλιν (i. e. in Megara).

Theaet. 142 A εἰς λιμένα καταβαίνων. 'As I went down to the harbour' (of Megara).

Rep. II. 371 C καθήμενος ἐν ἀγορᾷ.

(2) With a noun used in a general sense, but without pointed reference to others from which it is distinguished—

I. 332 E ἰατρός . . . κυβερνήτης.

II. 369 B γίγνεται . . . πόλις.

VI. 499 C ἄκροις εἰς φιλοσοφίαν . . . πόλεως . . . ἐπιμεληθῆναι.

VIII. 562 A τυραννίς τε καὶ τύραννος.

X. 611 B ὅτι μὲν τοίνυν ἀθάνατον ψυχή.

And sometimes arbitrarily to avoid cumbrous repetition (in many cases it *may* have accidentally been dropped, yet it is needless to restore it as H. Richards proposes in IV. 434 A ⟨τὰς⟩ τιμάς)—

IV. 438 C καὶ αὖ βαρύτερα πρὸς κουφότερα καὶ θάττω πρὸς τὰ βραδύτερα.

V. 475 A καὶ μὴν φιλοτίμους, κ.τ.λ.

VIII. 545 A καὶ ὀλιγαρχικὸν αὖ καὶ δημοκρατικὸν καὶ τὸν τυραννικόν (supra *Obs.* 1).

Phaedr. 254 A τῷ σύζυγί τε καὶ ἡνιόχῳ.

*Obs.* 3.—The substantival use of the neut. adj. does not always necessitate the article.

V. 478 C μὴ ὄντι μὴν ἄγνοιαν ἐξ ἀνάγκης ἀπέδομεν, ὄντι δὲ γνῶσιν.

VII. 518 A, B εἰς φανότερον ἰοῦσα ὑπὸ **λαμπροτέρου** μαρμαρυγῆς ἐμπέπλησται (where, even if βίον is to be supplied with φανότερον, λαμπροτέρου at least is neuter).

Symp. 218 A ὑπὸ ἀλγεινοτέρου.

*Obs.* 4.—The omission of the article with ἀνήρ so constant in MSS. is proved by the examples in tragedy, where the *a* is long (e. g. Soph. Aj. 9, 324, 783, &c. all in senarii), to be often due to the scribes; but it is uncertain whether in such instances as IX. 573 C γίγνεται . . . οὕτω καὶ τοιοῦτος ἀνήρ the Platonic idiom requires us to write ἀνήρ or not. Cp. Phaedr. 266 C ἄνδρες, 267 C δεινὸς ἀνὴρ γέγονε (this Thompson leaves unaltered), 268 C μαίνεται ἄνθρωπος.

## § 16.   2. THE PRONOUNS.

The pronouns, especially the demonstratives (with their adverbs οὕτως, ὧδε, ὡσαύτως, &c.) have a widespread use in the Platonic dialogues, in which resumption, reference, antithesis, are necessarily so frequent.

(*a*) *Demonstratives.*

a. The demonstratives and the oblique cases of αὐτός, as in Thucydides, often refer to an antecedent which although implied in the preceding context has not been fully expressed. The same thing happens in the case of the adverb αὐτόθι.

I. 334 A κινδυνεύεις παρ' Ὁμήρου μεμαθηκέναι **αὐτό**.

I. 339 A, B πρόσεστι δὲ δὴ **αὐτόθι** τὸ τοῦ κρείττονος.

II. 371 C τὴν διακονίαν . . . **ταύτην**.

II. 371 E τὴν τιμὴν **ταύτην**.

II. 373 C **τοῦτο** γὰρ (' the care of swine ') ἡμῖν ἐν τῇ προτέρᾳ πόλει οὐκ ἐνῆν.

III. 399 D ἢ οὐ **τοῦτο** (αὐλός from αὐλοποιούς) πολυχορδότατον.

IV. 424 D ἡ . . . παρανομία . . . **αὕτη** (sc. ἡ ἐν μουσικῇ).

VI. 491 C λαβοῦ . . . ὅλου **αὐτοῦ** ὀρθῶς.

VI. 507 D παρούσης δὲ χρόας ἐν **αὐτοῖς** (sc. τοῖς ὁρωμένοις).

X. 597 B τὸν μιμητὴν **τοῦτον**.

β. οὗτος is sometimes simply the thing or person in question.

VII. 523 C μηδὲν μᾶλλον **τοῦτο** ἢ τὸ ἐναντίον. Cp. Theaet. 180 A κἂν **τούτου** ζητῇς λόγον λαβεῖν, τί εἴρηκεν, ἑτέρῳ πεπλήξει, κ.τ.λ.

Theaet. 199 B μὴ γὰρ ἔχειν τὴν ἐπιστήμην **τούτου** οἷόν τε, ἀλλ' ἑτέραν ἀντ' ἐκείνης. Hence in Rep. IV. 436 A if we read with most MSS. εἰ τῷ αὐτῷ **τούτῳ** ἕκαστα πράττομεν, **τούτῳ** means the thing in question—having no distinct antecedent.

γ. ὅδε and οὗτος are less markedly distinguishable in § 17. Plato than, for example, in Xenophon. The familiar rule that ὅδε points to what is present in perception, οὗτος to what is present in thought, applies to the Platonic instances, but with modifications arising from the liveliness of the discourse and sudden changes of the aspect in which a thing is regarded.

Both pronouns are used to indicate what is familiar in daily experience, as distinguished from what is imaginary or remote.

III. 403 E **τῶνδε** τῶν ἀσκητῶν.

VIII. 544 C ἡ Κρητική τε καὶ Λακωνικὴ **αὕτη** (πολιτεία).

Gorg. 470 D τὰ . . . ἐχθὲς καὶ πρώην γεγονότα **ταῦτα**. So probably οὕτω in II. 377 B ἆρ' οὖν ῥᾳδίως **οὕτω** (' as is usually done ') παρήσομεν, although this may be merely idiomatic like νῦν οὕτως, &c. (VI. 490 A σφόδρα **οὕτω**).

δ. In the same spirit the antithesis of οὗτος and ἐκεῖνος does not necessarily correspond to what is 'latter' and 'former' in the sentence. But whichever term is imagined as in some way nearer to the mind is marked with οὗτος, and that which in the same aspect is more remote, with ἐκεῖνος. Thus, in the opening of the Euthydemus (p. 271), it is a mistake to suppose, because Critobulus is last mentioned, that he is meant by οὗτος. Crito modestly speaks of his own son as 'gawky' (σκληφρός), and admiringly of the stranger who is more immediately in question.

II. 370 A οὕτω ῥᾷον ἢ 'κείνως, 'the familiar way is easier than the novel plan proposed,' i. e. οὕτω and 'κείνως do not refer to the order in which they have been mentioned but to the order in which they occur to the mind or which is more familiar in use and experience.

III. 416 A πῶς, ἔφη, αὖ τοῦτο λέγεις διαφέρειν ἐκείνου ; ' How does the plan you now prefer differ from that which you condemn? '

IV. 421 B εἰς τὴν πόλιν ὅλην βλέποντας θεατέον εἰ ἐκείνῃ ἐγγίγνεται.

In VI. 511 A ἐκείνοις πρὸς ἐκεῖνα *both* terms are remote, because they are the segments of τὸ ὁρατόν, and τὸ νοητόν is immediately in question. See note in loco.

ε. The vividness of Plato's style sometimes anticipates, as already present to the mind, something to which attention is for the first time directed. Hence οὗτος (ἐνταῦθα, &c.) are sometimes used where ὅδε (ἐνθάδε, &c.) might rather have been expected.

IV. 430 E ὥς γε ἐντεῦθεν ἰδεῖν, 'from the point of view at which I am standing.'

VI. 510 C τούτων προειρημένων, 'when I have stated what I have now to state.'

VII. 514 A τοιούτῳ πάθει, 'to a condition such as I am now imagining.'

So probably VI. 488 A νόησον ... τοιουτονὶ γενόμενον, 'conceive the occurrence of such a situation as I (have in mind and) am about to describe.'

ζ. οὗτος is used vaguely for ὁ τοιοῦτος.

III. 395 C τὰ τούτοις προσήκοντα.

*Obs.* 1.—οὗτος occurs twice in the same sentence with different references in VII. 532 C πᾶσα αὕτη ἡ πραγματεία . . . ταύτην ἔχει τὴν δύναμιν, where αὕτη refers to the sciences, ταύτην to their educational effect.

*Obs.* 2.—ἐκεῖνος in the progress of a sentence often refers to what has previously been denoted by an oblique case of αὐτός or οὗτος. See especially III. 405 C, VI. 511 A, VII. 533 A.

η. τοιοῦτος (especially in ἕτερα τοιαῦτα) and ὁ τοιοῦτος are § 18. often used to avoid the repetition of an adjective.

IV. 424 A φύσεις χρησταὶ τοιαύτης (sc. χρηστῆς) παιδείας ἀντιλαμβανόμεναι.

Ib. E παρανόμου γιγνομένης αὐτῆς καὶ παίδων τοιούτων (sc. παρανόμων).

IV. 429 A δι' ὃ τοιαύτη (sc. ἀνδρεία) κλητέα ἡ πόλις.

VIII. 560 C κατέσχον τὸν αὐτὸν τόπον τοῦ τοιούτου (sc. τὴν τῆς ψυχῆς ἀκρόπολιν τοῦ ὀλιγαρχικοῦ γιγνομένου).

Similarly in VIII. 546 C ἑκατὸν τοσαυτάκις probably means ἑκατὸν ἑκατοντάκις.

*Obs.* 1.—τοιοῦτος is used euphemistically in V. 452 D πάντα τὰ τοιαῦτα: and in III. 390 C δι' ἕτερα τοιαῦτα the euphemism conveys also contempt.

*Obs.* 2.—υἷος, τοιοῦτος, &c., as in other Greek, gain a peculiar force from the context or intonation.

IX. 588 B οἷα ἔλεγεν, 'what a preposterous statement he was guilty of.'

*Obs.* 3.—The derisive use of ποῖος (Theaet. 180 B ποίοις μαθηταῖς, ὦ δαιμόνιε;) is applied in Rep. I. 330 B ποῖ' ἐπεκτησάμην; to express the gentle amusement of Cephalus at the suggestion that he may have augmented his ancestral fortune.

θ. The deictic form τουτοισί is rightly restored by Bekker in I. 330 B. Cp. τοιουτονί VI. 488 A.

(The deictic use of pronominal adverbs may be

illustrated from IV. 430 E ἐντεῦθεν, 445 B δεῦρο, V. 477 D, VII. 527 E αὐτόθεν. This adds vividness to the style.)

(*b*) *Indefinite Pronoun.*

§ 19.   *a.* Τὶς added to the predicate with the force of πού or πώς as in Soph. Ajax 1266 τοῦ θανόντος ὡς ταχεῖά τις βροτοῖς | χάρις διαρρεῖ.

II. 358 A ἀλλ' ἐγώ τις, ὡς ἔοικε, δυσμαθής, 'but I am a slow sort of person it would seem.'

VIII. 548 E δούλοις μέν τις ἂν ἄγριος εἴη.

β. Combined with other pronouns :

I. 346 C τινὶ τῷ αὐτῷ προσχρώμενοι.

III. 412 A τοῦ τοιούτου τινός.

VIII. 562 A τρόπον τινὰ τὸν αὐτόν.

γ. With indirect allusion to a person :

Phaedr. 242 B λόγῳ τινί, ' a speech of mine.'

Phaedo 63 A λόγους τινὰς ἀνερευνᾷ, ' one's arguments,' i. e. mine.

II. 372 E ταῦτα γὰρ δή τισιν ... οὐκ ἐξαρκέσει ('Glaucon and fine gentlemen like him ').

δ. Πότερος *indefinite.*

VI. 499 C τούτων δὲ πότερα γενέσθαι ἢ ἀμφότερα, κ.τ.λ.

This is rare in other writers but not infrequent in Plato. See IV. 439 E, Theaet. 145 A, 178 C.

ὁπότερον in IX. 589 A seems only to be a more emphatic πότερον.

(*c*) *Reflexive.*

§ 20.   *a.* Ἑαυτοῦ has sometimes an indefinite antecedent.

IV. 434 C τῆς ἑαυτοῦ πόλεως, ib. 443 D.

The authority of the MSS. about breathings is very slight, and it is sometimes difficult to decide whether to read αὑτοῦ or αὐτοῦ, &c., e. g. I. 344 A, II. 359 A, 367 C.

β. The personal is sometimes used for the reflexive pronoun, giving special point to a relation or antithesis.

V. 450 D πιστεύοντος ... ἐμοῦ ἐμοί.   Cp. Gorg. 482 B οὔ σοι ὁμολογήσει Καλλικλῆς, ὦ Καλλίκλεις.

(*d*) The *Relative Pronoun* ὅς is sometimes used where an indefinite antecedent is implied.

I. 352 C οὕς φαμεν, κ.τ.λ., 'any persons of whom we say,' &c.

This differs from οὓς ἂν φῶμεν in assuming that we do thus speak.

(*e*) *Indirect Interrogatives.*

When an interrogative is repeated, if there is any ground for using the indirect form, this is usually done.

IX. 578 E ἐν ποίῳ ἄν τινι καὶ ὁπόσῳ φόβῳ οἴει, κ.τ.λ. Even without repetition the indirect form is sometimes preferred—with the ellipse of εἰπέ or the like.

I. 348 B ὁποτέρως οὖν σοι . . . ἀρέσκει. Cp. Euthyd. 271 A ὁπότερον καὶ ἐρωτᾷς.

(*f*) *Personal Pronouns.*                                   § 21.

α. The explicit use of the nominative in such phrases as εὖ γε σὺ ποιῶν (I. 351 C), ἐγὼ δὲ λέγω (III. 382 B), where the sentence and not the subject of it is really emphasized, deserves a passing notice; also the idiomatic use of ἡμεῖς for ἐγώ (sometimes a cause of ambiguity).

β. One usage (though again rather rhetorical than grammatical) seems to claim notice as characteristic of the Platonic dialogue,—what may be termed the *condescending* use of the first person plural for the second person singular or plural, the speaker identifying himself with the person or persons addressed. It belongs to the ' maieutic ' manner of Socrates, who deals gently with his patient and asks at intervals ' How are we now ? ' A clear example occurs in Theaet. 210 B ἦ οὖν ἔτι κυοῦμέν τι καὶ ὠδίνομεν, ὦ φίλε, περὶ ἐπιστήμης, ἢ πάντα ἐκτετόκαμεν ;

Somewhat similar to this are such places in the Republic as

II. 368 D ἐπειδὴ οὖν ἡμεῖς οὐ δεινοί, κ.τ.λ.

II. 373 E πολεμήσομεν (i. e. πολεμήσουσιν ἡμῖν οἱ τρόφιμοι), and the more distinctly ironical use in

I. 337 C ἐάν τε ἡμεῖς ἀπαγορεύωμεν ἐάν τε μή.

In the mouth of the respondent this use becomes a mere *façon de parler*, II. 377 E πῶς . . . λέγομεν ;

(*g*) *Pronominal phrases*, i. e. phrases which take the place of nouns.

It is sufficient to glance at such expressions as ἀνήρ, οὗτος ἀνήρ, τοὐναντίον, τὸ εἰρημένον, τὸ πολλάκις ἤδη λεγόμενον and other such phrases which avoid the repetition of a noun. See especially II. 368 A ἐκείνου τοῦ ἀνδρός : VIII. 560 C τὸν αὐτὸν τόπον τοῦ τοιούτου (sc. τὴν τῆς ψυχῆς ἀκρόπολιν), and cp. Symp. 212 A ᾧ δεῖ . . . ᾧ ὁρατὸν τὸ καλόν.

This habit increases in the later dialogues and is especially frequent in the Philebus, when it has an effect of mannerism. Something like it occurs already in Thuc. VIII. 92, § 3 where the phrase ἐφ' οἷσπερ καὶ αὐτὸς ἀεὶ κατηγόρει is used to avoid repeating what Theramenes has been represented as saying twice before.

### IV. Adverbs and Prepositions.

§ 22.   1. ADVERBS.

(*a*) The predicative use of adverbs (cp. Thuc. I. 21, § 1 ἀπίστως) though not frequent is noticeable.

I. 332 A μὴ σωφρόνως (= μὴ σώφρων ὤν) ἀπαιτοῖ expressing the condition of the agent rather than the mode of the action

III. 406 C ὃ ἡμεῖς γελοίως (= γελοῖοι ὄντες).

(*b*) The adverb also takes the place of an epithet.

VII. 537 C τά τε χύδην μαθήματα (with γενόμενα following by an afterthought)—'the subjects indiscriminately taught.'

VIII. 564 A ἡ . . . ἄγαν ἐλευθερία . . . εἰς ἄγαν δουλείαν.

§ 23.   2. PREPOSITIONS.

(*a*) διά.

a. A questionable use of διά with the accusative occurs in IV. 440 C, D ξυμμαχεῖ τῷ δοκοῦντι δικαίῳ καὶ διὰ τὸ πεινῆν καὶ διὰ τὸ ῥιγοῦν . . . ὑπομένων καὶ νικᾷ καὶ οὐ λήγει . . . (so the MSS. and edd.), a place which Madvig has rewritten.   See notes and v. rr. On the whole it seems necessary to obviate the difficulty by reading διὰ *τοῦ in both places as is done in this edition. The use of διά will then be the same as in VI. 494 D ἆρ' εὐπετὲς οἴει εἶναι εἰσακοῦσαι διὰ τοσούτων κακῶν;

The notion of persistence and of obstacles overcome is common to both passages.

N.B.—To take διά = 'on account of' and the whole phrase as equivalent to ἕνεκα τοῦ πεινῆν . . . οὐ λήγει, κ.τ.λ. (καὶ νικᾷ being διὰ μέσου) is hardly a tenable view.

(*b*) ἐπί.

α. With gen. after λέγειν, = 'in the case of.' This seems a slight extension of the use after αἰσθάνεσθαι, νοεῖν, &c.

V. 475 A ἐπ' ἐμοῦ λέγειν.

VII. 524 E ὥσπερ ἐπὶ τοῦ δακτύλου ἐλέγομεν.

β. With accusative = 'extending to.'

VI. 491 A ἐπὶ πάντας, cp. Prot. 322 C. Tim. 23 B ἐπ' ἀνθρώπους.

(*c*) μετά. A frequent and characteristic use is that of § 24. conjoining correlated attributes.

IX. 591 B σωφροσύνην τε καὶ δικαιοσύνην μετὰ φρονήσεως κτωμένη, ἢ σῶμα ἰσχύν τε καὶ κάλλος μετὰ ὑγιείας λαμβάνον.

Theaet. 176 B, Phaedr. 249 A, 253 D.

Similarly with article prefixed.

VIII. 548 B Μούσης τῆς μετὰ λόγου, κ.τ.λ.

(*d*) παρά (with accusative).

α. 'In the course of.'

II. 362 B παρὰ ταῦτα πάντα ὠφελεῖσθαι: IV. 424 B; VII. 530 E. Cp. τὸ παράπαν, and see Hdt. II. 60 ταῦτα παρὰ πᾶσαν πόλιν . . . ποιεῦσι.

β. In VI. 492 E παρὰ τὴν τούτων παιδείαν πεπαιδευμένον, it is doubted whether παρά means 'in consequence of' (cp. Thuc. I. 141, § 7 παρὰ τὴν ἑαυτοῦ ἀμέλειαν, Xen. Hipparch, § 5), or 'contrary to.'

(*e*) περί.

α. Like ὑπέρ, 'on behalf of.'

II. 360 D ὁ περὶ τοῦ τοιούτου λόγου λέγων.

β. For περί pleonastic, see esp. :

IV. 427 A τὸ τοιοῦτον εἶδος νόμων πέρι.

VII. 539 C τὸ ὅλον φιλοσοφίας πέρι.

( *f* ) πρός.

α. πρός τινι εἶναι or γίγνεσθαι, 'to be engaged (or absorbed) in a thing.'

VIII. 567 A πρὸς τῷ καθ' ἡμέραν . . . εἶναι, 'to be engrossed with their daily avocations,' Phaedo 84 C, Phaedr. 249 C, D.

β. But in IX. 585 A πρὸς πληρώσει . . . γίγνεσθαι, 'to be close upon repletion.' So in Phaedr. 254 B πρὸς αὐτῷ τ᾽ ἐγένοντο, κ.τ.λ.

γ. With accusative.

VIII. 545 B πρὸς . . . ταύτην, 'in comparison with this' (emphatic).

§ 25.　( *g* ) ὑπέρ. The less common use with the genitive, nearly = περί, 'concerning,' is clearly present in II. 367 A ταῦτα . . . Θρασύμαχός τε καὶ ἄλλος πού τις ὑπὲρ δικαιοσύνης τε καὶ ἀδικίας λέγοιεν ἄν (Thrasymachus is not imagined as speaking *in behalf of* Justice). For other instances in Plato see Apol. 39 E ἡδέως ἂν διαλεχθείην ὑπὲρ τοῦ γεγονότος, κ.τ.λ., Laws VI. 776 E ὑπὲρ τοῦ Διὸς ἀγορεύων. And, for several in Aristotle, Bonitz' *Index Aristotel.* s. v. ὑπέρ, 1 *b*.

( *h* ) μεταξύ.

α. μεταξὺ τῶν λόγων, 'by the by,' Phaedr. 230 A.

β. With a participle, μεταξὺ ἀναγιγνώσκων Phaedr. 234 D.

γ. τὸ μεταξύ, 'during the interval until.'

See Mr. Herbert Richards' note in the *Classical Review* for December, 1888, p. 324 : 'Instead of a thing being between A and B, it is sometimes said to be between B, so that μεταξύ practically means "on this side of," "short of," "before reaching." '

Clear instances are Soph. O. C. 290, 291 τὰ δὲ | μεταξὺ τού- του, 'in the interval before Theseus arrives,' Dem. de Cor. p. 233 sub fin. τὸν μεταξὺ χρόνον τῶν ὅρκων, 'the interval before the ratification.'

For the same idiom in regard to place, see Thuc. III. 51, § 3.

Cp. also Eur. Hec. 436, 437, Aristoph. Ach. 433, 434, Arist. Rhet. III. 5, § 2.

So, probably, Rep. VI. 498 A ἄρτι ἐκ παίδων τὸ μεταξὺ οἰκονομίας καὶ χρηματισμοῦ, 'just after boyhood, in the interval before keeping house and engaging in business.'

## V. Particles and Conjunctions (*Digest*, §§ 132–178).

The use of particles acquires its full development in Plato, who employs them with extreme subtlety, variety and precision, not only to mark with minute clearness the progress of the argument, the degrees of assent and dissent, and the modes of inference, but also to give the light and life of oral conversation to each successive clause.

Platonic particles have lately been made a subject of 'statistical' investigation, and W. Dittenberger and others have attempted with some success to test the relative age of different dialogues by the absence or comparative frequency of certain particles in them. The results have been summed up by Constantin Ritter, *Untersuchungen über Plato*, Stuttgart, 1888. The Republic is shown to come with Phaedrus and Theaetetus about midway between the Symposium on the one hand and the Politicus Philebus Laws on the other.

### 1. Καί. § 26.

(*a*) Καί *adverbial.*

*a.* The anticipatory use, though common in Greek, is still worth noticing, from the liveliness which it adds to many sentences:

I. 327 A καλὴ μὲν οὖν μοι καὶ ἡ τῶν ἐπιχωρίων πομπὴ ἔδοξεν εἶναι, οὐ μέντοι ἧττον ἐφαίνετο πρέπειν ἣν οἱ Θρᾷκες ἔπεμπον.

II. 375 D ἴδοι μὲν ἄν τις καὶ ἐν ἄλλοις ζῴοις, οὐ μέντ' ἂν ἥκιστα ἐν ᾧ ἡμεῖς παρεβάλλομεν τῷ φύλακι.

β. ἵνα καί.

IV. 445 C δεῦρο . . . ἵνα καὶ ἴδῃς. 'Come hither . . . that you may really descry.'

γ. In interrogative phrases :

IV. 434 D τί . . . καὶ ἐροῦμεν ; 'What, after all, are we to say ? '

IV. 445 C ἵνα . . . ἴδῃς ὅσα καὶ εἴδη ἔχει ἡ κακία, 'that you may see how many, in point of fact, are the varieties of vice.'

Cp. Gorg. 455 A ἴδωμεν τί ποτε καὶ λέγομεν περὶ τῆς ῥητορικῆς.

δ. In affirmative sentences, giving additional emphasis :

I. 328 C διὰ χρόνου γὰρ καὶ ἑωράκη αὐτόν, 'for indeed it was long since I had seen him.'

ε. καὶ ταῦτα = 'in this too.'

I. 341 C οὐδὲν ὢν καὶ ταῦτα = 'discomfited as usual ;' or ' as you would be if you attempted to shave a lion.'

ζ. At once pointing and softening an asyndeton (cp. αὖ, πάντως).

I. 350 D τότε καὶ εἶδον ἐγώ, πρότερον δὲ οὔπω, Θρασύμαχον ἐρυθριῶντα. See note in loco.

η. With implied preference for an alternative :—'as well' = 'rather' (cp. Phil. 33 B ἔτι καὶ εἰσαῦθις).

III. 400 B ἀλλὰ ταῦτα μέν, ἦν δ' ἐγώ, καὶ μετὰ Δάμωνος βουλευσόμεθα. 'For the matter of that, said I, I had rather we conferred with Damon.'

V. 458 B ἀναβαλέσθαι καὶ ὕστερον ἐπισκέψασθαι.

IX. 573 D τοῦτο σὺ καὶ ἐμοὶ ἐρεῖς, '*that*, it would be as well (i. e. better) for *you* to tell *me*.'

θ. With ὥστε, emphasizing the *clause*.

IV. 421 D ὥστε καὶ κακοὺς γίγνεσθαι, 'I mean so as to deteriorate.'

Cp. the idiomatic use with ὡς εἰπεῖν in X. 619 D ὡς δὲ καὶ εἰπεῖν, where καί really belongs to the whole sentence.

ι. Displacement (hyperbaton or trajection) of καί. A possible instance is VI. 500 A ἦ, καὶ ἐὰν οὕτω θεῶνται, where (see note in loco) the difficulty may be solved by joining καὶ οὕτω,— 'If they look at it in this light rather (supra § 5) than in the other.' But the reading is doubtful, and perhaps ἦ οὐκ, ἐάν should be read, with q, merely changing τοι in what follows to τε.

(*b*) Καί *conjunctive.*

α. In narrative, indicating prompt sequence (as in the § 27. familiar phrase καὶ ἐγὼ εἶπον).

I. 327 B κελεύει ὑμᾶς, ἔφη, Πολέμαρχος περιμεῖναι. καὶ ἐγὼ μετεστράφην τε, κ.τ.λ. ʻWhereupon I turned about,ʼ &c.

β. In abrupt questions with a tone of surprise (as in καὶ πῶς;) to which καί gives emphasis.

I. 338 C τὸ τοῦ κρείττονος φῂς ξυμφέρον δίκαιον εἶναι. καὶ τοῦτο, ὦ Θρασύμαχε, τί ποτε λέγεις; ʻPray, Thrasymachus, what can you mean by that?ʼ

*Obs.*—Similarly καίτοι interposes a sudden question.

I. 350 E καίτοι τί ἄλλο βούλει; ʻWhat else in the name of common sense would you have?ʼ

II. 376 B καίτοι πῶς οὐκ ἂν φιλομαθὲς εἴη;

VII. 522 D καίτοι ποῖόν τιν' αὐτὸν οἴει στρατηγὸν εἶναι;

(*c*) καί virtually *disjunctive* (§ 7).

III. 411 A δειλὴ καὶ ἄγροικος, ʻ*either* cowardly *or* rudeʼ (the former being the effect of music without gymnastic, the latter of gymnastic without music).

VII. 518 B καὶ εἰ γελᾶν, κ.τ.λ.

In these cases καί is possibly preferred to ἤ on account of euphony. The result is a slight inexactness of expression.

*Obs.*—The former of two correlatives καί . . . καί = ʻ both . . . and ʼ is brought in after the beginning of the sentence in VII. 536 B τἀναντία πάντα καὶ πράξομεν καὶ φιλοσοφίας ἔτι πλείω γέλωτα καταντλήσομεν. This gives additional emphasis = ʻnot only . . . but also.ʼ Cp. IV. 440 D ὑπομένων καὶ νικᾷ καὶ οὐ λήγει, κ.τ.λ. ʻ It not only prevails but perseveres,ʼ &c.

## 2. Ἀλλά. § 28.

(*a*) In animated conversation ἀλλά often opposes what is now advanced to the position *attributed in thought* to the other speaker. Thus in the opening scene of the Republic (327 B) — ἀλλὰ περιμένετε. ἀλλὰ περιμενοῦμεν — the first ἀλλά opposes the entreaty that they should remain to their apparent intention of departing; the second ἀλλά opposes their willingness to remain to the supposed necessity of further entreaty. So on the following page (328 B) the first ἀλλά emphasizes entreaty as before, the second opposes Socrates' present assent to his previous show of reluctance. Cp. 338 C ἀλλὰ τί οὐκ ἐπαινεῖς; ἀλλ' οὐκ ἐθελήσεις.

(*b*) ἀλλ' ἤ. This familiar idiom occurs frequently after negatives, e. g. IV. 427 C οὐδὲ χρησόμεθα ἐξηγητῇ ἀλλ' ἢ τῷ πατρίῳ, 'we will consult no other authority, but only that which our fathers consulted.'

Also after an interrogative with negative meaning, IV. 429 B τίς ἂν . . . εἰς ἄλλο τι ἀποβλέψας . . . εἴποι ἀλλ' ἢ εἰς τοῦτο, κ.τ.λ. See L. and S., s. v. ἀλλ' ἤ.

(*c*) Since δέ often takes the place of ἀλλά in the Laws and in Aristotle (see Bonitz, *Ind. Ar.* s.v. δέ, p. 167 *a* l. 19), it is worth while to notice the use of δέ after the negative in—

I. 349 B, C εἰ τοῦ μὲν δικαίου μὴ ἀξιοῖ πλέον ἔχειν . . . τοῦ δὲ ἀδίκου.

I. 354 A ἄθλιόν γε εἶναι οὐ λυσιτελεῖ, εὐδαίμονα δέ.

IV. 422 D οὐδ' ἡμῖν θέμις, ὑμῖν δέ.

§ 29.                3. Μέντοι.

Μέντοι is a particle having a distinct and prominent office in Platonic dialogue.

(*a*) In *affirmation* it marks that what is now said alters the case.

I. 328 C χρῆν **μέντοι.** Cephalus pleads that Socrates should make an exception to his general rule by visiting the Piraeus:—'But you really should.'

I. 331 E ἀλλὰ **μέντοι** . . . τοῦτο **μέντοι.** **μέντοι** here is not merely adversative, but implies *reflection*.

IV. 440 A οὗτος **μέντοι,** ἔφην, ὁ λόγος σημαίνει, κ.τ.λ.

(*b*) In *questions* it calls attention to some fact or previous statement which has been overlooked and is inconsistent with what has just been said.

I. 339 B οὐ καὶ πείθεσθαι **μέντοι** τοῖς ἄρχουσι δίκαιον φὴς εἶναι; 'But, by the by, is it not your view that it is right to obey authority?'

I. 346 A οὐχὶ ἑκάστην μέντοι φαμὲν ἑκάστοτε τῶν τεχνῶν τούτῳ ἑτέραν εἶναι;

In such expressions μέντοι not only, like δήπου, claims assent, but also implies that the new statement is one which affects the argument.

(c) In *replies*, it often expresses deliberate assent (after reflection) to an objection or suggestion which alters the point of view.

I. 332 A ἄλλο μέντοι νὴ Δί’, ἔφη. 'There you are right, he said ; he meant something different from that.'

II. 374 E ἡμέτερον μέντοι.

### 4. Τοι. § 30.

Τοι, 'I may tell you.' For idiomatic uses see

I. 330 B οὗ τοι ἕνεκα ἠρόμην. 'Well, that was just my motive for asking.'

I. 343 A ὅτι τοί σε, ἔφη, κορυζῶντα περιορᾷ. 'Why,' said he, 'because she lets you drivel.'

Gorg. 447 B ἐπ’ αὐτό γέ τοι τοῦτο πάρεσμεν. 'Indeed, that is just why we are here.'

Prot. 316 B ὦ Πρωταγόρα, πρὸς σέ τοι ἤλθομεν ἐγώ τε καὶ Ἱπποκράτης οὑτοσί.

The use of τοι is often a delicate way of bespeaking attention to what is said.

### 5. Μέν.

Μέν is used without δέ following not only in the phrases εἰκὸς μέν, δοκῶ μέν, but in other connexions, as in III. 403 E ἀθληταὶ μὲν γὰρ οἱ ἄνδρες τοῦ μεγίστου ἀγῶνος. 'For, to begin with,' &c. V. 466 C ἐμοὶ μὲν . . . ξυμβούλῳ χρώμενος, κ.τ.λ.

*Obs.*—In v. 475 E ἀλλ’ ὁμοίους μὲν φιλοσόφοις the δέ is supplied by the respondent ; τοὺς δὲ ἀληθινούς, ἔφη, τίνας λέγεις; Cp. II. 380 E ὑπὸ μὲν ἄλλου . . . 381 B ’Αλλ’ ἆρα αὐτὸς αὑτόν, κ.τ.λ.

### 6. Γε. § 31.

Besides its ordinary use (very frequent in Plato) in giving a qualified or intensified assent, γε also

(a) limits the application of a statement :

I. 331 B ἀλλά γε ἐν ἀνθ' ἑνός, κ.τ.λ.

VI. 506 E τοῦ γε δοκοῦντος ἐμοὶ τὰ νῦν, and

(*b*) usually with participles it emphasizes what is put forward as the ground of a preceding statement.

Polit. 260 C ἢ μᾶλλον τῆς ἐπιτακτικῆς ὡς ὄντα αὐτὸν τέχνης θήσομεν, δεσπόζοντά γε; 'Or shall we rather assign him to the preceptive art, since he commands?'

Rep. VIII. 547 A ἀνάγκη Μούσας γε οὔσας.

So also perhaps

V. 478 B μὴ ὄν γε (sc. τὸ μὴ ὄν). ' Not-being, *since non-existent*, should be called no-thing.'

And, without a participle :

I. 331 D τῶν γε σῶν, i. e. ' of the argument, since it is your property.'

VI. 485 E ὅ γε τοιοῦτος, ' since that is the description of him.'

(*c*) δέ γε (' yes, but ') often introduces a second statement, which in some way modifies the first.

I. 335 D ὁ δέ γε δίκαιος ἀγαθός.

VIII. 547 E, 549 B, 553 C, 556 B, 561 E, &c.

### 7. Γάρ.

(γε ἄρα remain uncompounded in Theaet. 171 C.)

(*a*) Explaining something implied or understood. Cp. Hdt. IX. 92, § 2 μετὰ σφέων γάρ, κ.τ.λ.: VI. 111, § 2 ἀπὸ ταύτης γάρ σφι τῆς μάχης, κ.τ.λ.

Rep. II. 365 D ἐπὶ γὰρ τὸ λανθάνειν (' there is a difficulty, but it is not insuperable; for,' &c.).

III. 413 B νῦν γάρ που μανθάνεις ; ' (I have said enough) ; for I suppose you understand me now.'

VI. 491 C ἔχεις γὰρ τὸν τύπον ὧν λέγω.

So commonly in replies =' yes, for —,' ' no, for —,' &c.

(*b*) Introducing an inference under the form of a reason, ' the truth is,' ' the fact is.'    Lit. ' That is because.'

I. 338 D βδελυρὸς γὰρ εἶ, ' that shows your malignity.'

Cp. Gorg. 454 D δῆλον γὰρ αὖ ὅτι οὐ ταὐτόν ἐστιν, ' that is another proof of their difference.'

## 8. Δή.

Δή marks what is said as manifest, either in itself, or in connexion with a preceding statement : 'you know,' 'of course,' 'to be sure.' Sometimes *ironicè*, 'forsooth' (as in ὡς δή). In questions it demands proof or certainty, or asks for something more explicit.

(*a*) Idiomatic combinations of δή with adverbs and conjunctions :

α. With adverbs of time = 'just,' νῦν δή, 'just now' (passim), αὐτίκα δὴ μάλα, 'just immediately' (I. 338 B), τότε δή, 'even then' (Symp. 184 E).

β. καὶ . . . δή and καὶ δὴ καί, singling out the most prominent *item* in an enumeration or series :

I. 352 A (ᾧ ἂν ἐγγένηται, εἴτε πόλει τινὶ εἴτε γένει εἴτε στρατοπέδῳ . . .) καὶ ἐν ἑνὶ δή.

II. 367 C οἷον ὁρᾶν, ἀκούειν, φρονεῖν, καὶ ὑγιαίνειν δή, 'and in particular the being well and strong.'

VIII. 563 E, 564 A ἐν ὥραις τε καὶ ἐν φυτοῖς καὶ ἐν σώμασι, καὶ δὴ καὶ ἐν πολιτείαις οὐχ ἥκιστα (καὶ δή om. Par. A). Cp. Men. 87 E, Theaet. 156 B.

γ. δὴ οὖν : οὖν δή.

II. 382 D κατὰ τί δὴ οὖν τούτων τῷ θεῷ τὸ ψεῦδος χρήσιμον ; 'On which, *then*, of these grounds, *in particular*, is falsehood useful to God ?'

VI. 497 C δῆλος δὴ οὖν εἰ ὅτι μετὰ τοῦτο ἐρήσει . . . '*Now, then*, I see plainly that the next thing you will ask is . . .'

VII. 526 D ἀλλ' οὖν δή, εἶπον, πρὸς μὲν τὰ τοιαῦτα βραχύ τι ἂν ἐξαρκοῖ . . . , 'Howbeit, it is manifest, said I . . .'

VIII. 545 D πῶς οὖν δή, εἶπον, . . . ἡ πόλις ἡμῖν κινηθήσεται ; 'How, then, in point of fact, shall our city be disturbed ?'

(*b*) δή, with imperatives, giving peremptory emphasis :

φέρε δή, ἴθι δή (passim), σκόπει δή (I. 352 D), ἔχε δή (ib. 353 B).

Hence Baiter's emendation of V. 450 C πειρῶ *δή for πειρῶ ἄν (Par. A) is at least plausible, although the reading of Π M πειρῶ οὖν is perhaps preferable, because less abrupt.

(*c*) ὡς δή, 'since forsooth!'

I. 337 C **ὡς δὴ** ὅμοιον τοῦτο ἐκείνῳ, 'as if there was any comparison between the two cases.' Quite different from this is the effect of ὡς δή τοι.

II. 366 C **ὡς δή** τοι . . . πολλήν πού συγγνώμην ἔχει, κ.τ.λ., 'since truly, as you are aware.'

§ 33.                                    9. Μήν.

Μήν bespeaks attention for a fresh topic, generally in combination with a conjunction, καὶ μήν, ἀλλὰ μὴν . . . γε, οὐδὲ μήν, &c.

Plato shows a growing fondness for this particle, and employs it in new ways, especially in questions, asking for something fresh or different from what has been said.

(*a*) μήν alone :

VII. 520 E παντὸς **μὴν** μᾶλλον ὡς ἐπ' ἀναγκαῖον . . . εἶσι τὸ ἄρχειν, 'let me observe, however.'

VII. 524 C μέγα **μὴν** καὶ ὄψις καὶ σμικρὸν ἑώρα, 'you will observe that vision too had perception of great and small.'

VII. 528 A φθονοῖς **μὴν** οὐδ' ἂν ἄλλῳ, κ.τ.λ., 'though, to be sure, you would not grudge any incidental benefit which another may reap.' Cp. Phaedr. 244 B, Theaet. 193 D.

(*b*) Ἀλλὰ μὴν . . . γε :

VI. 485 D **ἀλλὰ μὴν ὅτῳ γε** εἰς ἕν τι αἱ ἐπιθυμίαι σφόδρα ῥέπουσιν, κ.τ.λ., 'well but, observe —.'

(*c*) μήν in combination with an interrogative :

α. In such expressions there is generally an ellipse of ἄλλο—i. e. an implied contrast or antithesis. In other words, μήν gives to the interrogative an intonation = 'what else ?' or 'what then ?'

I. 362 D ἀλλὰ τί **μήν**; εἶπον, 'but what more, then, would you desire ? said I.'

VII. 523 B οὐ πάνυ, ἦν δ' ἐγώ, ἔτυχες οὗ λέγω. ποῖα **μήν**, ἔφη, λέγεις ; 'You have not hit my meaning.'   'But what, then, are the things you mean ?'

β. Hence τί μήν ; acquires the force of strong assent :
' what else ? ' i. e. 'that, certainly.'

VI. 508 D ὅταν δέ γ', οἶμαι, ὧν ὁ ἥλιος καταλάμπῃ, σαφῶς
ὁρῶσι, κ.τ.λ. τί μήν ; ' of course.'

*Obs.*—W. Dittenberger has shown (*Hermes*, xvi. pp. 321 ff.) that
τί μήν; is absent from two-thirds of the Platonic dialogues, but increasingly frequent in Phaedr. (12 times), Rep. (35), Theaet. (13),
Soph. (12), Polit. (20), Phileb. (26), Laws (48).

The combination γε μήν, which is very frequent in the
later dialogues, above all in the Laws, occurs only twice in
the Republic :

I. 332 E μὴ κάμνουσί γε μήν, κ.τ.λ., 'well but, if men are
not ill,' &c.

V. 465 B τά γε μὴν σμικρότατα τῶν κακῶν, κ.τ.λ.

## 10. Αὖ and πάντως. §§ 34.

Αὖ and πάντως, though not conjunctions, serve to connect
sentences which are otherwise in asyndeton.

IV. 427 B τελευτησάντων αὖ θῆκαι, ' moreover, how the dead
are to be buried ' (v. r. τε αὖ).

VI. 504 E πάντως αὐτὸ οὐκ ὀλιγάκις ἀκήκοας.

Theaet. 143 C, Symp. 174 B, Gorg. 497 B, Polit. 268 E.

So εἶτα—as in other Greek—expressing impatience :

I. 338 D εἶτ' οὐκ οἶσθα, κ.τ.λ., Protag. 359 E :

and αὐτίκα in adducing an example, Protag. 359 E, &c.

This last idiom occurs also in a subordinate clause,

I. 340 D ἐπεὶ αὐτίκα ἰατρὸν καλεῖς, κ.τ.λ.

## 11. Ἄρα. §§ 35.

Ἄρα is not only a particle of inference (like οὖν) but also,
and in Plato more frequently, a sign of reference. This
has sometimes been overlooked by interpreters. Socrates
and other speakers are often engaged in developing
opinions which they do not endorse, or in relating what

is matter of hearsay. In such passages, ἄρα is constantly used to direct attention to the fact that the speaker is not uttering his own thought. The light particle enables Plato to dispense with such clumsy additions as (*a*) 'as my informant said,' (*b*) 'according to the theory I am expounding,' or (*c*) with reference to other speakers, 'according to the theory which they uphold,' or 'which you uphold,' or 'as we are expected to think.'

(*a*) II. 364 B ὡς ἄρα καὶ θεοὶ πολλοῖς . . . βίον κακὸν ἔνειμαν, 'that, as they declare,' &c.

(*b*) II. 362 A τὸ δὲ τοῦ Αἰσχύλου πολὺ ἦν ἄρα (' is really, according to their view ') ὀρθότερον λέγειν κατὰ τοῦ ἀδίκου.

X. 598 E ἀνάγκη . . . εἰδότα ἄρα ποιεῖν, 'he must, according to them, make his poetry with perfect knowledge.'

(*c*) I. 332 E χρήσιμον ἄρα καὶ ἐν εἰρήνῃ δικαιοσύνη ; ' Justice is useful in peace also, according to you ? '

X. 600 C, D Πρωταγόρας μὲν ἄρα (' according to the view in question ') . . . Ὅμηρον δ' ἄρα, κ.τ.λ.

### 12. που.

που =' I presume,' appealing to the knowledge or recollection of the respondent ; often used in recalling what has been previously said.

VI. 490 C μέμνησαι γάρ που.

IX. 582 D διὰ λόγων που ἔφαμεν δεῖν κρίνεσθαι.

Hence perhaps also in VIII. 562 B we should read τοῦτο δ' ἦν *που πλοῦτος.

§ 36.      ### 13. Negative Particles—and Interrogative Phrases.

It is needless to do more than to cite a few scattered uses which appear to be specially Platonic. (Uses of μὴ οὐ, for example, in Plato fall under the headings now given in L. and S. s.v. μή)—

(*a*) Οὐ in negation.

α. There is a courteous, reassuring use of οὐδέν, οὐδαμῶς,

&c., which is not intended to be taken seriously, but only to prepare for a modified restatement. This may in some cases be formally accounted for by supplying ἄλλο, &c. (below, p. 216 β), but not, for example, in

IX. 578 D τί γὰρ ἂν φοβοῖντο ;

Οὐδέν, εἶπον· ἀλλὰ τὸ αἴτιον ἐννοεῖς; 'Why indeed?' said I. 'But do you know the cause?'

V. 472 B ἀλλὰ τί τοῦτό γ'; ἔφη.

Οὐδέν· ἀλλ' ἐὰν εὕρωμεν, κ.τ.λ., 'Oh, merely to find,' &c.

The courtesy is sometimes ironical : as in

IV. 424 D Οὐδὲ γὰρ ἐργάζεται, ἔφη, ἄλλο γε ἢ κατὰ σμικρόν, κ.τ.λ., 'Oh!' said he, 'it is innocent enough, I dare say. All that it does is to undermine morality,' &c.

These examples may justify a similar rendering of

V. 461 C, D πατέρας δὲ καὶ θυγατέρας ... πῶς διαγνώσονται ἀλλήλων ;

Οὐδαμῶς, ἦν δ' ἐγώ. ἀλλ' ἀφ' ἧς, κ.τ.λ., 'Oh! simply in this way, said I.'

Although it is of course possible to take the words to mean literally 'not at all,' i. e. they will never know their actual parents.

β. **Οὐ πάνυ** in Plato has various shades of meaning, from (1) 'not quite,' to (2) 'not at all.'

(1) V. 474 D **οὐ γὰρ πάνυ γε ἐννοῶ**, 'I cannot quite recall it,' rather than, 'I have it not at all in mind.'

(2) VI. 504 E οἴει τιν' ἄν σε ... ἀφεῖναι ... ;

**Οὐ πάνυ**, ἦν δ' ἐγώ, 'Certainly not, said I.'

The stronger meaning may, however, be sometimes indirectly implied,—the speaker, as so often in Greek, saying less than he means.

IV. 429 A **οὐ πάνυ χαλεπόν**, 'not so very difficult,' i.e. 'surely not difficult at all.'

(*b*) *Interrogatives.* 37.

a. The regular interrogative use of οὐ in confident questions (='don't you think' &c.) is to be distinguished from the negative assertion with interrogative meaning, assuming a negative reply (=' you don't think so, surely?'):

II. 362 D οὖ τί που οἴει, ..., ὦ Σώκρατες, ἱκανῶς εἰρῆσθαι περὶ τοῦ λόγου;

β. Slightly different from both is the use in

V. 455 E (again assuming an affirmative answer) γυμναστικὴ δ' ἄρα οὔ, οὐδὲ πολεμική; ' And (will you tell me that) there is not an athletic nor yet a warlike woman?' Cp. Theaet. 145 A ἆρ' οὐδὲ γεωμετρικός; 'But will you tell me that he is not a geometrician?'

γ. ἦ and ἆρα, emphatically interrogative, commonly anticipate a negative reply.

(1) I. 348 C ἦ τὴν δικαιοσύνην κακίαν; 'Do you mean to tell me that Justice is Vice?' (The particle here might ironically anticipate an affirmative answer, but the following examples confirm the above rendering.)

III. 396 B τὰ τοιαῦτα ἦ μιμήσονται; 'Shall we allow them to imitate such things as these?'

V. 469 C ἦ καλῶς ἔχει; 'Is that an honourable thing?'

VIII. 552 A ἦ δοκεῖ ὀρθῶς ἔχειν;

(2) VII. 523 E τί δὲ δή; τὸ μέγεθος . . . ἆρα ἱκανῶς ὁρᾷ; (resumed with ἆρ' οὐκ ἐνδεῶς immediately afterwards).

δ. But ἆρα; with ironical emphasis is sometimes practically equivalent to ἆρ' οὐ;

VI. 484 C τόδε δέ, ἦν δ' ἐγώ, ἆρα δῆλον . . . ; Καὶ πῶς, ἔφη, οὐ δῆλον;

Cp. Soph. 221 D ἆρ', ὦ πρὸς θεῶν, ἠγνοήκαμεν, κ.τ.λ., 'Can it be that we have failed to recognize their kinship?' i.e. 'Are they not, after all, akin?'

ε. And ἦ in ἦ γάρ; 'Surely that is so?' puts a strong affirmation with an interrogative tone (cp. supra a).

Gorg. 449 D ἡ ὑφαντικὴ περὶ τὴν τῶν ἱματίων ἐργασίαν· ἦ γάρ; 'Surely that is so?'

In X. 607 C, however, this use is 'mixed' with the ordinary interrogative use of οὔ.

ἦ γάρ . . . οὐ κηλεῖ ὑπ' αὐτῆς καὶ σύ ; 'Do not you feel her charm ? Surely you do ? '

*Obs.*—This use of ἦ may be pressed into service to account for VI. 500 A ἦ, καὶ ἐὰν οὕτω θεῶνται. But ἦ καὶ ἐάν may be corrupted from ἦ οὐκ ἐάν, through dittographia of ε and dropping of ου.

ζ. For ἆρα μή, μῶν, μῶν μή (I. 351 E, VI. 505 C) in doubtful questions, see the Lexica.

(c) Exceptional uses of μή. These mostly occur where § 38. either some generalized notion, or some idea of prohibition, has been implied.

a. Where a relative has preceded :

II. 357 B ὅσαι ἀβλαβεῖς καὶ μηδὲν . . . γίγνεται ἄλλο, κ.τ.λ. (See above, p. 174, 2 (*b*).)

VIII. 559 B ᾗ τε μὴ παῦσαι ζῶντα δυνατή (so *q*). See note.

X. 605 E οἷον ἑαυτὸν . . . μὴ ἀξιοῖ εἶναι. Μή is here used in putting the case generally.

In Hipp. Maj. 295 C οἱ ἂν δοκῶσι τοιοῦτοι εἶναι οἷοι μὴ δυνατοὶ ὁρᾶν, the hypothetical turn of expression follows οἱ ἂν δοκῶσιν.

β. In *oratio obliqua* (*M. and T.*, § 685).

I. 346 E διὰ δὴ ταῦτα ἔγωγε . . . καὶ ἄρτι ἔλεγον μηδένα ἐθέλειν ἑκόντα ἄρχειν—recalling the *general* statement in 345 E τὰς ἄλλας ἀρχὰς . . . ὅτι οὐδεὶς ἐθέλει ἄρχειν ἑκών.

X. 602 A πότερον ἐκ τοῦ χρῆσθαι ἐπιστήμην ἕξει ὧν ἂν γράφῃ, εἴτε καλὰ καὶ ὀρθὰ εἴτε μή ;

Theaet. 155 A μηδέποτε μηδὲν ἂν μεῖζον . . . γενέσθα . . . τοῦτο μήτε αὐξάνεσθαί ποτε μήτε φθίνειν. Socrates is recording the ' postulates' or *a priori determinations* of the mind. Ἄν in the former sentence adds the notion of impossibility. So τίς ἄν in Apol. 27 D τίς ἂν ἀνθρώπων θεῶν μὲν παῖδας ἡγοῖτο εἶναι, θεοὺς δὲ μή ;

γ. A shadowy sense of prohibition seems present in VIII. 553 D where οὐδέν . . . ἐᾷ λογίζεσθαι is followed by τιμᾶν μηδέν, as if ἀναγκάζει or some such word had preceded. So possibly in III. 407 D οὐκ ἐπιχειρεῖν . . . μὴ οἴεσθαι δεῖν θεραπεύειν, the change to μή is occasioned by some reminiscence of καταδεῖξαι . . . προστάττειν, preceding. See note in loco.

*Obs.*—For idiomatic accumulation of negatives, see especially x. 610 A–C ἢ τοίνυν . . . ἀπόλλυσθαι.

§ 39.                   **14. Formulae.**

(*a*) Of question—ἢ οὔ ; τίς μηχανὴ μὴ οὐ, &c. For ἦ γάρ ; see above p. 210, ε.

(*b*) Of reply—πάνυ γε, σφόδρα γε, καὶ μάλα. πάνυ μὲν οὖν, παντάπασι μὲν οὖν, κομιδῇ μὲν οὖν. φαίνεται, οὐ φαίνεται, δοκεῖ γε δή. πῶς γάρ ; πῶς γὰρ οὔ ; τί μὴν (sc. ἄλλο) ; (See above, under μήν, p. 206.)

The degree of assent or dissent implied in each case varies somewhat with the context.

(*c*) Of connexion, τί δέ ; τὸ δὲ γε, ἄλλο τι ἤ (cp. Herod. II. 14, &c.), ἄλλο τι ; ἄλλο τι οὖν ;

α. The question whether τί δέ and τί δὲ δή are to form a separate sentence, or to be joined to the words that follow them, is one that can only be determined by the immediate context. See especially I. 349 B, C, E ; V. 468 A and notes in locis.

β. For ἄλλο τι in apposition to the sentence, see below, p. 221.

*Obs.* 1.— Single words habitually used in parenthesis are not treated as breaking the unity of a clause, but may be immediately followed by an enclitic. This applies, not only to οἴει and the like (for which see especially VIII. 564 A), but to a vocative, e. g. I. 337 E πῶς γὰρ ἄν, ἔφην ἐγώ, ὦ βέλτιστε, τὶς ἀποκρίναιτο ;

*Obs.* 2.—For the common transference of ἤδη, ἔτι, πω from temporal to logical succession, see especially II. 370 D, IV. 430 D— 432 B.

*Obs.* 3.—ἀληθῶς, τῇ ἀληθείᾳ, ὄντως, τῷ ὄντι may be taken under the present head. M. Schanz has shown that in the later dialogues ὄντως gradually takes the place of τῷ ὄντι. But when he argues that because ὄντως occurs five times in Bb. V–VII while it is absent from

Bb. i–iv, Bb. v–vii are 'late,' he loses sight of his own observation that τῷ ὄντι is naturally avoided in conjunction with other cases of ὤν.

## VI. Ellipse and Pleonasm. § 40.

1. ELLIPSE.

To maintain the effect of conversation and to avoid monotony, Plato constantly represents his speakers as omitting what, although essential to the meaning, is assumed to be obvious to the hearers. Hence a frequent duty of the interpreter is to supply the word or words 'understood' :—especially (*a*) in references, (*b*) in replies, (*c*) in antitheses, (*d*) in transitions, and (*e*) where a word of simple meaning is *absorbed* in some neighbouring word. Under this head should also be noticed (*f*) familiar abbreviations.

(*a*) *In references.*

I. 341 B τὸν ὡς ἔπος εἰπεῖν (sc. οὕτω προσαγορευόμενον). The incomplete expression is explained by the reference to 340 D λέγομεν τῷ ῥήματι οὕτως.

(*b*) *In replies.*

I. 334 D μηδαμῶς (sc. οὕτω τιθῶμεν).

I. 349 B οὐδὲ τῆς δικαίας (sc. πράξεως).

IV. 428 E πολύ, ἔφη, χαλκέας (sc. πλείους οἶμαι ἐνέσεσθαι τῇ πόλει).

V. 451 D κοινῇ, ἔφη, πάντα (sc. οἰόμεθα δεῖν αὐτὰς πράττειν τοῖς ἄρρεσιν).

V. 468 A λέγ᾽, ἔφη, ποῖ ἄν (sc. καταφαίνοιτό σοι).

V. 473 A ἃ σὺ ἐπιτάττεις (sc. ἀποφαίνειν ὡς δυνατά ἐστι καὶ ᾗ).

VI. 508 C ὅταν δέ γ᾽, οἶμαι, ὧν ὁ ἥλιος καταλάμπῃ (sc. ἐπ᾽ ἐκεῖνά τις τρέπῃ τοὺς ὀφθαλμούς).

VIII. 552 C ἐδόκει (sc. τῶν ἀρχόντων εἶναι).

IX. 585 D σῶμα δὲ αὐτὸ ψυχῆς οὐκ οἴει οὕτως ; (sc. ἧττον ἀληθείας τε καὶ οὐσίας μετέχειν).

Cp. Phaed. 73 A ἐνὶ μὲν λόγῳ, ἔφη ὁ Κέβης, καλλίστῳ (sc.

ταῦτα ἀποδείκνυται supplied from ποῖαι τούτων αἱ ἀποδείξεις; preceding).

*Obs.* 1.—In continuing a conversation, the indirect form is sometimes used with the ellipse of εἰπέ. Rep. I. 348 B ὁποτέρως ... ἀρέσκει; Euthyd. 271 B. Cp. Polit. 261 E ὁπότερον ἂν ἐν τῷ λόγῳ ξυμβαίνῃ (sc. ὀνομάσομεν).

*Obs.* 2.—A special idiom is the ellipse of the apodosis with a new protasis, participial or otherwise.

Phaedr. 228 D δείξας γε πρῶτον, ὦ φιλότης (see above, p. 179, *Obs.* 3).

Rep. I. 338 C ἐὰν μάθω γε πρῶτον;

I. 340 A ἐὰν σύ γ', ἔφη, αὐτῷ μαρτυρήσῃς.

*Obs.* 3.—Note the occasional omission of a comparative with ἤ following.

I. 335 A προσθεῖναι ... ἢ ... ἐλέγομεν.

Symp. 220 E ἐμὲ λαβεῖν ἢ σαυτόν.

### (c) *In antitheses.*

II. 360 A ἔξω δὲ δήλῳ (sc. **ἔξω δὲ** αὐτῷ στρέφοντι τὴν σφενδόνην **δήλῳ** γίγνεσθαι).

III. 412 D μὴ δέ, τοὐναντίον (sc. εἰ δὲ οἴοιτο ἐκείνου μὴ εὖ πράττοντος, ξυμβαίνειν καὶ ἑαυτῷ κακῶς πράττειν).

IV. 444 D τὸ δὲ νόσον παρὰ φύσιν, κ.τ.λ. (sc. **τὸ δὲ νόσον** ποιεῖν ἐστὶ τὰ ἐν τῷ σώματι **παρὰ φύσιν** καθιστάναι, κ.τ.λ.).

### (d) *In transitions* :—i. e. in passing from one alternative to another, or to a new topic.

I. 351 B ἢ ἀνάγκη αὐτῇ μετὰ δικαιοσύνης (sc. τὴν δύναμιν ταύτην ἔχειν);

II. 366 D ὡς δέ (sc. οὕτως ἔχει), δῆλον.

IV. 428 C τί δέ; τὴν ὑπὲρ τῶν ἐκ τοῦ χαλκοῦ (sc. διὰ τὴν ... σκευῶν ἐπιστήμην);

VI. 493 D ὅτι μὲν γάρ, κ.τ.λ. (sc. δῆλόν ἐστι, from δοκεῖ preceding).

*Obs.*—In Plato, as in other Greek, the affirmative notion is often assumed in passing from a negative—e. g. ἕκαστος supplied from οὐδείς in

II. 366 D οὐδεὶς ἑκὼν δίκαιος, ἀλλ' ὑπὸ ἀνανδρίας ... ψέγει τὸ ἀδικεῖν.

VI. 500 B οὐδὲ γάρ ... σχολὴ ... βλέπειν ... ἀλλὰ (καιρὸς) μιμεῖσθαι

And sometimes the word to be supplied is more *general* than that which precedes—e. g.

v. 469 c μηδὲ ″Ελληνα ἄρα δοῦλον ἐκτῆσθαι (sc. δεῖ from δοκεῖ δίκαιον, κ.τ.λ. preceding).

Somewhat similarly in VIII. 557 E μηδὲ αὖ, ἐάν τις ἄρχειν νόμος σε διακωλύῃ ἢ δικάζειν, μηδὲν ἧττον καὶ ἄρχειν καὶ δικάζειν, the general notion of 'no compulsion' (sc. ἐξεῖναι) is continued from μηδεμίαν ἀνάγκην supra. 'There is nothing to compel you any the less for that to be a ruler and judge,' i. e. there is nothing any more on that account to prevent you from exercising both functions.

(*e*) *Absorption by a neighbouring word.*   The want of the § 41. word omitted is not felt because of another word which suggests it to the mind.   Cp. Herod. II. 87 τοὺς τὰ πολυτελέστατα (sc. σκευαζομένους) σκευάζουσι νεκρούς.

II. 358 D εἴ σοι βουλομένῳ (sc. λέγω) ἃ λέγω.

II. 364 A πονηροὺς πλουσίους (sc. ὄντας) καὶ ἄλλας δυνάμεις ἔχοντας.

II. 366 E ἄλλως ἢ δόξας (sc. ἐπαινοῦντες, κ.τ.λ.).

II. 372 E καὶ ὄψα (sc. ἔχειν) ἅπερ καὶ οἱ νῦν ἔχουσι.

IV. 421 B ὁ δ' ἐκεῖνο λέγων . . . (sc. ἔλεγεν).

IV. 439 A τῶν τινός (sc. ὄντων suggested by εἶναι following). See note in loco.

V. 452 A παρὰ τὸ ἔθος (sc. φαινόμενα) γελοῖα ἂν φαίνοιτο.

VI. 488 A ναύκληρον (sc. μὲν) μεγέθει μέν, κ.τ.λ.

VI. 510 B ἀλλ' αὖθις, ἦν δ' ἐγώ (sc. μαθήσει, which follows soon).

VII. 517 D φαίνεται . . . γελοῖος (sc. ὢν) . . . ἀμβλυώττων.

IX. 589 C ὁ δὲ ψέκτης οὐδὲν ὑγιὲς (sc. λέγει, from ἀληθεύει preceding or ψέγει following) οὐδ' εἰδὼς ψέγει ὅ τι ψέγει.

X. 615 B, C τῶν δὲ εὐθὺς γενομένων (sc. ἀποθανόντων: the whole passage relating to the dead).   See Essay on Text, p. 121.

*Obs.*—Such omissions are not purely accidental, but are due to instinctive avoidance of cumbrous tautology.

(*f*) *Familiar abbreviations.*

α. Certain adjectives readily dispense with the verb substantive. The idiom is frequent with ἄξιος and ἕτοιμος (Parm. 137 C ἕτοιμός σοι, ὦ Παρμενίδη) but is extended by Plato to other words.

II. 358 A ἀλλ' ἐγώ τις, ὡς ἔοικε, δυσμαθής.

III. 407 B ἀβίωτον τῷ μὴ μελετῶντι.

X. 598 D εὐήθης τις ἄνθρωπος.

*Obs.*—The substantive verb is similarly omitted with ἀνάγκη, τίς μηχανή, &c., also in εἰ μὴ εἴ, κ.τ.λ. : III. 411 E, IX. 581 D.   In II. 370 E ὧν ἂν αὐτοῖς χρεία, the subjunctive ᾖ is dropped.

β. Ἄλλος is constantly omitted with interrogatives and negatives.

I. 332 C ἀλλὰ τί οἴει (sc. ἄλλο) ;

I. 348 C ἀλλὰ τί μήν (sc. ἄλλο) ;

V. 461 D οὐδαμῶς (sc. ἄλλως).

V. 472 B οὐδέν (sc. ἄλλο).

Also in the hypothetical formula εἰ μή τι ἀλλά.

On ἄλλο τι, which is sometimes called an ellipse, see below, p. 221, *Obs.* 2.   Another phrase which is appositional not elliptical is ἐν ἀνθ' ἑνός (I. 331 B).

γ. The indefinite subject is dropped, as in the common idiom, κωλύει ἐν τῷ νόμῳ, &c.

IV. 445 A ἐάν τε λανθάνῃ ἐάν τε μή (sc. ὁ δίκαιά τε πράττων καὶ καλὰ ἐπιτηδεύων).

V. 478 B ἆρ' οὖν τὸ μὴ ὂν **δοξάζει** (sc. ὁ δοξάζων).

VI. 498 B, C ὅταν δέ ... πολιτικῶν δὲ καὶ στρατειῶν ἐκτὸς γίγνηται (sc. ὁ ἄνθρωπος).   Cp. Cratylus 410 B ἴσως οὖν **λέγει** (sc. ὁ ἀέρα λέγων).

δ. Transitive verbs used absolutely, i. e. without express object.

I. 335 D ψύχειν . . . ὑγραίνειν . . . βλάπτειν.

II. 368 B ὅ τι **χρήσωμαι** (sc. ὑμῖν or τῷ λόγῳ).

III. 392 D περαίνουσιν.

III. 411 A ὅταν μέν τις . . . **παρέχῃ**.

III. 411 E διαπράττεται.

IV. 420 C ἀπολαβόντες.

VII. 525 D οὐδαμῇ ἀποδεχόμενον.

IX. 585 E χαίρειν ἂν ποιοῖ (sc. τὸν ἄνθρωπον).

*Obs.*—Several of these words (χρῆσθαι, περαίνειν, ἀπολαμβάνειν, ἀποδέχεσθαι) belong to the technical language of the dialectical method. See also

V. 467 B οἷα . . . φιλεῖ (sc. γίγνεσθαι).

VIII. 565 E οἷα δὴ φιλοῦσι (sc. ποιεῖν).

ε. In some technical phrases a feminine abstract substantive is suppressed, as e. g. τέχνη in ἡ ἰατρική, &c. (*sexcenties*). Similarly

III. 397 B πρὸς τὴν αὐτήν (sc. χορδήν), 'in the same tone.' See note in loco.

IV. 432 A δι' ὅλης (sc. τῆς λύρας).

Ibid. διὰ πασῶν (sc. τῶν χορδῶν).

ζ. One of two alternative or correlative expressions is sometimes dropped.

VI. 486 C (πότερον) εὐμαθὴς ἢ δυσμαθής.

*Obs.*—Thus ὁ μέν is omitted where ὁ δέ follows, e. g. Phaedr. 266 A σκαιά, τὰ δὲ δεξιά. This idiom appears more frequently in the later dialogues (Tim. 63 E &c.).

N.B.—For the special idiom with μεταξύ (VI. 498 A) see above, p. 198, γ.

η. Other conversational ellipses are

I. 343 C οὕτω πόρρω εἶ (sc. τῆς γνώσεως).

V. 467 C ὅσα ἄνθρωποι (γιγνώσκουσιν).

## 2. PLEONASM.                                                    § 42.

As the omission of words gives an impression of ease and familiarity, so their redundancy enhances the appearance of leisure and freedom (cp. Theaet. 172 C foll.). Plato's periods 'are not made but grow' (cp. Phaedr. 264); he drifts down the wind of his discourse (Rep. II. 365 D). Hence when a new thought or mode of expression has occurred to the speaker, he does not wait to round off the sentence before introducing it, but weaves it into that which is half finished, often to the sacrifice of formal coherency. Thus rhetoric interferes with grammar.

A good instance of Plato's love of amplification occurs in II (380 A foll.), where Socrates insists that evil must not be attributed to God:

'Αλλ' ἐάν τις ποιῇ ἐν οἷς ταῦτα τὰ ἰαμβεῖα ἔνεστι, τὰ τῆς Νιόβης πάθη, ἢ τὰ Πελοπιδῶν ἢ τὰ Τρωϊκὰ ἤ τι ἄλλο τῶν τοιούτων, ἢ οὐ θεοῦ ἔργα ἐατέον αὐτὰ λέγειν, ἢ εἰ θεοῦ, ἐξευρετέον αὐτοῖς σχεδὸν ὃν νῦν ἡμεῖς λόγον ζητοῦμεν, καὶ λεκτέον, ὡς ὁ μὲν θεὸς δίκαιά τε καὶ ἀγαθὰ εἰργάζετο, οἱ δὲ ὠνίναντο κολαζόμενοι· ὡς δὲ ἄθλιοι μὲν οἱ δίκην διδόντες, ἦν δὲ δὴ ὁ δρῶν ταῦτα θεός, οὐκ ἐατέον λέγειν τὸν ποιητήν. ἀλλ', εἰ μὲν ὅτι ἐδεήθησαν κολάσεως λέγοιεν, ὡς ἄθλιοι οἱ κακοί, διδόντες δὲ δίκην ὠφελοῦντο ὑπὸ τοῦ θεοῦ, ἐατέον· κακῶν δὲ αἴτιον φάναι θεόν τινι γίγνεσθαι ἀγαθὸν ὄντα, διαμαχητέον παντὶ τρόπῳ μήτε τινὰ λέγειν ταῦτα ἐν τῇ αὐτοῦ πόλει, εἰ μέλλει εὐνομήσεσθαι, μήτε τινὰ ἀκούειν, μήτε νεώτερον μήτε πρεσβύτερον, μήτε ἐν μέτρῳ μήτε ἄνευ μέτρου μυθολογοῦντα, ὡς οὔτε ὅσια ἂν λεγόμενα, εἰ λέγοιτο, οὔτε ξύμφορα ἡμῖν οὔτε σύμφωνα αὐτὰ αὑτοῖς.

Here observe (1) the accumulation of examples characteristically summed up with ἤ τι ἄλλο τῶν τοιούτων, (2) the disjunctive mode of statement, put first affirmatively (*either one or other*), then negatively (*not both*); then affirmatively again, then once more negatively with increased explicitness and emphasis, and with the characteristic qualification εἰ μέλλει εὐνομήσεσθαι. Observe also (3) the addition of the participle μυθολογοῦντα, and of εἰ λέγοιτο. Note further (4) the pleonastic φάναι anticipating λέγειν, and (5) the clinching of the argument in the last clause, ὡς οὔτε ὅσια, κ.τ.λ. The examination of this one passage may prepare the student for much that he will find elsewhere. Cp. especially VI. 489; II. 374 B–D 'Αλλ' ἄρα . . . παρασχομένῳ; IV. 421 B–C. A simile or illustration is often expanded in this way, e. g. III. 402 A ὥσπερ ἄρα, κ.τ.λ. See also the pleonastic use of participles in Symp. 218 A, B.

(*a*) The most ordinary pleonasms are those in which § 43. a notion already implied is made explicit in a subsequent phrase.

II. 358 E πλέονι δὲ κακῷ ὑπερβάλλειν, κ.τ.λ.

II. 371 D καπήλων . . . γένεσιν ἐμποιεῖ.

VI. 486 D ζητῶμεν δεῖν.

VI. 490 A παρὰ δόξαν τοῖς νῦν δοκουμένοις.

VIII. 555 B τοῦ προκειμένου ἀγαθοῦ, τοῦ ὡς πλουσιώτατον δεῖν γίγνεσθαι.

(*b*) Specially Platonic is the expletive use of ἐπιχειρεῖν, φιλεῖν, κινδυνεύειν, ἔχομαι and other verbs as auxiliaries. See also VI. 500 D μελετῆσαι εἰς ἀνθρώπων ἤθη . . . τιθέναι: VII. 520 B ἐκτίνειν . . . προθυμεῖσθαι. So Cephalus, in his garrulous talk about old age, speaks of the time when one *comes near* to *thinking* that he is about to die, ἐπειδάν τις ἐγγὺς ᾖ τοῦ οἴεσθαι τελευτήσειν (I. 330 D). For the pleonastic or expletive use of participles (ἔχων, &c.) see above, p. 177 (*f*).

(*c*) The amplifying, expansive tendency of Plato's language has a distinct bearing on the treatment of the text. The excision of supposed 'glosses' and 'accretions' by which editors have tried to prune away such redundancies, must be carried far beyond the limit of even plausible conjecture, if the tendency itself is to be disproved. (See Essay on Text, p. 110.)

V. 477 B, C φήσομεν δυνάμεις εἶναι γένος τι τῶν ὄντων, αἷς δὴ καὶ ἡμεῖς δυνάμεθα ἃ δυνάμεθα καὶ ἄλλο πᾶν ὅ τί περ ἂν δύνηται, οἷον λέγω ὄψιν καὶ ἀκοὴν τῶν δυνάμεων εἶναι, εἰ ἄρα μανθάνεις ὃ βούλομαι λέγειν τὸ εἶδος.

*Obs.*—The addition of an equivalent phrase often adds a touch of admiration or scorn.

I. 331 A ἡδεῖα ἐλπίς . . . καὶ ἀγαθὴ γηροτρόφος.

II. 364 E διὰ θυσιῶν καὶ παιδιᾶς ἡδονῶν.

(*d*) A special idiom, not exclusively Platonic (see L. and S., s. v. II. 8), is the pleonastic (or adverbial) use of ἄλλος.

Cp. especially Hom. Odys. IX. 367 μήτηρ ἠδὲ πατὴρ ἠδ'

ἄλλοι πάντες ἑταῖροι: Herod. IV. 179, § 1 ἄλλην τε ἑκατόμβην καὶ δὴ καὶ τρίποδα χάλκεον.

a. ἄλλος attributive.

II. 368 B ἐκ τοῦ **ἄλλου** τοῦ ὑμετέρου τρόπου, 'from your manner of life, not from your words.'

II. 371 A γεωργῶν τε καὶ τῶν ἄλλων δημιουργῶν ... καὶ δὴ καὶ τῶν **ἄλλων** διακόνων, 'and *also* of that ministering class.'

III. 404 A, B πολλὰς μεταβολὰς ... μεταβάλλοντας ὑδάτων τε καὶ τῶν **ἄλλων** σίτων, 'enduring many changes of drinking-water and *also* of food.'

β. In other cases ἄλλος is predicative or adverbial, but still pleonastic:

X. 617 B **ἄλλας** δὲ καθημένας πέριξ, κ.τ.λ., 'and sitting there, *moreover*, round about.'

The Fates are thus contradistinguished from the Sirens (or perhaps 'there were others ... daughters of necessity,' &c.). Cp. the idiomatic ἄλλως in Gorg. 470 D συγγενόμενος ἂν γνοίης, **ἄλλως** δὲ αὐτόθεν οὐ γιγνώσκεις.

(*e*) Αὐτός τε καί, with expansion of the correlative phrase:

III. 398 A αὐτός τε καὶ τὰ ποιήματα **βουλόμενος ἐπιδείξασθαι**, 'bringing his poems for exhibition with him too.'

IV. 427 D αὐτός τε καὶ **τὸν ἀδελφὸν παρακάλει**, 'and call your brother also to assist.'

VII. 535 E ᾗ ἂν ... χαλεπῶς φέρῃ αὐτή τε καὶ ἑτέρων ψευδομένων **ὑπεραγανακτῇ**.

(*f*) Double comparative and superlative:

I. 331 B οὐκ ἐλάχιστον ... χρησιμώτατον.

II. 362 C θεοφιλέστερον ... εἶναι μᾶλλον προσήκειν.

§ 44.                    **VII. Apposition.**

One very frequent consequence of Plato's discursiveness is what may be loosely termed the apposition of sentences, —the second being often not the exact equivalent, but an explanation or expansion of the first. Cp. Herod. I. 23, § 2 θώυμα μέγιστον . . . .'Αρίονα . . . ἐπὶ δελφῖνος ἐξενειχθέντα:

VI. 117, § 2 θώνμα γενέσθαι τοιόνδε, 'Αθηναῖον ἄνδρα 'Επίζηλον
. . . τῶν ὀμμάτων στερηθῆναι.

Three cases may be distinguished :—

1. Where a pronoun or a pronominal phrase or adverb
resuming a preceding statement is followed by a restatement of the same thing, more or less expanded or modified.

I. 337 C καὶ σὺ οὕτω ποιήσεις ; ὧν ἐγὼ ἀπεῖπον, τούτων τι ἀποκρινεῖ ;

II. 365 C ἐπὶ τοῦτο δὴ τρεπτέον ὅλως· πρόθυρα μὲν καὶ σχῆμα
κύκλῳ περὶ ἐμαυτὸν σκιαγραφίαν ἀρετῆς περιγραπτέον, κ.τ.λ.

III. 416 B μὴ τοιοῦτον . . . ποιήσωσι πρὸς τοὺς πολίτας, ἐπειδὴ
αὐτῶν κρείττους εἰσίν, ἀντὶ ξυμμάχων εὐμενῶν δεσπόταις ἀγρίοις
ἀφομοιωθῶσιν.

IV. 429 E, 430 A τοιοῦτον . . . ὑπόλαβε . . . ἐργάζεσθαι καὶ ἡμᾶς
. . . μηδὲν οἷον ἄλλο μηχανᾶσθαι ἤ, κ.τ.λ.

VII. 517 B τὰ δ' οὖν ἐμοὶ φαινόμενα οὕτω φαίνεται, ἐν τῷ
γνωστῷ . . . μόγις ὁρᾶσθαι, κ.τ.λ.

VII. 532 A οὕτω καὶ ὅταν τις τῷ διαλέγεσθαι ἐπιχειρῇ, ἄνευ
πασῶν τῶν αἰσθήσεων διὰ τοῦ λόγου ἐπ' αὐτὸ ὃ ἔστιν ἕκαστον
ὁρμᾷ (*subjunctive*) καὶ μὴ ἀποστῇ, κ.τ.λ.   Here the *protasis*
is expanded.

X. 605 B ταὐτὸν καὶ τὸν μιμητικὸν ποιητὴν φήσομεν κακὴν
πολιτείαν . . . ἐμποιεῖν.

*Obs.* 1.—The frequent formula of transition with the interrogative
follows the analogy of this mode of construction—

I. 332 E τί δὲ ὁ δίκαιος ; ἐν τίνι πράξει, κ.τ.λ. *et passim.*

This form is better suited to the majority of cases than the other
punctuation τί δέ; ὁ δίκαιος ἐν τίνι πράξει, κ.τ.λ.

VII. 515 B τί δὲ τῶν παραφερομένων ; οὐ ταὐτὸν τοῦτο ;
although the latter is also sometimes required by the context :

VII. 517 D τί δέ ; τόδε οἴει τι θαυμαστόν, κ.τ.λ.

*Obs.* 2.—So ἄλλο τι, when not followed by ἤ, forms virtually
a separate clause in apposition.

I. 337 C ἄλλο τι οὖν, ἔφη, καὶ σὺ οὕτω ποιήσεις ; 'You mean to say
that that is what you are going to do ?'

So I. 331 B ἐν ἀντ' ἑνός : VI. 498 B πᾶν τοὐναντίον.

Also τὸ δέ (Soph. 248 D ; Laws III. 676 c).

VII. 527 A τὸ δ' ἔστι που πᾶν τὸ μάθημα, κ.τ.λ. (*Digest*, § 22).

*Obs.* 3.—Similarly, the relative pronoun, although not forming a separate clause, often introduces a long sentence, towards which it stands in apposition. (*Digest*, §§ 10 ff.)

II. 368 D οἷανπερ ἂν εἰ, κ.τ.λ. 'A method similar to that we should have adopted, if' &c.

IV. 434 D ἐκτελέσωμεν τὴν σκέψιν, ἣν ᾠήθημεν, κ.τ.λ.

Cp. Phaedr. 249 D περὶ τῆς τετάρτης μανίας, ἥν, κ.τ.λ.

Protag. 352 E, 353 A τὸ πάθος, ὅ φασιν ὑπὸ τῶν ἡδονῶν ἡττᾶσθαι.

So οἷον, VI. 488 A οἷον οἱ γραφῆς, κ.τ.λ. 'As painters do, when they delineate monsters.'

§ 45.     2. Apposition of Clauses,—where a statement is immediately followed by a parallel statement, in the same construction, with no conjunction between (Asyndeton).

I. 329 C, D παντάπασι γὰρ τῶν γε τοιούτων ἐν τῷ γήρᾳ **πολλὴ εἰρήνη** γίγνεται καὶ ἐλευθερία, ἐπειδὰν αἱ ἐπιθυμίαι παύσωνται κατατείνουσαι καὶ χαλάσωσι, παντάπασι τὸ τοῦ **Σοφοκλέους** γίγνεται, **δεσποτῶν** πάνυ πολλῶν ἔστι καὶ μαινομένων **ἀπηλλάχθαι.** (Some MSS. insert γάρ after ἐπειδάν.)

II. 359 B, C **εἰ τοιόνδε ποιήσαιμεν** τῇ διανοίᾳ· **δόντες ἐξουσίαν** ... **ἐπακολουθήσαιμεν.**

V. 457 C λέγε δή, ἴδω.

VII. 530 A οὐκ οἴει . . . τὰ ἐν αὐτῷ ;

VII. 540 E **διασκευωρήσωνται** . . . **ἐκπέμψωσιν.**

VIII. 557 C κινδυνεύει . . . καλλίστη αὕτη τῶν πολιτειῶν εἶναι· ὥσπερ ἱμάτιον ποικίλον . . . καὶ αὕτη . . . καλλίστη ἂν φαίνοιτο.

IX. 589 D τοιόνδε τι γίγνεται, λαμβάνων, κ.τ.λ. Cp. Phaedo 95 C ; Gorg. 493 E.

*Obs.* 1.—Between clauses thus related a question is sometimes interposed,

VII. 540 E ὅταν . . . διασκευωρήσωνται . . . : **Πῶς** ; ἔφη : . . . ἐκπέμψωσιν.

*Obs.* 2.—Slightly different from the foregoing is the emphatic repetition, with asyndeton, of what has been said—

(*a*) giving the effect of a second apodosis :

I. 339 E οἶον τοίνυν . . . ὡμολογῆσθαι . . . ὅταν . . ., ἆρα τότε . . . οὐκ ἀναγκαῖον συμβαίνειν, κ.τ.λ.

I. 340 B τοῦτο ποιητέον εἶναι, κ.τ.λ.

II. 372 B θρέψονται . . . εὐωχήσονται.

So III. 413 c; VI. 497 B.

N.B.—The case of VIII. 545 B ὄνομα γὰρ οὐκ ἔχω ... ἄλλο· ἢ τιμοκρατίαν, κ.τ.λ. is peculiar and should probably be met as W. H. Thompson suggested by reading ἀλλ' ἢ τιμοκρατίαν, κ.τ.λ.

(β) The protasis is likewise (1) repeated with variation, or (2) an additional protasis subjoined.

(1) VII. 529 B ἐάν τέ τις ἄνω κεχηνὼς ... ἐπιχειρῇ μανθάνειν, οὔτε μαθεῖν ἄν ποτέ φημι αὐτόν, κ.τ.λ.

(2) I. 331 C εἴ τις λάβοι ... εἰ μανεὶς ἀπαιτοῖ. Cp. Theaet. 210 B, C ἐὰν τοίνυν ... ἐγκύμων ἐπιχειρῇς γίγνεσθαι ... ἐάν τε γίγνῃ ... ἐάν τε κενὸς ᾖς, where the two alternative hypotheses are subordinate to the principal one.

*Obs.* 3.—This, like other Platonic idioms, is used with greater abruptness in the Laws. See especially, Laws IV. 708 B ὅταν μὴ τὸν τῶν ἑσμῶν γίγνηται τρόπον, ἓν γένος ἀπὸ μιᾶς ἰὸν χώρας οἰκίζηται.

## VIII.  Co-ordination (Parataxis).  § 46.

While in all syntax the subordination of clauses gradually supersedes their co-ordination, this tendency is checked in Greek by the fondness for analytical and antithetical expression, not only giving to co-ordination a temporary survival, but also favouring some independent developments of it, which interfere with the complete regularity of subordination.   The crossing of the two methods may confuse the interpreter, but it enriches the style.

1. Interposition of one or more co-ordinate or parallel clauses with μέν or τέ after the sentence is begun.

(*a*) μέν.

II. 367 E καὶ ἐγὼ ἀκούσας, ἀεὶ μὲν δὴ τὴν φύσιν τοῦ τε Γλαύκωνος καὶ τοῦ Ἀδειμάντου ἠγάμην, ἀτὰρ οὖν καὶ τότε πάνυ γε ἤσθην.

III. 407 C, D φῶμεν καὶ Ἀσκληπιὸν τοὺς μὲν φύσει ... τὰ δ' εἴσω ... θεραπεύειν (see notes in loco).

III. 415 A ἅτε οὖν ξυγγενεῖς ὄντες πάντες τὸ μὲν πολὺ ὁμοίους ἂν ὑμῖν αὐτοῖς γεννῷτε, ἔστι δ' ὅτε ἐκ χρυσοῦ γεννηθείη ἂν ἀργυροῦν καὶ ἐξ ἀργυροῦ χρυσοῦν ἔκγονον καὶ τἄλλα πάντα οὕτως ἐξ ἀλλήλων.

IV. 421 A, B εἰ μὲν οὖν ἡμεῖς μὲν ... ὁ δ' ἐκεῖνο λέγων ... ἄλλο ἄν τι ἢ πόλιν λέγοι.

VIII. 552 B ἢ ἐδόκει μὲν τῶν ἀρχόντων εἶναι, τῇ δὲ ἀληθείᾳ οὔτε ἄρχων οὔτε ὑπηρέτης ἦν αὐτῆς, ἀλλὰ τῶν ἑτοίμων ἀναλωτής; Cp. Laws VI. 765 E ἄνθρωπος δέ, ὥς φαμεν, ἥμερον, κ.τ.λ., where although μέν is omitted, the mode of expression is virtually the same.

(b) τέ.

II. 357 A ὁ γὰρ Γλαύκων ἀεί τε ἀνδρειότατος ὢν τυγχάνει πρὸς ἅπαντα, καὶ δὴ καὶ τότε ... οὐκ ἀπεδέξατο.

III. 404 C καὶ ὀρθῶς γε, ἔφη, ἴσασί τε καὶ ἀπέχονται.

See also II. 359 D ἄλλα τε δὴ [ἃ] μυθολογοῦσι θαυμαστά, κ.τ.λ., when the same idiom may perhaps justify the omission of ἅ. as in Par. A.

2. Δέ *in apodosi.*

The use of δ' οὖν in resumption is a special case of this. The general idiom is too common to require further illustration. See, however, Symp. 183 C ἐπειδὰν δέ ... μὴ ἐῶσι ... εἰς δὲ ταὐτά τις αὖ βλέψας, κ.τ.λ., for a striking example of its effect.

Δέ is also added to a participle subjoined to a sentence, VIII. 544 C δευτέρα καὶ δευτέρως ἐπαινουμένη, **καλουμένη δ'** ὀλιγαρχία : IX. 572 E εἰς πᾶσαν παρανομίαν, **ὀνομαζομένην δ'** ... ἐλευθερίαν ἅπασαν.

3. Two complex sentences, opposed with μέν and δέ, are bound together by a single interrogative or negative. This may fairly be regarded as a speciality of Platonic syntax, though not unknown to other Greek writers. In a simpler form it occurs, e. g. in Aesch. Prom. 507, 508—

> μή νυν βροτοὺς μὲν ὠφέλει καιροῦ πέρα,
> σαυτοῦ δ' ἀκήδει δυστυχοῦντος.

Eur. Bacch. 311, 312—

> μηδ', ἢν δοκῇς μέν, ἡ δὲ δόξα σου νοσεῖ,
> φρονεῖν δόκει τι.

Cp. Shakespeare, *M. of V.*, i. 3, 180 :

> 'I like not fair terms and a villain's mind.'

*Macb.* ii. 2, 12 :

> 'The attempt and not the deed confounds us ;'

and a complete example occurs in Lysias, contra Eratosth. § 36 οὐκοῦν δεινόν, εἰ τοὺς μὲν στρατηγούς, οἳ ἐνίκων ναυμαχοῦντες ... θανάτῳ ἐζημιώσατε ... τούτους δέ, οἳ ... ἐποίησαν ἡττηθῆναι ναυμαχοῦντας ... οὐκ ἄρα χρή ... ταῖς ἐσχάταις ζημίαις κολάζεσθαι. (See also Xen. Mem. I. 4, § 17 : III. 4, § 1.) This form is employed where the combination of the two statements is deprecated or denied, i. e. to signify either that they ought not to be true together or cannot be so. The enormity or impossibility is marked more pointedly by the union of the two contradictories in a continuous sentence.

I. 336 E μὴ γὰρ δὴ οἴου, εἰ μὲν χρυσίον ἐζητοῦμεν, οὐκ ἄν ποτε ἡμᾶς ἑκόντας εἶναι ὑποκατακλίνεσθαι ἀλλήλοις ἐν τῇ ζητήσει καὶ διαφθείρειν τὴν εὕρεσιν αὐτοῦ, δικαιοσύνην δὲ ζητοῦντας, πρᾶγμα πολλῶν χρυσίων τιμιώτερον, ἔπειθ' οὕτως ἀνοήτως ὑπείκειν ἀλλήλοις καὶ οὐ σπουδάζειν ὅ τι μάλιστα φανῆναι αὐτό.

II. 374 B, C Ἀλλ' ἄρα τὸν μὲν σκυτοτόμον ... ἢ οὕτω ῥάδιον, ὥστε καὶ γεωργῶν τις ἅμα πολεμικὸς ἔσται ... πεττευτικὸς δὲ ἢ κυβευτικὸς ἱκανῶς οὐδ' ἂν εἷς γένοιτο μὴ αὐτὸ τοῦτο ἐκ παιδὸς ἐπιτηδεύων ;

III. 406 C ὃ ἡμεῖς γελοίως ἐπὶ μέν ... ἐπὶ δέ ... οὐκ, κ.τ.λ.

III. 407 A, B ἀλλ' ἡμᾶς αὐτοὺς διδάξωμεν, πότερον μελετητέον τοῦτο τῷ πλουσίῳ καὶ ἀβίωτον τῷ μὴ μελετῶντι, ἢ νοσοτροφία τεκτονικῇ μὲν καὶ ταῖς ἄλλαις τέχναις ἐμπόδιον τῇ προσέξει τοῦ νοῦ, τὸ δὲ Φωκυλίδου παρακέλευμα οὐδὲν ἐμποδίζει.

IV. 445 A γελοῖον ἔμοιγε φαίνεται τὸ σκέμμα γίγνεσθαι ἤδη, εἰ τοῦ μὲν σώματος τῆς φύσεως διαφθειρομένης δοκεῖ οὐ βιωτὸν εἶναι . . , τῆς δὲ αὐτοῦ τούτου ᾧ ζῶμεν φύσεως ταραττομένης καὶ διαφθειρομένης βιωτὸν ἄρα ἔσται, κ.τ.λ.

V. 456 C οὐκ ἄλλη μὲν ἡμῖν ἄνδρας ποιήσει παιδεία, ἄλλη δὲ γυναῖκας.

IX. 589 D, E εἰ μέν ... εἰ δέ ... οὐκ ἄρα ; and, without μέν, V. 456 A.

Similarly, but with the second statement deferred, VIII. 556 B, C σφᾶς δὲ αὐτοὺς καὶ τοὺς αὐτῶν—ἆρ' οὐ τρυφῶντας μὲν τοὺς νέους, κ.τ.λ. (three lines), αὐτοὺς δὲ πλὴν χρηματισμοῦ τῶν ἄλλων ἠμεληκότας, κ.τ.λ.

X. 600 C ἀλλ' οἴει, ὦ Γλαύκων, κ.τ.λ.

N.B.—Such introductory words as δεινὸν εἰ, γελοῖον εἰ, have the force of a negative.

*Obs.* 1.—A clause is sometimes prefixed or appended to such composite sentences, just as if the meaning had been simply expressed, e. g.

V. 456 C πρός γε τὸ φυλακικὴν γυναῖκα γενέσθαι, οὐκ ἄλλη μέν, κ.τ.λ.

*Obs.* 2.—Sometimes instead of introducing the sentence with a negative, two alternative suppositions are co-ordinated and followed by an apodosis relating to both combined ; so as to point the antithesis between what is preferred and its opposite.

IV. 421 A, B εἰ μὲν οὖν ἡμεῖς μέν ... ποιοῦμεν ... ὁ δ' ἐκεῖνο λέγων ... —ἄλλο ἄν τι ἢ πόλιν λέγοι.

§ 47. **4. *Disjunctives.***

A clause, apparently pleonastic, is often introduced with ἤ to enforce a rule by adding to it the sanction of a penalty. This formula is especially frequent in the Republic.

III. 401 B προσαναγκαστέον τὴν τοῦ ἀγαθοῦ εἰκόνα ἤθους ἐμποιεῖν τοῖς ποιήμασιν ἢ μὴ παρ' ἡμῖν ποιεῖν, 'else they shall be prohibited.'

III. 401 B διακωλυτέον τὸ κακόηθες ... μήτε ... ἐμποιεῖν, ἢ ὁ μὴ οἷός τε ὢν οὐκ ἐατέος παρ' ἡμῖν δημιουργεῖν. See p. 219 (a).

V. 463 D περί ... τοῦ ὑπήκοον δεῖν εἶναι τῶν γονέων, ἢ μήτε πρὸς θεῶν μήτε πρὸς ἀνθρώπων αὐτῷ ἄμεινον ἔσεσθαι.

VI. 490 A ἣν (sc. ἀλήθειαν) διώκειν ... ἔδει ἢ ἀλαζόνι ὄντι μηδαμῇ μετεῖναι φιλοσοφίας.

VI. 503 A τὸ δόγμα τοῦτο μήτ' ἐν πόνοις μήτ' ἐν φόβοις ... φαίνεσθαι ἐκβάλλοντας, ἢ τὸν ἀδυνατοῦντα ἀποκριτέον.

VII. 525 B τῆς οὐσίας ἁπτέον εἶναι γενέσεως ἐξαναδύντι, ἢ μηδέποτε λογιστικῷ γενέσθαι.

(Cp. Isocr. Aeginet. § 27 οὐδὲ γὰρ ἀπελθεῖν οἷόν τ᾽ ἦν, ἢ δοκεῖν ἀμελεῖν.)

*Obs.*—Another mode of introducing such a sanction,—not falling under the same grammatical heading,—is the incidental assertion of a condition in a hypothetical or participial clause, in which the word μέλλω generally occurs—

II. 365 C, D ἀλλ᾽ ὅμως, εἰ μέλλομεν εὐδαιμονήσειν, ταύτῃ ἰτέον, ὡς τὰ ἴχνη τῶν λόγων φέρει.

II. 372 D ἐπί τε κλινῶν κατακεῖσθαι, οἶμαι, τοὺς μέλλοντας μὴ ταλαιπωρεῖσθαι, κ.τ.λ.

So in VI. 491 B εἰ τελέως μέλλοι φιλόσοφος γενέσθαι, words unduly suspected by Cobet.

### 5. *Minute or verbal antithesis.* § 48.

The Greek love of antithesis gives rise to forms of expression which, if taken literally, are over-emphatic or even inaccurate.

(*a*) Thus αὐτός is sometimes emphatically used where the antithesis is too minute to be pressed.

II. 370 E ἀλλὰ μήν . . . κατοικίσαι γε αὐτὴν τὴν πόλιν εἰς τοιοῦτον τόπον, κ.τ.λ. ' The city,' as distinguished from the citizens.

II. 371 B ἐν αὐτῇ τῇ πόλει.

Antithetical formulae are also used ironically to suggest the equivalence of an alternative of which one side is tacitly preferred.

II. 373 E μήτ᾽ εἴ τι κακὸν μήτ᾽ εἰ ἀγαθὸν ὁ πόλεμος ἐργάζεται (cp. Herod. VIII. 87, § 5 οὔτε εἰ . . . οὔτε εἰ).

Cp. I. 339 B σμικρά γε ἴσως, ἔφη, προσθήκη. οὔπω δῆλον οὐδ᾽ εἰ μεγάλη.

Such antithetical redundancies as I. 346 A ἑκάστην . . . ἑκάστοτε, V. 462 D μέρους πονήσαντος ὅλη, VII. 516 B αὐτὸν καθ᾽ αὑτὸν ἐν τῇ αὑτοῦ χώρᾳ, and such reduplications in climax as III. 406 A, B πρῶτον μὲν καὶ μάλιστα, V. 449 D μέγα . . . καὶ ὅλον are extremely frequent.

The following are more noticeable :

IV. 441 C τὰ αὐτὰ μὲν ἐν πόλει, τὰ αὐτὰ δ' ἐν . . . τῇ ψυχῇ.

X. 605 B, C οὔτε τὰ μείζω οὔτε τὰ ἐλάττω διαγιγνώσκοντι.

X. 618 C βίον καὶ χρηστὸν καὶ πονηρὸν διαγιγνώσκοντα.

(*b*) The love of antithesis often gives a negative turn to a sentence ; VIII. 556 C, D ὅταν . . . μηδαμῇ . . . καταφρονῶνται . . . ἀλλά, κ.τ.λ.

6. Introduction of the reverse or contrary statement. In dwelling on one side of a distinction or antithesis the other side is introduced with apparent irrelevancy where it is not immediately in point. This is another way in which *co-ordination* breaks the smoothness of *subordination*.

A clear example is VII. 528 A ἀλλὰ σαυτοῦ ἕνεκα τὸ μέγιστον ποιεῖ τοὺς λόγους, φθονοῖς μὴν οὐδ' ἂν ἄλλῳ, κ.τ.λ.

See also :

I. 349 B, C εἰ τοῦ μὲν δικαίου μὴ ἀξιοῖ πλέον ἔχειν μηδὲ βούλεται ὁ δίκαιος, τοῦ δὲ ἀδίκου ;

II. 358 A πάλαι ὑπὸ Θρασυμάχου ὡς τοιοῦτον ὂν ψέγεται, ἀδικία δ' ἐπαινεῖται (*om.* Par. A).

II. 371 D ἢ οὐ καπήλους καλοῦμεν τοὺς . . . διακονοῦντας ἱδρυμένους ἐν ἀγορᾷ, τοὺς δὲ πλάνητας ἐπὶ τὰς πόλεις ἐμπόρους ;

II. 374 C μὴ αὐτὸ τοῦτο ἐκ παιδὸς ἐπιτηδεύων, ἀλλὰ παρέργῳ χρώμενος ;

V. 455 E, 456 A πολεμική, ἡ δ' ἀπόλεμος.

VI. 490 E τὰς φθοράς, ὡς διάλλυται ἐν πολλοῖς, σμικρὸν δέ τι ἐκφεύγει.

VII. 520 D οὐκ ἐθελήσουσι ξυμπονεῖν ἐν τῇ πόλει ἕκαστοι ἐν μέρει, τὸν δὲ πολὺν χρόνον μετ' ἀλλήλων οἰκεῖν ἐν τῷ καθαρῷ ;

VIII. 546 D (if the text is sound) ἡμῶν (τῶν Μουσῶν) πρῶτον ἄρξονται ἀμελεῖν . . . ἔλαττον τοῦ δέοντος ἡγησάμενοι τὰ μουσικῆς, δεύτερον δὲ τὰ γυμναστικῆς (δεύτερά τε γυμν. Madv. cj.).

VIII. 552 A τὸ ἐξεῖναι πάντα τὰ αὑτοῦ ἀποδόσθαι, καὶ ἄλλῳ κτήσασθαι τὰ τούτου.

VIII. 559 C ὃν νῦν δὴ κηφῆνα ὠνομάζομεν, τοῦτον ἐλέγομεν τὸν τῶν τοιούτων ἡδονῶν καὶ ἐπιθυμιῶν γέμοντα καὶ ἀρχόμενον ὑπὸ τῶν μὴ ἀναγκαίων, τὸν δὲ ὑπὸ τῶν ἀναγκαίων φειδωλόν τε καὶ ὀλιγαρχικόν ;

*Obs.* 1.—The same love of completeness shows itself in the frequent addition of limiting or qualifying clauses, such as ὅταν γίγνηται, ἂν μὴ πᾶσα ἀνάγκη, ὅσα ἄνθρωποι, ὅσον γέ μ' εἰδέναι, κατὰ τὸ δυνατόν or εἰς τὸ δυνατόν and the like, also in the addition of single words which remind the reader that there is another point of view, especially of δοκῶν, καλούμενος, λεγόμενος, or νῦν λεγόμενος, &c. to mark what belongs to ordinary unphilosophic opinion. For other examples of similar fulness of expression, see

IV. 430 C καὶ γὰρ ἀποδέχου, ἦν δ' ἐγώ, πολιτικήν γε.

VI. 492 A ὅ τι καὶ ἄξιον λόγου.

VII. 523 A τό γ' ἐμοὶ δοκοῦν.

*Obs.* 2.—Note also, as illustrating the same over-emphatic or exaggerating tendency, the multiplication of pronominal words in the same sentence :—τοιούτους γε καὶ οὗτω (III. 416 A), μηδαμῇ μηδαμῶς (Laws VI. 777 E), εἴτε ὅπῃ ἔχει καὶ ὅπως,—also the addition of the negative side in such expressions as ἀλλὰ σμικρὸν οἴει διαφέρειν, καὶ οὐκ ἄξιον κινδύνου, θεωρεῖν ἢ μή. A striking example of this sort of thing occurs in II. 369 C where in introducing the division of labour, Socrates is not contented with saying that different men have different wants and need various helpers, ἄλλον ἐπ' ἄλλου ... χρείᾳ, but adds τὸν δ' ἐπ' ἄλλου, 'and this man yet another, for another want,' to show not only that different men need different helpers, but that each requires more than one.

## IX. Deferred Apodosis.
### *Digression and Resumption.* §49.

1. It is a natural consequence of the expansion of sentences, and especially of the tendency of parentheses [1] and subordinate clauses to take an independent form, that the main statement at first intended is thrust aside, and, if not wholly lost, can no longer be expressed in strict continuation of the original construction. The sentence becomes like a tree whose leading stem has been distorted or broken. This is particularly apt to occur in the course of those elaborate similes of which Plato is fond. Cp. Lysias, contra Eratosth. § 6, Xen. Mem. IV. 2, § 25.

[1] See Prof. Jowett's note on Rom. ii. 16.

I. 337 A, B εὖ οὖν ᾔδησθα ὅτι εἴ τινα ἔροιο, κ.τ.λ. (four lines intervene) δῆλον οἶμαί σοι ἦν, κ.τ.λ.   Cp. V. 471 C.

I. 352 B–D ὅτι μὲν γὰρ (twelve lines intervene) ταῦτα μὲν οὖν ὅτι οὕτως ἔχει, κ.τ.λ.

III. 402 A, B ὥσπερ ἄρα . . . γραμμάτων πέρι τότε ἱκανῶς εἴχομεν, ὅτε . . . (eight lines intervene) . . . ἆρ᾽ οὖν, ὃ λέγω, . . . οὐδὲ μουσικοὶ πρότερον ἐσόμεθα.

IV. 428 A ὥσπερ τοίνυν, κ.τ.λ.

VI. 495 D, E οὗ δὴ ἐφιέμενοι πολλοὶ ἀτελεῖς μὲν τὰς φύσεις, ὑπὸ δὲ τῶν τεχνῶν τε καὶ δημιουργιῶν ὥσπερ τὰ σώματα λελώβηνται, οὕτω καὶ τὰς ψυχὰς ξυγκεκλασμένοι τε καὶ ἀποτεθρυμμένοι διὰ τὰς βαναυσίας τυγχάνουσιν, κ.τ.λ.   The apodosis, if any, comes half a page below, ποῖ᾽ ἄττα φῶμεν γεννᾶν . . . ἆρ᾽ οὐ . . . σοφίσματα ;

VIII. 562 B ὃ προὔθεντο, κ.τ.λ.

X. 609 C ὥσπερ σῶμα, κ.τ.λ.

Theaet. 197 C ὥσπερ εἴ τις ὄρνιθας ἀγρίας, κ.τ.λ

Hence τε occurs without a distinct correlative.

V. 463 D περί τε τοὺς πατέρας, κ.τ.λ.

VII. 522 B αἵ τε γὰρ τέχναι, κ.τ.λ.

VIII. 568 D ἐάν τε ἱερὰ χρήματα, κ.τ.λ. (if *πωλουμένων is read.   See note in loco).

IX. 575 A τὸν ἔχοντά τε αὐτόν, κ.τ.λ.

*Obs.*—The apodosis is sometimes given in the reply ;

IX. 577 A, B εἰ οὖν οἰοίμην . . . : Ὀρθότατ᾽ ἄν . . . προκαλοῖο.

IX. 582 E ἐπειδὴ δ᾽ ἐμπειρίᾳ . . . : Ἀνάγκη . . . εἶναι.

§ 50.   2. As in all conversation the consciousness of imperfect expression is apt to occasion the attempt to recover preciseness by the introduction of superfluous words, so in the conversational style of Plato it often happens that what has been already stated or implied is resumed with some increase of explicitness, often with the addition of a formula of reference, such as ὃ λέγω, ὅπερ εἶπον, &c.   Thus the effort to be exact leads to further irregularity of structure and sometimes even to a degree of confusion.

(*a*) The simplest case is where the antecedent to a relative or correlative clause is made explicit with τοῦτο, ταῦτα or some other demonstrative word. This is common in Greek and is used more for emphasis than for clearness.

The same remark applies to αὐτός τε καί and to καὶ ταῦτα. See above, p. 220 (*e*).

In some instances, however, the demonstrative is thus inserted from the fear of losing the thread of the discourse, when the phrase that has been put emphatically foremost has been amplified :

IV. 440 B ταῖς δ᾽ ἐπιθυμίαις αὐτὸν κοινωνήσαντα . . . οἶμαί σε οὐκ ἂν φάναι . . . τοῦ τοιούτου αἰσθέσθαι, where the construction also becomes more definite.

So I. 331 B τὸ γὰρ μηδὲ ἄκοντά τινα ἐξαπατῆσαι . . . μέγα μέρος εἰς τοῦτο, κ.τ.λ.

Or, where there is no amplification, but the order has been disturbed by emphasis, the chief word is resumed with an oblique case of αὐτός.

V. 477 D ἐπιστήμην πότερον δύναμίν τινα φῂς εἶναι αὐτήν, κ.τ.λ.

Cp. Gorg. 483 E where the construction is disturbed by the substitution of a general for a particular expression, ἢ ἄλλα μυρία ἄν τις ἔχοι τοιαῦτα λέγειν.

(*b*) In an explanatory clause, the chief word in the sentence to be explained is often resumed by a synonym :

II. 359 B ἀγαπᾶσθαι . . . τιμώμενον.

II. 359 C εἴη δ᾽ ἂν ἡ ἐξουσία . . . οἵαν ποτέ φασι δύναμιν, κ.τ.λ.

X. 611 C, D τεθεάμεθα . . . ὥσπερ οἱ . . . ὁρῶντες οὐκ ἂν . . . ἴδοιεν . . . , οὕτω . . . θεώμεθα, κ.τ.λ.

(*c*) In resuming a deferred apodosis, a conjunction is often introduced ; and, as μὲν οὖν usually introduces a digression, so δ᾽ οὖν is the regular formula for resumption.

I. 330 E καὶ αὐτός,—ἤτοι ὑπὸ τῆς τοῦ γήρως ἀσθενείας ἢ καὶ ὥσπερ ἤδη ἐγγυτέρω ὢν τῶν ἐκεῖ μᾶλλόν τι καθορᾷ αὐτά— ὑποψίας δ᾽ οὖν καὶ δείματος μεστὸς γίγνεται καὶ ἀναλογίζεται ἤδη καὶ σκοπεῖ, εἴ τινά τι ἠδίκηκεν.

This, reduced to normal syntax, might be thus expressed:—ἤτοι ὑπὸ τῆς τοῦ γήρως ἀσθενείας, ἢ ὑπὸ τοῦ μᾶλλόν τι καθορᾶν τὰ ἐκεῖ, ὑποψίας καὶ δείματος μεστὸς γίγνεται.   But the addition of ὥσπερ ἐγγυτέρω ὤν, by occasioning the change to the indicative, disturbs this orderly arrangement and requires the insertion of δ' οὖν.

Cp VIII. 562 B ὃ προὔθεντο . . . ἀγαθόν . . . τοῦτο δ' ἦν *που πλοῦτος . . . ἡ πλούτου τοίνυν ἀπληστία, κ.τ.λ.

## X.  Remote Reference.

§ 51.   The power of holding firmly by a complex thought appears (1) in the continuation of the main construction in spite of interruptions; and (2) in the pertinence of replies, showing that the respondent has fully grasped the main question, although the previous statement has been complicated by digressions.

(1) III. 413 E, 414 A τόν . . . ἀκήρατον ἐκβαίνοντα καταστατέον ἄρχοντα . . . καὶ τιμὰς δοτέον καὶ ζῶντι καὶ τελευτήσαντι, . . . μέγιστα γέρα λαγχάνοντα.   Cp. Phaedo 81 A οὕτω μὲν ἔχουσα . . . ἀπέρχεται . . . οἷ ἀφικομένῃ ὑπάρχει αὐτῇ εὐδαίμονι εἶναι, πλάνης . . . ἀπηλλαγμένη ὥσπερ δὲ λέγεται κατὰ τῶν μεμνημένων . . . μετὰ τῶν θεῶν διάγουσα[1].

VII. 540 D ξυγχωρεῖτε . . . εἰρηκέναι.   Then follows a sentence of nineteen lines with a break and appositional asyndeton in the middle, then the construction with the infinitive is resumed with πλεῖστα ὀνήσειν 541 A.

(2) III. 405 B, C ἦ δοκεῖ σοι . . . τούτου αἴσχιον εἶναι . . . (ten lines) . . . οὔκ, ἀλλὰ τοῦτ', ἔφη, ἐκείνου ἔτι αἴσχιον.

IV. 439 D οὐ δὴ ἀλόγως . . . (five lines) . . . οὔκ, ἀλλ' εἰκότως.

VI. 491 E οὔκ, ἀλλά, ἦ δ' ὅς, οὕτως (see note in loco).

VIII. 558 B, C ἡ δὲ συγγνώμη . . . (nine lines) . . . πάνυ γ', ἔφη, γενναία.

IX. 573 E ἆρα οὐκ ἀνάγκη . . . (six lines) . . . σφόδρα γ', ἔφη.

---

[1] διάγουσα is supported by the Petrie papyrus against διαγούσῃ, Heindorf's conjecture.

## XI.  Imperfect Constructions.

### *Attraction, Hypallage, Zeugma.*

Very often, however, as in all Greek, the attraction of the § 52. nearest word, or an agreement that is apparent only, prevails over logic. The speaker is contented with a prima facie appearance of concord. The frequent redundancy of expression causes this anomaly to be more common than it would otherwise be.

1. *Construction with the nearest word.* (What is commonly known as *Attraction* is a special case of this.)

II. 370 E ἵνα οἵ τε γεωργοὶ ἐπὶ τὸ ἀροῦν ἔχοιεν βοῦς, οἵ τε οἰκοδόμοι πρὸς τὰς ἀγωγὰς μετὰ τῶν γεωργῶν **χρῆσθαι ὑποζυγίοις** (i. e. ἔχοιεν ὑποζύγια ὥστε χρῆσθαι αὐτοῖς).

III. 392 D **πάντα, ὅσα** . . . λέγεται, διήγησις οὖσα τυγχάνει.

III. 409 D ἀρετὴ δὲ φύσεως παιδευομένης χρόνῳ. Mr. H. Richards would read παιδευμένη. But if precise exactness is required, should it not be χρηστὴ φύσις παιδευομένη?

III. 416 A **αἴσχιστον ποιμέσι** τοιούτους . . . *τρέφειν κύνας* (ποιμέσι in construction with αἴσχιστον takes the place of ποιμένας the subject of τρέφειν). Ib. ἐπιχειρῆσαι τοῖς προβάτοις κακουργεῖν. Madvig would omit κακουργεῖν. But the pleonastic infinitive is rendered easier by the frequent use of ἐπιχειρεῖν with infinitive in Plato so that ἐπιχειρεῖν κακουργεῖν τὰ πρόβατα is also suggested.

IV. 421 C ἐατέον **ὅπως** ἑκάστοις τοῖς ἔθνεσιν ἡ φύσις ἀποδί-δωσι τοῦ μεταλαμβάνειν εὐδαιμονίας (where the meaning is ἐατέον τὰ ἔθνη μεταλαμβάνειν εὐδαιμονίας οὕτως ὅπως ἡ φύσις ἑκάστοις ἀποδίδωσιν).

V. 454 D **διαφέρον** sing. agreeing with γένος, instead of plur.

V. 459 B δεῖ **ἄκρων** εἶναι τῶν ἀρχόντων.

V. 472 D **παράδειγμα** οἷον ἂν εἴη ὁ κάλλιστος ἄνθρωπος (οἷον is neuter because of παράδειγμα).

V. 473 D καὶ τοῦτο εἰς ταὐτὸν συμπέσῃ, δύναμίς τε πολιτικὴ καὶ φιλοσοφία. τοῦτο is singular by prolepsis. H. Richards would read ταῦτα. But cp. IV. 435 A ὅ γε ταὐτὸν ἄν τις προσείποι, κ.τ.λ.

VII. 520 D ἐν πόλει ᾗ ἥκιστα πρόθυμοι ἄρχειν . . . ταύτην ἄριστα . . . ἀνάγκη οἰκεῖσθαι (for πόλιν ἐν ᾗ, κ.τ.λ.).

VII. 526 C ἅ γε μείζω πόνον παρέχει . . . οὐκ ἂν ῥᾳδίως οὐδὲ πολλὰ ἂν εὕροις ὡς τοῦτο (ὡς is said as if οὕτω μέγαν and not μείζω had preceded; and this is occasioned by οὐδὲ πολλά coming between. 'You will not *easily* find any that give *more* trouble; not *many* that give *as much.*'

VII. 534 A ἵνα μὴ ἡμᾶς πολλαπλασίων λόγων ἐμπλήσῃ ἢ ὅσων οἱ παρεληλυθότες—a place at which the critics have stumbled. It may no doubt be explained by supplying ἢ ὅσων λόγων οἱ παρεληλυθότες λόγοι ἐνέπλησαν ἡμᾶς. But it seems more probable that ὅσων (for ὅσοι) follows the case of πολλαπλασίων.

*Obs.* 1.—In comparisons the antecedent is often attracted into the relative clause.

VI. 485 D αἱ ἐπιθυμίαι . . . ἀσθενέστεραι, ὥσπερ ῥεῦμα . . . ἀπωχετευμένον.

VII. 539 D μὴ ὡς νῦν ὁ τυχὼν καὶ οὐδὲν προσήκων ἔρχεται ἐπ' αὐτό.

X. 610 D μή, ὥσπερ νῦν διὰ τοῦτο ὑπ' ἄλλων . . . ἀποθνήσκουσιν οἱ ἄδικοι. A striking example in Phaedo 84 A is supported by the Petrie papyrus, Πηνελόπης τινὰ ἐναντίως ἱστὸν μεταχειριζομένης.

*Obs.* 2.—The mood of a verb is affected by an intervening conjunction, though not strictly in construction with it.

IX. 591 C, D οὐχ ὅπως . . . ἐνταῦθα τετραμμένος ζήσει, ἀλλ' οὐδέ . . . τοῦτο πρεσβεύων, ὅπως . . . καλὸς ἔσται, ἐὰν μή . . . μέλλῃ . . . ἀλλ' ἀεὶ . . . φαίνηται. φαίνηται should have been φανεῖται depending on the first ὅπως. Cp. V. 466 E διακονεῖν, sc. δεήσει.

*Obs.* 3.—The verb of a relative clause is often attracted into the infinitive of *oratio obliqua*: VI. 492 C; X. 614 C; 619 C &c., cp. Herodotus.

*Obs.* 4.—The conclusion or answer, instead of following the main sentence, sometimes takes the nearer construction:

I. 336 E μὴ γὰρ δὴ οἴου . . . (five lines intervene) ὑπείκειν . . . καὶ οὐ σπουδάζειν . . . οἴου γε σύ (sc. σπουδάζειν ἡμᾶς):—the original sentence μὴ γὰρ δή, κ.τ.λ., is lost sight of.

IV. 421 E ἕτερα δή . . . εἰρήκαμεν . . . ποῖα ταῦτα ; Πλοῦτός τε, ἦν δ᾽ ἐγώ, καὶ πενία.

The nominatives really answer to the accusative ἕτερα, but this is lost sight of, the case of ταῦτα being ambiguous.

VI. 492 C, D ἐν δὴ τῷ τοιούτῳ τὸν νέον . . . τίνα οἴει καρδίαν ἴσχειν; ἢ *ποίαν αὐτῷ παιδείαν . . . ἀνθέξειν, ἣν οὐ . . . οἰχήσεσθαι . . . καὶ ἐπιτηδεύσειν, κ.τ.λ.

Πολλή . . . ἀνάγκη.

The answer refers to the last clauses of the preceding sentence, and takes no notice of the question.

## 2. *Parallelism.* § 53.

(*a*) The action of a verb is extended to several nouns although it is strictly applicable to one only ('zeugma').

VIII. 553 C τιάρας τε καὶ στρεπτοὺς καὶ ἀκινάκας παραζωννύντα : the participle is strictly applicable only to ἀκινάκας.

(*b*) On the other hand, a preceding construction is continued, although some other construction is really required.

V. 453 D ἤτοι δελφῖνα . . . ὑπολαβεῖν ἂν ἤ τινα ἄλλην ἄπορον σωτηρίαν (φανῆναι ἄν).

IV. 431 C τὰς δέ γε ἁπλᾶς τε καὶ μετρίας . . . ἐν ὀλίγοις τε ἐπιτεύξει, κ.τ.λ. The accusative is carried on from ἁπλᾶς τε καὶ παντοδαπὰς ἐπιθυμίας, supra.

V. 467 C προσμηχανᾶσθαι governed by δεῖ in ὑπαρκτέον.

VI. 510 B τὸ μὲν αὐτοῦ . . . ψυχὴ ζητεῖν ἀναγκάζεται ἐξ ὑποθέσεων . . . τὸ δ᾽ αὖ ἕτερον τὸ ἐπ᾽ ἀρχὴν ἀνυπόθετον . . . ἰοῦσα (sc. ζητεῖ) where to two parallel clauses a single expression is applied, which is only suitable to the former of them. The higher dialectic is above Necessity.

VII. 528 C ὑπὸ τῶν πολλῶν . . . κολουόμενα, ὑπὸ δὲ τῶν ζητούντων, λόγον οὐκ ἐχόντων καθ᾽ ὅ τι χρήσιμα.

(*c*) In replies the construction is sometimes continued from the previous sentence, although involving some harshness in the immediate context.

VI. 507 E τίνος δὴ λέγεις ; here the genitive may be explained as = περὶ τίνος ; see above, p. 184 (*b*), but it is more probably occasioned by a reference to what precedes : τίνος, sc. μὴ παραγενομένου.

VII. 531 D τοῦ προοιμίου . . . ἢ τίνος λέγεις ; A construction may be found for τίνος by supplying τὸ ἔργον, but the genitive is more probably occasioned by assimilation to the preceding construction.

VIII. 547 E τῷ δέ γε φοβεῖσθαι, κ.τ.λ. The dative is parallel to πᾶσι τοῖς τοιούτοις (supra D) but is inconsistent with what follows (548 A) τὰ πολλὰ τῶν τοιούτων ἴδια ἕξει ;

VIII. 558 A. The words αὐτῶν μενόντων have a possible construction with εἶδες, supra, but really follow the case of ἀνθρώπων which is genitive absolute.

*Obs.* 1.—An imperfect construction is sometimes supplemented by epexegesis.

v. 464 B ἀπεικάζοντες . . . πόλιν σώματι πρὸς μέρος αὐτοῦ . . . ὡς ἔχει.

*Obs.* 2.—The parallelism not only of cases and moods, but also of adverbs should be noted.

v. 475 E πῶς αὐτὸ λέγεις ;

Οὐδαμῶς . . . ῥᾳδίως (' not in a way easy to explain '). Cp. Symp. 202 C πῶς τοῦτο, ἔφην, λέγεις ; καὶ ἥ, ʻΡᾳδίως, ἔφη.

§ 54.   3. *Interchange of subject and attribute (Hypallage).*

The common idiom by which the attribute of a subordinate word (such as an infinitive) is attached to the subject of the main verb,—e. g. δίκαιός εἰμι ποιεῖν,—has an extended use in Plato.

VII. ʼ537 B οὗτος γὰρ ὁ χρόνος . . . ἀδύνατός τι ἄλλο πρᾶξαι.

VIII. 559 B ἦ τε μὴ παῦσαι ζῶντα δυνατή, 'in that one cannot suppress it while one lives.' See note in loco.

Hence VI. 489 A ταῖς πόλεσι . . . τὴν διάθεσιν ἔοικε = τῇ τῶν πόλεων διαθέσει ἔοικε, and in VIII. 562 A τίς τρόπος τυραννίδος . . . γίγνεται ; appears to be equivalent to τίνα τρόπον γίγνεται τυραννίς ;

See also VI. 496 A προσήκοντα ἀκοῦσαι σοφίσματα = οἷς προσήκει ἀκοῦσαι σ. (' to be so described '). Cp. Eur. Or. 771 οὐ προσήκομεν κολάζειν τοῖσδε = οὐ προσήκει τοῖσδε κολάζειν ἡμᾶς.

4. *Mixed Constructions.* § 55.

As a word is sometimes attracted out of its proper construction, so the speaker sometimes hesitates between two constructions and fuses both into one. Familiar instances are—

I. 347 A ὧν δὴ ἕνεκα, ὡς ἔοικε, μισθὸν δεῖν ὑπάρχειν.

VI. 485 A ὁ . . . ἐλέγομεν, τὴν φύσιν . . . δεῖν καταμαθεῖν.

VIII. 560 D ὡς ἀγροικίαν . . . οὖσαν πείθοντες ὑπερορίζουσι (πείθοντες . . . εἶναι, ὑπερορίζουσιν ὡς . . . οὖσαν).

Cp. Theaet. 157 A (B. Gildersleeve, *American Journal of Philology*, vii. 2, No. 26, p. 175) ὅπερ ἐξ ἀρχῆς ἐλέγομεν, οὐδὲν εἶναι ἐν αὐτὸ καθ᾽ αὐτό.

(*a*) *Apparent solecisms.*

I. 351 C εἰ μέν, ἔφη, ὡς σὺ ἄρτι ἔλεγες, ἔχει, ἡ δικαιοσύνη σοφία. Cp. Theaet. 204 A ἐχέτω δή, ὡς νῦν φαμέν, μία ἰδέα . . . γιγνομένη ἡ συλλαβή.

II. 378 C πολλοῦ δεῖ γιγαντομαχίας τε μυθολογητέον, κ.τ.λ. (πολλοῦ δεῖ is treated as an adverbial phrase = οὐδαμῶς).

III. 414 C οὐδ᾽ οἶδα εἰ (i.e. μόλις) γενόμενον ἄν. Cp. Tim. 26 B οὐκ ἂν οἶδα εἰ δυναίμην.

IV. 444 B τοιούτου ὄντος . . . οἵου πρέπειν αὐτῷ δουλεύειν. 'Τοιούτου ὄντος οἵου δουλεύειν would be Greek. So would τοιούτου ὄντος ὥστε π. α. δουλεύειν. But the text as it stands is not Greek at all.' H. Richards. It may stand as Platonic Greek.

V. 478 D εἴ τι φανείη οἷον ἅμα ὄν τε καὶ μὴ ὄν (confusion of οἷον εἶναι with φανείη ὄν).

X. 615 D οὐδ᾽ ἂν ἥξει (expressing more of certainty than ἥκοι ἄν, more of modality than ἥξει: Cobet cj. οὐδὲ *μὴ ἥξει).

Perhaps also in the doubtful passage, I. 333 E λαθεῖν . . . δεινότατος ἐμποιῆσαι, there is a confusion of δεινότατος λαθεῖν ἐμποιήσας with δεινότατος λαθὼν ἐμποιῆσαι, the position of δεινότατος suggesting the construction of ἐμποιῆσαι. But see note in loco.

(*b*) Fusion of the objective and subjective aspects of the same notion.

IV. 434 D ἐὰν ... εἰς ἕνα ἕκαστον τῶν ἀνθρώπων ἰὸν τὸ εἶδος τοῦτο ὁμολογῆται, κ.τ.λ. ('It is not the εἶδος which goes or turns to individual men.' H. Richards, who proposes ἰοῦσιν.)

IV. 442 D μή πῃ ἡμῖν ἀπαμβλύνεται ... δικαιοσύνη. 'Justice' here is the *notion* of justice as formerly conceived.

V. 450 E θαρραλέον, 'fearless,' i.e. not dangerous, a thing to be attempted without fear. Cp. Soph. Phil. 106 οὐκ ἄρ' ἐκείνῳ γ' οὐδὲ προσμῖξαι θρασύ;

(c) *Abstract and concrete.*

a. Attributes are personified.

II. 382 D ποιητὴς ... ψευδὴς ἐν θεῷ οὐκ ἔνι, 'The lying poet has no place in our idea of God.'

VIII. 554 D τὰς τοῦ κηφῆνος ξυγγενεῖς ... ἐπιθυμίας.

IX. 575 C, D ὃς ἂν ... πλεῖστον ἐν τῇ ψυχῇ τύραννον ἔχῃ.

β. In X. 617 D ἀρχὴ ἄλλης περιόδου θνητοῦ γένους, 'the beginning of another cycle of mortal race' is put abstractedly for 'the beginning of your time for again belonging to the race of mortals.'

γ. Name and thing.

V. 470 B ὥσπερ καὶ ὀνομάζεται δύο ταῦτα ὀνόματα, πόλεμός τε καὶ στάσις, οὕτω καὶ εἶναι δύο, ὄντα ἐπὶ δυοῖν τινοῖν διαφοραῖν.

(d) *General with particular.*

IV. 435 A ὅ γε ταὐτὸν ἄν τις προσείποι, κ.τ.λ. 'That which receives the same appellation' is the just, whether just man or just state, but these, although univocal, are not one thing. Cp. V. 473 D καὶ τοῦτο εἰς ταὐτὸν συμπέσῃ, κ.τ.λ. (p. 233).

(e) *Part with whole* (synecdoche).

II. 371 E πλήρωμα ... πόλεώς εἰσι ... καὶ μισθωτοί, 'Hirelings will *help* to make up our population.'

(f) Constructions κατὰ σύνεσιν may be included here.

V. 455 D κρατεῖται takes a genitive in the sense of ἡττᾶται.

## XII.  Changes of Construction.

§ 56.  1. From the relative to the definitive pronoun.

It is a well-known peculiarity of Greek syntax that in

continuing a relative sentence, a definitive or demonstrative pronoun takes the place of the relative.

I. 353 D ἔσθ' ὅτῳ ἄλλῳ ἢ ψυχῇ δικαίως ἂν αὐτὰ ἀποδοῖμεν καὶ φαῖμεν ἴδια **ἐκείνης** εἶναι.

VI. 511 C **αἷς** αἱ ὑποθέσεις ἀρχαὶ καὶ διανοίᾳ μὲν ἀναγκάζονται . . . **αὐτὰ** θεᾶσθαι οἱ θεώμενοι.

IX. 578 C **ὃς ἄν** . . . ᾖ καὶ **αὐτῷ** . . . ἐκπορισθῇ, κ.τ.λ.

Gorg. 452 D **ὃ** φῂς σὺ μέγιστον ἀγαθὸν εἶναι . . . καὶ σὲ δημιουργὸν εἶναι **αὐτοῦ.**

*Obs.*—In Plato although the sentence passes out of the relative construction it is still partially affected by it.

II. 357 B αἱ ἡδοναὶ **ὅσαι** ἀβλαβεῖς καὶ **μηδὲν** . . . διὰ **ταύτας** γίγνεται ἄλλο. See above, p. 211, *a.*

So in passing from a participial clause which is equivalent to a relative.

I. 337 E πρῶτον μὲν **μὴ εἰδὼς** . . . ἔπειτα . . . ἀπειρημένον **αὐτῷ εἴη,** where μὴ εἰδώς = ὃς μὴ εἰδείη.

2. Another consequence of the comparative laxity of the Greek sentence is the frequent change from a dependent to an independent construction. (See esp. Hom. Il. XV. 369, Lysias, c. Eratosth, § 38.)   § **57.**

II. 383 A **ὡς** μήτε αὐτοὺς γόητας **ὄντας** . . . μήτε ἡμᾶς ψεύδεσι **παράγειν.** Here παράγειν returns to construction with λέγειν, the subordinate clause, ὡς . . . ὄντας, being ignored.

IV. 426 C τὴν μὲν κατάστασιν . . . **μὴ κινεῖν** . . . **ὃς δ' ἄν** . . . θεραπεύῃ . . . **οὗτος ἄρα** ἀγαθὸς . . . **ἔσται** (H. Richards would read οὗτος ⟨ὡς⟩ ἄρα).

V. 465 E γέρα δέχονται . . . **ζῶντές** τε καὶ τελευτήσαντες ταφῆς ἀξίας **μετέχουσιν.** Here μετέχουσιν is co-ordinated with δέχονται, passing out of the subordinate participial construction.

VIII. 549 C, D **ὅταν** . . . τῆς μητρὸς **ἀκούῃ** ἀχθομένης . . . ἔπειτα **ὁρώσης** . . . **καί** . . . **αἰσθάνηται.** αἰσθάνηται which has the same subject with ὁρώσης, κ.τ.λ., passes out of the participial construction, and is construed immediately with ὅταν.

IX. 590 C **ὅταν** τις ἀσθενὲς . . . **ἔχῃ** τὸ . . . εἶδος, ὥστε μὴ ἂν δύνασθαι **ἄρχειν** . . . ἀλλὰ **θεραπεύειν** . . . καὶ τὰ θωπεύματα . . .

μόνον **δύνηται** μανθάνειν; **δύνηται** passes out of the construction with ὥστε, and returns to the construction with ὅταν. The last two instances might also be referred to mistaken parallelism: see above, p. 235. The reading of II. 364 C (βλάψει) may be sustained as an example of this tendency, and, in the same passage, 365 A περιμένει is to be retained.

*Obs.*—Note also the converse return from the finite verb to the participle.

VII. 531 A φασὶν . . . ἀμφισβητοῦντες.

and from inf. to partic.

III. 403 B, C οὕτως **ὁμιλεῖν** . . . εἰ δὲ μή . . . ὑφέξοντα.

§ 58. 3. *Change of subject.*

This frequently occurs when there is some alternation between the active and passive voice.

I. 333 C ὅταν μηδὲν δέῃ **αὐτῷ χρῆσθαι** ἀλλὰ **κεῖσθαι**;

II. 359 E, 360 A ἀφανῆ **αὐτὸν γενέσθαι** . . . καὶ **διαλέγεσθαι** ὡς περὶ οἰχομένου.

II. 377 B μάλιστα γὰρ δὴ τότε **πλάττεται** καὶ **ἐνδύεται τύπος**.

III. 409 E, 410 A. The subject changes from the *arts* to the professors of either art respectively.

III. 414 D ταῦτα . . . πάσχειν τε καὶ γίγνεσθαι περὶ αὐτούς.

4. *Limitation of subject.*

V. 465 C ὧν ἀπηλλαγμένοι ἂν **εἶεν** (sc. οἱ πολῖται) . . . κολακείας τε πλουσίων πένητες, κ.τ.λ.

VIII. 556 C, D ὅταν . . . ἀλλήλους θεώμενοι (sc. οἱ πολῖται) μηδαμῇ ταύτῃ καταφρονῶνται οἱ πένητες ὑπὸ τῶν πλουσίων.

5. From the dative in regimen to the accusative in agreement with the subject of an infinitive. (This change occurs in other Greek writers from Homer downwards.

Il. IV. 341, 342 σφῶϊν μέν τ' ἐπέοικε μετὰ πρώτοισιν ἐόντας | ἑστάμεν.)

IV. 422 B, C εἰ ἐξείη . . . **ὑποφεύγοντι** . . . ἀναστρέφοντα κρούειν;

6. *Suspended constructions.*

In many sentences, the notion which it is intended to

make prominent is put forward either in the nominative or accusative (see above, p. 183, γ), and is left with no definite construction, the turn of the sentence being subsequently modified. (Cp. Soph. El. 1364–1366 τοὺς γὰρ ἐν μέσῳ λόγους, | πολλαὶ κυκλοῦνται νύκτες ἡμέραι τ᾽ ἴσαι, | αἳ ταῦτά σοι δείξουσιν, Ἠλέκτρα, σαφῆ.)

II. 365 A ταῦτα πάντα . . . λεγόμενα . . . τί οἰόμεθα ἀκουούσας νέων ψυχὰς ποιεῖν. Here the shadow of a construction is supplied by ἀκουούσας.

II. 365 B τὰ μὲν γὰρ λεγόμενα . . . ὄφελος οὐδέν φασιν εἶναι.

III. 391 B τὰς τοῦ . . . Σπερχειοῦ ἱερὰς τρίχας Πατρόκλῳ ἥρωϊ, ἔφη, κόμην ὀπάσαιμι φέρεσθαι.

V. 474 E μελιχλώρους δὲ καὶ τοὔνομα, κ.τ.λ.

VI. 487 B παραγόμενοι . . . μέγα τὸ σφάλμα . . . ἀναφαίνεσθαι.

VIII. 565 D, E ὡς ἄρα ὁ γευσάμενος . . . ἀνάγκη δὴ τούτῳ λύκῳ γενέσθαι.

VIII. 566 E πρὸς τοὺς ἔξω ἐχθροὺς τοῖς μὲν καταλλαγῇ, κ.τ.λ.

7. Addition of a summary expression, without a con- § 59. junction, to clinch a series or enumeration which has been given whole or in part.

II. 373 A κλῖναί τε προσέσονται . . . ἕκαστα τούτων παντοδαπά.

IV. 434 A πάντα τἄλλα μεταλλαττόμενα.

VIII. 547 D πᾶσι τοῖς τοιούτοις.

X. 598 B τοὺς ἄλλους δημιουργούς.

*Obs.*—A conjunction is sometimes inserted.

VII. 523 D καὶ πᾶν ὅ τι τοιοῦτον.

8. In resumption after a digression (see above, pp. 229 ff.) the construction is often changed. See especially, in the rambling speech of Pausanias in the Symposium, the passage 182 D–183 D ἐνθυμηθέντι γὰρ . . . ἐνθάδε νομίζεσθαι, where, amongst other irregularities, the dative ἐνθυμηθέντι is in no construction, because the 'deferred apodosis' is resumed (183 C) with a fresh turn of expression, ταύτῃ μὲν οὖν οἰηθείη

ἄν τις, κ.τ.λ., in which the original construction is forgotten.
(Badham proposed to read γε for γάρ.)

Rep. VII. 532 B, C ἡ δέ γε ... λύσις τε ἀπὸ τῶν δεσμῶν καὶ
μεταστροφὴ ... πᾶσα αὕτη ἡ πραγματεία ... ταύτην ἔχει τὴν δύναμιν.

The passage has been already quoted above, p. 183 γ, but
it is a strong instance of the peculiarity here spoken of.

§ 60.　9. From interrogative with negative meaning to direct
negative :—

III. 390 A–C τί δέ; ποιεῖν ἄνδρα ... (fifteen lines) ; οὐδὲ
Ἄρεώς τε καὶ Ἀφροδίτης ... δεσμὸν δι᾽ ἕτερα τοιαῦτα.

10. *Other anacolutha.*

The laxity of the conversational style admits of changes
which can hardly be brought under the preceding heads.
Some words have only the ' shadow' of a construction, the
sentence continuing as if that had been expressed which is
only implied, or else returning to a connexion from which
the intervening clauses have broken loose; or some new
connexion or antithesis is suggested in the act of speaking.

II. 362 B τὰ κεδνὰ βλαστάνει βουλεύματα, πρῶτον μὲν ἄρχειν
... ἔπειτα γαμεῖν ... ἐκδιδόναι ... ξυμβάλλειν, κοινωνεῖν οἷς ἂν
ἐθέλῃ ... εἰς ἀγῶνας τοίνυν ἰόντα ... περιγίγνεσθαι ... Here
ἄρχειν and the following infinitives are in apposition with
βουλεύματα, but in περιγίγνεσθαι the sentence has reverted to
the construction with φήσουσι (supra A).

III. 387 D, E φαμὲν δὲ δή, ὅτι ... τὸ τεθνάναι οὐ δεινὸν ἡγήσεται ... οὐκ ἄρα ... ὀδύροιτ᾽ ἄν ... ἀλλὰ μὴν καὶ τόδε λέγομεν.
ὡς ... ἥκιστα ἑτέρου προσδεῖται ... ἥκιστα ἄρ᾽ αὐτῷ δεινὸν
στερηθῆναι ... ἥκιστ᾽ ἄρα καὶ ὀδύρεσθαι (sc. φήσομεν). (Cp. VI.
501 D ἢ ἐκείνους φήσειν μᾶλλον, where see note.) The last
infinitive, while perhaps occasioned by στερηθῆναι, which is
in a different construction, must borrow its government
from φαμέν and λέγομεν preceding. Others would supply
προσήκει from δεινόν.

III. 388 E, 389 A οὔτε ἄρα ἀνθρώπους ... ἄν τις ποιῇ, ἀπο-
δεκτέον, πολὺ δὲ ἧττον, ἐὰν θεούς.

III. 389 C κάμνοντι . . . λέγειν . . . μὴ τὰ ὄντα λέγοντι (the participle co-ordinate with the infinitive).

III. 399 A, B κατάλειπε . . . τὴν ἁρμονίαν, ἣ ἔν τε πολεμικῇ πράξει ὄντος ἀνδρείου . . . μιμήσαιτο φθόγγους . . . καὶ ἀποτυχόντος . . . ἀμυνομένου τὴν τύχην· καὶ ἄλλην αὖ ἐν εἰρηνικῇ . . . πράξει ὄντος, ἢ . . . πείθοντος . . . ἢ . . . ἄλλῳ . . . μεταπείθοντι ἑαυτὸν ἐπέχοντα. To obtain a construction for ἐπέχοντα one must go back to μιμήσαιτο or to κατάλειπε.

III. 407 C, D φῶμεν καὶ Ἀσκληπιὸν τοὺς μὲν . . . ὑγιεινῶς ἔχοντας . . . τούτοις μὲν . . . καταδεῖξαι ἰατρικήν . . . τὰ νοσήματα ἐκβάλλοντα . . . προστάττειν δίαιταν . . . τὰ δ' εἴσω . . . νενοσηκότα σώματα οὐκ ἐπιχειρεῖν διαίταις . . . ἀπαντλοῦντα . . . μακρὸν καὶ κακὸν βίον ἀνθρώπῳ ποιεῖν, καὶ ἔκγονα αὐτῶν . . . ἕτερα τοιαῦτα φυτεύειν, ἀλλὰ τὸν μὴ δυνάμενον . . . ζῆν μὴ οἴεσθαι δεῖν θεραπεύειν.

Goodwin (*M. and T.*, 685) quotes several instances of the exceptional use of μή in oratio obliqua after φαίην ἄν, πάντες ἐροῦσι, τίς ἂν . . . ἡγοῖτο. (I omit those in which μή is combined with ἄν, and also Rep. I. 346 E ἔλεγον μηδένα ἐθέλειν, for which see above, p. 211 β.)

These examples may justify the supposition that the change from οὐκ ἐπιχειρεῖν to μὴ οἴεσθαι is merely capricious. But I would suggest, 1st, that it is occasioned by the *sound* of μὴ δυνάμενον, and 2nd, more doubtfully, that while ἐπιχειρεῖν is *parallel* to ἐπιδεῖξαι, οἴεσθαι is in regimen after it— he prescribed that the physician should not think, &c. A further doubt occurs whether the subject of φυτεύειν is Ἀσκληπιόν, τὸν ἰατρόν, or τοὺς ἀνθρώπους from ἀνθρώπῳ, supra. See note in loco.

IV. 424 B ὅπως ἂν . . . φυλάττωσι, τὸ μὴ νεωτερίζειν . . . ἀλλ' ὡς οἷόν τε μάλιστα φυλάττειν.

The infinitive φυλάττειν is co-ordinate with νεωτερίζειν, but the construction is forgotten. Plato would not consciously have said φυλάττωσι τὸ φυλάττειν. The infinitive is taken as a vague imperative, or as depending on ἀνθεκτέον.

VI. 488 C αὐτοὺς δὲ . . . περικεχύσθαι δεομένους, κ.τ.λ.

In what follows the infinitive takes the place of the

participle, e. g. ἄρχειν, πλεῖν. Then there is a return to the participle in ἐπαινοῦντας . . . ψέγοντας. Then, if the MSS. are right, the nominative takes the place of the accusative in ἐπαΐοντες . . . οἰόμενοι possibly suggested by the nominatives, πείθοντες and βιαζόμενοι, which have intervened.

VI. 492 C ἦν οὐ κατακλυσθεῖσαν . . . οἰχήσεσθαι . . . καὶ φήσειν. The subject is changed, and the sense continued as if no negative particle had preceded.

VI. 510 E τούτοις μὲν . . . χρώμενοι, ζητοῦντές τε αὐτὰ ἐκεῖνα ἰδεῖν. But perhaps δέ should be read.

VII. 517 A ἆρ' οὐ γέλωτ' ἂν παράσχοι . . . καὶ . . . ἀποκτιννύναι ἄν. If the text is sound the͵ construction reverts to ἐννόησον supra 516 E.

VII. 530 B καὶ ζητεῖν appears to depend immediately on ἄτοπον ἡγήσεται, losing count of the intermediate words.

VIII. 556 C, D ὅταν παραβάλλωσιν . . . ἢ καὶ . . . ἀλλήλους θεώμενοι μηδαμῇ ταύτῃ καταφρονῶνται. θεώμενοι really takes the place of a subj. θεῶνται καὶ ἔπειτα, κ.τ.λ.

IX. 581 D ὅ τε χρηματιστικὸς . . . τί δὲ ὁ φιλότιμος . . . τὸν δὲ φιλόσοφον.

*Obs.*—A curious instance of wilful ambiguity occurs in

I. 344 E ἐγὼ γὰρ οἶμαι . . . τουτὶ ἄλλως ἔχειν ; Ἔοικας, ἦν δ' ἐγώ.

Thrasymachus says, ' you see, my view is different from yours,' meaning that injustice is profitable.

Socrates replies, ' You do seem to take a different view,' meaning ' you seem to think the question unimportant.'

In several of the above instances, those who do not allow for the extent of irregularity in Platonic syntax have recourse to conjecture.

§ 61.   11. Specially noticeable are the frequent interchanges or combinations (*a*) of singular and plural, (*b*) of masculine or feminine and neuter (in speaking of abstractions), (*c*) of the artist with his art, (*d*) of a city with her citizens, (*e*) of the soul (or some part or function of the soul) with the person ; and, what is equally noticeable, the opposition of the soul to the man.

(*a*) Singular and plural—

I. 344 B, C ἐπειδὰν δέ τις πρὸς τοῖς τῶν πολιτῶν χρήμασι καὶ αὐτοὺς ἀνδραποδισάμενος δουλώσηται, ἀντὶ τούτων τῶν αἰσχρῶν ὀνομάτων εὐδαίμονες καὶ μακάριοι κέκληνται . . . ὅσοι ἂν πύθωνται αὐτόν, κ.τ.λ.

III. 399 D αὐλοποιοὺς ἢ αὐλητὰς . . . ἢ οὐ τοῦτο πολυχορδότατον.

III. 411 B, C καὶ ἐὰν μὲν . . . λάβῃ . . . ἔμπλεῳ.

VI. 496 C, D τούτων . . . οἱ γενόμενοι, . . . λογισμῷ λαβών, κ.τ.λ.

VI. 498 B, C ὅταν . . . ἐκτὸς γίγνηται . . . ἀφέτους νέμεσθαι, κ.τ.λ.

VIII. 554 B, C ἐν αὐτῷ . . . αὐτῶν.

VIII. 558 A ἀνθρώπων καταψηφισθέντων . . . περινοστεῖ ὥσπερ ἥρως.

IX. 571 C τὰς περὶ τὸν ὕπνον . . . ἐκείνου.

Cp. II. 376 E ; III. 411 B, C τὸν θυμὸν ὀξύρροπον ἀπειργάσατο . . . ἀκρόχολοι οὖν, κ.τ.λ.: IV. 426 A τόδε αὐτῶν οὐ χαρίεν . . . ἔχθιστον ἡγεῖσθαι τὸν . . . λέγοντα, ὅτι πρὶν ἂν μεθύων, κ.τ.λ.: ib. 426 C ἀποθανουμένους ὃς ἂν τοῦτο δρᾷ.

So with transition from particular to general VIII. 554 A θησαυροποιὸς ἀνήρ· οὓς δὴ καὶ ἐπαινεῖ τὸ πλῆθος.

*Obs.* 1.—A collective plural has sometimes a singular verb (v. 462 E, 463 A ἔστι μέν . . . ἄρχοντές τε καὶ δῆμος) and a collective singular, a plural relative (VI. 490 E σμικρὸν δέ τι . . . οὕς, κ.τ.λ.). In III. 399 D, quoted above, τοῦτο is a collective singular.

*Obs.* 2.—When two things are joined or brought under a single notion, they are spoken of as one (IV. 435 A ταὐτὸν . . . μεῖζόν ε καὶ ἔλαττον: v. 473 D καὶ τοῦτο . . . δύναμίς τε . . . καὶ φιλοσοφία). Hence we have the part in apposition to the whole (VII. 526 A τὸ ἕν . . . ἴσον . . . ἕκαστον πᾶν παντί), and singular and plural are correlated where the former is universal, the latter particular (X. 601 D χρώμενον ἑκάστῳ . . . οἷα ἀγαθὰ ἢ κακὰ . . . ᾧ χρῆται).

(*b*) Masculine or feminine alternating with neuter—

II. 359 C πλεονεξίαν, ὃ πᾶσα φύσις, κ.τ.λ.

II. 363 A αὐτὸ δικαιοσύνην.

III. 401 D ὅ τε ῥυθμὸς καὶ ἁρμονία . . . **φέροντα.**

III. 410 E ἀνεθέντος **αὐτοῦ** (sc. τῆς φύσεως).

IV. 428 A κατάδηλον . . . ἡ σοφία.

IV. 428 B τοῦτό γε αὐτό, ἡ εὐβουλία.

V. 449 D κοινωνίαν . . . ὀρθῶς . . . γιγνόμενον.

X. 611 B τοιοῦτον εἶναι ψυχήν, κ.τ.λ.

*Obs.*—Even where a concrete masculine noun is used abstractly, it has a neuter correlative.

II. 382 E ὁ θεὸς ἁπλοῦν.

VI. 494 D **νοῦς** οὐκ ἔνεστιν αὐτῷ . . . **τὸ** δὲ οὐ κτητόν.

(*c*) The artist and his art.

III. 409 E, 410 A οὐκοῦν καὶ ἰατρικήν . . . μετὰ τῆς τοιαύτης δικαστικῆς κατὰ πόλιν νομοθετήσεις, αἳ τῶν πολιτῶν σοι τοὺς μὲν εὐφυεῖς . . . θεραπεύσουσι, τοὺς δὲ μή . . . αὐτοὶ ἀποκτενοῦσιν ;

Mr. H. Richards would read αὐταί. But observe that in that case ἐάσουσιν and ἀποκτενοῦσιν would *both* refer as θεραπεύσουσι does to ἰατρική and δικαστική combined.

The plural here is κατὰ σύνεσιν as the dual in VIII. 550 E πλούτου ἀρετὴ διέστηκεν . . . τοὐναντίον ῥέποντε. So dialectic and the dialecticians in VII. 537 E τὸ νῦν περὶ τὸ **διαλέγεσθαι** κακὸν . . . : παρανομίας . . . ἐμπίπλανται.

(*d*) The city and her citizens.

IV. 435 E **ἐν ταῖς πόλεσιν** . . . οἳ δὴ καὶ ἔχουσι ταύτην τὴν αἰτίαν.

VIII. 551 D τὴν μὲν πενήτων, τὴν δὲ πλουσίων, οἰκοῦντας ἐν τῷ αὐτῷ.

On the other hand the city is opposed to the citizens (as in Thuc.) : II. 370 E αὐτὴν τὴν πόλιν, IV. 428 C, D οὐχ ὑπὲρ **τῶν ἐν τῇ πόλει τινὸς** βουλεύεται, ἀλλ᾽ ὑπὲρ **ἑαυτῆς ὅλης.**

(*e*) The man and his mind. (This may also be regarded as a point of style. Cp. esp. Phaedo, pp. 82, 83.)

III. 411 A, B οὗτος τὸ μὲν πρῶτον . . . ὥσπερ σίδηρον ἐμάλαξε (τὸ θυμοειδὲς) . . . ὅταν δ᾽ ἐπέχων μὴ ἀνίῃ . . . τήκει . . . ἕως ἂν . . . ἐκτέμῃ ὥσπερ νεῦρα ἐκ τῆς ψυχῆς, κ.τ.λ. (with ἄθυμον infra ψυχήν is to be supplied).

IV. 440 C, D ὅταν τις οἴηται . . . πραϋνθῇ.

VI. 486 A ᾗ οὖν ὑπάρχει διανοίᾳ . . . οἷόν τε οἴει τούτῳ μέγα τι δοκεῖν εἶναι τὸν ἀνθρώπινον βίον;

VI. 503 C, D τὰ βέβαια αὖ ταῦτα ἤθη . . . χάσμης ἐμπίπλανται. The plural requires a masculine subject.

VI. 503 D, E δεῖν αὐτῷ (masc.) μεταδιδόναι . . . σπάνιον αὐτὸ οἴει ἔσεσθαι . . . βασανιστέον δὴ . . . εἰ . . . δυνατή (sc. ἡ φύσις αὕτη).

X. 620 E ἄγειν αὐτὴν . . . κυροῦντα ἣν λαχὼν εἵλετο μοῖραν.

## XIII. Rhetorical Figures. § 62.

1. *Personification* enters largely into Greek idiom and is very characteristic of Plato. The argument (λόγος) is of course continually personified. A strong instance occurs in

VI. 503 A παρεξιόντος καὶ παρακαλυπτομένου τοῦ λόγου, πεφοβημένου κινεῖν τὸ νῦν παρον.

Hence in VI. 484 A διὰ μακροῦ τινὸς διεξελθόντος λόγου, 'this reading (A Π M) is probably to be retained in preference to διεξελθόντες (x v).

Amongst many personifications perhaps the most striking is that in VIII. 568 D describing the difficulty experienced by tragic poetry in mounting 'constitution hill,' ὥσπερ ὑπὸ ἄσθματος ἀδυνατοῦσα πορεύεσθαι. Books VIII and IX indeed also abound with bold personifications : see esp. IX. 573 A δορυφορεῖταί τε ὑπὸ μανίας, IX. 587 C δορυφόροις ἡδοναῖς.

The use of personifying words often adds a touch of liveliness to the style.

ἐθέλω (cp. Herod.) : IV. 436 B ταὐτὸν τἀναντία ποιεῖν ἢ πάσχειν . . . οὐκ ἐθελήσει ἅμα. Cp. II. 370 B.

V. 459 C μὴ δεομένοις μὲν σώμασι φαρμάκων, ἀλλὰ διαίτῃ ἐθελόντων ὑπακούειν.

νοεῖν (I. 335 E), λέγειν, ἐπαινεῖν, ψέγειν, καλεῖν of words and phrases (IV. 431 A τοῦτο λέγειν τὸ κρείττω αὐτοῦ, κ.τ.λ.).

ἀμφισβητῶ : IV. 442 E εἴ τι ἡμῶν ἔτι ἐν τῇ ψυχῇ ἀμφισβητεῖ.

ζητῶ : III. 388 E ἰσχυρὰν καὶ μεταβολὴν ζητεῖ τὸ τοιοῦτον.

To this head belongs the adjectival use of ἀδελφός, ἑταῖρος III. 404 B, IV. 439 D.

ποιῶ : a special use of ποιεῖν (intrans.='to behave') may be noticed here because occurring sometimes with an impersonal subject.

II. 365 A τί οἰόμεθα ἀκουούσας νέων ψυχὰς ποιεῖν.

IV. 432 A οὐχ οὕτω ποιεῖ ('acts') αὕτη.

So probably in VII. 523 E ὧδε ποιεῖ ἑκάστη αὐτῶν (τῶν αἰσθήσεων).

For the same use with a personal subject see V. 474 D ἢ οὐχ οὕτω ποιεῖτε πρὸς τοὺς καλούς; 'Is not this your way?'

III. 416 B μὴ τοιοῦτον . . . ποιήσωσι, κ.τ.λ.

V. 469 B πρὸς τοὺς πολεμίους πῶς ποιήσουσιν ;

§ 63.　2. *Continued Metaphor.*　The two chief examples in the Republic of this figure, which serves at once to enliven and to connect discourse, are the image of the wave in Book V, and the allegory of the cave in Book VII. The former is a good instance of the way in which an image *grows* in Plato.

It may possibly have been suggested by some preparatory hints in Book IV. See esp. 441 C ταῦτα . . . μόγις διανενεύκαμεν. This renders more natural the incidental remark in V. 453 D ἄν τέ τις εἰς κολυμβήθραν μικρὰν ἐμπέσῃ ἄν τε εἰς τὸ μέγιστον πέλαγος μέσον, ὅμως γε νεῖ οὐδὲν ἧττον : (ibid.) οὐκοῦν καὶ ἡμῖν νευστέον καὶ πειρατέον σώζεσθαι ἐκ τοῦ λόγου, ἤτοι δελφῖνά τινα ἐλπίζοντας ἡμᾶς ὑπολαβεῖν ἂν ἤ τινα ἄλλην ἄπορον σωτηρίαν. So far, although the image of a 'sea of difficulty' has appeared in connexion with the fear of ridicule and the mockery of comic poets (452 B), there is no hint of combining the notion of laughter with that of the waves. Four pages afterwards (457 B, C) we are found to have escaped from the first great 'wave' which had threatened to swamp us. And, after a still longer interval,—the digression about usages of war having intervened,—it appears at 472 A that the three stages of difficulty are distinctly thought of as a τρικυμία, of which the third and greatest wave is now impending. Hence, as the result of all this, when the discussion culminates, and the moment has arrived for the audacious figure of the laughing wave, it is introduced without any effect of violence, (473 C) εἰρήσεται δ' οὖν, εἰ καὶ μέλλει γέλωτί τε ἀτεχνῶς ὥσπερ κῦμα ἐκγελῶν (' bursting in laughter ') καὶ ἀδοξίᾳ κατακλύσειν.

Similarly, the descriptions of the evil states in Books VIII, IX are linked together by the growing image of the *drones* in the hive (distinguished as stinging and stingless) which culminates in the description of the master passion in the tyrannical individual as a mighty winged drone— ὑπόπτερον καὶ μέγαν κηφῆνά τινα (IX. 573 A).

Again, the incidental phrase βίου κατασκευή (VIII. 557 B) helps to render more natural the impressive conception of the inward πολιτεία, 'the kingdom of Heaven within,' at the close of Book IX. 592 B ἐν οὐρανῷ . . . παράδειγμα ἀνάκειται τῷ βουλομένῳ ὁρᾶν καὶ ὁρῶντι ἑαυτὸν κατοικίζειν. Also in IX. 588 E the words καὶ τὰ περὶ τὸν λέοντα serve to make less abrupt the introduction of the serpent element— τὸ ὀφεῶδες (ib. 590 B).

Other instances of Plato's love of climax and gradation are the elaborate account of the misery of the tyrant in IX. 576–588, and the demonstration of the unreality of poetry in x. 598, 599. (Cp. the treatment of Pleasure in the Philebus.)

3. *Cumulative illustration.* The effect of liveliness and § 64. also of fertility of conception is often produced by the substitution of one illustration for another before there has been time for the first to be applied. Thus in the quick succession of examples with which Socrates poses Polemarchus, after showing that the just man is inferior to the draught-player as a partner in draughts, to the builder in the laying of bricks, &c., instead of simply asking, 'to whom then is he superior, and in what?' he brings in a fresh example at the moment of asking.

I. 333 B ἀλλ᾽ εἰς τίνα δὴ κοινωνίαν ὁ δίκαιος ἀμείνων κοινωνὸς τοῦ κιθαριστικοῦ, ὥσπερ ὁ κιθαριστικὸς τοῦ δικαίου εἰς κρουμάτων; Cp. Theaet. 147 A where in showing the absurdity of the definition of πηλός—πηλὸς ὁ τῶν χυτρέων καὶ πηλὸς ὁ τῶν ἱπνοπλαθῶν καὶ πηλὸς ὁ τῶν πλινθουργῶν—an unexpected addition is made to it,—εἴτε ὁ τῶν κοροπλαθῶν προσθέντες, εἴτε ἄλλων ὡντινωνοῦν δημιουργῶν.

So in IV. 421 A—where he has been arguing from the examples of the husbandman and potter that the life of the guardians must be arranged so as to secure their devotion to their proper work,—instead of proceeding to say that this is the more necessary in proportion to the high importance of their function, he suddenly introduces to our notice the class of 'botchers,' whose work is the least important of all:—νευρορράφοι γὰρ φαῦλοι γενόμενοι, κ.τ.λ.

Hence it is probable that in V. 479 B—τοῖς ἐν ταῖς ἐστιά-σεσιν, κ.τ.λ.—there are *two* illustrations and not one only. See note in loco.

§ 65.  4. *Irony and Litotes.* The tendency to under-statement, which in Thucydides and elsewhere renders οὐχ ἧσσον = μᾶλλον and the like, is strengthened by the peculiar irony of Plato. In a few places this irony has been a cause of obscurity, e. g.—

(*a*) I. 337 C ἄλλο τι οὖν, ἔφη, καὶ σὺ οὕτω ποιήσεις; 'I suppose, then, that is what you mean to do?'

IV. 423 C–E φαῦλον . . . φαυλότερον . . . φαῦλα.

V. 451 A ὥστε εὖ με παραμυθεῖ.

VII. 529 A οὐκ ἀγεννῶς (cp. Phaedr. 264 B).

It gives rise to doubt about οὐ πάνυ, μὴ πάνυ τι, &c. See above, p. 209 β.

*Obs.*—The alternation between irony and seriousness, which Plato sometimes introduces with marked effect, has also given rise to misapprehension.

I. 344 E ἐγὼ γὰρ οἶμαι, ἔφη ὁ Θρασύμαχος, τουτὶ ἄλλως ἔχειν. Ἔοικας, ἦν δ᾽ ἐγώ. (See note in loco.)

(*b*) The constant insertion of qualifying phrases, to avoid the appearance of dogmatism, belongs to the same tendency. To this may be referred the frequent use of τάχ᾽ ἄν, ὡς ἔπος εἰπεῖν, εἰς τὸ δυνατόν, ἂν μὴ πᾶσα ἀνάγκη, εἰς ὅσον ἐνδέχεται, and VII. 527 A καὶ σμικρά.

(*c*) Ironical collocation of words (παρὰ προσδοκίαν) II. 373 A ἑταῖραι καὶ πέμματα. (See note on II. 373 B θηρευταί.)

5. *Recurring phrases.*

Besides the qualifying expressions mentioned in the last paragraph, Plato employs certain recurring phrases or *façons de parler*, partly (*a*) to maintain the resemblance to ordinary conversation, and partly (*b*) to keep before the mind the pervading antithesis between the actual and the ideal.

(*a*) Of the former sort are ὥρα ἂν εἴη, τίς μηχανή ; τὸ λεγόμενον, πάσῃ τέχνῃ, εἰ μὴ ἀδικῶ, εἰ μή τι (sc. ἄλλο), εἰ μὴ σὺ κελεύεις, and the 'pronominal' phrases noticed above, p. 196 (*g*).

The frequent use of ὦ δαιμόνιε, ὦ θαυμάσιε, ὦ πρὸς Διός, &c. marks the rising interest of the discussion. See esp. IX. 574 B ἀντεχομένων δὴ καὶ μαχομένων, ὦ **θαυμάσιε**, γέροντός τε καὶ γραός, κ.τ.λ. A similar effect is produced by the repetition of ἦ δ᾽ ὅς in the course of a reported speech. Cp. ἔφη λέγων in Herodotus.

(*b*) To the latter motive,—the contrast of actual and ideal,—is to be ascribed the constant use of δοκῶν, λεγόμενος, καλούμενος, δοξαζόμενος εἶναι, οἰόμενος (I. 336 A, III. 395 D &c.) : also of ποιούμενος = 'esteemed' in VI. 498 A, VII. 538 C, —where see notes. Special uses of οὗτος, ἐκεῖνος, ὅδε, ἐνθάδε, ἐκεῖ, νῦν (VI. 489 C τοὺς νῦν πολιτικοὺς ἄρχοντας) are grounded on the same antithesis.

6. *Tautology and Repetition.*                    § 66.

(*a*) Plato is not in the least afraid of repeating the same word and often does so accidentally in the same passage with a difference of meaning. This happens very frequently with δοκεῖν, δόξα, and other words which have both a vernacular and a philosophical sense. Especially noticeable are :

III. 415 C τὴν ... προσήκουσαν τιμὴν ἀποδόντες ... τιμήσαντες :
where H. Richards would read τιμήσαντες ⟨κατ' ἀξίαν⟩.

V. 449 D ἄλλης ἐπιλαμβάνει πολιτείας, 'You are taking up
another form of State,' with V. 450 A ἐπιλαβόμενοί μου,
'taking me up,' i. e. 'checking my discourse' immediately
following.

VIII. 546 D ἄρχοντες . . . καταστήσονται, 'rulers will be
appointed' (passive).

Ibid. καταστήσονται . . . τοὺς ἀρίστους, 'they will appoint
the best men to be their rulers' (middle voice).

Cp. Laws VIII. 840 E, 841 A τίνα δὴ συμβουλεύεις αὐτοῖς
τίθεσθαι νόμον, ἐὰν ὁ νῦν τιθέμενος αὐτοὺς ἐκφύγῃ; where
τίθεσθαι is middle, and τιθέμενος passive.

For Rep. VIII. 547 E ἁπλοῦς . . . ἁπλουστέρους see note
in loco.

*Obs.*—There are limits to this as to other anomalies and it is
very improbable that in VI. 499 E ff. ἀλλοίαν . . . δόξαν should mean,
first, 'a different opinion from what they now have' and then
'a different opinion from that which we maintain,' or that in
X. 601 D, E τὸν χρώμενον . . . ἄγγελον γίγνεσθαι τῷ **ποιητῇ οἷα ἀγαθὰ
ἢ κακὰ ποιεῖ** . . . ᾧ χρῆται· οἷον αὐλητής . . . περὶ τῶν αὐλῶν . . . ἐπι-
τάξει οἵους δεῖ **ποιεῖν**, the words οἷα ἀγαθὰ ἢ κακὰ ποιεῖ . . . ᾧ χρῆται
should mean 'what *the instrument does* well or ill,' and not 'what
specimens of the instrument *the maker makes* well or ill.'

(*b*) On the other hand the language is varied without
apparent reason.

VII. 530 E ἐξῆκον . . . ἀφήκειν and often elsewhere.

§ 67.                    **XIV.  Order of Words.**

(Cp. *Digest*, §§ 287–311.)

The freedom of conversation allows of great variety in
the order of words, and Plato has used this liberty for
purposes of effect, sometimes putting words to the front to
give importance to them, sometimes reserving a surprise,
and sometimes merely avoiding harsh collocations.  Thus

unusual order is employed (1) for emphasis, (2) for euphony, or (3) for both together. (The general rule that the more emphatic notion stands *first* in Greek—not *last*, as often in English—of course holds in Plato as in other writers.)

1. (*a*) A phrase is rendered more emphatic by separating the words of which it is composed and placing unemphatic words between. (Phaedr 247 B ἄκραν . . . ἀψῖδα.)

I. 339 E ἆρα τότε . . . οὐκ ἀναγκαῖον συμβαίνειν αὐτὸ οὑτωσὶ δίκαιον εἶναι ποιεῖν τοὐναντίον ἢ ὃ σὺ λέγεις (see note in loco).

VI. 492 A ἐὰν μή τις αὐτῇ βοηθήσας θεῶν τύχῃ.

VI. 499 C πόλεώς τις ἀνάγκη ἐπιμεληθῆναι.

IX. 572 B καὶ πάνυ δοκοῦσιν ἡμῶν ἐνίοις μετρίοις εἶναι.

IX. 582 C ἀπό γε τοῦ τιμᾶσθαι, οἷόν ἐστι, πάντες τῆς ἡδονῆς ἔμπειροι (i. e. πάντες ἔμπειροι τῆς γε ἀπὸ τοῦ τιμᾶσθαι ἡδονῆς, οἷόν ἐστι).

(*b*) In order to bring an emphatic notion into prominence, a relative, interrogative, or negative word is postponed.

II. 363 A τοῖς ὁσίοις ἅ φασι θεοὺς διδόναι.

II. 377 E ὅ τε αὖ Κρόνος ὡς ἐτιμωρήσατο.

III. 390 B μόνος ἐγρηγορὼς ἃ ἐβουλεύσατο.

III. 413 C τοῦτο ὡς ποιητέον.

IV. 437 D οἷον δίψα ἐστὶ δίψα ἆρά γε, κ.τ.λ., where the inversion has led to an error of punctuation (see v. rr.).

V. 453 D οὐ μὰ τὸν Δία, ἔφη, οὐ γὰρ εὐκόλῳ ἔοικεν (= οὐ γὰρ εὐκόλῳ ἔοικεν, οὔ, μὰ τὸν Δία).

2. Euphony.                                                              § 68.

(*a*) The interlacing of clauses has sometimes no obvious motive except a more euphonious rhythm.

III. 396 C ὁ μέν μοι δοκεῖ, ἦν δ᾽ ἐγώ, μέτριος ἀνήρ.

Phaedo 99 C τὴν δὲ τοῦ ὡς οἷόν τε βέλτιστα αὐτὰ τεθῆναι δύναμιν οὕτω νῦν κεῖσθαι.

(*b*) A special case is the displacement of adverbs through the adherence of the preposition to its noun. (See Vahlen on Ar. Poet. 1457 A, 31 μὴ ἐκ σημαινόντων : 'quae collocatio et apud Ar. ipsum multa habet *exx.*, et apud alios.')

Cp. Herod. II. 27 κάρτα ἀπὸ θερμῶν χωρέων : Dem. de Cor. § 288 ὡς παρ᾽ οἰκειοτάτῳ.

III. 391 D ὥρμησαν οὕτως ἐπὶ δεινὰς ἁρπαγάς.

VI. 492 A μὴ ἐν προσηκούσῃ.

IX. 590 A πολὺ ἐπὶ δεινοτέρῳ ὀλέθρῳ.

§ 69.    3. Both emphasis and euphony seem to be consulted in the displacement or trajection of αὖ, ἤδη, καί.

(*a*) The habitual postponement of αὖ to the negative at once emphasizes the negation, and, in the case of οὐκ αὖ, avoids an undesirable hiatus. The use of μὴ αὖ probably follows the other idiom by assimilation.

III. 393 D ἵνα δὲ μὴ εἴπῃς, ὅτι οὐκ αὖ μανθάνεις.

IV. 442 A ὃ τηρήσετον μὴ . . . πολὺ καὶ ἰσχυρὸν γενόμενον οὐκ αὖ τὰ αὑτοῦ πράττῃ.

VI. 499 D τοῖς δὲ πολλοῖς . . . ὅτι οὐκ αὖ δοκεῖ, ἐρεῖς;

Cp. Theaet. 161 A οἴει . . . ἐρεῖν ὡς οὐκ αὖ ἔχει οὕτω ταῦτα.

Crat. 391 C ἀλλ' εἰ μὴ αὖ σε ταῦτα ἀρέσκει, κ.τ.λ.

Aristoph. Pax 281 τί ἔστι; μῶν οὐκ αὖ φέρεις;

Αὖ comes even between the preposition and the noun:

II. 371 D τοῖς δὲ ἀντὶ αὖ ἀργυρίου.

IX. 577 B καὶ ἐν αὖ τοῖς δημοσίοις κινδύνοις.

(*b*) An emphatic ἤδη is placed foremost although in meaning really attached to a word from which it is thus separated. In some cases this arrangement avoids cacophony.

V. 452 B ἀλλ' καὶ ἤδη τὰς πρεσβυτέρας.

VII. 531 E ἀλλὰ ἤδη, εἶπον, [οἱ] μὴ δυνατοί τινες (s. τινος) ὄντες, κ.τ.λ. (avoiding μὴ ἤδη).

(*c*) Similarly καί is sometimes separated (ὑπερβάτως) from its word.

V. 470 B, C ὅρα δὴ καὶ εἰ τόδε πρὸς τρόπου λέγω.

[VI. 500 A ἦ, καὶ ἐὰν οὕτω θεῶνται, κ.τ.λ. (joining καὶ οὕτω, but see note in loco and supra, p. 200 ι).]

In IX. 573 D τοῦτο σὺ καὶ ἐμοὶ ἐρεῖς, καί although joined to ἐμοί really emphasizes both pronouns.

Cp. Laws III. 680 A Πολιτείας δέ γε ἤδη καὶ τρόπος ἐστί τις οὗτος.

It is sometimes postponed together with the interrogative, though belonging to the whole sentence.

IX. 571 C λέγεις δὲ καὶ τίνας ... ταύτας (i. e. τίνας καὶ λέγεις) ;
Cp. Hdt. VIII. 89, § 1 ὀλίγοι δέ τινες καὶ Ἑλλήνων, where
καί belonging to the whole clause is attracted by the
emphasis to Ἑλλήνων. See also ib. III. 36, § 4 Σὺ καὶ ἐμοὶ
τολμᾷς συμβουλεύειν.

(*d*) ἀλλά ... δή are widely separated in V. 467 D ἀλλὰ γάρ,
φήσομεν, καὶ παρὰ δόξαν πολλὰ πολλοῖς δὴ ἐγένετο.

(*e*) Observe the position of τε in λέγειν λόγον τε in V. 472 A,
according to Par. A, and of μέν in VI. 508 E, but see notes
in locis.

4. Words introduced διὰ μέσου by an afterthought may
sometimes disturb the order of the sentence.

IV. 425 E ὥσπερ τοὺς κάμνοντάς τε καὶ οὐκ ἐθέλοντας ὑπὸ ἀκολασίας ἐκβῆναι πονηρᾶς διαίτης, where the position of ὑπὸ
ἀκολασίας belongs to the whole phrase οὐκ ἐθέλοντας ἐκβῆναι.

V. 467 C καὶ οὐκ ἄξιον κινδύνου (see note in loco).

5. Parenthetical words are introduced sometimes before
an enclitic, sometimes between a preposition and its case.

I. 337 E πῶς γὰρ ἄν ... ὦ βέλτιστε, τὶς κ.τ.λ.

VIII. 564 A ἐξ οἶμαι τῆς ἀκροτάτης ἐλευθερίας.

So in Phaedr. 227 B οὐκ ἂν οἴει, κ.τ.λ. the parenthetical
word divides ἄν from the verb.

N.B.—All these peculiarities of rhythmical arrangement
become more marked in the later dialogues, especially the
Timaeus and Laws.

## XV. Grammatical irregularities considered in relation § 70. to the text.

It will probably be objected that in these remarks too
little account has been taken of the alterations introduced by
recent editors into the Platonic text. The emendations of
Cobet, Madvig, Badham, and W. H. Thompson are manifestly deserving of attention. But before adopting them
wholesale, or even to the extent to which they were embodied
in the fourth Zürich edition, several considerations should be

carefully weighed.  (1) The balance of anterior probability
is against the best founded conjecture when this is opposed
to the consent of the MSS.  (2) How few of the changes
confidently proposed by Schleiermacher, van Heusde, Ast,
Heindorf, and K. F. Hermann, are at this moment accepted
as certain !  (3) In the last resort the context must decide.
But in judging of the context, it is not enough to be well
skilled in grammar and logic, or in the law of parsimony
that presides over a terse literary style.   The special
conditions of Attic dialogue should be taken into account,
and, as these are chiefly to be learned from Plato, some
such synoptical survey as has been here attempted is
required to assist the student in comparing Plato with
himself.   If the result of such an endeavour, based on the
traditional text, is to bring out a series of phenomena
which to those who are intimately acquainted with Greek
and with the nature of language commend themselves even
in their irregularities as *natural* and consistent, it follows
that the number of places in which conjecture is found
necessary will be considerably reduced.   If, on the contrary, the redundancies and anomalies to which reference
has been made are to be regarded as unworthy of the
great stylist and dialectician, and the acknowledgement of
them inconsistent with true reverence for him, the process
of conjectural emendation, precarious as it is at best, must
be largely extended before all such unsightlinesses can be
removed.   And should this labour be completed, the doubt
may ultimately recur whether Plato's image has not
suffered like that of the great English poet, whose bust
(according to Sir Henry Taylor) was 'sadly smoothed
away into nothingness at the instance of some country
neighbour of Wordsworth's, whose notions of refinement
could not be satisfied without the obliteration of everything that was characteristic and true.'

There is an extreme to be avoided in both directions,
and rational critics will probably be found to admit that

the distinction between what is sound and unsound often turns upon a question of degree. There are emendations which secure acceptance by their convincing quality— which 'jump to the eyes' of the reader as well as of the emender at the first flash. Such is Schneider's ἐτίμα μάλιστα for ἔτι μάλιστα in Rep. VIII. 554 B, such is Geer's παισίν for πᾶσιν in VI. 494 B, and Mr. Archer Hind's ἐν τῷ μέρει for ἐπὶ τῶν ἐν μέρει Theaet. 190 C. There are others of which a high degree of probability may be safely predicated, such as van Prinsterer's ἑκάστας for ἕκαστος (v. r. ἑκάστοτε) in VI. 493 B. Such simple changes as πάντων for πάντως (VI. 497 D), κατηκόῳ for κατήκοοι (VI. 499 B), τὼ δ' αὖ, τό for τὸ δ' αὐτό (VIII. 547 B), when they have the effect of restoring a smooth and idiomatic context, may be accepted without cavil. The transposition of χαίρων καί in III. 401 E (based on a reference in Aristotle—but cp. Laws VI. 751 D) although supported by the similar syllables in δυσχεραίνων, and even Graser's τί οἰώμεθα in IX. 581 D can only be regarded as highly probable (the same may be said of ὅσοι for ὅσων in VII. 534 A, οἰκείου ἐνόντος for οἰκεῖον ἔχοντος in IX. 590 D, αὐτόχειρος for αὐτόχειρας in X. 615 C), and there is good reason for rejecting the seemingly simple alteration of διδόντες to ᾄδοντες (II. 365 D)[1], and that of βλάψει to βλάψειν (a MS. emendation) in the preceding context, II. 364 C. Madvig's ingenious conjecture in X. 608 A, ᾀσόμεθα for αἰσθόμεθα, may well appear convincing at first sight. It gets rid of a non-classical form; it merely presupposes the miswriting of CΘO for CO; and it seems naturally enough to echo ἐπᾴδοντες in the sentence immediately preceding. But on closer inspection, the use of δ' οὖν requires the resumption not of what immediately precedes (with only εὐλαβούμενοι ... τὸν τῶν πολλῶν ἔρωτα coming between) but of the main apodosis answering to the words in the comparison, ὥσπερ ... βίᾳ μέν, ὅμως δὲ ἀπέχονται.

---

[1] Although supported by the v. r. διδομένου (Ven. Π) for ᾀδομένου in III. 398 D. But there is no reason for assuming corruption. See note in loco.

Either ἀφεξόμεθα, therefore, or some equivalent word, and not ᾀσόμεθα, is what the context requires.

§ 71.     Accretions consequent on the admission of glosses into the text, are a form of corruption to which all classical writers [1] are liable.   The assumption of such alteration has been of late extensively applied to Plato.   It is supported by such manifest instances as Theaet. 190 C, Rep. IX. 580 D, and it cannot be denied to have a legiti-mate place, although the condition of some dialogues, such as the Phaedo and Cratylus, is found in point of fact to give more scope for it than is the case with others. But the editors who, after the manner of Hirschig, have bracketed or excised every phrase that could not conveni-ently be tied upon the trellis-work of logic, should be asked to pause and consider whether these 'overgrowths' do not belong to the native exuberance of the Athenian language in its times of leisure (Theaet. 172 C, D).   Their ideal of trimness seems too like that of the old English (or Dutch) gardener—

> ' Go thou, and like an executioner,
> Cut off the heads of too fast growing sprays,
> That look too lofty in our commonwealth.
> All must be even in our government [2].'

But, it will be said, some superfluous clauses in the Republic are omitted in Par. A, the earliest and most authoritative MS.   This is perfectly true, but, before drawing conclusions from the fact, it is right to under-stand the nature and extent of it.   First, then, account should be taken of the observation, which is easily verified, that in most of these instances there is present either 'homoeoteleuton' or some other condition slippery for scribes ; e. g.—

II. 358 A ψέγεται [ἀδικία ἢ ἐπαινεῖται].

360 A τῶν ἀγγέλων γενέσθαι [τῶν παρὰ τὸν βασιλέα, add. in mg.].

---

[1] See especially Hdt. iv. 127, § 5.
[2] Shakespeare, *Richard II*, iii. 4, 33–36.

II. 364 A ἡ σωφροσύνη [τε καὶ δικαιοσύνη].

366 A αἱ τελεταὶ [αὖ μέγα δύνανται].

367 C ψέγειν [ἀλλὰ τὸ δοκεῖν add. in mg.] with ἀλλὰ τὸ δοκεῖν in preceding line.

373 A [καὶ τὴν ποικιλίαν], καὶ χρυσόν, κ.τ.λ.

„ E [καὶ ἰδίᾳ καὶ δημοσίᾳ] κακὰ γίγνεται add. in mg.

376 C [φιλόσοφον] καὶ φιλομαθῆ.

378 C τοιαῦτα [λεκτέα].

379 A ἐάν τέ τις αὐτὸν ἐν ἔπεσι ποιῇ [ἐάν τε ἐν μέλεσιν] ἐάν τε ἐν τραγῳδίᾳ.

This argument is greatly strengthened by considering the omissions in Ven. Π, also due to homoeoteleuton, or in some cases to the dropping of a line. See E on Text, pp. 103, 104.

Secondly, it is by no means an indifferent circumstance § 72. that these omissions all come within a certain limited space in the Republic. We should have to search far in order to gather an equal number from elsewhere, and those which do occur in the later portions of the dialogue for the most part involve the loss of indispensable words, and are to be accounted for by the accidental dropping of a line.

Thirdly, that some of them at least were the errors of a scribe appears from the omitted words being supplied in the margin by the diorthotes, either from the archetype of A or from another MS. And it should be observed that the words bracketed are *not* in every case superfluous. It would be rash to cancel αὖ μέγα δύνανται (II. 366 A), though they had been omitted in more MSS. than one, and the clause ἀλλὰ τὸ δοκεῖν (ib. 367 C) would have to be supplied if it had been omitted by all the scribes. But if these omissions are due to the copyists, the others can not be assumed not to be so. And the redundance, even where indisputable, has been shown to be not inconsistent with the manner of Plato. The case of IX. 580 D where A reads τὸ λογιστικὸν δέξεται, and another MS. (Par. K) λογιστικὸν ἐπιθυμητικὸν θυμικὸν δέξεται, for the simple δέξεται, stands on a different footing (see note in loco), and it may be admitted that a somewhat similar corruption may have crept into VII. 533 E ὃ ἂν μόνον δηλοῖ πρὸς τὴν ἕξιν σαφηνείᾳ ὃ λέγει ἐν ψυχῇ, though the interpolation is here less manifest and correction consequently more difficult, if not impossible. The whole sentence is omitted in Ven. Ξ. (E. on Text, pp. 112, 113.)

---

## PART II.

### PLATONIC DICTION.

i. NEW DERIVATIVES AND COMPOUNDS.
ii. SELECTION AND USE OF WORDS.
iii. PHILOSOPHICAL TERMINOLOGY.

§ 1.   Plato's vocabulary is that of highly educated Athenians of the fourth century B.C., enriched with special elements derived (*a*) from the Socratic love of homely illustration, (*b*) from poetic and other literature, in the way of quotation, adaptation, imitation, and allusion, (*c*) from the innovations of the Sophists, both rhetorical and eristic, and (*d*) from habits of speech fostered within the Academy as a philosophical school.

### i. New Derivatives and Compounds.

The restrictive or selective tendency of Attic Greek, reserving one word for one idea, and rejecting many synonyms, has been repeatedly illustrated [1].

'No Attic writer would have used it (Εὐφρόνη) for νύξ: but not only does it occur in Herodotus more frequently than the soberer term, but even a scientific writer like Hippocrates employs it. Again, if we compare the usage of πάλος and κλῆρος, it will be seen that the more picturesque of the two words has in all Attic, but that of Tragedy,

---

[1] See Rutherford, *New Phrynichus*, pp. 13 ff.

been ousted by the colourless term, though in Ionic prose
the former remained the commoner.'

The converse or complementary tendency, to have
a word for everything and to invent new terms to express
novel distinctions, has been less observed. Yet in comparing Plato's language with that of Thucydides or Antiphon, or the tragic poets, or even Lysias or Isocrates, it is
impossible not to be aware that the discarding of picturesque
or 'coloured' synonyms was accompanied with the invention of many novelties in the expression of abstract
notions. This increasing copiousness, forming part of the
improvement and development of prose-writing, is of
unquestionable significance, and exercised a marked influence
on all the subsequent literature.

Plato himself remarks on the introduction of new-fangled
terms by Protagoras and others [1], and on Prodicus' affected
love of minute verbal distinctions. He himself might have
been asked by a malicious questioner why he should
employ δικαιότης and διαφορότης when such old friends as
δικαιοσύνη and διαφορά were available. The answer is that
similar changes were multiplying on every side, and had
become a part of the natural medium of cultivated expression. 'Correct' writers like Isocrates might be sparing
in their use, but the extent to which they had found their
way into general currency may be estimated from Xenophon. Δικαιότης, for example, is one of a large number of
derivative words that are found in Plato and Xenophon,
and *in no earlier writer*.

A few others, of which the same remark is true, may be      § 2.
cited here in passing. To name them all would occupy
more space than can be fitly given to a mere collateral
illustration.

| | |
|---|---|
| ἀνδρείκελον | ἀμελέτητος |
| ἀπειροκαλία | ἀνυπόστατος |
| ἀνυποδησία | ἀνύσιμος |

[1] Ὀρθοέπειά γέ τις . . . καὶ ἄλλα πολλὰ καὶ καλά Phaedr. 267 c.

| | |
|---|---|
| ἀξιομνημόνευτος | δυσωπέομαι |
| ἀπατητικός | ζημιώδης |
| ἀπειλητικός | εὐαγωγός |
| ἀπορρᾳθυμεῖν | θεραπευτής |
| ἄπταιστος | θυμοειδής |
| ἀμεταστρεπτί | ἰδιωτεία |
| βαλλαντιοτομεῖν | κηδεστής |
| βλακικός | κυβερνητικός |
| βουλευτικός | λιχνεία |
| γενειάσκω | μεγάλειος |
| γεώδης | ξεναγέω |
| δαπανηρός | παιδοτροφία |
| δημηγορικός | τεχνίτης |
| διευκρινέομαι | |

**§ 3.** Some doubt is thrown on the whole inquiry, because it is necessarily limited to the extant remains of Greek literature. It is impossible to trace the steps by which the change referred to was gradually realized. But the following list of derivative and compound words which are found in Plato and in no earlier writer [1] may serve roughly to indicate the general fact that in the time of Plato a large class of words had recently come into use (he may even have added to the number) to express abstract notions of various kinds. This effervescence of language is naturally correlated to the stir and eager alacrity of thought which the Sophists set in motion and to which Socrates himself contributed. We may trace the beginnings of it in Antiphon's use of such derivative words as μιαρία, αἰτίασις, βιαιότης [2]. It would be interesting, were it only possible, to ascertain how far the language of Democritus or of Hippocrates had advanced in this direction. But Democritus is too often paraphrased by those who quote him, and the works ascribed

---

[1] It has been assumed for the purpose of this Essay that the first occurrence of a word in Greek literature is pretty sure to have been noted in the edition of Stephanus' *Thesaurus* by Dindorf and others.

[2] Or, to go further back, in the use of ἀπορία by Herodotus IV. 134.

to Hippocrates are of doubtful authenticity. For this reason no account is taken here of many words which are common to Plato and Hippocrates, or the Pseudo-Hippocrates. Where a word recurs in later writers, I have added the names of those by whom it is used. The influence of Plato on the subsequent usage is often apparent.

## (a)  *New Derivatives.*

α. Substantives in                                                  § 4.

-ειᾰ :—

ἀπρέπεια Rep. 465 C : Aristot., Athenaeus.
ἀπρομήθεια Lach. 197 B : Josephus.
ἀσάφεια Rep. 478 C : Plutarch : Dionys. Hal.
ἀψεύδεια Rep. 485 C : Aristotle.
εὐμάθεια Rep. 490 C : Callimachus.
νώθεια Phaedr. 235 D, Theaet. 195 C : Lucian.
ὀρθοέπεια (due to Protagoras) Phaedr. 267 C : Dionys. Hal.
φιλομάθεια Rep. 499 E, Tim. 90 B : Plut., Strabo.

-εία :—

γοητεία Rep. 584 A : Diodor., Lucian, Dio C.
ἐθελοδουλεία Symp. 184 C : Lucian.
εἰρωνεία Rep. 337 A : Aristot., Plut., Dionys. Hal.
ἐπιτροπεία Phaedr. 239 E (ἐπιτροπία (sic) occurs in a fragment of Lysias) : Dionys. Hal.
κολακεία Gorg. 463, 465, Rep. 590 B : Dem., Lucian.
προπαιδεία Rep. 536 D : Clem. Alex.

-ία :—

ἀβελτερία Theaet. 174 C, Symp. 198 D : Aristot., Plut.
ἀθεραπευσία Rep. 443 A : Diodor., Polyb.
ἀκαιρία Symp. 182 A : Dem., Aristot.
ἀλληλοφθορία Prot. 321 A : Joseph., Dionys. Hal.
ἀλλοδοξία (-έω) Theaet. 189 B : Dio C.
ἀμελετησία Phaedr. 275 A, Theaet. 153 B : Philo.
ἀμετρία Rep. 486 D : Lucian, Plut.

ἀναλογία Rep. 534 A.    Frequent in later Greek.

ἀναρμοστία Phaedo 93 C : Lucian, Plut.

ἀπεργασία Prot. 312 D : Plut.

ἀρρενωπία Symp. 192 A : Zeno Stoic.

ἀρρυθμία Rep. 401 A : Lucian.

ἀσυμμετρία Gorg. 525 A : Aristot., Theophr.

βασκανία Phaedo 95 B : Aristot., Philo.

βωμολοχία Rep. 606 C : Aristot., Plut.

γιγαντομαχία Rep. 378 C : Plut., Diodor.

γνωμολογία Phaedr. 267 C : Aristot., Plut.

γυμνασία Theaet. 169 C : Aristot., Dionys. Hal., Dio C.,
Polybius.

*εἰκονολογία Phaedr. 267 C, 269 A.

ἐλεεινολογία Phaedr. 272 A : Schol. in Sophocl.

εὐθυωρία Rep. 436 E : Aristot., Plut.

θεολογία Rep. 379 A : Aristot. Meteor., Theodoret.

ἰσορροπία Phaedo 109 A : Plut.

ἱστουργία Symp. 197 A : Theophr.

κηδεμονία Rep. 463 D : Dio C., Philo.

μακρολογία Prot. 335 B, Gorg. 449 C : Aristot.

μεγαλαυχία Lys. 206 A, Theaet. 174 D : Plut.

μελοποιία Symp. 187 D : Aristot.

μετεωρολογία Phaedr. 270 A : Plut.

μισανθρωπία Phaedo 89 D : Dem., Stobaeus.

μισολογία Phaedo 89 D : Plut.

*νεκροσυλία Rep. 469 E.

νοσοτροφία Rep. 407 B : Aelian.

οἰκειοπραγία Rep. 434 C : Porphyr., Stobaeus.

οἰκοφθορία Phaedo 82 C : Plut.

*ὀλιγογονία Prot. 321 B.

ὁμοδοξία Rep. 433 C : Aristot., Olympiod.

παιδεραστία (-έω) Symp. 181 C : Plut., Athen., Lucian (the
verb only).

παιδογονία Symp. 208 E : Heliod., Theodoret.

παραμυθία Phaedo 70 B, Rep. 450 D, al. : Plut., Longin.

* Words marked with an asterisk are found in Plato only.

πιθανολογία Theaet. 163 A : Euseb., Phot., St. Paul.

πολυγονία Prot. 321 B : Aristot., Plut., Galen.

πολυειδία Rep. 580 D : Cyrill. Alex.

πολυχορδία Rep. 399 C : Plut., Athen.

ῥαψῳδία Ion 533 B, Tim. 21 B : Aristot., Athen., Lucian, &c.

σκιαγραφία Phaedo 69 B, Rep. 365 C : Aristot., Euseb.

συμφωνία Crat. 405 D, al. : Aristot., Plut.

συντομία Phaedr. 267 B : Aristot., Diodor., Dionys. Hal.

φαντασία Theaet. 161 E, al. : Aristot., Plut.

φιλεραστία (-ής) Symp. 213 D : Aristaen. (-ία), Aristot. (-ής).

φιλογυμναστία (-έω, -ικός) Symp. 182 C, al. : Athen., Plut.
(verb only).

ψυχαγωγία Phaedr. 261 A, 271 C : Plut., Polyb., Lucian.

-ιον (Diminutives):—                                                   § 5.

ῥηματίσκιον Theaet. 180 A : Theodoret., Themist. ap.
Budaeum.

σκολύθριον Euthyd. 278 B : Pollux.

τεχνίον Rep. 495 D : Athen., Dio C.

τεχνύδριον Rep. 475 E : Clem. Alex.

ψυχάριον Rep. 519 A, Theaet. 195 A : Julian, Lucian, Galen.

-μα (neut.):—

αἴτημα Rep. 566 B : Aristot., Dionys. Hal., Plut., Lucian.

ἀμφισβήτημα Theaet. 158 B : Plut.

*ἀναλόγισμα Theaet. 186 C.

*ἀπείκασμα Crat. 402 D, 420 C.

ἀποβλάστημα Symp. 208 B : Theophr.

ἀπολόγημα Crat. 436 C : Plut.

ἀπόσπασμα Phaedo 113 B : Galen.

*ἀφομοίωμα Rep. 395 B.

διακόνημα Theaet. 175 E : Aristot.

δυσχέρασμα Phileb. 44 D : Suidas.

*καρτέρημα Meno 88 C.

κοινώνημα Rep. 333 A : Aristot., Plut.

κύημα Rep. 461 C : Aristot., Plut., Galen.

*λήρημα Gorg. 486 C.

μυθολόγημα Phaedr. 229 C : Plut., Lucian.
νεανί(σκ)ευμα Rep. 390 A : Lucian.
ὁμολόγημα Phaedo 93 D, al.
*περίπτωμα Prot. 345 B.
πρόσρημα Charm. 164 E, Phaedr. 238 B : Plut.
*σκιαγράφημα Theaet. 208 E.
χειρούργημα Gorg. 450 B : Dionys. Hal.

-μός :—

βαδισμός Charm. 160 C, al.
νεωτερισμός Rep. 422 A, al. : Plut., Lucian.
σφαδασμός Rep. 579 E : Eustath.
σχηματισμός Rep. 425 B, 494 D : Plut.
χωρισμός Phaedo 67 D : Theophr., Plut.

§ 6.     -της (fem.) :—

ἀθλιότης Rep. 545 B, al. : Plut.
ἀλλοτριότης Symp. 197 C : Dem., Plut.
ἀνισότης Phaedo 74 B : Aristot.
ἀνωμαλότης Tim. 57 E, al. : Plut.
διαφορότης Theaet. 209 A, Rep. 587 E, Parm. 141 B, C :
Stobaeus.
ἑτεροιότης Parm. 160 D : Eustath.
μαλακότης Theaet. 186 B, Rep. 523 E : Plut.
ὀλιγότης Theaet. 158 D, Rep. 591 E : Aristot., Theophr.
ὁμαλότης Tim. 57 E : Aristot., Plut.
πιθανότης Crat. 402 A : Aristot., Plut., Philo, Polyb.
ποιότης Theaet. 182 A : Aristot., Hermog.
στρογγυλότης Meno 73 E : Aristot., Theophr.
ὠχρότης Rep. 474 E : Aristot., Plut., Lucian.

-σύνη :—

ἀλλοτριοπραγμοσύνη Rep. 444 B : Proclus.
φιλοπραγμοσύνη Rep. 549 C : Dem., Pollux, Strabo.

§ 7.     -σις :—

ἀλλοίωσις Rep. 454 C : Aristot., M. Aurel., Theodoret.
ἀνάδυσις Euthyd. 302 E : Theophr., Plut.
*ἀνομοίωσις Theaet. 166 B.

ἀντιβόλησις Symp. 183 A : Themist.

ἀπόφασις Crat. 426 D : Aristot., Themist.

αὔλησις Prot. 327 B : Aristot., Stobaeus.

διακόσμησις Symp. 209 A : Plut.

διήγησις Phaedr. 246 A : Aristot., Hermog., Polyb.

*ἐπιπίστωσις Phaedr. 266 E.

εὐδοκίμησις Rep. 358 A, 363 A : Themist., Phot., Lucian.

ἡνιόχησις Phaedr. 246 B : Philostr., Philo, Dio Chrys.

ἰάτρευσις Rep. 357 C : Aristot.

ἰδίωσις Rep. 462 B : Plut.

ἵδρυσις Rep. 427 B : Plut., Strabo.

καρτέρησις Symp. 220 A : Musonius ap. Stob.

κατάλειψις Phaedr. 257 E : C. I. 4369 : Hesych.

κήλησις Euthyd. 290 A, Rep. 601 B : Plut., Phot., Lucian,
Diog. Laert., Porphyr.

κοίμησις Symp. 183 A : Josephus, Sirach.

κόλασις Apol. 26 A, Prot. 323 E, al.: Aristot.,Theophr., Plut.

κόσμησις Gorg. 504 D : Aristot., Plut., Dionys. Alex. ap.
Euseb.

κύησις Menex. 238 A, Polit. 274 A : Plut., Eustath., Galen.

μετάληψις Theaet. 173 B, Rep. 539 D, Parm. 131 A :
Aristot., Plut., Polyb.

*μετάσχεσις Phaedo 101 C.

*μετοίκησις Apol. 40 C, Phaedo 117 C.

*νώμησις Crat. 411 D.

ὁμοίωσις Theaet. 176 B, Rep. 454 C : Aristot., Theophr.,
Ep. of James.

ὄσφρησις Phaedo 111 B, Theaet. 156 B : Aristot., Theophr.,
Galen.

πολλαπλασίωσις Rep. 587 E : Aristot., Iambl. ap. Stob.

*προήσθησις Rep. 584 C.

*προλύπησις Rep. 584 C.

*πρόσεξις Rep. 407 B. Def.

πρόσληψις Theaet. 210 A : Plut., Diog. L., St. Paul.

πτόησις Prot. 310 D, Symp. 206 D, Crat. 404 A : Aristot.,
Hesych., 1 Ep. Pet.

πτῶσις Rep. 504 C : Aristot., Plut., Lucian, &c.

ῥῖψις Rep. 378 : · Plut., Pollux.

συγκοίμησις Phaedr. 255 E, Rep. 460 B : Plut., Dio C.

*συμπίεσις Crat. 427 A.

σύναψις Theaet. 195 D, Tim. 40 C : Aristot., Plut., Suidas, Porphyr.

σύνερξις Rep. 460 A, Tim. 18 D : L/ C., Galen, Plotinus.

σύνοψις Rep. 537 C, al.: Polyb., Pollux, Dionys. Hal., &c.

σχίσις Phaedo 97 A, 101 C : Aristot., Theophr., Plut.

§ 8.    -της (masc.) :—

*αἰσθητής Theaet. 160 D.

ἀναλωτής Rep. 552 B, C : Dio C.

ἀποπληρωτής Rep. 620 E : Hierocl., Iambl., Plotinus.

ἀποστερητής Rep. 344 B : Antioch., Theophil. (Cp. Ar. Nub. 730 ἀποστερητρίς.)

παγκρατιαστής Rep. 338 C, al. (C. I.) : Plut., Polyb., Lucian.

παιδευτής Rep. 493 C : Plut., Polyb., Diog. L.

παρασκευαστής Gorg. 518 C : Ep. regis Antigoni ad Zenonem, Jo. Chrys.

πλάστης Rep. 588 C : Plut., Philo.

φοιτητής Rep. 563 A : Theodoret., Eustath.

-τήριον :—

δικαιωτήριον Phaedr. 249 A : Philostr., Suidas, Hesych.

-ιον :—

παντοπώλιον Rep. 557 D : Plut., Jo. Chrys.

Verbals in -α or -η:—

ἄνθη Phaedr. 230 B : Theophr., Philostr., Aelian, Pollux.

κολυμβήθρα Rep. 453 D : Diodor. Sic. ap. Athen., Galen, Philostr.

*μεταστροφή Rep. 525 C, 532 B.

συμπλοκή Soph. 262 C : Aristot., Polyb., Lucian, Dionys. H.

§ 9.    β. Adjectives in

-δης :—

ἀειδής Phaedo 79 A, al.: Aristot., Theophr., Plut., Philo, Dio C.

ἀλιτηριώδης Rep. 470 D : Plut., Pollux, Dio C.

θνητοειδής Phaedo 86 A : Plut., Julian.

κηφηνώδης Rep. 554 B : Cleomedes.

κολλώδης Crat. 427 B : Aristot., Theophr., Plut., Athen., Galen.

λεοντώδης Rep. 590 B : Aristot., Plut.

μονοειδής Phaedo 78 D, al. : Theophr., Polyb.

*σειληνώδης Symp. 217 D.

-ιος :—

αἰώνιος Rep. 363 D, al. : Diodor., Porphyr., Hebr., John, Peter, Clem. Alex., Olympiod.

-κός :—                                                                    § 10.

ἀγανακτητικός Rep. 604 E : Clem. Alex., Aelian, Lucian.

ἀγορανομικός Rep. 425 D : Aristot., Dionys. Hal., Plut.

*ἀγοραστικός Crat. 408 A.

ἀναλωτικός Rep. 558, 559 : Clem. Alex.

ἀνατρεπτικός Rep. 389 D : Euseb., Pollux.

ἀπεργαστικός Rep. 527 B : Diodor., Clem. Alex., Galen.

ἀριθμητικός Gorg. 453 E : Aristot., Plut.

ἀριστοκρατικός Rep. 587 D : Aristot., Plut., Polyb., &c.

ἀστρονομικός Rep 530 A : Theophr., Philo.

ἀστυνομικός Rep. 425 D : Aristot.

*αὐλοποιϊκός Euthyd. 289 C.

γεωμετρικός Rep. 546 C : Aristot., Plut., Athen.

δοξαστικός Theaet. 207 C : Aristot.

*ἐλλιμενικός Rep. 425 D.

ἐπιθυμητικός Rep. 439 E : Aristot., Plut.

ζητητικός Meno 81 D, Rep. 528 B : Philo, Photius.

ἡνιοχικός Phaedr. 253 C : Philo, Eustath.

κολακευτικός Gorg. 464 C : Pollux, Lucian.

κολακικός Gorg. 502 D, al.: Polyb. (superlative).

λογογραφικός Phaedr. 264 B : Pollux, &c.

*λογοποιϊκός Euthyd. 289 C.

*μεταστρεπτικός Rep. 525 A : Iambl. (μετατρεπτικός).

μετρητικός Prot. 357 D.

μιμητικός Rep. 395 A, al. : Aristot., Plut., Lucian.

*μισθωτικός Rep. 346 A.

μυθικός Phaedr. 265 C : Plut., Athen., Dionys. Hal.

μυθολογικός Phaedo 61 B : Pollux.

νομοθετικός Gorg. 464 C, al. : Aristot., Theodorus Metoch.

οἰκοδομικός Charm. 170 C : Aristot., Theophr., Plut.

ὁμονοητικός Phaedr. 256 B, Rep. 554 E : Aristot.

παρακελευστικός Euthyd. 283 B : Pollux.

παρακλητικός Rep. 523 D : Dionys. Hal. (-κῶς, Clem. Alex., &c.).

πεττευτικός Charm. 174 B, al. : Eustath.

πιστευτικός Gorg. 455 A : Aristot.

ποιμενικός Rep. 345 D : Theocr., Opp., Galen.

*προμνηστικός Theaet. 150 A.

προστατικός Rep. 565 D : Plut., Polyb.

πυκτικός Gorg. 456 D : Aristot., Plut.

*ῥαψῳδικός Ion 538 B.

*σειληνικός Symp. 222 C.

σπουδαστικός Rep. 452 E : Aristot., Plut.

στατικός Charm. 166 B : Aristot., Strabo, Arrian.

στοχαστικός Gorg. 463 A : Aristot., Clem. Alex.

συνοπτικός Rep. 537 C : Budaeus in Dionys. Areop.

σφενδονητικός Lach. 193 B : Schol. in Lyc. 633.

τελεστικός Phaedr. 248 D : Plut., Tetrab. in Ptolemaeum, Budaeus.

ὑφαντικός Crat. 388 C : Aristot., Plut., Pollux, Aelian, Theodoret.

*φιλογυμναστικός Rep. 456 A.

   -λός :—

αἰσχυντηλός Charm. 160 E : Aristot., Plut.

   -ρός :—

αἰσχυντηρός Gorg. 487 B : Hesych.

   -τος :—

*ἀναμνηστός Men. 87 B.

ἁπτός Rep. 525 D : Aristot., Plut., Galen.

*παιδευτός Prot. 324 B.

παραληπτός Meno 93 B : Plut.

*παρασκευαστός Prot. 319 B, 324 A, C.

πλανητός Rep. 479 D : Hesych.

πρόκριτος Rep. 537 D : Aristot., Dio C.

προσποίητος Lys. 222 A : Aristot., Dem., Dio C., Philo, Dionys. Hal., &c.

σκευαστός Rep. 510 A : Aristot., Theophr., Euseb.

σταθμητός Charm. 154 B : Pollux, Suidas.

σύσπαστος Symp. 190 E : Athen., Pollux, Hesych.

γ. Adverbs in                                                § II.

-ως :—

ἀγαμένως [1] Phaedo 89 A : Aristot.

ἀπαρακαλύπτως Euthyd. 294 D : Heliodorus.

*ἀπταίστως Theaet. 144 B.

*ἐμποδιζομένως [1] Crat. 415 C.

*ἐπιθυμητικῶς Phaedo 108 A.

*ἡμαρτημένως [1] Meno 88 E.

*καρτερούντως [1] Rep. 399 B.

*μεμελημένως [1] Prot. 344 B.

παγίως Rep. 434 D : Aristot.

παρακινδυνευτικῶς Rep. 497 E : Longinus.

παρατεταγμένως [1] Rep. 399 B : Iamblichus.

πεπλασμένως [1] Rep. 485 D : Aristot.

προσποιήτως Theaet. 174 D : Dio C.

*συγγραφικῶς Phaedo 102 D.

*ὑφαντικῶς Crat. 388 C.

-ί :—

ἀγελαστί Euthyd. 278 E : Plut., Lucian.

ἀψοφητί Theaet. 144 B : Aristot., Themist., Lucian.

-ῇ :—

*πλεοναχῇ Rep. 477 A.

-σε :—

*μηδαμόσε Rep. 499 A.

[1] From participles.

-κις :—

ἀρτιάκις Parm. 144 A : Plut.

§ 12.    δ. Verbs in

-αίνω :—

ἀμαθαίνω Rep. 535 E : Themist., Plotinus.

-είω :—

γελασείω Phaedo 64 B : Damasc. ap. Suid., Euseb.

-εύω :—

γνωματεύω Rep. 516 E : Eustath., Philostratus.
γοητεύω Phaedo 81 B : Plut., Lucian.

-έω, -έομαι :—

ἀβουλέω Rep. 437 C : Plut., Dio C., Philo.
αἰσχρολογέω Rep. 395 E : Aristot., Diod. Sic.
ἀκριβολογέομαι Rep. 340 E, Crat. 415 A : Dem., Aeschin.,
Theophr., Dionys. Hal., Lucian.
ἀλλοτριονομέω Theaet. 195 A : Dio C.
*ἀναρμοστέω Rep. 462 A.
ἐρεσχηλέω Rep. 545 E : Lucian, Philo.
λευχειμονέω Rep. 617 C : Herodian, Strabo.
μετεωροπορέω Phaedr. 246 C : Plotinus, Philostr., Aelian.
ὁμοδοξέω Phaedo 83 D : Theophr., Strabo, Polyb.
παιδοσπορέω Phaedr. 250 E : Aelian.
παρασιτέω Lach. 179 C : Diphilus ap. Athen., Plut.
ταριχοπωλέω Charm. 163 B : Lucian.
ὑψηλολογέομαι Rep. 545 E : Themist.
φιλογυμναστέω Prot. 342 C : Plut., Athen., Iambl.
φιλοτεχνέω Prot. 321 E : Epictetus, Athen., Aelian, Polyb.,
Diod.

§ 13.    -ζω, -ζομαι :—

ἀποστοματίζω Euthyd. 277 A : Aristot., Plut., Themist.,
Athen., St. Luke.
αὐθαδίζομαι Apol. 34 D : Themist.
γαργαλίζω Phaedr. 251 C : Clem. Alex.
*ἐνθουσιάζω Apol. 22 C, al. (elsewhere -άω).

ἐπαμφοτερίζω Rep. 479 B : Aristot., Plut., Lucian.

μεσημβριάζω Phaedr. 259 A : Porphyr.

τετραγωνίζω Theaet. 148 A, Rep. 527 A : Aristot., Pseudo-Lucian.

ψελλίζομαι Gorg. 485 B: Aristot., Plut., Philostr., Heliodor.

-όω, -όομαι :—

ἀνομοιόω Rep. 546 B : Themist.

### (*b*) *New Compounds.* § 14.

*a.* Substantives :—·

ἀντίστασις Rep. 560 A : Aristot., Plut., Plotinus.

ἀπόλογος Rep. 614 B : Aristot., Plut., Aristid.

κλινοποιός Rep. 596 E : Dem.

\*κλινουργός Rep. 597 A.

συνοπαδός Phaedr. 248 C : Themist., Iambl., Clem. Al.

φιλοχρηματιστής Rep. 551 A : Pollux.

ψευδόμαρτυς Gorg. 472 B : Aristot., Athanas., Cyrill., Pollux.

*β.* Adjectives :—

ἀδιανόητος Soph. 238 C : Athen., Olympiod.

ἀδιάφθορος Phaedo 106 D : Dem., Plut., Aelian.

\*ἄθερμος Phaedo 106 A.

ἄκεντρος Rep. 552 C : Plut., Philo, Athen.

ἀκροσφαλής Rep. 404 B : Plut., Hesych., Themist., Polyb., Clem. Al.

ἀμερής Theaet. 205 E : Aristot., Lucian, Plotinus.

ἀμέριστος Theaet. 205 C : Aristot., Pollux, Hierocl., Clem. Al., Iambl., Dionys. A.

ἀμετάστατος Rep. 361 C : Plut., Themist., Pollux.

ἀμετάστροφος Rep. 620 E : Themist.

ἄναιμος Prot. 321 B : Aristot., Plut.

ἀναφής Phaedr. 247 C : Plut., Lucian, Philo, Dionys. A.

ἀνέγγυος Rep. 461 B : Plut., Dio C.

ἀνεμέσητος Symp. 195 A : Aeschin., Plut., Lucian, Heliod.

ἀνεξέταστος Apol. 38 A : Aeschin., Dem., Plut., Themist.

ἀνερμάτιστος Theaet. 144 A : Plut., Themist., Theodoret., Dio C.

ἀνομολογούμενος Gorg. 495 A : Aristot.

ἀνυπόθετος Rep. 510 B : Aristot., Plut., Iambl.

ἀνώλεθρος Phaedo 88 B : Aristot., Theophr., Plut., Plotinus, Lucian.

*ἀξιοκοινώνητος Rep. 371 E.

*ἄρρατος Rep. 535 C, Crat. 407 D.

ἀρτιμελής Rep. 536 B : Dio C., Themist.

ἀρτιτελής Phaedr. 251 A : Himer., Nonn.

ἀσύμφωνος Rep. 402 D : Theophr., Plut., Lucian.

ἀσύνθετος Phaedo 78 C : Dem., Aristot., Theodor., Polyb.

ἀσχημάτιστος Phaedr. 247 C : Plut., Plotin.

ἀσώματος Phaedo 85 E : Aristot., Plut.

ἄτηκτος Phaedo 106 A : Aristot., Galen.

αὐλοποιός Rep. 399 D : Aristot., Plut., Galen.

ἄφρουρος Phaedr. 256 C : Aristot., Plut.

*ἄψυκτος Phaedo 106 A.

βραχυλόγος Gorg. 449 C : Plut., Suid.

βραχύπορος Rep. 546 A : Plut., Philostr.

βραχυτράχηλος Phaedr. 253 E : Aristot., Diodor.

δοξόσοφος Phaedr. 275 B : Aristot., Clem. Al

*δυσγοήτευτος Rep. 413 E.

δυσδιερεύνητος Rep. 432 C : Dio C., Themist.

δυσκοινώνητος Rep. 486 B : Plut., Themist., Pollux.

*δωδεκάσκυτος Phaedo 110 B.

ἐθελόδουλος Rep. 562 D : Aristaen., Philo.

*ἐπεισαγώγιμος Rep. 370 E.

ἐπεξέλεγχος Phaedr. 267 A : Aristot.

*θησαυροποιός Rep. 554 A (quoted by Pollux).

κακόσιτος Rep. 475 C : Aelian, Arrian.

λογοδαίδαλος Phaedr. 266 E : Pollux.

μεγαλόθυμος Rep. 375 C : Eustath.

μελανόμματος Phaedr. 253 D : Aristot., Pollux.

μελίρρυτος Ion 534 A : Eustath., Nonn.

μελίχλωρος Rep. 474 E : Nicand., Theocr.

μετεωρολέσχης Rep. 489 C: Plut., Lucian.

*μετεωροσκόπος Rep. 488 E.

μισόλογος Phaedo 89 C, al. : Galen, Pollux.

*μυθολογικός Phaedo 61 B (Pollux).

μυθολόγος Rep. 392 D: Manetho.

μυθοποιός Rep. 377 B : Lucian.

νεοτελής Phaedr. 250 E : Lucian, Phot., Hesych., Himer. ap. Phot.

νομογράφος Phaedr. 278 E : Suid., Diodor.

νυμφόληπτος Phaedr. 238 D : Plut., Pollux, Synes.

*οἰκτρόγοος Phaedr. 267 C.

ὁλόκληρος Phaedr. 250 C : Aristot., Polyb., Philo.

ὁμοήθης Gorg. 510 C: Aristot., Eustath., Pollux.

ὁμοιοπαθής Rep. 409 B : Aristot., Theophr., Plotin., Acta Apost.

ὁμοπαθής Rep. 464 D : Aristot., Plut., Plotin.

ὁμοφυής Phaedo 86 A : Theodoret., Cyrill., Psellus.

ὀξύρροπος Theaet. 144 A, Rep. 411 B : Theophr., Pollux, Aristaen., Theodoret.

*παγγέλοιος Phaedr. 260 C, al.

πάμμεγας Phaedr. 273 A, al. : Lucian.

παμπάλαιος Theaet. 181 B: Aristot., Plut., Athen.,Themist.

παναρμόνιος Phaedr. 277 C, Rep. 399 C : Lucian, Dio C., Suidas, Jo. Chrys.

πάνδεινος Rep. 610 D : Dem., Dio C., Lucian, Galen.

περιαλγής Rep. 462 B : Aristot., Plut., Philo.

πολλαπλοῦς Rep. 397 E : Themist., Aristid., Hesych.

πολυήκοος Phaedr. 275 A : Philostr., Cleobul. ap. Stob., Damasc. ap. Suid.

πολυθεάμων Phaedr. 251 A: Bud., Stob., Pollux.

πολυθρύλητος Phaedo 100 B, Rep. 566 B : Polyb., Lucian, Galen, Theodoret.

πολυκέφαλος Rep. 588 C : Aristot., Plut., Lucian, Julian.

πολυμελής Phaedr. 238 A : Pollux.

*πτερώνυμος Phaedr. 252 C.

*σιμοπρόσωπος Phaedr. 253 E (Pollux).

συμμαθητής Euthyd. 272 C : Pollux, Phryn.

*συμπεριαγωγός Rep. 533 D.

σύμψηφος Gorg. 500 A : Dem., Plut., Diodor.

τερατολόγος Phaedr. 229 E : Philostr., Liban.

τετανόθριξ Euthyphr. 2 B : Aristaen., Clem. Al., Pollux.

ὑπόχρυσος Rep. 415 C: Lucian, Heliodor., Jo. Chrys., Philo.

ὑψηλόνοος Phaedr. 270 A : Plut., Themist., Damasc.

φιλαναλωτής Rep. 548 B : Pollux, Dio C.

φιλεραστής Symp. 192 B : Aristot.

φιλήκοος Rep. 535 D : Plut., Lucian, Polyb.

φιλογέλως Rep. 388 E : Aristot., Diodor., Athen., Philostr.

φιλογυμναστής Rep. 535 D, al. : Philo, Pollux.

φιλογύναιξ Symp. 191 D : Aristaen.

φιλοθεάμων Rep. 475 D : Plut., Lucian.

*φιλοποιητής Rep. 607 D.

*φιλόρτυξ Lys. 212 D.

φιλοσώματος Phaedo 68 B : Plut., Pollux, Philo, Euseb.

φιλότεχνος Rep. 476 A : Plut., Diodor., Pollux.

χιλιέτης Phaedr. 249 A, Rep. 615 A, 621 D : Athen., Strabo, Iambl.

ψοφοδεής Phaedr. 257 D : Plut., Lucian, Dionys. Hal.

§ 15.  γ. Verbs:—

ἀναβιώσκομαι Phaedo 71 E : Theophr.

ἀναβρυχάομαι Phaedo 117 D : Philostr., Suid.

ἀνακαγχάζω Euthyd. 300 D : Plut., Lucian, Athen.

ἀναπεμπάζομαι Lys. 222 E : Aristid., Plut., Lucian, Clem. Al.

ἀνασοβέω Lys. 206 A : Plut., Lucian, Polyb., Aristaen.

ἀνείλλω Symp. 206 D : Hesych., Suid.

ἀνερευνάω Phaedo 63 A : Plut., Dio C., Lucian, Philo.

ἀνομολογέομαι Symp. 200 E : Dem., Plut., Lucian.

ἀνταδικέω Theaet. 173 A : Dem. ap. Polluc.

ἀντερωτάω Euthyd. 295 B : Plut., Clem. Al.

ἀντιδέομαι Lach. 186 D : Liban., Herenn.

ἀντιδοξάζω Theaet. 170 D : Diog. L.

*ἀντικακουργέω Crit. 49 C.

ἀντικαταλείπω Rep. 540 B : Iambl.

ἀντιπαρατείνω Phaedr. 257 C : Iambl., Dio C.

ἀντίφημι Gorg. 501 C : Aristot., Polyb., Diodor.

*ἀντοίομαι Theaet. 178 C.

ἀπαθανατίζω Charm. 156 D : Aristot., Lucian, Diodor.

ἀπαναισχυντέω Apol. 31 C : Dem., Cyrill., Porphyr.

ἀπανθαδίζομαι Apol. 37 A : Plotin., Euseb., Olympiod.

ἀποδέω Symp. 190 E : Aristot., Theophr.

ἀποθρύπτω Rep. 495 E : Joseph.

ἀπομαντεύομαι Rep. 505 E : Dio C., Galen, Iambl.

ἀπομεστόομαι Phaedr. 255 C : Plotin.

ἀπομηκύνω Prot. 336 C : Plut., Lucian, Themist., Dionys. Hal.

ἀπονεύω Theaet. 165 A : Aristot., Theophr., Plut., Polyb., Lucian.

ἀποπληρόω Prot. 329 C : Aristot., Plut., Lucian.

*ἀποπολεμέω Phaedr. 260 B.

ἀποσαφέω Prot. 348 B : Lucian, Dio C., Galen, Joseph.

ἀποσκιάζω Rep. 532 C : Dio C., Budaeus.

ἀποσκώπτω Theaet. 174 A : Lucian, Dio C.

ἀποστοματίζω Euthyd. 277 A : Aristot., Plut., St. Luke, Pollux, Themist., Athen.

ἀποτίκτω Theaet. 150 C : Aristot., Lucian, Philostr.

ἀποτοξεύω Theaet. 180 A : Dio C., Lucian.

ἀποτορνεύω Phaedr. 234 E : Plut., Dionys. Hal., Hermog.

ἀποτυπόω Theaet. 191 D : Theophr., Lucian, Porphyr.

ἀποχετεύω Rep. 485 D : Plut., Philostr., M. Anton.

ἀποχραίνω Rep. 586 B : Theophr., Pollux, Budaeus.

*διαμαστιγόω Gorg. 524 E.

*διασκευωρέω Rep. 540 E.

ἐξαγριαίνω Lys. 206 B : Plut., Philo, Joseph., Dio C.

*μεταδοξάζω Rep. 413 C.

μεταρρέω Theaet. 193 C : Aristot., Galen, Athen., Joseph., Philostr.

παραζώννυμι Rep. 553 C : Theophr., Lucian, Dio C., Dionys. Hal.

παρακαλύπτομαι Rep. 440 A : Plut., Lucian, Aristaen.

*παραποδύομαι Theaet. 162 B.

περικρούω Rep. 611 E : Plut., Themist., Plotin.

περιπλάττω Rep. 588 D: Aristot., Theophr., Athen., Nicand.

προδοξάζω Theaet. 178 E : Aristot.

προθεραπεύω Rep. 429 E : Plut., Joseph., Clem. Al.

προκολακεύω Rep. 494 C : Plut.

προλυπέομαι Phaedr. 258 E : Aristot., Dio C.

προομολογέω Phaedo 93 D : Aristot., Philo.

προπαιδεύω Rep. 536 D : Aristot., Plut., Clem. Al., Synes.

προσανατρίβω Theaet. 169 C : Theophr., Plut., Aelian.

προσδιατρίβω Theaet. 168 A : Plut., Aristid., Joseph.

προσηλόω Phaedo 83 D : Dem., Plut., Lucian, Diodor., Galen, Joseph., Iambl. ap. Stob.

προσκρούω Phaedo 89 E : Alciphr., Dem., Aeschin., Aristot., Plut., Themist.

προσλάμπω Rep. 617 A : Plut.

συγκορυβαντιάω Phaedr. 228 B : Euseb., Suid., Synes.

συμπαρακαθίζομαι Lys. 207 B : Dem., Themist.

*συμπένομαι Meno 71 B.

συμπεριπατέω Prot. 314 E : Plut., Themist., Lucian, Athen.

συμπεριφέρω Phaedr. 248 A : Aeschin., Aristot., Lucian, Polyb., Diog. L.

*συμπροσμίγνυμι Theaet. 183 E.

συναιωρέομαι Phaedo 112 B : Plut., Aristaen.

συναπεργάζομαι Rep. 443 E : Aristot., Plut.

συναποτίκτω Theaet. 156 E : Pollux.

συνδέομαι Parm. 136 D : Dem., Plut., Dio C.

συνδιαπεραίνω Gorg. 506 B : Gregor.

*συνδιαπέτομαι Theaet. 199 E.

συνδιασκοπέω Prot. 349 B : Philo, Joseph., Athanas.

συνδιατελέω Phaedo 91 B : Dem.

συνεξερευνάω Theaet. 155 E : Act. Anon. Combefis. Hist. Monothel.

συνεπιστατέω Rep. 528 C : Eustath.

συνεπιστρέφω Rep. 617 C : Plut., Philo.

\*συνθαμβέω Ion 535 E.

συνοδύρομαι Menex. 247 C : Plut., Gregor.

\*συνοίομαι Rep. 500 A.

*Obs.*—The above list is not exhaustive, and in particular, it does § **16.** not include what has been characterised as the peculiar vocabulary of the later dialogues [1].

This is marked (1) by a further stage of the process which has now been described. Such words as the following are foreign not only to earlier Greek, but to most of the dialogues of Plato.

| | |
|---|---|
| ἀδιάπλαστος Tim. 91 D. | ἐπιτηδειότης Laws VI. 778 A. |
| ἀθεότης Polit. 308 E, Laws XII. | ἐψευσμένως Laws X. 897 A. |
| 967 C. | θεώρησις Phil. 48 A. |
| ἀναζήτησις Critias 110 A. | κάμψις Tim. 74 A. |
| ἀναισθησία Phil. 34 A, Tim. 52 B, | κωμῴδημα Laws VII. 816 D. |
| 74 E. | νομοθέτησις Laws IX. 876 D. |
| ἀνοηταίνω Phil. 12 D. | παραφορότης Tim. 87 E. |
| ἀπταισία Laws II. 669 E. | ῥύψις Tim. 65 E. |
| ἀστρωσία Laws I. 633 C. | στασιωτεία Laws IV. 715 B, VIII. |
| ἀφοβία Laws I. 649 A, B, C. | 832 C. |
| βλάψις Laws XI. 932 E. | συγκαταγήρασις Laws XI. 930 B. |
| γεώργημα Laws II. 674 C. | φάντασις Tim. 72 B. |
| δυσχέρασμα Phil. 44 D. | φιλοχρημονέω Laws V. 729 A. |
| ἑόρτασις Laws II. 657 D. | φιλοχρημοσύνη Laws XI. 938 C. |
| ἐπίστημα Laws XII. 958 E. | |

(2) The late dialogues show an increasing tendency to return to earlier Attic or Ionic, and especially to tragic forms. When Dionysius couples Plato with Thucydides as employing the earlier Attic style, he must be thinking of the Laws and kindred dialogues. The occasional use of τέκνον for παιδίον is one of many examples of this. Another is the preference of φλαῦρος to φαῦλος [2]. Note also the increasing frequency of the Dative Plural of the first and second declension in -σι(ν).

(3) Certain changes in Plato's philosophical terminology will be noticed under a separate head.

---

[1] For a full treatment of this subject see Sophistes and Politicus of Plato, edited by L. Campbell, Oxford University Press, 1867, and compare the Essay on Structure, &c., Excursus, above, p. 46 ff.

[2] See also αἰνιγμός, κλαυμονή, πάθη, τέρψις, χαρμόνη, &c.

§ 17.　　　　　ii. **Selection and Use of Words.**

The foregoing enumeration serves to illustrate some
novelties of diction which had become rife in Plato's time.
Certain peculiarities in his choice of words, and in his
special employment of them, may be treated more briefly
under the following heads :—

(*a*) Vernacular words, including those borrowed from
the arts of life.

(*b*) Picturesque uses (1) borrowed, or (2) imitated from
Epic, Tragic, and Lyric poetry.

(*c*) Metaphorical Generalization.

(*d*) Playing with words (1) ironically, and (2) etymo-
logically.

(*a*) *Vernacular words.*

Words of common life.

Plato's use of such expressions may be illustrated by
reference to the writers of the Old Comedy.　Compare,
for example, the use of the following words in Plato and
Comic poets.

| | | |
|---|---|---|
| ἀμέλει | Phaedo 82 A | Ar. Nub. 877 |
| ἀνακογχυλιάζω | Symp. 185 D | Eupolis Phil. 5 |
| ἀστεῖος | Phaedo 116 D, | Ar. Ach. 811 |
| | Rep. I. 349 B | |
| βαλανεύς | Rep. I. 344 D | ,, Ran. 710 |
| βδελυρός | Rep. I. 338 D | ,, ,, 465 |
| βλίττω | Rep. VIII. 564 E | ,, Eq. 794 |
| εἶτα | Theaet. 148 E | ,, Plut. 79 |
| ἐξ ἑωθινοῦ | Phaedr. 227–8 | ,, Thesm. 2 |
| κανθήλιος | Symp. 221 E | ,, Lys. 290 |
| κροῦμα | Rep. I. 333 B | ,, Thesm. 120 |
| κύρβεις | Polit. 298 D | ,, Av. 1354 |
| λαβή | Phaedr. 236 B | ,, Eq. 841 |
| λυγίζομαι | Rep. III. 405 C | Eupolis incert. 44 |
| μᾶζα | Rep. II. 372 B | Ar. Eq. 55 |

| | | |
|---|---|---|
| μελαγχολᾶν | Phaedr. 268 E | Ar. Av. 14 |
| μινυρίζω | Rep. III. 411 A | „ „ 1414 |
| μορμολυκεῖον | Phaedo 77 E | „ Thesm. 417 |
| μορμολύττομαι | Gorg. 473 D | „ Av. 1245 |
| ναυτιάω | Theaet. 191 A | „ Thesm. 882 |
| νεοττιά | Rep. VIII. 548 A | „ Av. 642 |
| νευρορράφος | Rep. IV. 421 A | „ Eq. 739 |
| περινοστέω | Rep. VIII. 558 A | „ Plut. 494 |
| πόπανον | Rep. V. 455 C | „ Thesm. 285 |
| σκίμπους | Prot. 310 C | „ Nub. 254 |
| σποδίζω | Rep. II. 372 C | „ Vesp. 329 |
| τέλμα | Phaedo 109 B | „ Av. 1593 |
| τίτθη | Rep. I. 343 A | „ Eq. 716 |
| τρίβων | Prot. 335 D | „ Ach. 184 |
| χώνη (χοάνη) | Rep. III. 411 A | „ Thesm. 18 |
| ψῆττα | Symp. 191 D | „ Lys. 115 |

We may distinguish (α) trivial or familiar expressions, (β) 'household words,' in the literal sense (τὰ οἰκετικὰ ὀνό-ματα Soph. 226 A, B), (γ) words belonging to special arts and handicrafts. And we shall not depart from Plato's own view of the matter if we include under this head the 'cant' or 'slang' terms of the rhetorical schools.

(α) Amongst the familiar idioms which Plato adopted to give the natural effect of conversation to his writings, the following may be specially noted:—

The insertion of ὦ δαιμόνιε, ὦ θαυμάσιε, ὦ μακάριε, ὠγαθέ, ὦ τᾶν, and other appellative formulae, some probably the humorous inventions of Socrates or Plato.

The familiar ἦ δ' ὅς &c. (found in Cratinus and Aristophanes). The phrase is a survival from the Old Attic speech.

Socrates' familiar oath νὴ τὸν κύνα.

The pleonastic use of ἥκω with participles to denote recurrence (Phaedo 60 C ἥκειν δή, κ.τ.λ.: Rep. V. 456 B ἥκομεν ἄρα εἰς τὰ πρότερα περιφερόμενοι).

ποῖος, denoting various moods of amusement or scorn, as in Rep. I. 330 A ποῖ᾽ ἐπεκτησάμην; Gorg. 490 D ποίων ἱματίων;

The epexegetic ἰδεῖν with adj. (Phaedr. 253 D λευκὸς ἰδεῖν &c.).

The deictic οὑτοσί Rep. I. 330 B.

πολλάκις (=‘perhaps’), ποιέω (‘I behave myself so and so’), ποιοῦμαι pass. (‘I am accounted so and so’), αἰτίαν ἔχω, ‘I am reputed’ (Theaet. 169 A): the words ἀγαπῶ (‘I am content’), ἀδολέσχης, ἀκκίζομαι, κινδυνεύω (‘I am likely,’ cp. Hdt. IV. 105), μελαγχολῶ, ναρκῶ, ναυτιῶ, νεανικός, περικρούω, σκληφρός, τρίβων, χαμαίζηλος, χαμεύνιον, and the expletive use of ἐπιχειρεῖν.

*Obs.* 1.—The idiomatic use of ποιῶ with adverbs = ‘*I behave myself* so and so,’—cp. Thuc. II. 59 ποιοῦντας ἅπερ αὐτὸς ἤλπιζεν— occurs in Rep. I. 330 C, II. 360 C, 365 A, III. 416 B, VI. 494 C.

*Obs.* 2.—The special use of ποιοῦμαι (passive) is more dubious, but see the notes on Rep. VI. 498 A, VII. 538 C, where it appears that the meaning ‘are esteemed or held to be’ is alone suitable.

But in Laws XI. 930 D τῶν ποιουμένων = ‘of those who claim it as their child.’

*Obs.* 3.—Plato sometimes quotes vernacular idioms from other dialects—

Rep. IX. 575 D μητρίδατε, Κρῆτές φασι.

Phaedo 62 A ἴττω Ζεύς, ἔφη, τῇ αὑτοῦ φωνῇ εἰπών.

*Obs.* 4.—Other idiomatic uses, obviously derived from common parlance, are the following:—

λαμπρός, of a distinguished entrance, ‘making a great impression,’ Rep. VIII. 560 E (cp. Soph. El. 685, Eur. Heracl. 280, Phoen. 1246, Dem. de Cor. § 313 ἐν τίσιν οὖν σὺ νεανίας καὶ πηνίκα λαμπρός ;).

παιδαγωγέω, ‘I conduct personally’ (I. Alc. 135 D): cp. Rep. X. 600 E αὐτοὶ ἂν ἐπαιδαγώγουν. ‘They would have been his insepar-able followers.’

κεῖμαι, ‘I am ruined’ or ‘undone’ (cp. Herod. VII. 176, § 8 τὸ πλέον αὐτοῦ (τοῦ τείχους) ἤδη ὑπὸ χρόνου ἔκειτο), Rep. IV. 425 A, V. 451 A.

νεανικός, 'glorious,' Rep. II. 363 C, 'vehement' (cp. Hippocr. Vet. Med. 15, 79) Rep. VI. 491 E.

αἱρέω, 'I gain an advantage,' Rep. II. 359 A, III. 410 B. αἱροῦντος λόγου, the common idiom, Rep. IV. 440 B, slightly modified, Rep. X. 607 B ὁ γὰρ λόγος ἡμᾶς ᾕρει.

οὐ δοκῶν, 'pretending not,' VIII. 555 E οὐ . . . δοκοῦντες . . . ὁρᾶν, 'pretending not to see' (cp. Eur. Med. 67 οὐ δοκῶν κλύειν).

δράττομαι, 'I seize by handfuls,' Lys. 209 E.

ἔλυτρον, 'case,' 'outside,' Rep. IX. 588 E.

(β) 'Household words.' Cooking, nursing, familiar ob-  § 18. jects, &c.

| | |
|---|---|
| ἀμφιδρόμια Theaet. 160 E. | λύγξ Symp. 185 D. |
| ἀνεμιαῖον Theaet. 151 E. | οὖλα Phaedr. 251 C. |
| ἄνθη Phaedr. 230 B. | ὄψον Gorg. 518 B. |
| ἀπομύττω Rep. I. 343 A. | πέμμα Rep. II. 373 A. |
| βαλανεύς Rep. I. 344 D. | σκίμπους Prot. 310 C. |
| βράττω Soph. 226 B. | σκολύθριον Euthyd. 278 B. |
| γυρῖνος Theaet. 161 D. | σποδίζω Rep. II. 372 C. |
| διαττῶ Soph. 226 B, Crat. 402 C. | τεμάχιον Symp. 191 E. |
| ἕψω Euthyd. 285 C. | τίτθη Rep. I. 343 A. |
| ἥδυσμα Rep. I. 332 D. | φορμίσκος Lys. 206 E. |
| λίσπη Symp. 193 A. | χαλεστραῖον Rep. IV. 430 A. |
| | χώνη Rep. III. 411 A. |

*Obs.* 1.—Words belonging to games of strength or skill are intermediate between this and the next heading,—i.e. they are at once vernacular and technical—

| | |
|---|---|
| ἀπὸ τῶν ἄνω θεῖν (?) Rep. X. 613 B. | λαβή Phaedr. 236 B. |
| ἀποδειλιάω Prot. 326 B, Rep. VI. 504 A. | λυγίζομαι Rep. III. 405 C. |
| | ὀλυμπικῶς Rep. IX. 583 B. |
| ἀποκλείομαι Rep. VI. 487 C (as a term in draughts). | παρακινέω ('flinch') Rep. VII. 540 A. |
| ἀρτιάζω Lys. 206 E. | παρακρούω Lys. 215 C. |
| ἀσκωλιάζω Symp. 190 D. | στρόβιλος Rep. IV. 436 D. |
| ἀστραγαλίζω Lys. 206 E. | ὕσπληξ Phaedr. 254 E. |
| δρόμου ἀκμή Rep. V. 460 E. | |

*Obs.* 2.—Allusions to banqueting customs are of course frequent ;

and amongst these may possibly be reckoned τοῖς ἐν ταῖς ἑστιάσεσιν
… ἐπαμφοτερίζουσιν ἔοικε Rep. v. 479 B.　See note in loco.

## § 19.　(γ) Handicrafts and other arts.

### Agriculture.

ἀποχετεύω Rep. VI. 485 D.

ἄφετος Rep. VI. 498 C.　Cp.
Prot. 320 A.

βδάλλω Theaet. 174 D.

βλίττω Rep. VIII. 564 E.

[δίνω] Soph. 226 B (MS. διακρίνειν).

κανθήλιος Symp. 221 E.

κυρίττω Rep. IX. 586 B.

μελιττουργός Rep. VIII. 564 C
(v.l. μελιτουργός).

νεοττιά Rep. VIII. 548 A.

σμινύη Rep. II. 370 D.

σύνερξις Rep. V. 460 A.

τέλμα Phaedo 109 B.

### Hunting.

θάμνος Rep. IV. 432 B.

ἴχνος Rep. IV. 432 D.

κυνηγέσιον Rep. III. 412 B.

### Medicine.

ἰλιγγιάω Phaedo 79 C.

ἴλιγγος Rep. III. 407 C.

κατάρρους Crat. 440 D.

ναρκῶ Meno 80 B.

ὀμφαλητομία Theaet. 149 D.

ῥεῦμα Rep. III. 405 D.　Cp.
Crat. 440 D.

σφύζω Phaedr. 251 D.

φλέγμα Rep. VIII. 564 B.

φλεγμαίνω Rep. II. 372 E.

φλεγματώδης Rep. III. 406 A.

φῦσα Rep. III. 405 D.

χάσμη Rep. VI. 503 D (χασμά-
ομαι Charm. 169 C).

χολή Rep. VIII. 564 B.

ψωράω Gorg. 494 C.

### Music, dancing, the drama.

ἁρμονία Theaet. 175 E.

διὰ πασῶν Rep. IV. 432 A [1].

δρᾶμα Rep. V. 451 C.　Cp.
Symp. 222 D.

ἐργολάβος Rep. II. 373 B.

λυδιστί &c. Laches 188 D.

μελοποιΐα Symp. 187 D.

νεάτη Rep. IV. 443 D.

ποιεῖν, 'to dramatize' (a
fable), Rep. II. 379.

ῥαψῳδός Ion 530 C.

ὑπάτη Rep. IV. 443 D.

---

[1] Prob. also πρὸς τὴν αὐτήν (sc. χορδήν) Rep. III. 397 B.

ὑποκριτής Charm. 162 D.
χορευτής Phaedr. 252 D.
χορός Euthyd. 279 C.

ὁ διὰ πάντων κριτής Rep.
IX. 580 B (see note in
loco).

Painting, statuary, pottery.

ἀνδρείκελον Crat. 424 E.
ἀποχραίνω Rep. IX. 586 B.
διαγράφω Rep. VI. 500 E.
διαζωγραφῶ Tim. 55 C.
ἐκκαθαίρω Rep. II. 361 D.
ἐκμαγεῖον Tim. 72 C.
ζῷον, 'a figure,' Rep. IV.
  420 C, VII. 515 A, and

probably Phaedr. 264 C.
Cp. Polit. 277 C.
ἱπνοπλάθος Theaet. 147 A.
κοροπλάθος Theaet. 147 B.
μελίχλωρος Rep. V. 474 E.
πλινθουργός Theaet. 147 A.
σμίλη Rep. I. 353 A.
χυτρεύς Rep. IV. 421 D.

Spinning, weaving and clothes-making.

ἤτριον Phaedr. 268 A.
κατάγω Soph. 226 B.
κερκίζω Soph. 226 B, Crat.
  388 A.

νευρορράφος Rep. IV. 421 A.
νῆσις Rep. X. 620 E.

*Obs.*—Allusions to the arts of the fuller (γναφεύς), currier (ἐκλεαίνω), dyer, ἁλουργόν, ἄνθος, δευσοποιόν, ἐκκλύζειν, βαφεύς, &c., are also frequent.

Navigation.

κελεύειν, to act as coxswain,
  Rep. III. 396 A.
θέοντες ἤδη τότε ἐγγύτατα
  ὀλέθρου Rep. III. 417
  sub fin.

κυβερνήτης Rep. I. 341 C.
ναύκληρος Prot. 319 D.
πλωτήρ Rep. VI. 489 A.
τὸν δεύτερον πλοῦν Phaedo
  99 D.

The Mysteries.

ἐποπτεύω Laws XII. 951 D.
ἐποπτικά Symp. 209 E.
θρόνωσις Euthyd. 277 D.
μυεῖσθαι Symp. 209 E, Phaedr.

250 C, Gorg. 497 C,
  Phaed. 81 A, Men. 76 E.
ναρθηκοφόρος, βάκχος Phaed.
  69 C.

Rhetorical Schools.

δείνωσις Phaedr. 272 A.
διπλασιολογία Phaedr. 267 C.

εἰκονολογία Phaedr. 267 C.
ἐπιπίστωσις Phaedr. 266 E.

ὀρθοέπεια Phaedr. 267 C.　　πιθανολογία Theaet. 162 E.

παράψογος Phaedr. 267 A.　　ὑπερβατόν Prot. 343 E.

παρέπαινος Phaedr. 267 A.

§ 20.　(*b*)　Epic, Lyric, and Tragic elements.

(Rep. VIII. 545 E φῶμεν αὐτὰς τραγικῶς, ὡς πρὸς παῖδας ἡμᾶς παιζούσας καὶ ἐρεσχηλούσας, ὡς δὴ σπουδῇ λεγούσας, ὑψηλολο-γουμένας λέγειν ;)

Plato's dialect is for the most part the purest Attic. But, besides quotations from poetry, which he occasionally weaves (with adaptations) into his prose, he frequently makes conscious use of words borrowed from the poets, and properly belonging to the diction of an earlier time. In adorning his style with these, sometimes half-humorously, sometimes in genuine earnest, he not unfrequently modifies their meaning by adding an ethical significance to what in the earlier and simpler use was merely physical. (E. g. βλοσυρός in Homer means 'rugged in appearance,' in Plato 'sturdy in character,' &c.)

(*a*)　It must suffice here to give a short list of the more striking examples : the graphic language of Herodotus being counted for this purpose as poetic diction

| | |
|---|---|
| ἀδελφός (adj.) Rep. IV. 421 C[1]. | ἴκταρ Rep. IX. 575 C. |
| ἀκτίς Tim. 78 D. | ἰνδάλλομαι Rep. II. 381 E. |
| ἀλγηδών Phaedo 65 C. | καθαιμάσσω Phaedr. 254 E. |
| ἄλκιμος Rep. X. 614 B. | κυμαίνω Phaedo 112 B. |
| ἀνακηκίω Phaedr. 251 B. | μελίγηρυς Phaedr. 269 A. |
| ἀπτώς Rep. VII. 534 C. | μήνιμα Phaedr. 244 D. |
| εἱμαρμένη Phaedo 115 A. | ναυτίλλομαι Rep. VIII. 551 C. |
| θαμίζω Rep. I. 328 C. | οἶμος Rep. IV. 420 B. |
| θέμις Symp. 188 D. | ὅμαδος Rep. II. 364 E. |
| θεοειδής Phaedo 95 C. | παραπαίω Symp. 173 E. |
| θεοείκελος Rep. VI. 501 B. | πολυάρατος Theaet. 165 E. |
| θεσπέσιος Rep. II. 365 B. | πόριμος Symp. 203 D. |

---

[1] This use is rare in Attic prose, but see Isocrates, Paneg. p. 55, § 71 (Bekker).

πότιμος Phaedr. 243 D.

σταθερός Phaedr. 242 A.

ταυρηδόν Phaedo 117 B.

ὑπηχέω Phaedr. 230 C.

ὑψηλόφρων Rep. VIII. 550 B.

χαμαιπετής Symp. 203 D.

χαρτός Prot. 358 A.

χήτει Phaedr. 239 D.

χθόνιος Rep. X. 619 E.

χλιδή Symp. 197 D.

(β) In this connexion it is right to observe the frequent transference from a physical to an ethical meaning.

ἄβυθος Parm. 130 D.

ἀδαμαντίνως Rep. X. 618 E.

αἴθων Rep. VIII. 559 D.

ἀκέραιος Rep. I. 342 B.

ἀντιλαμβάνεσθαι Rep. I. 336 B.

ἀντίτυπος Crat. 420 D.

ἀπομαραίνομαι Theaet. 177 B.

ἀρρενωπία Symp. 192 A.

αὐστηρός Rep. III. 398 A.

αὐχμός Meno 70 C.

βλοσυρός Rep. VII. 535 B.

ἐκκαθαίρω Rep. II. 361 D.

ἐπιλαμβάνεσθαι (cp. Herodot.) Phaedo 79 A.

ἐσμός Rep. V. 450 B.

κερματίζω Rep. VII. 525 E,

(κατα-) Rep. III. 395 B.

καταχώννυμι Gorg. 512 B.

μετάβασις Rep. VIII. 547 C.

νυστάζω Rep. III. 405 C.

A similar (although more naïve) use of graphic words to express mental things is observed in Herodotus: e.g. χαλεπῶς ἐλαμβάνετο (II. 121 δ), &c.

(γ) Poetic Allusions. These will be mentioned in the notes. In a few cases the reference is doubtful, as in ἡ Διομηδεία λεγομένη ἀνάγκη in Rep. VI. 493 D.

Καδμεία νίκη (Laws I. 641 C) involves some mythical allusion to which the key is lost. The supposed reference to the σπαρτοί is not sufficiently clear.

(δ) Parody and Imitation.

For humorous imitations of poetic diction, see especially Rep VIII. 545 E ὅπ(π)ως δὴ πρῶτον στάσις ἔμπεσε.

Phaedr. 237 A, B ἄγετε δή, ὦ Μοῦσαι, . . . ξύμ μοι λάβεσθε τοῦ μύθου.

Ibid. 252 B, C (ἐκ τῶν ἀποθέτων ἐπῶν) τὸν δ' ἤτοι θνητοὶ μὲν Ἔρωτα καλοῦσι ποτηνόν, | ἀθάνατοι δὲ Πτέρωτα, διὰ πτερόφοιτον ἀνάγκην.

Rep. VIII. 550 C ἄλλον ἄλλῃ πρὸς πόλει τεταγμένον.

In a similar spirit, if the reading be sound, a humorous turn is given to the quotation from Homer in Rep. III. 388 A τοτὲ δ' ὀρθὸν ἀναστάντα | πλωΐζοντ' ἀλύοντ' ἐπὶ θῖν' ἁλὸς ἀτρυγέτοιο.

§ 21.    (*c*) Metaphorical Generalization.

In all philosophical writing, thought inevitably reacts on language. The effort to define, distinguish, generalize, leads insensibly to novel uses of words. And Plato's method, like that of his master Socrates, largely consists in the attempt to rise to universal conceptions through the analysis of ordinary speech. At the same time he casts his thoughts in an imaginative mould, and his turn of mind, as exhibited in his writings, is eminently plastic and creative. Hence it is difficult, in describing his use of words, to draw an exact line between the work of fancy and that of logic, between metaphor and classification.

The extension of the meaning of θηρευτής, for example, in Rep. II. 373 B (side by side with that of μιμητής) appears at first sight to justify the remark ταῦτ' ἐστὶ ποιητικὰς λέγειν μεταφοράς. But in the Sophistes it is gravely stated that the genus *Huntsman* comprises several species, as General, Lover, Sophist, Fisherman, &c. Thus what a modern reader would assign to fancifulness — in this particular instance tinged with irony — Plato himself attributes to συναγωγή.

α. The use of μουσική in the Republic is here directly in point. Because in Plato's view melody is inseparable from words, and words from thoughts, not only μουσική, but the cognate terms ἁρμονία and ῥυθμός are used by him in a greatly extended sense. See especially

Prot. 326 B πᾶς γὰρ ὁ βίος τοῦ ἀνθρώπου εὐρυθμίας τε καὶ εὐαρμοστίας δεῖται.

Phaedo 61 A ὡς φιλοσοφίας μὲν οὔσης μεγίστης μουσικῆς.

Theaet. 175 E οὐδέ γ' ἁρμονίαν λόγων λαβόντος, κ.τ.λ.

β. Under the same heading of figurative abstraction may be fairly brought the graphic use of words denoting physical states to indicate mental phenomena. See above, p. 287 (*b*).

(1) ἀνατίθεμαι, ' I retract,' literally 'take back a move' (in draughts), Phaedo 87 A.

διαβολή, ' prejudice,' lit. ' calumny,' Rep. VI. 489 D.

ἕταιρος (adj.), ' akin to,' lit. ' companion of,' Rep. X. 603 B.

θήρα, ' pursuit,' lit. ' chase,' Phaedo 66 C.

θρέμμα, ' creature ' (used of an argument personified), Phaedr. 260 B.

κέρας, ' an offensive weapon,' Rep. IX. 586 B.

κυρίττω, ' I attack,' Rep. IX. 586 B.

μοῦσα, extended to include philosophy, Rep. VI. 499 D.

ὄναρ, ' dream,' i.e. ' impression,' Rep. VIII. 563 D.

ὀνειρώττω, ' I have vague (unverified) impressions,' Rep. VII. 533 C ; cp. V. 476 C.

ὄχημα, ' vehicle,' i.e. ground of belief, Phaedo 85 D.

παναρμόνιος, transferred from music to discourse, Phaedr. 277 C.

συλλαβή, transferred from letters to ideas, Theaet. 203 C.

ὕπαρ, ' with clear thoughts,' Rep. V. 476 C, D.

φυτόν, ' organized being,' ' organism,' Rep. II. 380 E, VI. 491 D.

ψυχαγωγία, extended to include rhetoric, Phaedr. 261 A. (The usual meaning appears in ψυχαγωγός Aesch. Pers. 687, Eur. Alc. 1128.)

*Obs.*—A word which properly belongs to an aggregate is applied to a constituent part, which is thus regarded in a more general aspect.

πλήρωμα Rep. II. 371 E.

So ἱκανὸν λόγον, Rep. II. 376 D, means one which is necessary to completeness.

(2) For bold graphic uses, see

ἀναζωπυρέω, ' to re-illumine ' (the eye of the mind), Rep. VII. 527 D.

ἄρρατος, 'indefatigable' (in Cratyl. 407 D = σκληρός), Rep. VII. 535 B.

θόρυβος, 'turmoil,' Phaedo 66 D ; cp. Rep. VIII. 561 B, IX. 571 E.

§ 22.   (*d*) Playing with words.

The Cratylus shows what might be made of the Greek language by 'victorious analysis' at play. The freedom which is there sportively abused has left many traces in other dialogues. Sometimes ironically, but sometimes also quite gravely, words are employed in new senses suggested by analytical reflexion.

α. Ironical Catachresis.

β. Etymological Analysis.

α. The exact meaning is made evident by the context. A good instance is the singular use of νεωκορεῖν in Rep. IX. 574 D, to denote an act of sacrilege, 'He will industriously clean out some temple.' For other instances consult the Lexicon under the 'facetious words' ἀγεννής, ἀστεῖος, γεννάδας, γενναῖος, γλισχρός, εὐδαίμων, καλός (especially VIII. 562 A), κομψός, ὑγιαίνω, φαῦλος, χαρίεις, χρηστός.

It may be observed by the way that the word εἰρωνεία, from meaning 'dissimulation,' generally acquires in Plato the specific meaning of 'pretended ignorance.'

*Obs.* 1.—A return is sometimes made (above, p. 250) from the ironical to the serious meaning.

Rep. I. 339 B **Σμικρά** γε ἴσως, ἔφη, προσθήκη : οὔπω δῆλον οὐδ' εἰ μεγάλη.

Rep. IV. 426 A, B τόδε αὐτῶν οὐ **χαρίεν**; . . . . οὐ πάνυ χαρίεν.

*Obs.* 2.—The constant use of ἐπιεικής for χρηστός or ἀγαθός, although not ironical, partakes somewhat of the general tendency to understatement. So also μετρίως, ἱκανῶς (Rep. VI. 499 A), &c.

β. Etymological Analysis.

(1) Sometimes a word is used quite simply in the etymological sense, which, however, is indicated by the context : Theaet. 149 B ὅτι ἄλοχος οὖσα τὴν λοχείαν εἴληχε, 'the goddess of childbirth, although not a mother.'

Other examples are : Theaet. 199 D ἀγνωμοσύνη, Symp. 197 D ἄδωρος (active), Rep. III. 411 B ἄθυμος, Phaedr. 230 A ἄτυφος, Rep. VI. 500 A ἄφθονος, Rep. I. 348 D, III. 400 E εὐήθεια, Theaet. 157 E παραισθάνεσθαι, Rep. X. 596 D ποιητής, Rep. VII. 521 D προσ-έχειν.

(2) More frequently the play on words takes the form of an oxymoron or a downright pun.

Rep. II. 382 A τό γε ὡς ἀληθῶς ψεῦδος.

Symp. 198 A ἀδεὲς . . . δέος.

Phaedr. 247 C, D τό γε ἀληθὲς εἰπεῖν, ἄλλως τε καὶ περὶ ἀληθείας.

Rep. VI. 509 D ἵνα μὴ οὐρανὸν εἰπὼν δόξω σοι σοφίζεσθαι.

Rep. VI. 507 A κίβδηλον ἀποδιδοὺς τὸν λόγον τοῦ τόκου.

Rep. VII. 527 A, IX. 574 B, C ἀναγκαῖος.

Rep. VII. 540 C δαίμοσιν . . . εὐδαίμοσι.

Rep. IX. 580 B, C ὁ ᾿Αρίστωνος υἱὸς τὸν ἄριστον, κ.τ.λ.

*Obs.* 1.—This tendency becomes exaggerated in Plato's later manner:—Soph. 254 A τριβῇ, Tim. 90 C εὐδαίμων, Phileb. 64 E ξυμφορά, Tim. 55 C ἄπειρος, Laws II. 656 C παιδεία, ib. IV. 717 B νόμος.

*Obs.* 2.—Plato's fanciful etymologies afford no real ground for critical judgement on his text. See note on Rep. I. 338 A, B φιλο-νεικεῖν (cp. IX. 581 A, B), E. on Text, p. 131.

### iii. **Philosophical expression.**

It has been suggested in the preceding section that § 23. the growth of reflexion and, in particular, the Socratic search for definitions had in Plato's time already exercised a natural and inevitable influence on words. This was the beginning of a process which tended ultimately to give an approximately fixed connotation to the chief terms of constant use in mental and moral philosophy. But the result was still far distant, and even in Aristotle the appearance of definiteness is often illusory.

In all ages philosophers have been apt to dream of a language which should be the exact, unvarying counterpart of true conceptions[1]. The dream has not been realized, and if it were, would not the very life and progress of thought be arrested? Philosophy reacts on common language, and in employing it again, is sure to modify it further. But the process cannot have, and ought not to have, either finality or absolute fixity. In some departments of knowledge, Mathematics, Chemistry, Astronomy, Anatomy, Jurisprudence, such an aim is obviously legitimate;—the use of technical terms in them is clearly necessary. But Mental Philosophy is in danger of becoming hidebound, if it be not permitted to her to draw afresh, and to draw freely, from the fountains of common speech.

In Plato, at all events, philosophical terminology is incipient, tentative, transitional. And although this remark applies with especial force to what have been called the 'dialogues of search,' where the method is 'peirastic' or 'maccutic,' leading to an avowedly negative result, it is a serious error even in dealing with the more positive and constructive dialogues to assume strict uniformity of expression. In a few rare instances the metaphysical significance acquired by a word or phrase in one dialogue may be thought to have influenced the use or application of the same term in another. Thus in the Timaeus the meaning attached to οὐσία (35 B), and to θατέρου φύσις (35 B, 74 A), may bear some relation to the definitions in the Philebus (26 D) and Sophist (257 D). But even where such connexion may doubtfully be traced, it by no means precludes the occurrence of other philosophical uses, still less the continued employment of the word or phrase in its ordinary vernacular sense. And the instances which have been adduced are quite exceptional. The contrary

---

[1] See Ward in *Encyc. Brit.* ed. ix. Art. *Psychology*: 'It seems the fate of this science to be restricted in its terminology to the ill-defined and well-worn currency of common speech, with which every psychologist feels at liberty to do what is right in his own eyes, at least within the wide range which a loose connotation allows.'

practice is more frequent. The special meanings assigned
to διάνοια and πίστις in Rep. VI. 511, VII. 534 A are not
to be found elsewhere in Plato. Even the definition of
Justice, so carefully elaborated in Rep. IV, though once
alluded to in IX. 586 E, can hardly be said to affect the
connotation of the term elsewhere [1]. Nor does the definition of δύναμις by the young mathematicians in Theaet.
148 B for a moment supplant either the ordinary or the
scientific uses of the word.

Thus, while attempts are made to give a precise meaning
to words denoting philosophical conceptions, such attempts
are inchoate, intermittent and casual. The very nature of
dialectic, as an 'interrogation' of language, forbids the
assumption of technicalities, nor can Plato's literary instinct
tolerate the air of pedantry, which such buckram stiffening
involves. The formal terminology of Rhetors and Sophists
(ὀρθοέπεια, ἀπορροή, &c.) is the object of his frequent ridicule. In two of the most elaborate of his dialogues [2] he
reminds the reader that precise verbal distinctions, such as
Prodicus affected, are rarely of any use in philosophy, and
warns young men that a liberal indifference to mere words
is the condition of growth in wisdom ; just as in the
Cratylus he had long since pronounced against looking for
the truth of things in words [3]. That second course (δεύτερος
πλοῦς), for which Socrates declares in the Phaedo [4] as
preferable to the bare assertion of an unapplied first cause,
—the endeavour to find in the mirror of language, however
confusedly, some reflexion of eternal truths,—is really
a method which dissolves the apparent fixity of ordinary
speech, and awakens thought to new conceptions which,
the more firmly they are held, can be more freely and
variously expressed.

These remarks are here to be exemplified by the con-

---

[1] See esp. Laws I. 631 c.     [2] Theaet. 184 c ; Polit. 261 E.
[3] Cratylus 439 A, B.    [4] Phaedo 99 D.

sideration of a few cardinal expressions [1], which may be roughly classified as (*a*) Metaphysical, (*b*) Psychological, and (*c*) Dialectical, although such distinctions are not clearly present to the mind of Plato.

§ 24.  (*a*) METAPHYSICAL TERMS.

Εἶδος.

This word, which Aristotle and others have made the symbol of Platonism, is used by Plato himself with entire freedom, and very seldom with a pronounced metaphysical intention. He has nowhere defined it.

*Ordinary meanings.*

The word was in common use amongst contemporary writers.

a. Εἶδος was still used, as in Homer, in the literal sense of 'outward appearance,' 'visible form.'

(1) Xen. Cyrop. IV. 5, § 57 ἐκλεξάμενος αὐτῶν τοὺς τὰ εἴδη βελτίστους.

(2) In Xenophon (Cyn. 3, § 3 αἱ δὲ σκληραὶ τὰ εἴδη [κύνες] : ib. 4, § 2 ἰσχυραὶ τὰ εἴδη), εἶδος nearly = δέμας, bodily constitution or condition.

b. But it had acquired the secondary meaning—

(1) Of 'a mode of action or operation'; so in Thuc. II. 41, § 1 ἐπὶ πλεῖστ' ἂν εἴδη . . . τὸ σῶμα αὔταρκες παρέχεσθαι, 'to adapt himself to the most varied forms of action,' ib. 50, § 1 τὸ εἶδος τῆς νόσου, 'the course of the disease,' III. 62, § 3 ἐν οἵῳ εἴδει . . . τοῦτο ἔπραξαν, 'the peculiarity of the course they took,' VI. 77, § 2 ἐπὶ τοῦτο τὸ εἶδος τρεπομένους, 'betaking themselves to this policy,' VIII. 56, § 2 τρέπεται ἐπὶ τοιόνδε εἶδος, 'had recourse to such a method of proceeding,' ib. 90, § 1 ἐναντίοι ὄντες τῷ τοιούτῳ εἴδει, 'opposed to this policy' or 'platform' (εἶδος here seems more definite than ἰδέα in τῇ αὐτῇ ἰδέᾳ preceding).

(2) In the language of rhetoric this use was naturally transferred from action to speech, so that in Isocrates,

---

[1] ἵνα μὴ ταραττώμεθα ἐν πολλοῖς (Soph. 254 c).

Antid. § 80 ὅλοις εἴδεσι προειλόμην χρῆσθαι πρὸς ὑμᾶς, it seems to mean an entire course or line of argument, as distinguished from a single phrase.

c. Εἶδος was already used in common speech, with associations from the primary meaning, in a still more general sense, approaching to the abstract notion of ' mode,' ' sort,' ' kind.' Hippocrates περὶ ἀρχαίης ἰατρικῆς, § 15 αὐτό τι ἐφ' ἑωυτοῦ θερμόν, ἢ ψυχρὸν . . . μηδενὶ ἄλλῳ εἴδεϊ κοινωνέον.

Thuc. III. 82 τοῖς εἴδεσι διηλλαγμένα, 'differing in character.'

Isocr. 190 D, E (Evagoras, § 10) τοῖς μὲν γὰρ ποιηταῖς πολλοὶ δέδονται κόσμοι . . . καὶ περὶ τούτων δηλῶσαι μὴ μόνον τοῖς τεταγμένοις ὀνόμασιν, . . . ἀλλὰ πᾶσι τοῖς εἴδεσι διαποικῖλαι τὴν ποίησιν.

Isocr. 294 D (κατὰ τῶν σοφιστῶν § 20 Bekker) δεῖν τὸν μὲν μαθητὴν πρὸς τῷ τὴν φύσιν ἔχειν οἵαν χρὴ τὰ μὲν εἴδη τῶν λόγων μαθεῖν, κ.τ.λ.

These, the ordinary uses of the word, may all be readily § 25. exemplified out of Plato.

a. (1) Rep. X. 618 A ἐπὶ εἴδεσι καὶ κατὰ κάλλη.

Charm. 154 D τὸ εἶδος πάγκαλος.

Symp. 189 E τὸ εἶδος στρογγύλον.

Prot. 352 A ἄνθρωπον σκοπῶν ἐκ τοῦ εἴδους.

(2) Rep. III. 402 D ἔν τε τῇ ψυχῇ . . . ἐνόντα καὶ ἐν τῷ εἴδει, ' in mind and body.'

Symp. 196 A ὑγρὸς τὸ εἶδος, ' of flexible make.'

b. (1) Rep. IX. 572 C ὁρμήσας εἰς ὕβριν τε πᾶσαν καὶ τὸ ἐκείνων εἶδος, ' their way of life ' (where ἦθος has been needlessly conjectured).

(2) Rep. V. 449 C εἶδος ὅλον οὐ τὸ ἐλάχιστον ἐκκλέπτειν τοῦ λόγου, ' a whole chapter.'

III. 392 A τί . . . ἡμῖν . . . ἔτι λοιπὸν εἶδος ; (cp. Laws VI. 751 A).

II. 363 E ἄλλο αὖ εἶδος λόγων.

See also Phaedr. 263 C καλὸν γοῦν ἂν . . . εἶδος εἴη κατανενοηκώς.

c. Rep.·II. 357 C τρίτον δὲ ὁρᾷς τι . . . εἶδος ἀγαθοῦ, ' a third kind of good.'

Gorg. 473 E ἄλλο αὖ τοῦτο **εἶδος** ἐλέγχου ἐστίν;

Rep. III. 406 C οὐδὲ ἀπειρίᾳ τούτου τοῦ **εἴδους** τῆς ἰατρικῆς, 'this mode of practice.'

IV. 424 C **εἶδος** ... καινὸν μουσικῆς μεταβάλλειν, 'a new style in music.'

And therefore in passages of more distinctly philosophical import the interpreter is by no means bound to drag in a ready-made 'doctrine of ideas' (εἰσαγαγεῖν τὰ εἴδη) wherever the word εἶδος happens to occur. This can hardly be done without violence, for example, in the following places :—

Rep. II. 380 D ἀλλάττοντα τὸ αὑτοῦ **εἶδος** εἰς πολλὰς μορφάς.

VI. 511 A τοῦτο τοίνυν νοητὸν μὲν τὸ **εἶδος** ἔλεγον.

VII. 530 C οὐ μὴν ἔν, ἀλλὰ πλείω ... **εἴδη** παρέχεται ἡ φορά.

VII. 532 E (ἡ τοῦ διαλέγεσθαι δύναμις) κατὰ ποῖα δὴ **εἴδη** διέστηκε.

VIII. 544 D ὅτι καὶ ἀνθρώπων **εἴδη** τοσαῦτα ἀνάγκη τρόπων εἶναι, ὅσαπερ καὶ πολιτειῶν.

And in the concluding passage in Book VI, where εἶδος is the cardinal term, it is applied to the visible forms as well as to the invisible (510 D **τοῖς ὁρωμένοις εἴδεσι προσχρῶνται**, compared with 511 B, C αἰσθητῷ παντάπασιν οὐδενὶ προσχρώμενος, ἀλλ' **εἴδεσιν αὐτοῖς δι' αὐτῶν εἰς αὐτά, καὶ τελευτᾷ εἰς εἴδη**).

*Obs.*—In Phaedr. 249 B where εἶδος has been used in the logical sense (infra p. 298, γ) it recurs in the same passage (1) for the imaginary form or nature of the soul, and (2) for the form and appearance of the noble steed.

§ 26.　*Platonic uses.*

Εἶδος as employed by Plato is a word of extremely wide significance, and even where its use is avowedly technical (as in Phaedo 102 A) it receives not a new meaning but a new application. It is applied so variously that it can hardly be defined more closely, as a philosophical term in Plato, than by saying that it denotes *the objective reality of any and every abstract notion.* Nor is·the word in this its philosophical sense by any means confined to

the Platonic 'ideas.' The crude idealists of Soph. 246 are
no less than Plato himself believers in εἴδη. And in the
passage of the Republic just referred to (VI. 510, 511) the
connotation of εἶδος is not confined to the classification of
natural objects, nor to mathematical principles, nor to
moral truths. It includes also ἐπιστήμη, ἀλήθεια, οὐσία, ἡ
τοῦ ἀγαθοῦ ἰδέα and all other philosophical conceptions to
which the mind of Plato had attained when the book was
written.

The application of the term in different passages, even
within the limits of one dialogue, is by no means uniform.

*a.* Εἶδος is an ethical notion regarded as an object of § **27.**
thought.

The chief instance of this use in the Republic is III. 402 B, C
οὐδὲ μουσικοὶ πρότερον ἐσόμεθα . . . πρὶν ἂν τὰ τῆς **σωφροσύνης**
**εἴδη καὶ ἀνδρείας καὶ ἐλευθεριότητος καὶ μεγαλοπρεπείας καὶ ὅσα**
**τούτων ἀδελφὰ** καὶ τὰ τούτων αὖ ἐναντία πανταχοῦ περιφερόμενα
γνωρίζωμεν καὶ ἐνόντα ἐν οἷς ἔνεστιν αἰσθανώμεθα καὶ αὐτὰ καὶ
εἰκόνας αὐτῶν, καὶ μήτε ἐν σμικροῖς μήτε ἐν μεγάλοις ἀτιμά-
ζωμεν, ἀλλὰ τῆς αὐτῆς οἰώμεθα τέχνης εἶναι καὶ μελέτης; where
observe that two lines lower down the word is used in the
vernacular meaning of 'bodily constitution' (ἔν τε τῇ ψυχῇ
. . . καὶ ἐν τῷ εἴδει: supra p. 294, ɑ (2)).

Cp. Parm. 130 B δικαίου τι εἶδος αὐτὸ καθ' αὐτὸ καὶ καλοῦ
καὶ ἀγαθοῦ καὶ πάντων . . . τῶν τοιούτων.

Ib. 135 C καλόν τε τί καὶ δίκαιον καὶ ἀγαθὸν καὶ ἓν ἕκαστον
τῶν εἰδῶν.

*β.* This meaning is extended from ethical universals to
all universals, implying at once the abstract notion and
the essential nature of the thing.

Phaedo 100 B, C εἶναί τι καλὸν αὐτὸ καθ' αὐτὸ καὶ ἀγαθὸν
**καὶ μέγα** καὶ τἆλλα πάντα, resumed in ib. 102 B with εἶναί τι
**ἕκαστον τῶν εἰδῶν.**

Crat. 440 B εἰ δὲ καὶ αὐτὸ τὸ εἶδος μεταπίπτει τῆς γνώσεως,
ἅμα τ᾽ ἂν μεταπίπτοι εἰς ἄλλο εἶδος γνώσεως, κ.τ.λ.

Rep V. 476 A, X. 596 A **εἶδος** γάρ πού τι ἓν ἕκαστον

εἰώθαμεν τίθεσθαι περὶ ἕκαστα τὰ πολλά, οἷς ταὐτὸν ὄνομα ἐπιφέρομεν.

Parm. 135 D. (See also ib. 130 C, D where the doubt is raised whether there is any such essential nature attaching to dirt, mud, hair, and other insignificant things.)

γ. Εἶδος is the reality of a general concept.

Phaedr. 249 B δεῖ γὰρ ἄνθρωπον ξυνιέναι κατ᾽ εἶδος λεγόμενον, κ.τ.λ.

Ib. 277 C, Rep. VIII. 544 D ἥτις καὶ ἐν εἴδει . . . κεῖται; Men. 72 C.

(1) Εἶδος is thus a logical whole, containing the particulars under it. Rep. V. 475 B παντὸς τοῦ εἴδους, Theaet. 178 A, ib. 148 D.

(2) But it is also a part, i.e. a subordinate species: Phaedr. 265 E κατ᾽ εἴδη δύνασθαι τέμνειν, Rep. V. 454 A διὰ τὸ μὴ δύνασθαι κατ᾽ εἴδη διαιρούμενοι . . . ἐπισκοπεῖν, Theaet. 181 C, 187 C.

Obs. 1.—Εἶδος when thus employed signifies a true and natural, as opposed to an arbitrary division. Cp. Polit. 262, 263.

Obs. 2.—In the passage of the Phaedrus p. 265 ff., the word is also used in the familiar idiomatic sense of a line of argument or mode of reasoning (see above, p. 295 b (2)) τούτων δέ τινων ἐκ τύχης ῥηθέντων δυοῖν εἰδοῖν . . . . τὸ δ᾽ ἕτερον δὴ εἶδος τί λέγεις; See also ib. 263 B, C.

δ. Εἶδος is applied, not only to the species into which a genus is divided, but also to the parts of an organic whole. These two conceptions are, in fact, not clearly kept apart by Plato.

Thus the Soul in Rep. IV. 435 ff. is shown to have three forms or natures (εἴδη), which are her parts (μέρη, p. 442), but are also species, having varieties under them (VIII. 559 E, alib.), and are repeatedly spoken of as γένη.

ε. Εἶδος is the type of any natural kind, comprising its essential attributes.

Theaet. 157 B, C ἄνθρωπόν τε τίθενται καὶ λίθον καὶ ἕκαστον ζῷόν τε καὶ εἶδος.

Parm. 130 C ἀνθρώπου εἶδος χωρὶς ἡμῶν καὶ τῶν οἷοι ἡμεῖς ἐσμὲν πάντων, αὐτό τι εἶδος ἀνθρώπου ἢ πυρὸς ἢ καὶ ὕδατος.

*Obs.*—This is the μονάς of Phileb. 15 A ἕνα ἄνθρωπον . . . καὶ βοῦν ἕνα, κ.τ.λ., about which there, as in Parm. 130 C, D, Socrates expresses himself doubtfully.

ζ. Εἶδος is also used of an abstract whole, conceived as separable from the parts, as in

Theaet. 204 A ἢ καὶ τὸ ὅλον ἐκ τῶν μερῶν λέγεις γεγονὸς ἕν τι εἶδος ἕτερον τῶν πάντων μερῶν ;

η. Εἶδος is used not only for the type of a natural kind § 28. (man, horse, stone, &c.),—though on this point, as we have seen, there is in Plato's mind a lingering doubt,—not only for generic attributes (good, beautiful, wise, &c., Phileb. 15), but also to denote an idea of relation, as for example, the idea of similarity.

Parm. 128 E αὐτὸ καθ᾽ αὑτὸ εἶδός τι ὁμοιότητος.

In Rep. V. 454 B τί εἶδος τὸ τῆς ἑτέρας τε καὶ τῆς αὐτῆς φύσεως καὶ πρὸς τί τεῖνον ὡριζόμεθα ; the meaning of εἶδος is further explained by πρὸς τί τεῖνον. And in Phaedo 74, 75, although the term εἶδος is not expressly used of αὐτὸ τὸ ἴσον, yet the whole course of reasoning implies that this, together with μεῖζον καὶ ἔλαττον, is included amongst the εἴδη spoken of in ib. 102 A.

θ. Lastly, εἶδος is applied to each of the primary forms or elements of thought. These come into question most in the dialectical dialogues (Theaet., Soph., Polit., Phileb.), but the use referred to is much the same with that which occurs already in Phaedr. 263 B εἰληφέναι τινὰ χαρακτῆρα ἑκατέρου τοῦ εἴδους. See especially Parm. 129 D, E, Theaet. 184, 185, 197 D, 202 A, Soph. 254 C, Phileb. 23 B, C, and again Soph. 258, where the θατέρου φύσις is described as an εἶδος, and also as *having* an εἶδος (i. e. a real nature corresponding to its definition).

The chief meanings or applications of εἶδος as a philosophical term in Plato may accordingly be thus tabulated :—
Εἶδος is

1. an ethical notion, Rep. III. 402 C, D, &c.

2. a universal nature, Phaedo 1co B, C.

3. a logical whole, Phaedr. 249 B.    *a.* genus Rep. V.
474;  *β.* species, Phaedr. 265 E.

4. a part of an organic whole : an organ, Rep. IV. 435.

5. the type of a natural kind, Theaet. 157 B.

6. a pure abstraction, e. g. the whole as separable from
the parts, Theaet. 204 A.

7. an idea of relation, Rep. V. 454 C.

8. any primary form or element of thought, Theaet.
184, 185, Parm. 129 C–E, Soph. 254 C, &c.

### Γένος.

γένος often occurs in the Republic, Parmenides, and later
dialogues, interchangeably with εἶδος, though suggesting
rather the notion of *kind,* than of *form* or *nature.*

Rep. V. 477 B, C φήσομεν δυνάμεις εἶναι γένος τι τῶν ὄντων
. . . εἰ ἄρα μανθάνεις ὃ βούλομαι λέγειν τὸ εἶδος . . . ib. D, E εἰς
τί γένος . . . ἢ εἰς ἄλλο εἶδος ;

Parmenides 129 C αὐτὰ τὰ γένη τε καὶ εἴδη.

See also Polit. 285 C, 286 D.

This use is especially frequent in the Sophistes.

γένος is combined with ἰδέα in Laws VIII. 836 D τὸ τῆς
σώφρ῾ινος ἰδέας γένος.

*Obs.*—The use of γένος becomes more frequent in the later
dialogues and at the same time the applications of εἶδος and ἰδέα
become more varied.  For confirmation of these assertions the
student may consult the following passages :—

εἶδος Soph. 219–230 (where εἶδος occurs fifteen times), 236, 239,
246, 248, 252, 254, 255, 256, 258, 259, 260, 261, 264, 265, 267 :
Polit. 258, 262, 263, 267, 278, 285, 286, 287, 288, 289, 291, 304,
306, 307 :  Phil. 18, 19, 20, 23, 32, 33, 35, 48, 51 :  Tim. 30, 37,
40, 42, 48, 50, 51, 52, 53, 54, 55, 56, 57, 58, 59, 60, 62, 64, 66,
67, 68, 69, 75, 77, 81, 83, 87, 88, 89, 90 :  Laws I. 630 E, VI. 751 A.

ἰδέα Soph. 235, 253, 254, 255 :  Polit. 258, 289, 307, 308 :  Phil.

16, 25, 60, 64 (twice), 67: Tim. 28, 35, 39, 40, 58, 60, 70, 71, 75, 77 : Laws VIII. 836 D (τὸ τῆς σώφρονος ἰδέας γένος).

γένος Soph. 228 (three times), 229, 235, 253, 254, 256, 257, 259, 260, 261, 267, 268 : Polit. 260, 262, 263, 266, 267, 279, 285, 287, 288, 289, 291, 305 : Phil. 12, 23, 25, 26, 27, 28, 30, 31, 32, 44, 52, 65: Tim. 41, 42, 43, 46, 47, 48, 49, 50, 51, 52, 53, 54, 55, 56, 57, 58, 59, 60, 61, 63, 67, 69, 73, 74, 77, 78, 81, 82, 83, 85, 86, 92 : Laws VII. 797 A, VIII. 836 D, 897 B, XI. 916 D.

## Ἰδέα.                                                                    § 29.

ἰδέα is the feminine form of εἶδος. It is naturally the more picturesque word and is accordingly more frequent in the more imaginative and exalted passages. From this cause, and from its adoption as a term of Stoicism, the word has passed over into Latin and thence into modern literature and philosophy.

*Ordinary meanings.*

α. In the literal sense, = 'form,' 'appearance,' ἰδέα is used by Pindar, Theognis, Euripides, Aristophanes, Herodotus, and Thucydides (VI. 4 ὅτι δρεπανοειδὲς τὴν ἰδέαν τὸ χωρίον ἐστί).

β. In Herodotus it has the slightly more abstract meaning of Nature, description (I. 203 φύλλα τοιῆσδε ἰδέης, 'leaves of such a nature'; II. 71 φύσιν . . . παρέχονται ἰδέης τοιήνδε, 'their nature and description is as follows'; VI. 119), and even of a line of thought or policy, VI. 100 ἐφρόνεον δὲ διφασίας ἰδέας.

c. In Thucydides, where (acc. to Bétant) the word occurs fourteen times (see esp. III. 81, § 5 πᾶσά τε ἰδέα κατέστη θανάτου), it has acquired the further meaning of a plan, or mode of operation (see above, εἶδος, p. 294, β (1)).

II. 77, § 2 πᾶσαν ἰδέαν ἐπενόουν, 'they devised every plan.'
III. 62, § 2 τῇ . . . αὐτῇ ἰδέᾳ ὕστερον . . . ἀττικίσαι, 'on the same principle.'

δ. In Isocrates ἰδέα already signifies a form (1) of life, (2) of speech, (3) of thought (see also Aristoph. Nub. 547 ἀλλ' ἀεὶ καινὰς ἰδέας εἰσφέρων σοφίζομαι, Ran. 384, Av. 993).

(1) Isocr. p. 21 D (Nicocl. § 46) δεῖ δὲ χρῆσθαι μὲν ἀμφοτέραις ταῖς ἰδέαις ταύταις (dignity and urbanity).

32 E τὰς μὲν μὴ μετεχούσας τούτων τῶν ἰδεῶν (ἀρετὰς) μεγάλων κακῶν αἰτίας οὔσας, 'those virtues that have no share of temperance and justice.'

The ἰδέαι referred to are σωφροσύνη and δικαιοσύνη.

36 A ἐν ταῖς αὐταῖς ἰδέαις (explained by ἐν ταῖς ἀπορίαις, ἐν ταῖς δυναστείαις, &c.).

259 E (Panathen. § 141) τὰς . . . ἰδέας τῶν πολιτειῶν τρεῖς εἶναι.

(2) 42 C (Panegyr. § 7) εἰ μὲν μηδαμῶς ἄλλως οἷόν τ' ἦν δηλοῦν τὰς αὐτὰς πράξεις ἀλλ' ἢ διὰ μιᾶς ἰδέας.

210 E (Helen. Encom. § 16) ἔστι δ' οὐκ ἐκ τῶν αὐτῶν ἰδεῶν . . . ὁ λόγος, 294 C (Sophist. § 18).

(3) 312 C (Antid. § 12) τοσαύτας ἰδέας καὶ τοσοῦτον ἀλλήλων ἀφεστώσας συναρμόσαι καὶ συναγαγεῖν, 'notions so important and so remote from one another.'

(4) A special use occurs in 216 E (Helen. Encom. § 62) ὅσα ταύτης τῆς ἰδέας κεκοινώνηκε, where αὕτη ἡ ἰδέα is the *attribute* of beauty.

(The word is hardly, if at all, used by Xenophon.)

§ 30.     Thus it is evident that by the time of Plato the word ἰδέα was ready for his philosophical use. But before touching on this, it is important to observe, as in the case of εἶδος, (1) that he also employs it freely in all the senses (except perhaps that marked ϲ) above-mentioned, and (2) that even in philosophical passages it is by no means always used with a scientific or technical intention. Such an intention is only to be assumed when the context places it beyond doubt.

α. Protag. 315 E τὴν . . . ἰδέαν πάνυ καλός.

Phaedr. 251 A ἤ τινα σώματος ἰδέαν.

Phaedo 108 D τὴν . . . ἰδέαν τῆς γῆς.

Polit. 291 B ταχὺ δὲ μεταλλάττουσι τάς τε ἰδέας καὶ τὴν δύναμιν εἰς ἀλλήλους.

β. Rep. II. 369 A τὴν τοῦ μείζονος ὁμοιότητα ἐν τῇ τοῦ

ἐλάττονος ἰδέᾳ ἐπισκοποῦντες, 'the resemblance of the greater in the form of the less.'

Rep. II. 380 D φαντάζεσθαι ἄλλοτε ἐν ἄλλαις **ἰδέαις**.

Tim. 58 D τὴν τοῦ σχήματος **ἰδέαν**, 'the shape of the figure.'

c. This meaning is possibly approached in Rep. VI. 507 E οὐ σμικρᾷ ἄρα **ἰδέᾳ**, κ.τ.λ., 'by a notable expedient' (?); Phaedr. 237 D, 238 A. But it is hard to find in Plato an exact parallel for the Thucydidean use.

b. Phaedr. 253 B εἰς τὸ ἐκείνου ἐπιτήδευμα καὶ **ἰδέαν** ἄγουσιν, 'into conformity with his practices and way of life.' Cp. εἶδος, p. 294, b (1).

Even where the context is highly philosophical, ἰδέα often retains its usual, vernacular, meaning. Thus in Phaedr. 246 A it is used not of absolute Justice, Beauty, &c., but of the nature or conformation of the soul, as it is there figuratively described. And in Theaet. 184 C, D the word is similarly applied, not to Being, sameness, difference, and the other primary notions, but to the nature of the mind perceiving them—εἰς μίαν τινὰ **ἰδέαν**, εἴτε ψυχὴν εἴτε ὅ τι δεῖ καλεῖν, πάντα ταῦτα ξυντείνει.

*Platonic uses.* § 31.

The transition to the specially Platonic use is well marked in Parm. 131 E, 132 A οἶμαί σε ἐκ τοῦ τοιοῦδε ἓν ἕκαστον **εἶδος** οἴεσθαι εἶναι. ὅταν πόλλ' ἄττα μεγάλα σοι δόξῃ εἶναι, μία τις ἴσως δοκεῖ **ἰδέα** ἡ αὐτὴ εἶναι ἐπὶ πάντα **ἰδόντι**, ὅθεν ἓν τὸ μέγα ἡγεῖ εἶναι, 'when you look at them together, there appears to you one and the same form (or idea) in them all.'

a. Ἰδέα, as a philosophical term, signifies rather *form* than *kind*. The meaning of a *class*, which εἶδος often essentially connotes, attaches only accidentally to ἰδέα. The latter term immediately suggests the unity of a complex notion as present to the mind. It is thus used to describe the work of συναγωγή, where εἶδος denotes the result of διαίρεσις :—

Phaedr. 265 D, E εἰς μίαν τε **ἰδέαν** συνορῶντα ἄγειν τὰ

πολλαχῇ διεσπαρμένα, κ.τ.λ. . . . τὸ πάλιν κατ᾽ εἴδη δύνασθαι τέμνειν.

Theaet. 205 D, E, Soph. 253 C, D, Phileb. 60 D.

Observe the frequent combination of μία ἰδέα.

See also Phaedo 103 D, E—where at first sight the terms may seem to be interchanged—μὴ μόνον αὐτὸ τὸ εἶδος ἀξιοῦσθαι τοῦ ἑαυτοῦ ὀνόματος εἰς τὸν ἀεὶ χρόνον, ἀλλὰ καὶ ἄλλο τι, ὃ ἔστι μὲν οὐκ ἐκεῖνο, ἔχει δὲ τὴν ἐκείνου μορφὴν ἀεὶ ὅτανπερ ᾖ . . . 104 C οὐδὲ ταῦτα ἔοικε δεχομένοις ἐκείνην τὴν ἰδέαν ἢ ἂν τῇ ἐν αὐτοῖς οὔσῃ ἐναντία ᾖ. On a closer inspection it is seen that ἰδέαν corresponds not to εἶδος but to μορφήν in the preceding sentence.

§ 32.    It follows that each εἶδος, or distinct and definite kind, has its own ἰδέα, or notional form.

Euthyphr. 5 D τὸ ἀνόσιον . . . αὐτὸ δὴ αὑτῷ ὅμοιον καὶ ἔχον μίαν τινὰ ἰδέαν κατὰ τὴν ὁσιότητα.

Phil. 25 B τὸ μικτὸν (εἶδος) . . . τίνα ἰδέαν φήσομεν ἔχειν;

β. In Rep. VI, where Plato dwells on the unity of knowledge and characterizes the philosopher as a spectator of all time and all existence, the term ἰδέα, in the more precise philosophical sense, occurs with special frequency.

VI. 486 D, E ἣν (διάνοιαν) ἐπὶ τὴν τοῦ ὄντος ἰδέαν ἑκάστου τὸ αὐτοφυὲς εὐάγωγον παρέξει.

VI. 507 B, C τὰς . . . ἰδέας νοεῖσθαι μέν, ὁρᾶσθαι δ᾽ οὔ.

And the process so indicated naturally culminates in the contemplation of the ἰδέα τοῦ ἀγαθοῦ. Closely akin to this last is the use in Phil. 67 B οἰκειότερον . . . τῇ τοῦ νικῶντος ἰδέᾳ.

And in the more imaginative description of the parts of the Soul towards the end of Book IX ἰδέα again takes the place of εἶδος :—

588 C, D μίαν μὲν ἰδέαν θηρίου ποικίλου . . . μίαν δὴ τοίνυν ἄλλην ἰδέαν λέοντος, μίαν δὲ ἀνθρώπου (he had just said in illustration συχναὶ λέγονται ξυμπεφυκυῖαι ἰδέαι πολλαὶ εἰς ἓν γενέσθαι) [1].

---

[1] To estimate Plato's freedom in the use of terms, words like ὅρος, τύπος,

γ. 'Ιδέα is also preferred in speaking of an organic whole, in which the parts or elements are merged :—

Theaet. 204 A μία ἰδέα ἐξ ἑκάστων τῶν συναρμοττόντων στοιχείων γιγνομένη.

The word ἰδέα may be regarded as symbolizing the union of thought and imagination in Plato.

### Αὐτός.

a. The emphatic use of αὐτός is the most constant and characteristic of the various modes in which Plato expresses his belief in the absolute reality of universals. The term ἰδέα in its technical sense is absent both from the myth in the Phaedrus and from the discourse of Diotima in the Symposium, where εἶδος, too, only comes in by the way. But the pronominal use now in question perpetually recurs. It is needless to quote passages at length: it is enough to refer to Lys. 220 B, Crat. 439 C, D, Phaedr. 247 D, Phaedo 74 B, 76 C, 100 B, C (αὐτὸ καθ' αὐτό, cp. Rep. VI. 485 D, X. 604 A), Symp. 211 B (αὐτὸ καθ' αὐτὸ μεθ' αὐτοῦ), ib. D (θεωμένῳ αὐτὸ τὸ καλόν), Rep. I. 342 A, II. 363 A, IV. 438 C, V. 472 C, 476 A–C, 479 A, VI. 493 E, 506 D, E, VII. 532 A, X. 612 A, Parm. 133 D, &c., Theaet. 175 B, C (αὐτῆς δικαιοσύνης τε καὶ ἀδικίας). § 33.

β. Yet, while thus consecrated to special use, the pronoun is far from losing its proper idiomatic sense. Words like αὐτοδικαιοσύνην belong to later Platonism, although, through a not unnatural error, they have found their way into MSS. of Plato (E. on Text: above, p. 71). Such a form as αὐτοάνθρωπος nowhere occurs, and, though the neuter pronoun is often joined to a feminine abstract word, frequent changes of the order clearly prove that they do not adhere together as in a compound. See for example § 34.

μορφή, μονάς (Phileb.), μοῖρα, φῦλον (Polit.), μέρος, μέλος, στοιχεῖον, μόριον, σχῆμα, ἑνάς, should be considered. This is more noticeable in later dialogues. The expression is more varied, as the philosopher becomes more sure of his ground.

Rep. I. 331 C τοῦτο δ' αὐτό, τὴν δικαιοσύνην . . .

Theaet. 146 E ἐπιστήμην αὐτὸ ὅ τί ποτ' ἐστίν.

And consider the context of II. 363 A οὐκ αὐτὸ δικαιοσύνην ἐπαινοῦντες, ἀλλὰ τὰς ἀπ' αὐτῆς εὐδοκιμήσεις, where Par. A reads αὐτοδικαιοσύνην.

Once more, the Platonic student must often refrain from Platonizing. Even in passages where the 'doctrine of ideas' is immediately in question the emphatic αὐτός occurs in the ordinary vernacular sense. The context must decide. Thus in Rep. VI. 510 E αὐτὰ μὲν ταῦτα . . . 511 A αὐτοῖς τοῖς ὑπὸ τῶν κάτω ἀπεικασθεῖσι, the pronoun refers to τοῖς ὁρωμένοις εἴδεσι supra, individual objects *themselves* as opposed to their shadows or reflexions, although in the words τοῦ τετραγώνου αὐτοῦ ἕνεκα . . . καὶ διαμέτρου αὐτῆς, what has here been called the special use of αὐτός has intervened. Compare Parm. 130 D χρὴ φάναι καὶ τούτων ἑκάστου εἶδος εἶναι χωρίς, ὃν ἄλλο αὐτῶν ὧν ἡμεῖς μεταχειριζόμεθα,—' the *actual* hair, mud, dirt, &c., of common life': Soph. 241 E (περὶ) εἰδώλων . . . εἴτε φαντασμάτων αὐτῶν, ἢ καὶ περὶ τεχνῶν τῶν, κ.τ.λ., 'illusions *themselves* or the arts concerned with them.'

γ. It follows that there is nothing specially Platonic in such uses as Crat. 432 D τὸ μὲν αὐτό, τὸ δὲ ὄνομα ('name and thing'), or Theaet. 202 A αὐτὸ ἐκεῖνο μόνον τις ἐρεῖ ('the term by itself apart from attributes').

§ 35.    Εἶναι, ὃ ἔστι, τὸ ὄν, τὰ ὄντα, τὸ ὂν ἕκαστον, ὄντως, οὐσία.

(Theaet. 186 A τοῦτο γὰρ μάλιστα ἐπὶ πάντων παρέπεται.)

In all Greek philosophy, and not in Plato alone, meta-physical truths are expressed through εἶναι, its inflexions and derivatives. The cause of this is partly to be sought in Eleaticism, but largely also in the Socratic form of questioning, τί ἐστί;

The student who would learn of Plato in simplicity should clear his mind of Aristotelian distinctions, such as those in the third book of the Metaphysics, and, still more carefully of *Daseyn, Wesen, Ansich, Fürsich,*

*Anundfürsichseyn*, and other terms of modern German philosophy.

a. Οὐσία is the truth of predication, as sifted out by § 36. dialectical discussion (Prot. 349 B); in other words, it is the reality of definition :

Rep. X. 597 A ὃ δή φαμεν εἶναι ὃ ἔστι κλίνη.

Phaedo 75 D περὶ ἁπάντων οἷς ἐπισφραγιζόμεθα τοῦτο, ὃ ἔστιν : ib. 65 D.

Phaedo 78 C αὐτὴ ἡ οὐσία ἧς λόγον δίδομεν τοῦ εἶναι : Polit. 285 B.

Phaedr. 245 E ψυχῆς οὐσίαν τε καὶ λόγον τοῦτον αὐτόν τις λέγων οὐκ αἰσχυνεῖται.

Being, so conceived, is called in Phaedo 76 C, D ἡ τοιαύτη οὐσία.

β. τὰ ὄντα, τὸ ὂν ἕκαστον, have nearly the same force.

Phaedr. 247 E καὶ τἆλλα ὡσαύτως τὰ ὄντα ὄντως θεασαμένη : ib. 262 B ὁ μὴ ἐγνωρικὼς ὃ ἔστιν ἕκαστον τῶν ὄντων.

Theaet. 174 A τῶν ὄντων ἑκάστου ὅλου.

Rep. VI. 484 D τοὺς ἐγνωκότας μὲν ἕκαστον τὸ ὄν.

γ. But sometimes, in moments of exaltation, the whole § 37. of Being (like the sea of Beauty in the Symposium) is spoken of as one *continuum*, which, as the object of intellectual contemplation, exists in a region above the Visible :—

Phaedr. 247 C ἡ γὰρ ἀχρώματός τε καὶ ἀσχημάτιστος καὶ ἀναφὴς οὐσία ὄντως ψυχῆς οὖσα κυβερνήτῃ μόνῳ θεατὴ νῷ : ib. D, E ἐπιστήμην, οὐχ ᾗ γένεσις πρόσεστιν, οὐδ' ᾗ ἐστί που ἑτέρα ἐν ἑτέρῳ οὖσα ὧν ἡμεῖς νῦν ὄντων καλοῦμεν, ἀλλὰ τὴν ἐν τῷ ὃ ἔστιν ὂν ὄντως ἐπιστήμην οὖσαν. (Cp. Tim. 29 C, 35 A.)

The white light of Being so conceived is parted into the primary colours, as it were, of Knowledge and Truth, as for example in Rep. VI. 508, 509, where, however, the ἰδέα τοῦ ἀγαθοῦ dominates over οὐσία as well as over ἐπιστήμη and ἀλήθεια. See also for the totality of Being, VI. 486 A θεωρία παντὸς μὲν χρόνου, πάσης δὲ οὐσίας. And, for οὐσία as abstract truth, VII. 525 C ἐπ' ἀλήθειάν τε καὶ οὐσίαν.

§ **38.**    δ. In the dialectical dialogues οὐσία and τὸ ὄν have again the more logical meaning, 'Reality, answering to truth of conception:' or the essence of a thing as defined (Polit. 283 E, Phil. 32).

For example, in the strikingly modern passage of the Theaetetus quoted above, this sentence occurs, 186 B τοῦ μὲν σκληροῦ τὴν σκληρότητα διὰ τῆς ἐπαφῆς αἰσθήσεται, καὶ τοῦ μαλακοῦ τὴν μαλακότητα ὡσαύτως . . . τὴν δέ γε **οὐσίαν** καὶ ὅ τι ἐστὸν καὶ τὴν ἐναντιότητα πρὸς ἀλλήλω καὶ τὴν **οὐσίαν** αὖ τῆς ἐναντιότητος αὐτὴ ἡ ψυχὴ ἐπανιοῦσα καὶ συμβάλλουσα πρὸς ἄλληλα κρίνειν πειρᾶται ἡμῖν. And, just below, τὰ δὲ περὶ τούτων ἀναλογίσματα πρός τε **οὐσίαν καὶ ὠφέλειαν** ('what they are and what good they do') μόγις καὶ ἐν χρόνῳ διὰ πολλῶν πραγμάτων καὶ παιδείας παραγίγνεται οἷς ἂν καὶ παραγίγνηται. And in the main argument of the Sophistes, τὸ ὄν is positive truth or reality, as opposed to negation. The verb of existence is attenuated to the copula, passing from the notion of essence to that of relation. Yet this dialectical procedure does not preclude a recurrence to the language of 'ontology':—

Soph. 254 A, B ὁ δέ γε φιλόσοφος, τῇ τοῦ **ὄντος** ἀεὶ διὰ λογισμῶν προσκείμενος ἰδέᾳ, διὰ τὸ λαμπρὸν αὖ τῆς χώρας οὐδαμῶς εὐπετῆς ὀφθῆναι· τὰ γὰρ τῆς τῶν πολλῶν ψυχῆς ὄμματα καρτερεῖν πρὸς τὸ θεῖον ἀφορῶντα ἀδύνατα.

A different shade of meaning is observable according as εἶναι is opposed to γίγνεσθαι or φαίνεσθαι (Tim. 27 D, Parm. 165 A).

ε. A special meaning of οὐσία = μικτὴ οὐσία, 'concrete reality,' is formulated in Phil. 27 B, and applied in Tim. 35 A. But to examine this at present would be to travel too far beyond the stage of Platonism embodied in the Republic.

ζ. If the philosophical meanings of εἶδος, ἰδέα, αὐτός, are crossed by the vernacular meaning, this happens inevitably also in the case of εἶναι in both its meanings, (1) as the copula and (2) as the substantive verb.

(1) Rep. VI. 507 B πολλὰ· καλά . . . καὶ πολλὰ ἀγαθὰ καὶ ἕκαστα οὕτως εἶναί φαμέν τε καὶ διορίζομεν τῷ λόγῳ.

(2) Parm. 135 D, E οὐδὲν χαλεπὸν . . . ὁτιοῦν τὰ ὄντα πάσχοντα ἀποφαίνειν.

So οὐσία in the sense of 'property' occurs in Phaedr. 252 A καὶ οὐσίας δι' ἀμέλειαν ἀπολλυμένης παρ' οὐδὲν τίθεται. And there is a play on both uses of the word (property and truth) in Gorg. 472 B ἐπιχειρεῖς ἐκβάλλειν με ἐκ τῆς οὐσίας καὶ τοῦ ἀληθοῦς.

Μετέχειν, μέθεξις, μετάσχεσις, ἔχειν, μεταλαμβάνειν, προσχρῆσθαι, § 39. μετάληψις, κοινωνία, μετεῖναι, παρεῖναι, παρουσία, ἀγγεῖον (Lys. 219 D), ἐνεῖναι, προσγίγνεσθαι, προσεῖναι, παραγίγνεσθαι, ἐγγίγνεσθαι, ὁμοίωσις, μίμησις, παράδειγμα, περιφέρεσθαι, περιτρέχειν, μετατίθεσθαι, πεπονθέναι, πάθος ἔχειν, συμπλοκή.

(εἴτε παρουσία, εἴτε κοινωνία, εἴτε ὅπῃ δὴ καὶ ὅπως προσαγορευομένη,—οὐ γὰρ ἔτι τοῦτο διισχυρίζομαι Phaedo 100 D, cp. Rep. V. 476 C, D.)

See Arist. Metaph. I. 6, § 4 τὴν μέντοι γε μέθεξιν ἢ τὴν μίμησιν, ἥτις ἂν εἴη τῶν εἰδῶν, ἀφεῖσαν ἐν κοινῷ ζητεῖν.

a. In his first discovery of the supreme reality of universals, Plato lightly assumes the correlation between them and the particulars of experience. He is more concerned in asserting this than in explaining it. And he expresses his conception in a variety of ways. When Socrates in the Phaedo substitutes a dialectical for a physical method, he implies a *causal* relation of idea to fact—ἔρχομαι γὰρ δὴ ἐπιχειρῶν σοι ἐπιδείξασθαι τῆς αἰτίας τὸ εἶδος ὃ πεπραγμάτευμαι (Phaedo 100 B), and he explains this by participation: ib. C εἴ τί ἐστιν ἄλλο καλὸν πλὴν αὐτὸ τὸ καλόν, οὐδὲ δι' ἓν ἄλλο καλὸν εἶναι ἢ διότι μετέχει ἐκείνου τοῦ καλοῦ. He does not, however, confine himself to the word μετέχειν, as if this were the chosen term of the school: μεταλαμβάνειν (102 B) is freely substituted, also κοινωνία (100 D). And it is observable that the abstract nouns, μέθεξις, μετάληψις (Parm. 131, 132, 151 E), do not seem to have been at this time in use.

§ 40.    β. The participation of the particular in the universal is otherwise spoken of as the *presence* of the universal in the particular : Phaedo 100 D ἡ ἐκείνου τοῦ καλοῦ εἴτε παρουσία, εἴτε κοινωνία. Cp. Lys. 217 D καὶ μὴν παρείη γ' ἂν αὐταῖς λευκότης : Charm. 158 E. 'Ενεῖναι—'to inhere' is similarly used in the Republic : III. 402 C τὰ τῆς σωφροσύνης εἴδη . . . ἐνόντα ἐν οἷς ἔνεστιν. In the same passage these moral attributes are spoken of as 'carried about' πανταχοῦ περιφερόμενα ; and in Theaet. 202 A, though not in stating Plato's own theory, general predicates are said to *run round about*, περιτρέχειν, amongst particular subjects.

§ 41.    γ. The relation of the universal to the particular is elsewhere regarded as the relation of the Perfect to the Imperfect, or of the Ideal to the Actual. Plato in the Phaedo does not feel this point of view to be inconsistent with the former. In that dialogue (p. 74) the reminiscence which is the germ of knowledge is accounted for by the *resemblance* of things transitory to eternal truths, known by us in a pre-existent state. The perception of equality and inequality, for example, is referred to the recollection of Ideal Equality (αὐτὸ τὸ ἴσον). Sense-perceived equality recalls this by resemblance, but falls short of it. ὅταν γε ἀπὸ τῶν ὁμοίων ἀναμιμνήσκηταί τίς τι, ἆρ' οὐκ ἀναγκαῖον . . . ἐννοεῖν, εἴτε τι ἐλλείπει τοῦτο κατὰ τὴν ὁμοιότητα εἴτε μή, κ.τ.λ. In Phaedo 69 B the ordinary Virtue is called a σκιαγραφία, and in 76 D occurs the phrase, ταῦτα (τὰ ἐκ τῶν αἰσθήσεων) ἐκείνῃ (τῇ οὐσίᾳ) ἀπεικάζομεν.

§ 42.    This form of Plato's Idealism appears principally (1) in passages marked by strong ethical aspiration, or (2) where his speculation takes a cosmological turn. The image often employed is that of pattern and copy, borrowed from the 'imitative' arts, especially from the art of painting.

(1) Moral improvement is continually represented as a process of assimilation to the Divine (see esp. Theaet. 176 B). And in this connexion Plato treats the notions of participation and assimilation as interchangeable. For

instance in Phaedr. 253 A the words καθ' ὅσον δυνατὸν θεοῦ ἀνθρώπῳ μετασχεῖν are immediately followed up with ποιοῦσιν ὡς δυνατὸν ὁμοιότατον τῷ σφετέρῳ θεῷ. See Arist. Met. I. 6, § 3 τὴν δὲ μέθεξιν τοὔνομα μόνον μετέβαλεν· οἱ μὲν γὰρ Πυθαγόρειοι μιμήσει τὰ ὄντα φασὶν εἶναι τῶν ἀριθμῶν, Πλάτων δὲ μεθέξει, τοὔνομα μεταβαλών. τὴν μέντοι γε μέθεξιν ἢ τὴν μίμησιν, ἥτις ἂν εἴη τῶν εἰδῶν, ἀφεῖσαν ἐν κοινῷ ζητεῖν.

In the Republic, the perfect or ideal state is more than once described as a pattern of which the actual state is to be a copy:—V. 472 D, E παράδειγμα ἐποιοῦμεν λόγῳ ἀγαθῆς πόλεως, VI. 500 E οἱ τῷ θείῳ παραδείγματι χρώμενοι ζωγράφοι. And the same ideal is to be the pattern for the individual, whether the perfect state is realized or not,—IX. 592 B ἀλλ' . . . ἐν οὐρανῷ ἴσως παράδειγμα ἀνάκειται τῷ βουλομένῳ ὁρᾶν καὶ ὁρῶντι ἑαυτὸν κατοικίζειν. This comes near to the exalted tone of Theaet. 176 E παραδειγμάτων . . . ἐν τῷ ὄντι ἑστώτων, τοῦ μὲν θείου εὐδαιμονεστάτου, τοῦ δὲ ἀθέου ἀθλιωτάτου . . . λανθάνουσι τῷ μὲν ὁμοιούμενοι διὰ τὰς ἀδίκους πράξεις, τῷ δὲ ἀνομοιούμενοι, where the conjunction of opposites has a similar effect to that in Phaedo 74 D.

And in the Politicus (273 B, 293 E, 297 C) the true states-man is represented as imitating from afar the principles of Divine Government.

Similarly in Rep. VI. 500 C, Timaeus 47 C, the philosopher is described as imitating the universal order. See also Tim. 88 C κατὰ δὲ ταὐτὰ . . . τὸ τοῦ παντὸς ἀπομιμούμενον εἶδος.

(2) In the last-mentioned passages there is a union of § 43. the ethical with the cosmological strain. The following may serve to illustrate the place which μίμησις holds from time to time in Plato's cosmogony. In the mythical description of the Earth in Phaedo 110 foll., the colours and the precious stones known in human experience are but meagre *samples* (δείγματα) of those on the upper surface of the globe as seen from above. In the vision of Judge-ment at the close of the Republic (not to dwell on the

βίων παραδείγματα) the orrery turning on Necessity's knees, although partly pictorial, is partly also an ideal pattern (and in some occult or inconsistent way an efficient cause) of the revolutions of the planets.

In the Phaedrus, 250 B, earthly realities are ὁμοιώματα τῶν ἐκεῖ; and each lover makes himself and his beloved like his god (ἄγαλμα).

And in the allegory of the Cave (Rep. VII) into which less of what is purely mythological enters, natural objects in their most essential forms are described as σκευαστὰ εἴδωλα, things manufactured after the supreme realities, and moved by hands unseen so as to cast their shadows on the wall. Elsewhere in the Republic, the figure of *substance versus shadow* repeatedly appears: II. 365 C, 382 D, III. 401 B, 402 B, C, IV. 443 C, V. 472 C, VI. 510, 511, VII. 516 A, 520 C, 534 C, IX. 587 D. Cp. Lysis 219 C, D, Phaedr. 250 A, B. And a similar strain of metaphor is carried further in the Timaeus, where the world is an εἰκών, or true image (not σκιά, an imperfect likeness) of the νοητὸν εἶδος, whose forms are stamped upon the chaotic receptacle of space 'in a strange and hardly explicable way.' (Tim. 50 C.)[1]

§ 44. Meanwhile the other metaphors of *participation* in the ideas, *real presence* of the ideas, *communion* with the ideas, are by no means discarded. For the Republic it is enough to quote V. 476 C, D, where indeed the two modes of expression (τὸ ὅμοιον . . . τὰ μετέχοντα) are conjoined,—as they are in Parm. 133 D. See also VI. 505 A ᾗ καὶ δίκαια καὶ τἄλλα προσχρησάμενα χρήσιμα καὶ ὠφέλιμα γίγνεται.

In the later dialogues (Soph., Polit., Phil., Tim., Laws) the relation of the individual to the universal is altogether less in question. See Excursus, Essay on Structure, p. 46 ff. But μέθεξις still takes place between subject and predicate, or between substance and attribute.

---

[1] Cp. Tim. 48 E, 49 A ἐν μὲν ὡς παραδείγματος εἶδος ὑποτεθέν, νοητὸν καὶ ἀεὶ κατὰ ταὐτὰ ὄν, μίμημα δὲ παραδείγματος δεύτερον, γένεσιν ἔχον καὶ ὁρατόν.

Soph. 247 A δικαιοσύνης ἕξει καὶ **παρουσίᾳ** (L. C.'s conjecture δ. ἕ. κ. φρονήσεως has been approved by Schanz, but see the words which follow, τό γε δυνατόν τῳ **παραγίγνεσθαι** καὶ ἀπογίγνεσθαι πάντως εἶναί τι φήσουσιν [1]), which show that the correction is not absolutely necessary.

Ib. 248 C ὅταν τῳ **παρῇ** . . . δύναμις.

Ib. 256 A διὰ τὸ **μετέχειν** αὖ πάντ᾿ αὐτοῦ.

Phil. 16 D μίαν ἰδέαν περὶ παντὸς . . . ζητεῖν· εὑρήσειν γὰρ **ἐνοῦσαν.**

Ib. 60 B, C τὴν τἀγαθοῦ διαφέρειν φύσιν τῷδε τῶν ἄλλων. τίνι ; ᾧ **παρείη** τοῦτ᾿ ἀεὶ τῶν ζῴων διὰ τέλους πάντως καὶ πάντῃ, μηδενὸς ἑτέρου ποτὲ ἔτι προσδεῖσθαι, τὸ δὲ ἱκανὸν τελεώτατον **ἔχειν.**

Polit. 268 B μουσικῆς . . . **μετείληφεν.**

Ib. 269 D πολλῶν μὲν καὶ μακαρίων παρὰ τοῦ γεννήσαντος **μετείληφεν,** ἀτὰρ οὖν δὴ **κεκοινώνηκέ** γε καὶ σώματος, κ.τ.λ.

Ib. 273 B, 275 D οὐ **μετόν.**

Tim. 34 E **μετέχοντες** τοῦ . . . εἰκῇ, 36 E, 58 E **μετίσχει** μᾶλλον κινήσεως, 77 A, B **μετάσχῃ** . . . **μετέχει,** 90 C καθ᾿ ὅσον . . . **μετασχεῖν** ἀνθρωπίνη φύσις ἀθανασίας ἐνδέχεται.

δ. The ἀπορήματα raised in the Parmenides, then (with **§ 45.** which cp. Phil. 15), have not had the effect of banishing 'participation' (see esp. the examples just quoted from Polit., Phileb.). Yet it was there shown that particulars could not partake in the universal εἶδος, either (1) wholly, or (2) in part, nor (3) as individuals in a common form, nor (4) as objects of thought, nor (5) as copies of a pattern (καὶ ἡ μέθεξις αὕτη τοῖς ἄλλοις γίγνεσθαι τῶν εἰδῶν οὐκ ἄλλη τις ἢ εἰκασθῆναι αὐτοῖς). Nor are these difficulties solved in the latter portion of that dialogue. What is really shown there is the inadequacy of the Zenonian dialectic, since by subjecting to it the Eleatic hypothesis of One Being, this is proved (1) to have no predicates, (2) to have all predi-

---

[1] In Parm. 133 D there are two stages in the descent from the ideas to individuals, (1) ὁμοίωσις, subsisting between the idea and its ὁμοίωμα or concrete type, and (2) μέθεξις τοῦ ὁμοιώματος.

cates, and (3) to have neither all nor none, but to be in
transition between them.  Plato thus hints indirectly at
the root-fallacy which he has ridiculed in the Euthydemus,
and of which he finally disposes in the Sophistes—the
blank absoluteness of affirmation and negation.  By the
series of inferences which Parmenides himself sums up in
the concluding paragraph, Plato, it may be fairly said,
ἐξημφοτέρικε τὸν τοῦ Ζήνωνος λόγον (cp. Euthyd. 360 D).

§ 46.    ε. This is not done without a motive, and the motive
may be gathered in the words of Socrates, Parm. 129 C–E εἰ
. . . αὐτὰ τὰ γένη τε καὶ εἴδη ἐν αὑτοῖς ἀποφαίνοι τἀναντία ταῦτα
πάθη πάσχοντα, ἄξιον θαυμάζειν . . . ἐὰν . . . πρῶτον μὲν διαι-
ρῆται χωρὶς αὐτὰ καθ᾽ αὑτὰ τὰ εἴδη, οἷον ὁμοιότητά τε καὶ ἀνομοι-
ότητα καὶ πλῆθος καὶ τὸ ἓν καὶ στάσιν καὶ κίνησιν καὶ πάντα
τὰ τοιαῦτα, εἶτα ἐν ἑαυτοῖς ταῦτα δυνάμενα συγκεράννυσθαι καὶ
διακρίνεσθαι ἀποφαίνῃ, ἀγαίμην ἂν ἔγωγ᾽, ἔφη, θαυμαστῶς.  Cp.
Phileb. 14 D.  The discussion of those ἀπορίαι has cleared
the ground for truer modes of conception.  Something like
a theory of predication is at length formulated.  But even
in the Philebus the construction of ideas into a κόσμος τις
ἀσώματος is carried only a little way, and after the relativity
of ideas is proved, Plato still speaks of them as absolute,
and still employs metaphorical language to indicate metaphysical relations.  Yet the point of view is no longer
quite the same as before.

As the conception of the nature of predication becomes
more distinct, a new stage of inquiry is reached in the
search for an order and connexion of ideas.  A rational
psychology begins to clear away the confusions of a crude
ontology.  And while in the untried effort to account for
γένεσις, language is still affected with dualism and tinged
with mythological imagery, a far less dubious light is
already shining on the world of thought.

§ 47.    In the Phaedo and elsewhere, moral and other 'ideas'—
αὐτὸ τὸ καλόν, ἀγαθόν, δίκαιον, ὅσιον, ἴσον, μέγα—were ranked
together as coordinate, or summed up as ἡ ἀΐδιος οὐσία and

set over against the transitoriness of individual objects, τὰ τούτων (sc. τῶν εἰδῶν) μετέχοντα. But in the concluding passage of Book VI, and in what follows it, there is a revelation of the unity and organization of knowledge, implying (1) that there is an order in the intellectual world, and (2) that there is a way upward and downward[1] between intellect and sense: moreover that above knowledge, truth and being, there is the supreme domination of the good. But the statement is in general terms, and no account is taken of the difficulties which are raised, without being solved, in the Parmenides. In the Theaetetus (185 C) it is clearly seen that Being, Unity, Number, likeness, difference and goodness (even when relative) are notions of a higher order than other generalizations of experience—they are birds that fly everywhere about the cage[2]—and also that there are relations between them (Theaet. 186 B τὴν οὐσίαν ... τῆς ἐναντιότητος). The existence of such relations amongst the highest ideas (or primary forms of thought and being) is what the Stranger in the Sophistes undertakes to prove ; and here the long-familiar words κοινωνία, μετέχειν, μεταλαμβάνειν, ἐνεῖναι (also ξύμμιξις, ἐνοικεῖν, συνοικεῖν, δέχεσθαι, προσάπτειν, περιτρέχειν, μετατίθεσθαι, μιχθῆναι, ἁρμόττειν, προσαρτᾶσθαι, συμφωνεῖν, σύμφυτον ἔχειν)[3] are again in frequent use. Even the dim form of Space in the Timaeus, the γενέσεως τιθήνη, is spoken of as εἶδός τι ... μεταλαμβάνον ... πῃ τοῦ νοητοῦ, and again as (εἰκόνα) οὐσίας ἁμῶς γέ πως ἀντεχομένην[4]. At the same time the other metaphor of Pattern and Copy comes once more into service, not now, however, merely to express the relation of particular to universal, but to throw light upon another difficulty, the possibility

---

[1] Cp. Heracl. Fr. 69 (Bywater) ὁδὸς ἄνω κάτω μία καὶ ωὐτή.

[2] Theaet. 197 D : cp. Soph. 254 C.

[3] See Soph. 216, 223, 228 B, 235 A, 238, 248, 249 A, 250 E, 251, 252, 253, 255, 256, 259 ; Polit. 309 ; Phil. 15 24 37, 57, 60, 66.

[4] Tim. 45 D, 51 A, 52 C: cp. ib. 64 D λύπης δὲ καὶ ἡδονῆς οὐ μετέχον. The simple words ἔχειν, λαμβάνειν, κεκτῆσθαι are often similarly used. So too μὴ στέρεσθαι Phileb. 67.

of false opinion (ψευδὴς δόξα) and of falsity (ψευδὴς λόγος).
And as the idea of predication becomes more distinct,
other modes of expression of a more definite kind are
introduced—πεπονθέναι Parm. 148 A, πάθος ἔχειν Soph.
245 A, πάθημα πάσχειν, συλλαβή Theaet. 202, συμπλοκή
Theaet. 202 B, Soph. 262 C, 240 C, σύγκρασις Polit. 273 B, &c.,
Phil. 64 D, &c., κόσμος ἀσώματος Phil. 64 B.

§ 48.    We are at present concerned not with Plato's philosophy,
but with his use of Language.   Else more might be said
not only of his various modes of expression, but of the
increasing clearness of his thoughts, and of an approach to
system.

His expressions are various, because almost always
figurative.   Metaphorical language about philosophical
notions is necessarily broken and inconsistent, and cannot
without confusion be tested by a logical standard.   Many
phases of the Ideas occurred to Plato's mind.   They are
universals, realities, absolute, relative : they represent the
most abstract and the most concrete notions : they are
isolated, and also 'flying about' everywhere among objects :
they are akin to numbers, though not the same with them.
Plato does not attempt to harmonize all these different
views ; they are experimental conceptions of the Universal,
which he gradually brings back more and more to what
we term common sense,—to psychology and logic from
a fanciful ontology.   His language about them in the
Phaedrus, Meno, Phaedo, is different from that which he
uses in the Philebus and the Laws ; or rather in the
two latter dialogues the transcendental form of them has
almost disappeared.   If instead of dwelling on his use of
terms we consider his thought and intention [1], we find that
in the dialectical dialogues and those which go with them
(Tim., Critias, Laws), through grappling with the difficulties which his own theories have raised in relation to

---

[1] τί . . . διανοούμενος εἶπε (Theaet. 184 A).

contemporary opinion, he is confronted more and more closely with the great central questions of all philosophy, the essence of thought, the meaning of the Universe, the conditions and possibilities of human improvement for the individual and for communities. The last word of Plato on the nature of Mind is hardly different from the language of Modern Philosophy. What can be more 'modern,' for example, than the definition of Thought in Soph. 265 D, E, or than several of the psychological distinctions in the Philebus ?

Other terms having a metaphysical significance may be dismissed more briefly.

### φύσις.                                                              § 49.

The word φύσις (after appearing once in Hom. Od. X. 303, for the 'virtues' of a drug[1]) occurs in writers from Pindar to Aristophanes with various shades of meanings :— *birth, growth, stature, native character or disposition, inherent power or capacity*, as well as in the more general sense of *that which is natural, or in accordance with experience*, as opposed to what is artificial, acquired, conventional, or monstrous.

Herodotus II. 45 already has the idiomatic phrase φύσιν ἔχει (ἔνα ἐόντα τὸν Ἡρακλέα ... κῶς φύσιν ἔχει πολλὰς μυριάδας φονεῦσαι). Thucydides repeatedly speaks of 'human nature' (ἡ ἀνθρωπεία φύσις I. 76, II. 50, III. 45, 84 ; see also III. 82, § 2 ἕως ἂν ἡ αὐτὴ φύσις ἀνθρώπων ᾖ): and in V. 105, § 2 ὑπὸ φύσεως ἀναγκαίας, he alludes to the inevitableness of 'natural law.'

Professor Burnet in his able work on *Early Greek Philosophy* argues with much force in favour of the thesis that 'the word which was used by the early cosmologists to express the idea of a permanent and primary *substance* was none other than φύσις, and that the title περὶ φύσεως so commonly given to philosophical works in the sixth and

---

[1] Also in the Batrachomyomachia, in the sense of natural endowments.

fifth centuries B.C. does not mean " on the nature of things,"
—a far later use of the word,—but simply "concerning
the primary substance"'; and that 'in Greek philosophical
language φύσις always means that which is primary,
fundamental and persistent as opposed to that which is
secondary, derivative and transient, what is given as
opposed to what is made or becomes.'

The preciseness of this statement can hardly be borne
out by quotations, but it may be accepted as an expression
of the fact that the early philosophers in writing περὶ
φύσεως had given to the word a new depth of meaning by
choosing it as an expression for the uniformity of experience
for which they sought to account. Hence κατὰ φύσιν, φύσει,
παρὰ φύσιν, are phrases in common use. And the opposition of the natural to the conventional (φύσει to νόμῳ) was
a common-place of sophistical disputation, Isocr. Panegyr.
p. 62 d, § 121 (Bekker) φύσει πολίτας ὄντας νόμῳ τῆς πολιτείας
ἀποστερεῖσθαι.

§ 50.     In Plato the connotation of φύσις has not more fixity
than that of other philosophical terms. The particular
meaning is to be determined by the context in each case.

The following uses appear to be specially Platonic :—

1. Phaedo 103 C τότε μὲν γὰρ ἐλέγετο ἐκ τοῦ ἐναντίου πράγ-
ματος τὸ ἐναντίον πρᾶγμα γίγνεσθαι, νῦν δὲ ὅτι αὐτὸ τὸ ἐναντίον
ἑαυτῷ ἐναντίον οὐκ ἄν ποτε γένοιτο, οὔτε τὸ ἐν ἡμῖν οὔτε τὸ ἐν
τῇ φύσει.

Here are three grades of reality [1], (1) the actual thing or
object in which the idea is embodied (τὸ πρᾶγμα τὸ μετέχον
τοῦ εἴδους), (2) the idea as so embodied or 'immanent' (αὐτὸ
τὸ ἐν ἡμῖν), (3) the idea as self-existent, absolute, 'transcendent' (αὐτὸ τὸ ἐν τῇ φύσει). Φύσις, therefore, in this
passage is the sum of self-existences, the immutable nature
of things.

Compare Rep. X. 597 B μία μὲν ἡ ἐν τῇ φύσει οὖσα, ἣν

---

[1] As in Parm. 133 D, quoted above, p. 313, note.

φαῖμεν ἄν, ὡς ἐγῷμαι, θεὸν ἐργάσασθαι, ib. VI. 501 B πρός τε τὸ **φύσει** δίκαιον ... καὶ πρὸς ἐκεῖνο αὖ τὸ ἐν τοῖς ἀνθρώποις.

2. But elsewhere the supreme agency of Nature is regarded as an heretical doctrine, opposed to the sovereignty of Reason and of God. Soph. 265 C τῷ τῶν πολλῶν δόγματι ... τῷ τὴν **φύσιν** αὐτὰ γεννᾶν ἀπό τινος αἰτίας αὐτομάτης καὶ ἄνευ διανοίας **φυούσης**. 'Nature' is here not Eternal Law, but mere blind, unconscious energy, as opposed to Mind. Cp. Laws X. 892 C φύσιν βούλονται λέγειν γένεσιν τὴν περὶ τὰ πρῶτα, κ.τ.λ.[1]

3. In Phaedr. 270 φύσις is an extremely comprehensive word, including both worlds, the inward and the outward. This appears from the allusions to Anaxagoras and Hippocrates. Φύσις in this sense differs from οὐσία chiefly in referring more distinctly to the parts which make up the whole.

4. According to another mode of expression, the subject of philosophy is not *all* nature but *every* nature, Theaet. 173 E, Polit. 272 C.

In so denoting single or particular natures, φύσις is sometimes (*a*) the nature of the thing described, and sometimes (*b*) the thing itself as characterized, and the word in this sense is applied equally to natural kinds and to abstract notions.

(*a*) Rep. II. 359 B ἡ μὲν οὖν δὴ **φύσις** δικαιοσύνης ... αὕτη[2] (including both γένεσις and οὐσία, see context).

Phaedr. 245 E ἀθανάτου δὲ πεφασμένου τοῦ ὑφ' ἑαυτοῦ κινουμένου, ψυχῆς οὐσίαν τε καὶ λόγον τοῦτον αὐτόν τις λέγων οὐκ αἰσχυνεῖται. πᾶν γὰρ σῶμα, ᾧ μὲν ἔξωθεν τὸ κινεῖσθαι, ἄψυχον, ᾧ δὲ ἔνδοθεν αὐτῷ ἐξ αὐτοῦ, ἔμψυχον, ὡς ταύτης οὔσης **φύσεως** ψυχῆς (sc. τὸ αὐτὸ ἑαυτὸ κινεῖν).

---

[1] Plato here claims that if the study of *nature* is the study of *primary* substances, it ought to begin with the study of mind, since mind is prior to the elements. He tries to wrest from the natural philosophers their chief catch-word— more openly and disputatiously than in the Phaedrus.

[2] The 'Naturalist' theory is in question, see πεφυκέναι Rep. II. 358 E.

Rep. VI. 493 C τὴν δὲ τοῦ ἀναγκαίου καὶ ἀγαθοῦ **φύσιν**, κ.τ.λ.

Ib. VII. 525 C ἐπὶ θέαν τῆς τῶν ἀριθμῶν **φύσεως.**

Ib. X. 611 B μήτε γε αὖ τῇ ἀληθεστάτῃ **φύσει** τοιοῦτον εἶναι ψυχήν.

Soph. 245 C, 258 B, C ; Phil. 25 A, 44 E.

(*b*) In the following places the nature is identified with the thing :—

Rep. II. 359 C ὃ **πᾶσα φύσις** ('every creature') διώκειν πέφυκεν ὡς ἀγαθόν.

Ib. IV. 429 D **μίαν φύσιν** τὴν τῶν λευκῶν.

Ib. VI. 491 A οἷαι οὖσαι **φύσεις** ψυχῶν.

Polit. 306 E.

§ 51.  5. There is a pleonastic use of φύσις with a genitive, in this latter sense, which, like other periphrases, occurs more frequently in the later dialogues.   But the Phaedrus affords more than one example :—

Phaedr. 248 C ἡ . . . τοῦ πτεροῦ **φύσις.**

Ib. 254 B τὴν τοῦ κάλλους **φύσιν.**

Soph. 257 A ἡ τῶν γενῶν **φύσις.**

Ib. 257 C, D (bis) ἡ θατέρου **φύσις.**

Polit. 257 D τὴν τοῦ προσώπου **φύσιν.**

Phileb. 25 E τὴν ὑγιείας **φύσιν.**

Ib. 30 B τὴν τῶν καλλίστων καὶ τιμιωτάτων **φύσιν.**

Tim. 45 D τὴν τῶν βλεφάρων **φύσιν.**

Ib. 74 D τὴν τῶν νεύρων **φύσιν.**   Ib. 75 A τὴν τῶν ἰσχίων **φύσιν.**

Ib. 84 C ἡ τοῦ μυελοῦ **φύσις.**

(Cp. for similar periphrases ib. 75 A τὸ τῆς γλώττης εἶδος, 70 C τὴν τοῦ πλεύμονος ἰδέαν.)

Laws VIII. 845 D τὴν ὕδατος **φύσιν.**

Ib. IX. 862 D τὴν τοῦ δικαίου **φύσιν.**

The same use recurs in Aristotle.   See Bonitz' *Index Aristotelicus*, p. 837 b.

6.  Φύσις is constantly used in the Republic in the ordinary sense of natural disposition or capability (esp. Apol. 22 B, C) as distinguished from the complete development of mind or character :—

III. 410 D τὸ θυμοειδὲς . . . τῆς **φύσεως**.

VI. 485 A τὴν **φύσιν** αὐτῶν πρῶτον δεῖν καταμαθεῖν.

The great frequency of the term φύσις in Plato's dialogues represents, what has too often been ignored, the experiential aspect of his philosophy.

## (*b*) PSYCHOLOGICAL TERMS.

As Plato's philosophical language becomes (1) more § **52.** subjective and (2) more accurate, his use of words to signify mental states, processes, or faculties, becomes at once more frequent and more precise. It would be an error, however, even in his latest dialogues to look for consistency or finality. When it is found that the definition of δικαιοσύνη, obtained with so much labour in the Republic, is tacitly set aside in the Laws, and that the disjunctive-hypothetical method so energetically put forth in the Parmenides nowhere distinctly recurs, it need not surprise us that the significance of διάνοια in Theaet. 189 E, Soph. 265 D, E differs essentially from that assigned to the same word in Rep. VI. 511, or that αἴσθησις, δόξα, φαντασία, τέχνη, ἐπιστήμη, φιλοσοφία, can only be said to have an approximate fixity of meaning.

### Αἴσθησις.

*a.* Any immediate perception, intuition or consciousness.

Charm. 158 E, 159 A δῆλον γὰρ ὅτι, εἴ σοι πάρεστι σωφροσύνη, ἔχεις τι περὶ αὐτῆς δοξάζειν. ἀνάγκη γάρ που ἐνοῦσαν αὐτήν, εἴπερ ἔνεστιν, αἴσθησίν τινα παρέχειν, ἐξ ἧς δόξα ἄν τίς σοι περὶ αὐτῆς εἴη, ὅ τι ἐστὶ καὶ ὁποῖόν τι ἡ σωφροσύνη.

This is the ordinary meaning as exemplified in Antiphon, Herod. p. 134, § 44; Thuc. II. 50, 61; Eur. El. 290; Xen. Hell. V. 1, § 8; Anab. IV. 6, § 13.

*Obs.*—Euripides (Iph. Aul. 1243) already has αἴσθημα, which, though frequent in Aristotle, does not seem to occur in Plato. A special meaning = 'scent' as a hunting term occurs in Xen. Cyn. 3, § 5; cp. Rep. II. 375 A.

β. Sense-perception in general, as opposed to γνῶσις, cognition, νόησις, intellection, λογισμός, reasoning : imperfectly distinguished from δόξα and φαντασία.

Without entering here on the discussion of Plato's philosophy of sensation, it may be observed that a comparison of Phaedo 79, Phaedr. 249, 250, Rep. VII. 524, with Phileb. 33, 38, 43 A, B, Tim. 43 C, shows that the reasonings attributed to the disciples of Protagoras in the Theaetetus, though rejected as a definition of knowledge, exercise a decided influence on the evolution of Plato's psychology.

γ. Special modes of sensation, including the five senses, with others not separately named.

Phaedo 65 D ἤδη οὖν πώποτέ τι τῶν τοιούτων τοῖς ὀφθαλμοῖς εἶδες ; Οὐδαμῶς, ἦ δ' ὅς.   'Αλλ' ἄλλη τινὶ αἰσθήσει τῶν διὰ τοῦ σώματος ἐφήψω αὐτῶν ; Rep. VI. 507 E ἡ τοῦ ὁρᾶν αἴσθησις.

δ. A single act of sense-perception,—an impression of sense. Theaet. 156 D τὴν λευκότητά τε καὶ αἴσθησιν αὐτῇ ξύμφυτον : ib. B αἱ μὲν οὖν αἰσθήσεις τὰ τοιάδε ἡμῖν ἔχουσιν ὀνόματα, ὄψεις τε καὶ ἀκοαὶ καὶ ὀσφρήσεις, κ.τ.λ.

Thus the ἐναντία αἴσθησις of Rep. VII. 523 B, Soph. 266 C is an opposite impression of *the same* sense.

*Obs.*—Αἰσθητός in Men. 76 D is said to be an expression in the manner of Gorgias : otherwise the word occurs first in Plato ; and αἰσθητής, ἅπαξ εἰρημένον in Theaet. 160 D, appears to be invented on the spot. It is cited by Pollux as an unusual word.

§ 53.   Δόξα.

The opposition of δοκεῖν at once to εἶναι and ἐπίστασθαι leads to the association of δόξα as the lower faculty with αἴσθησις. For example in Rep. VI, VII, where the clearness of a faculty is said to be proportioned to the nature of its object, δόξα seems to be concerned with the shadows, i. e. the visible world ; in Phaedo 96 it is an involuntary judgement resulting from sense and memory, and in the Phaedrus the unlucky charioteer regales his steeds with τροφὴ δοξαστή, because of his poverty in the ideas.   But in

Theaet., Soph., Phil., it becomes manifest that δόξα is simply a judgement, given by the mind in answer to herself, which may or may not be coincident with an impression of sense, and may be either true or false. This is in accordance with the advance in psychological clearness which marks the dialectical dialogues.

In the earlier part of the Theaetetus, δόξα φαντασία αἴσθησις are very closely associated, although in such an expression as in 179 C τὸ παρὸν ἑκάστῳ πάθος, ἐξ ὧν αἱ αἰσθήσεις καὶ αἱ κατὰ ταύτας δόξαι γίγνονται, the distinction between αἴσθησις and δόξα is accurately preserved (cp. Charm. 159 A quoted above). It is only after the discussion in pp. 184–190, however, that the definition of δόξα as διανοίας ἀποτελεύτησις (Soph. 264 A) becomes possible. For it has now been clearly brought out that δόξα, opinion or judgement, is an operation of the mind, silently predicating one thing of another. Such predication or judgement may refer to any subject matter, but it may be false as well as true, and this gives occasion for the question, How is false opinion possible? See esp. Phileb. 37 C, D.

Opinion, so understood, is still distinguished from Knowledge (ἐπιστήμη) which is always true, although this opposition is not sufficiently accounted for by the definition of ἐπιστήμη as δόξα ἀληθὴς μετὰ λόγου. Δόξα ἀληθής holds a higher place in subsequent dialogues, Sophist, Philebus, Timaeus, than in the Republic, where it is condemned as ' blind.' Rep. VI. 506 C: cp. IV. 430 B.

For the vernacular crossing the specific meaning, see esp. VI. 490 A παρὰ δόξαν . . . δοξαζομένοις.

*Obs.*—The naturalness of the association of δόξα with αἴσθησις appears from the passage of the Charmides (159 A) above quoted. On the other hand, the constant use of δοκεῖ μοι in expressing a judgement of the mind, suggested the other meaning in which δόξα is opposed to ἐπιστήμη. As the two meanings were not consciously distinguished, a confusion arose which helped to accentuate

Plato's view of the uncertainty and fallaciousness of sensation ; to which, however, Philosophy had from the first been predisposed, as appears from well-known sayings of Heraclitus and Parmenides.

§ 54.    Φαντασία.

Φαντασία is properly the noun of φαντάζεσθαι (Soph. 260 E, Rep. II. 382 E), but is treated in Theaet. 152 C, 161 E as the noun of φαίνεσθαι. In Soph. 264 A, B τὸ φαίνεσθαι is defined as δόξα μετ᾽ αἰσθήσεως or σύμμιξις αἰσθήσεως καὶ δόξης. In Phileb. 39, however, there is a more elaborate description of imagination or presentation (Vorstellung). Opinion or judgement having been characterized under the figure of a scribe who writes down sentences in the mind, it is added that the scribe is corroborated by a painter, who illustrates what is written down. And the pictures of this artist may have reference to the past or future, and like the judgements which they accompany, they may be either false or true. The pleasures of Hope are thus accounted for. The word φαντασία does not occur in this passage. But it is obvious that the thing meant might be denoted by the term, and the mental images in question are spoken of as ζωγραφήματα (39 D) τὰ φαντάσματα ἐζωγραφη-μένα (40 A). In Rep. II. 382 E, where φαντάζεσθαι (380 D) has preceded, φαντασίαι are 'illusive apparitions.' The word carries a similar association in Soph. 260 E, &c.

The noun, although common (with its derivatives) in later writers, does not occur before the time of Plato.

§ 55.    Διάνοια.

In the concluding passage of Rep. VI the word διάνοια acquires a specific meaning, to denote the faculty, or attitude of mind, *intermediate* between δόξα and ἐπιστήμη, or between πίστις and νοῦς. This definition stands in close reference to the context in which it occurs, and it is observable that διάνοια in this exact sense is hardly to be found elsewhere in Plato. The definition appears to rest on a false etymology, viz. δια-νοια, 'mediate intellection,' 'thinking *through* something,' as distinguished from pure intuition on the one hand and mere impressions on the other ; because the abstract truths of mathematical science are studied *through* visible symbols (VI. 511 D ὡς μεταξύ τι δόξης τε καὶ νοῦ, cp. VII. 533 D, E). The psychology of the Theaetetus supplies a more accurate explanation of the term, as = 'mental discourse,' *passing between* subject and predicate, or predicate and subject. This view of διάνοια recurs in the Sophistes (263 D). Διάνοια, so understood, is not above and beyond δόξα, but is the necessary preliminary to it ; since the mind puts her questions before she answers them, and opinion, however seemingly instantaneous, is the consequence of thought. Thus δόξα rises in the scale, and διάνοια, as a subjective fact, is correctly analysed.

In the great majority of instances διάνοια (with its verb διανοεῖσθαι) is used in the ordinary Greek acceptations of (1) mental activity, (2) mind in act, (3) a particular thought or conception, (4) meaning, (5) intention.

Ἕξις. § 56.

Ἕξις, ἀπὸ τοῦ ἔχειν πως, is properly a state or condition whether bodily or mental. But the psychological use of this word also is affected in Plato by a false etymological association from the active use of ἔχω. The active use of ἕξις occurs in Rep. IV. 433 E ἡ τοῦ οἰκείου τε καὶ ἑαυτοῦ ἕξις τε καὶ πρᾶξις, Soph. 247 A δικαιοσύνης ἕξει καὶ παρουσίᾳ, Theaet. 197 A ἐπιστήμης . . . ἕξιν. And it seems probable that in such passages as Phaedr. 268 E τὸν τὴν σὴν ἕξιν ἔχοντα, Rep. VI. 509 A τὴν τοῦ ἀγαθοῦ ἕξιν, IX. 591 B ὅλη ἡ ψυχὴ . . . τιμιωτέραν ἕξιν λαμβάνει, although the ordinary meaning of 'condition' is present, Plato has the other association in his mind. For the more familiar meaning, see esp. Phileb. 11 D ἕξιν ψυχῆς καὶ διάθεσιν, κ.τ.λ.

Τέχνη—practical skill.

a. Skill as opposed to inexperience, Phaedo 89 E ἄνευ τέχνης τῆς περὶ τἀνθρώπεια.

β. Enlightened practice, as opposed to mere 'rule of thumb' (ἐμπειρία καὶ τριβή), Phaedr. 260 E, 270 B, Gorg. 463 B (see Rep. VI. 493 B).

γ. Professional practice, opposed to that of an amateur, Prot. 315 A ἐπὶ τέχνῃ μανθάνει.

δ. Art as opposed (1) to nature, Rep. II. 381 B; (2) to divine inspiration, Ion 536 D.

ε. A system of rules (Phaedr. 261 B).

ζ. τέχνη as distinguished from ἐπιστήμη is (1) a lower grade of knowledge (see the contemptuous diminutive τεχνύδριον in Rep. V. 475 E); (2) (chiefly in the later dialogues) Knowledge applied to production (γένεσις), Laws X. 892 B, C.

*Obs.*—The *actual sciences* (as distinguished from the same studies when enlightened by philosophy) are called τέχναι in Rep. VI. 511 C τὸ ὑπὸ τῶν τεχνῶν καλουμένων. The second (β) and sixth (ζ) of these definitions reappear in subsequent philosophy.

§ 57. Ἐπιστήμη.

As in other cases (above, p. 292 ff.) the philosophical is to be distinguished from the ordinary use.

a. (1) The proper note of ἐπιστήμη, as distinguished from δόξα, is *certainty* (Soph. Oed. Tyr. 1115):—

Rep. V. 477 B ἐπιστήμη . . . ἐπὶ τῷ ὄντι πέφυκε, γνῶναι ὡς ἔστι τὸ ὄν.

(2) Hence in the specially Platonic sense, ἐπιστήμη is distinguished from τέχνη as speculative from practical knowledge.

Rep. IV. 438 C ἐπιστήμη . . . αὐτὴ μαθήματος αὐτοῦ ἐπιστήμη ἐστίν.

Parm. 134 A αὐτὴ μὲν ὃ ἔστιν ἐπιστήμη, τῆς ὃ ἔστιν ἀλήθεια, αὐτῆς ἂν ἐκείνης εἴη ἐπιστήμη . . . ἑκάστη δὲ αὖ τῶν ἐπιστημῶν ἣ ἔστιν, ἑκάστου τῶν ὄντων, ὃ ἔστιν, εἴη ἂν ἐπιστήμη.

It is in this ideal sense that vain attempts are made in the Theaetetus to define ἐπιστήμη. And this is the meaning of the word in Rep. VI. 508 E and similar places.

β. The more ordinary use of the word, in which it is nearly equivalent to τέχνη, is sometimes guarded by the addition of the specific object :—

Rep. IV. 438 D ἐπειδὴ οἰκίας ἐργασίας ἐπιστήμη ἐγένετο, διήνεγκε τῶν ἄλλων ἐπιστημῶν, ὥστε οἰκοδομικὴ κληθῆναι.

Or by some qualifying word such as λεγομένη. See Rep. VII. 533 D ἃς ἐπιστήμας μὲν πολλάκις προσείπομεν διὰ τὸ ἔθος, δέονται δὲ ὀνόματος ἄλλου, ἐναργεστέρου μὲν ἢ δόξης, ἀμυδροτέρου δὲ ἢ ἐπιστήμης.

But this meaning of ἐπιστήμη also occurs without any qualification, especially in the plural, and quite as often in the later as in the earlier dialogues.

Rep. VII. 522 C ᾧ πᾶσαι προσχρῶνται τέχναι τε καὶ διάνοιαι καὶ ἐπιστῆμαι.

Polit. 308 C τῶν συνθετικῶν ἐπιστημῶν : Phileb. 62 D.

The singular also appears in the sense of ‘practical skill’ (as in Thucydides, &c.).

Phaedr. 269 D προσλαβὼν ἐπιστήμην τε καὶ μελέτην.

Gorg. 511 C ἡ τοῦ νεῖν ἐπιστήμη.

### Φιλοσοφία. §58.

The abstract noun as well as the adjective φιλόσοφος occurs in Isocrates, but not elsewhere before Plato, although φιλοσοφεῖν was in ordinary use (Herod. I. 30, Thuc. II. 40).

α. Φιλοσοφία is defined in the Republic (V. 475 E ff.) as the love of the whole, (VI. 486 A) θεωρία παντὸς μὲν χρόνου, πάσης δὲ οὐσίας, and is elsewhere (Sophist. 253 E) identified with διαλεκτική.

β. But the word is also used in the more ordinary sense of ‘mental culture,’ ‘scientific pursuit’ :—

Theaet. 143 D γεωμετρίαν ἤ τινα ἄλλην φιλοσοφίαν.

Tim. 88 C μουσικῇ καὶ πάσῃ φιλοσοφίᾳ προσχρώμενον.

In Theaet. 172 C οἱ ἐν ταῖς φιλοσοφίαις πολὺν χρόνον δια-τρίψαντες, the plural seems to include Theodorus as a man of *scientific culture.*

§ 59.    θυμός, τὸ θυμοειδές.

A tripartite division of ψυχή appears in the Phaedrus-myth (Phaedr. 246 foll.), in Rep. IV. 435 foll., IX. 580 foll., and in Tim. 70. On the other hand in Rep. X. 612 A a doubt is expressed whether the Soul in her true nature be divisible at all, and in Phaedo 80 B, C pure Soul is akin to the μονοειδές. In the Timaeus θυμός, or resentment, is expressly said to belong to the lower and mortal part, or aspect, of the Soul. But the function assigned to it is much the same as in Rep. IV [1]. In Rep. IX, l. c., this part of the soul is more exactly described as φιλότιμον, and in the same passage the love of honour is resolved into the love of power. In the imagery which follows, the θυμοειδές is further analysed into the nobler and meaner forms of anger, the 'lion' being reinforced with a crawling serpent brood : IX. 590 B τὸ λεοντῶδές τε καὶ ὀφεῶδες.

The conception mythically expressed in the Phaedrus is less distinct, and though closely akin to the psychology of the Republic and Timaeus, is not precisely the same. The white horse yoked to the winged chariot is *altogether* of a noble strain (καλὸς καὶ ἀγαθὸς καὶ ἐκ τοιούτων), 'a lover of honour, with temperance and chastity [2], a comrade of right thinking, obedient to the voice of Reason.' He thus corresponds rather to the ideal in conformity with which the θυμοειδές is to be trained than to the θυμοειδές as such. Nor is the nobler steed entrusted with control over his

---

[1] Tim. 70 A τὸ μετέχον οὖν τῆς ψυχῆς ἀνδρίας καὶ θυμοῦ, φιλόνεικον ὄν, κατῴκισαν ἐγγυτέρω τῆς κεφαλῆς . . . ἵνα τοῦ λόγου κατήκοον ὂν κοινῇ μετ' ἐκείνου βίᾳ τὸ τῶν ἐπιθυμιῶν κατέχοι γένος, ὁπότ' ἐκ τῆς ἀκροπόλεως τῷ ἐπιτάγματι καὶ λόγῳ μηδαμῇ πείθεσθαι ἑκὸν ἐθέλοι. τὴν δὲ δὴ καρδίαν . . . εἰς τὴν δορυφορικὴν οἴκησιν κατέστησαν.

[2] Shakespeare, *Macbeth* ii. 1 :

> *Macbeth.*        'When 'tis,
> It shall make honour for you.'
> *Banquo.*            'So I lose none
> In seeking to augment it, but still keep
> My bosom franchis'd and allegiance clear,
> I shall be counsell'd.'

baser yoke-fellow. His work is done if he run his own course obediently.

It is probable that in the partition of the Soul in the Republic, Plato has not forgotten the Phaedrus. But he has also in mind the special requirements (practical as well as speculative) of the work in hand, and in particular the close analogy between individual and state, and the position of ἀνδρεία amongst the cardinal (civic) virtues.

Now θυμοειδής, 'spirited,' is applied by Xenophon to a high-bred horse, such as that which symbolized the nobler passions in the Phaedrus—the word does not occur in earlier Greek: and θυμός is the crude form of ἀνδρεία. 'Ανδρεία is the virtue of the guardians, who are φύλακες τῶν τε ἐκτὸς πολεμίων καὶ τῶν ἐντὸς φιλίων, and τὸ θυμοειδές is now formulated as the corresponding part of the individual Soul.

(c) DIALECTICAL TERMS. §60.

No terms in Plato so nearly attain the fixity of technical use as those which bear on method, such for example as συνάγειν, 'generalize,' διαιρεῖσθαι, 'distinguish,' λαμβάνειν, 'apprehend,' διαλαμβάνειν, 'divide,' ἀπολαμβάνειν, 'specify,' μετιέναι, 'treat,' μέθοδος, 'treatment.' This is most apparent in dialogues which represent the conversation of Socrates with his disciples—as in the Phaedo, Republic and Philebus. See Rep. VII. 532 D where Glaucon says, οὐ γὰρ ἐν τῷ νῦν παρόντι μόνον ἀκουστέα, ἀλλὰ καὶ αὖθις πολλάκις ἐπανιτέον.

### Διαλεκτική—διαλέγεσθαι—διάλεκτος.

Διάλεκτος is *rational conversation*, with associations derived from the practice of Socrates, and is opposed to *barren disputation*:—Rep. V. 454 A ἔριδι, οὐ διαλέκτῳ πρὸς ἀλλήλους χρώμενοι. Hence ἡ διαλεκτική (sc. τέχνη, s. μέθοδος) is the Platonic ideal of method. But the connotation of the term inevitably varies with the shifting aspects of that ideal.

Meno 75 D εἰ μέν γε τῶν σοφῶν τις εἴη καὶ ἐριστικῶν τε καὶ ἀγωνιστικῶν ὁ ἐρόμενος, εἴποιμ᾽ ἂν αὐτῷ . . . κ.τ.λ., εἰ δὲ ὥσπερ ἐγώ τε καὶ σὺ νυνὶ φίλοι ὄντες βούλοιντο ἀλλήλοις **διαλέγεσθαι**, δεῖ δὴ πραότερόν πως καὶ **διαλεκτικώτερον** ἀποκρίνεσθαι.

In the sequel it is explained that a dialectical answer is one having a true relation to the respondent's previous admissions.

The word therefore has no reference here to any assumption of supra-sensual εἴδη, but only to that living intercourse of mind with mind, which was the secret of Socrates [1]. In the Phaedrus διαλεκτική is again associated with the same vivid reciprocity of thoughts. But both the Socratic method and its intellectual aim are now viewed under the glow of Platonic idealism at its most fervent heat, and the διαλεκτικός is now the master of knowledge that is at once comprehensive and distinct, seeing as one what is a whole in Nature, as different, what Nature parts asunder; overtaking the subtleties of reality with the movement of mind — his thought adequately grasping and following the Nature of things, at once in their infinity and unity. Thus he realizes the privilege which belongs at birth to every soul which takes the form of man: δεῖ γὰρ ἄνθρωπον ξυνιέναι κατ᾽ εἶδος λεγόμενον, ἐκ πολλῶν ἰὸν [2] αἰσθήσεων εἰς ἓν λογισμῷ ξυναιρούμενον. τοῦτο δέ ἐστιν ἀνάμνησις ἐκείνων, ἅ ποτε εἶδεν ἡμῶν ἡ ψυχὴ συμπορευθεῖσα θεῷ καὶ ὑπεριδοῦσα ἃ νῦν εἶναί φαμεν, καὶ ἀνακύψασα εἰς τὸ ὂν ὄντως. διὸ δὴ δικαίως μόνη πτεροῦται ἡ τοῦ φιλοσόφου διάνοια· πρὸς γὰρ ἐκείνοις ἀεί ἐστι μνήμῃ κατὰ δύναμιν, πρὸς οἷσπερ θεὸς ὢν θεῖός ἐστι. These latter words are of course taken from the myth (249 C), but in the later portion of the same dialogue (266 B, &c.) the method referred to, if not exactly formulated, is more precisely indicated. True eloquence, it is

---

[1] So in the Theaetetus Protagoras is made to claim fairness from a dialectical respondent. Theaet. 167 E χωρὶς μὲν ὡς ἀγωνιζόμενος . . . χωρὶς δὲ διαλεγόμενος. Cp. also Crat. 390 C for the simpler meaning.

[2] W. H. Thompson conjectured ἰόντ᾽.

there said, must be based on a scientific estimate of the human mind and of truth in all its aspects, and also of the mutual relations between these and various minds. This science is compared to that of Hippocrates, whose medical practice was based on profound study of the human body. Such an ideal, though vaguely sketched, is by no means severed from experience. Its unattainableness, indeed, lies rather in the infinity of nature than in the abstractedness of knowledge. In the Republic, on the other hand, the allegory of the cave and the ladder of the sciences carry off the mind into a region where actual experience seems of little account, and philosophic thought is imagined as moving among pure εἴδη,—εἴδεσιν αὐτοῖς δι᾽ αὐτῶν εἰς αὐτά. Yet here also, while the dualism is more evident, it is hard to tell how much is allegorical. For Socrates maintains that the philosopher, who has been trained in dialectic, will be no whit behind his fellow-citizens in practical wisdom, but on the contrary will be infinitely more capable, with equal opportunities, of dealing with any actual emergency [1].

Συναγωγή—συλλογισμός.                                  § 61.

The most pervading note of διαλεκτική, and this appears both in the Republic and the Phaedrus, is comprehensiveness accompanied with clearness.

VII. 537 C ὁ . . . γὰρ **συνοπτικὸς** διαλεκτικός, ὁ δὲ μὴ οὔ. Cp. Tim. 83 C where Socrates admires the man who gave the name of χολή to phenomena so diversified as those to which it is applied. This is again insisted on in Soph. 253 C, D— esp. in the words ὅ γε τοῦτο δυνατὸς δρᾶν **μίαν ἰδέαν** διὰ πολλῶν, . . . πάντη διατεταμένην ἱκανῶς διαισθάνεται—another *locus classicus* on the subject. By this time, however, the questions turning on predication have come to the front,

---

[1] In the Republic Socrates refuses to define διαλεκτική: but he describes it thus—ἦ καὶ διαλεκτικὸν καλεῖς τὸν λόγον ἑκάστου λαμβάνοντα τῆς οὐσίας; This follows a passage in praise of διαλεκτική in the light of the account of the mental faculties in Book VI.

and the method indicated is one of logical determination, according to the real participation of things in ideas, and of ideas or kinds in one another : τοῦτο δ' ἔστιν, ᾗ τε κοινωνεῖν ἕκαστα δύναται καὶ ὅπῃ μή, διακρίνειν κατὰ γένος ἐπίστασθαι. In the Politicus again, and also in the Philebus, the notion of method becomes still more concrete, involving not merely relation but proportion—τὸ μέτριον, μικτὴ φύσις, μέτρον. An increasing sense of the complexity of the world makes more apparent the hindrances to adequacy of method. At the same time dialectical improvement, the preparation and sharpening of the instrument, is prized apart from the immediate results. The notion of adapting logical weapons to the subject to be attacked is curiously expressed in Philebus 23 B φαίνεται δεῖν ἄλλης μηχανῆς ἐπὶ τὰ δευτερεῖα ὑπὲρ νοῦ πορευόμενον οἷον βέλη ἔχειν ἕτερα τῶν ἔμπροσθεν λόγων· ἔστι δὲ ἴσως ἔνια καὶ ταὐτά. And the conception of science, without losing the associations originally suggested by the conversations of Socrates, now includes not only the ascertainment of differences, but of finite differences, not only the one and many, but the 'how many,' Phil. 16 D.

Plato's 'dialectic,' then, is not merely an ideal method, but the ideal of a method, which at best is only approximately realized[1], and presents different aspects according to the scope and spirit of particular dialogues. It is a conception which grows with the growth of Plato's thoughts. In the Protagoras and Gorgias it is contrasted with popular rhetoric—the one exact and truthful, the other loose and careless of the truth ; in other places to ἐριστική (ἀντιλογική, ἀγωνιστική). Its end is neither persuasion nor refutation, but the attainment and communication of truth, of which the tests are universality and certainty.

§ 62.    'Εριστική.

The marks of ἀντιλογική or ἐριστική also vary with the stages of Platonism[2] ; but that which is most pervading,

---

[1] Theaet. 196 E, Rep. IV. 435 C.
[2] Phaedo 101 E, Rep. V. 454, Theaet. 197 A.

and which comes out most clearly where Plato's own philosophy is ripest, is the crudeness of affirmation and negation, the root fallacy of confounding *dictum simpliciter* with *dictum secundum quid.*

Διαίρεσις : διαιρεῖν, διαιρεῖσθαι, διαλαμβάνειν, διακρίνειν, τέμνειν, § 63. μέρος, μόριον, τμῆμα, τομή, διαφυή.

While διαιρεῖν or διαιρεῖσθαι is the term most commonly used for logical division, and μέρος for the result, it is observable that in the later dialogues, where classification becomes more frequent, the expression is varied, some other word from the list given above being used instead.

*Obs.* 1.—'Ἁπλοῦν has two meanings, (1) admitting no further division, (2) true without qualification or distinction. (Gorg. 503 A, Phaedr. 244 A.)

*Obs.* 2.—'Ἀπολαμβάνειν is to ' specify,' and for this ἀπονέμεσθαι is used in Polit. 276 D and elsewhere.

The aor. participle ἀπολαβών is used absolutely in Rep. IV. 420 C τὴν εὐδαίμονα πλάττομεν οὐκ ἀπολαβόντες.

Cp. ἀπομερίζω, ἀποχωρίζω.

Λαμβάνειν.                                                               § 64.

The simple λαμβάνειν has also a special use, nearly = ὑπολαμβάνειν, ' to conceive,' or ' formulate,' sometimes with the addition of λόγῳ.

Phaedr. 246 D τὴν . . . αἰτίαν . . . λάβωμεν.

Rep. VIII. 559 A ἵνα τύπῳ λάβωμεν αὐτάς.

Ion 532 E λάβωμεν γὰρ τῷ λόγῳ.

Rep. VI. 496 D ταῦτα πάντα λογισμῷ λαβών.

Rep. VII. 533 B οὐδεὶς ἡμῖν ἀμφισβητήσει λέγουσιν, ὡς αὐτοῦ γε ἑκάστου πέρι, ὃ ἔστιν ἕκαστον, ἄλλη τις ἐπιχειρεῖ μέθοδος ὁδῷ περὶ παντὸς λαμβάνειν.

Phileb. 50 D λαβόντα . . . τοῦτο παρὰ σαυτῷ.

'Υπόθεσις, ὑποτίθεσθαι.                                              § 65.

'Υπόθεσις in Plato is ' an assumption,' adopted as a basis of reasoning, either (α) dogmatic, or (β) provisional. Cp. Xen. Mem. IV. 6, § 13.

*a.* Theaet. 183 B ὡς νῦν γε πρὸς τὴν αὐτῶν ὑπόθεσιν οὐκ ἔχουσι ῥήματα, viz. the dogmatic assumption that all is motion: Soph. 244 C τῷ ταύτην τὴν ὑπόθεσιν ὑποθεμένῳ, the doctrine of ἓν τὸ πᾶν.

*β.* Meno 86 E ἐξ ὑποθέσεως ... σκοπεῖσθαι, εἴτε διδακτόν ἐστιν εἴτε ὁπωσοῦν. Here the nature of such hypothetical reasoning is illustrated by a geometrical example: 'If the figure applied to the base of the triangle is similar to it, then one thing follows, but not otherwise' . In this sense the word is used with reference to the Zenonian dialectic, of the proposition which is subjected to the indirect proof that it is untenable.

Accordingly, in Socratic reasoning, which proceeds by testing successive assumptions with negative examples, each proposed definition, while it maintains its ground, is called the ὑπόθεσις.

Euthyphr. 11 C νῦν δέ, σαὶ γὰρ αἱ ὑποθέσεις εἰσίν.

Phaedo 107 B οὐ μόνον γ', ἔφη, ὦ Σιμμία, ὁ Σωκράτης, ἀλλὰ ταῦτά τε εὖ λέγεις (Simmias has just spoken of the greatness of the subject and the feebleness of man), καὶ τὰς ὑποθέσεις τὰς πρώτας, καὶ εἰ πισταὶ ὑμῖν εἰσίν, ὅμως ἐπισκεπτέαι σαφέστερον· καὶ ἐὰν αὐτὰς ἱκανῶς διέλητε, ... ἀκουλουθήσετε τῷ λόγῳ, καθ' ὅσον δυνατὸν μάλιστ' ἀνθρώπῳ ἐπακολουθῆσαι· κἂν τοῦτο αὐτὸ σαφὲς γένηται, οὐδὲν ζητήσετε περαιτέρω.

We may remember that it is the same Simmias, who earlier in the dialogue (85 D) puts forth the touching image of a raft, to represent the provisional nature of every human theory, in the absence of a divine, or superhuman, principle.

Now of these primary hypotheses, or first premises, one of the chief is clearly that notion of true causes insisted on in Phaedo 100 B, 101 D, as the outcome of the procedure of Socrates, viz. that each thing is what it is by participation (μετάσχεσις) in the idea. 'All other modes of causation you will leave, says Socrates, to those who are cleverer than you are. Fearing, as the proverb says, your own shadow, you will hold on to that sure ground of the assumption (τῆς ὑποθέσεως). And if any one attacks you there, you will not answer him until you have tested all the consequences of the hypothesis itself. And if in the end you have to examine the grounds of your assumption, you will do so by a similar process, having framed a new and higher hypothesis, by the best lights you have, and so on until you reach a satisfactory result. But you will not, as the eristics do, confuse in argument the principle with its consequences; that is not the way to discover truth.'

Here the ἀρχή is the same with the ὑπόθεσις. It is therefore somewhat startling to find in Rep. VI. 511 C this very identification (αἷς αἱ ὑποθέσεις ἀρχαί) made a ground of objection to the actual condition of the sciences. It will be said that this applies only to the mathematical sciences, and to them only in so far as they work through visible symbols, but this view is inconsistent with VII. 517 D ; see the notes.

The apparent discrepancy arises out of what may be termed the overweening intellectualism of this part of the Republic, the same temper which prompts the notion of an astronomy without observations, and a science of harmony independent of sound. Plato is aware that he is setting forth an impossible ideal, but for the education of his 'airy burghers,' nothing short of the absolute will satisfy him. Allowing for this difference of spirit, the two passages just quoted from the Phaedo, for the very reason that they are less aspiring, throw light on the description of the true method in Rep. VII. 533 C ἡ διαλεκτικὴ μέθοδος μόνη ταύτῃ πορεύεται, τὰς ὑποθέσεις ἀναιροῦσα ἐπ' αὐτὴν τὴν ἀρχήν, ἵνα βεβαιώσηται, and the corresponding passage in VI. 511. For example, though it is by no means clear that by the ἱκανόν τι of Phaedo 101 D, Plato means the same thing with the ἀνυπόθετον or the ἰδέα τοῦ ἀγαθοῦ, yet the description of the progress from the lower to the higher hypothesis is parallel to the ladder of ideas in VI. 511 B τὰς ὑποθέσεις ποιούμενος οὐκ ἀρχάς, ἀλλὰ τῷ ὄντι ὑποθέσεις, οἷον ἐπιβάσεις τε καὶ ὁρμάς, ἵνα μέχρι τοῦ ἀνυποθέτου ἐπὶ τὴν τοῦ παντὸς ἀρχὴν ἰών, κ.τ.λ. The contrast between arguing about principles and their consequences also corresponds to this upward and downward way. And the words in Phaedo 107 B ἐὰν αὐτὰς (τὰς ὑποθέσεις) ἱκανῶς διέλητε . . . ἀκολουθήσετε τῷ λόγῳ, καθ' ὅσον δυνατὸν μάλιστ' ἀνθρώπῳ ἐπακολουθῆσαι, further illustrate the notion of a 'higher analytic,' which in both dialogues is imperfectly shadowed forth : while the ultimate cause in the Phaedo 98 A, 99 C the 'reason of the best,' is a conception not far removed from the Idea of Good. It becomes apparent, when the whole tenour of these kindred passages is considered, that what Plato censures in the actual methods of 'Science' is not the use of assumptions, but the habit of regarding them as fixed and self-evident, VII. 533 C ἕως ἂν ὑποθέσεσι χρώμεναι ταύτας ἀκινήτους ἐῶσι, μὴ δυνάμεναι λόγον διδόναι αὐτῶν.

*Obs.*—The simple τιθέναι (sometimes τίθεσθαι)—in frequent use —is to 'posit' or 'assume,' not necessarily as the first step in an argument. Theaet. 190 A δόξαν ταύτην τίθεμεν αὐτῆς.

## § 66.     ἓν καὶ πολλά—στοιχεῖον.

It is clear from the classical passage of the Philebus 16 ff., that 'one and many' had become a recognized formula in the Platonic school. But it is also clear from the passage itself, especially when other places are compared, that the formula had different meanings and applications. (a) Single objects have many attributes. (β) Many individuals 'partake' in common of one ἰδέα : the εἶδος is therefore one and many. (γ) Ideas themselves are complex, and variously correlated, yet many are bound in one under some higher notion, all partake of number and being, and Being is itself absorbed in the Good.

It is characteristic of Plato's later theory, that in the

Philebus he not only dwells on this last aspect of the truth, but also speaks of it as a πάθος τῶν λόγων . . . παρ' ἡμῖν, 'an affection or attribute of human discourse.' This point of view is all the more significant, when it is remembered that the discussions in the Parmenides, Theaetetus, and Sophist have intervened.

α. The first and simplest aspect of the ' one and many ' §67. appears in Plato, (1) as a Zenonian or Heraclitean paradox, (2) as a proof of the necessity of the Idea.

(1) Phileb. 14 C ὅταν τις ἐμὲ φῇ . . . ἕνα γεγονότα φύσει, πολλοὺς εἶναι πάλιν, τοὺς ἐμέ, κ.τ.λ., τιθέμενος.

Parm. 129 C εἰ δ' ἐμὲ ἕν τις ἀποδείξει ὄντα καὶ πολλά, κ.τ.λ.

Theaet. 166 B τὸν εἶναί τινα, ἀλλ' οὐχὶ τούς, καὶ τούτους γιγνομένους ἀπείρους, ἐάνπερ ἀνομοίωσις γίγνηται.

In the Protagorean theory, as the mind is a bundle or succession of momentary impressions, each substance is a bundle or aggregate of transient attributes or presentations, Theaet. 157 B, C ᾧ δὴ ἀθροίσματι ἄνθρωπόν τε τίθενται καὶ λίθον καὶ ἕκαστον ζῷόν τε καὶ εἶδος.

(2) In Rep. VII. 523 it is shown by an example how the mind passes through the consciousness of diversity to the perception of unity. The finger is both rough and smooth ; this awakens thought to the existence of roughness and smoothness, each as one several thing, and of their opposition as a reality. This is the psychological counterpart of many other passages where the diversities of sense are made the ground for assuming abstract unities.

β. One idea or form is shared by many objects. Beauty §68. is one, the beautiful are many, &c. This point of view, with the difficulties attending it has been already discussed (above, p. 309 ff.; Μέθεξις, &c.). It may be called the formula of crude realism.

γ. The problem of solving these difficulties emerges together with the third and highest aspect of the ἐν καὶ πολλά in the dialectical dialogues. It is now that, as we have seen, clearer views of predication, a more subjective point of view, and a higher comprehension of the ideas as forms of thought, of their interrelation and sequence, lead the way towards a rational metaphysic and psychology. The result is a scheme of thought, or as Plato himself terms it, a κόσμος τις ἀσώματος (Philebus 64 B), which is indeed empty of content, but has no insignificant bearing on the after progress of the Sciences.

In Theaet. 202, Plato deals tentatively with this later phase of the question through the contrast of στοιχεῖον and συλλαβή. Here συλλαβή is the complex idea, which is itself resolved into a higher unity—e. g. the harmony of treble and bass notes, or the art of music as comprising various harmonies.

But in Polit. 278 B–D [1], as well as in Rep. III. 402 A–C, the στοιχεῖον is the idea, while the συλλαβή is the combination of ideas in fact. Thus justice is justice, whether in commerce, war, judicial pleadings, or any other of the varied circumstances of human society.

## § 69.   παράδειγμα.

παράδειγμα has two very different meanings in Plato, one of which has been already discussed (above, p. 310 ff.). The artist copies from a *pattern* (1); the merchant, for convenience sake, carries about (2) *examples* of his wares (δείγματα Phaedo 110 B). The latter would seem to be the figure implied in the logical use of παράδειγμα for the illustration of one species by another of the same genus, the complex by the simple, the obscure by the familiar, the unknown by the known. A full account of this mode of argument is given by the Eleatic Stranger in Polit. 277 D ff. Cp. Prot. 330 A, Phaedr. 262 C, Theaet. 154 C, 202 E, Soph. 218 D.

For other ' dialectical ' terms, expressing various aspects of predication, such as προσαγορεύω, προσάπτω, προστίθημι,

---

[1] This passage is a good example of the concrete mode of conception which belongs to Plato's later style.

προσαρμόττω, συμπλέκειν, ὄνομα, ῥῆμα, πρόσρημα, φάσις, ἀπόφασις, see the Lexica.

---

The wide gap which separates Plato's use of philo- § 70.
sophical terms from Aristotle's may be briefly instanced
in the case of (1) οὐσία, (2) διαλεκτική, and (3) συλλογισμός.

(1) The chapter of Aristotle's Metaphysics, IV. 8, in
which various meanings of οὐσία both as *substance* and
*essence* are distinguished, would hardly have been intelligible to Plato, although between the transcendent Being of
Rep. VI, and the μικτὴ οὐσία of Phil. 27 B, a long step has
been made towards the conception of concrete existence.

(2) Διαλεκτική in Aristotle is intermediate between
philosophy and common sense, a sort of tentative philosophizing which falls short of certainty—Met. III. 2, § 20 ἡ
διαλεκτικὴ πειραστικὴ περὶ ὧν ἡ φιλοσοφία γνωριστική. To
Plato, as we know, the same term represented the highest
reach of philosophic method.

(3) The word συλλογισμός occurs only once in Plato,
Theaet. 186 D, where it is used quite simply, much as
ἀναλογίσματα (ib. supr. C), to express the action of the mind
in forming judgements from impressions of sense. The
verb συλλογίζεσθαι, 'to reason,' 'collect,' 'infer,' is not
infrequent, but is also used quite simply, as it might occur
in ordinary discourse :—

Rep. VII. 531 D καὶ ξυλλογισθῇ ταῦτα ᾗ ἐστὶν ἀλλήλοις οἰκεῖα,
'and these things are reasoned of from that general point
of view in which they are mutually akin.'

Ib. 516 B μετὰ ταῦτ' ἂν ἤδη συλλογίζοιτο περὶ αὐτοῦ, κ.τ.λ.,
'in the next place he would proceed to infer that it is the
Sun who,' &c.

How far such uses are removed from the Aristotelian
doctrine of the Syllogism appears on comparing any one of
numberless passages :

Rhetor. I. 2, § 8 ἀνάγκη συλλογιζόμενον ἢ ἐπάγοντα δεικνύναι ὁτιοῦν.

Analyt. Pr. I. 1, § 6 συλλογισμὸς δέ ἐστι λόγος ἐν ᾧ τεθέντων τινῶν ἕτερόν τι τῶν κειμένων ἐξ ἀνάγκης συμβαίνει τῷ ταῦτα εἶναι.

Met. IV. 3, § 3 συλλογισμοὶ οἱ πρῶτοι ἐκ τῶν τριῶν δι' ἑνὸς μέσου.

Analyt. Pr. I. 7, § 4 ἔστιν ἀναγαγεῖν πάντας τοὺς συλλο-γισμοὺς εἰς τοὺς ἐν τῷ πρώτῳ σχήματι καθόλου συλλογισμούς.

See also esp. Soph. Elench. c. 33 sub fin.

But it is observable that even in Aristotle both verb and noun occur elsewhere in the ordinary Greek sense. See Bonitz, *Index Aristotelicus*, s. vv.

# INDEX TO VOL. II.

—◆—

## I. ENGLISH.

*Contractions*: *Str.* = *Structure*; *R.* = *Relation to other dialogues*; *Ess.* = *Essay*; *Exc.* = *Excursus to Essay on Structure*; *T.* = *Text*; *App.* = *Appendices to Essay on Text*; *St.* = *Style*; *Syn.* = *Syntax*; *D.* = *Diction.*

# II. GREEK

# PHILOSOPHY
## OF
# PLATO AND ARISTOTLE

AN ARNO PRESS COLLECTION

Aristotle. **Aristotle De Sensu and De Memoria.** Text and Translation with Introduction and Commentary by G[eorge] R[obert] T[hompson] Ross. 1906.

Aristotle. **Aristotle Nicomachean Ethics.** Book Six, with Essays, Notes, and Translation by L. H. G. Greenwood. 1909.

Aristotle. **Aristotle's Constitution of Athens.** A Revised Text with an Introduction, Critical and Explanatory Notes, Testimonia and Indices Revised and Enlarged by John Edwin Sandys. Second Edition. 1912.

Aristotle. **The Ethics of Aristotle.** Edited, with an Introduction and Notes by John Burnet. 1900.

Aristotle. **The Ethics of Aristotle.** Illustrated with Essays and Notes by Alexander Grant. Fourth Edition. 1885.

Aristotle. **The Fifth Book of the Nicomachean Ethics of Aristotle.** Edited for the Syndics of the University Press by Henry Jackson. 1879.

Aristotle. **The Politics of Aristotle.** With an Introduction, Two Prefatory Essays and Notes Critical and Explanatory by W. L. Newman. 1887.

Aristotle. **The Rhetoric of Aristotle.** With a Commentary by Edward Meredith Cope. Revised and Edited for the Syndics of the University Press by Sir John Edwin Sandys. 1877.

Bywater, Ingram. **Contributions to the Textual Criticism of Aristotle's Nicomachean Ethics.** 1892.

Grote, George. **Aristotle.** Edited by Alexander Bain and G. Croom Robertson. Second Edition, with Additions. 1880.

Linforth, Ivan M. **The Arts of Orpheus.** 1941.

Onians, Richard Broxton. **The Origins of European Thought About the Body, the Mind, the Soul, the World, Time, and Fate.** 1951.

Pearson, A. C., editor. **The Fragments of Zeno and Cleanthes.** With Introduction and Explanatory Notes. 1891.

Plato. **The Apology of Plato.** With a Revised Text and English Notes, and a Digest of Platonic Idioms by James Riddell. 1877.

Plato. **The Euthydemus of Plato.** With Revised Text, Introduction, Notes, and Indices by Edwin Hamilton Gifford. 1905.

Plato. **The Gorgias of Plato.** With English Notes, Introduction, and Appendix by W. H. Thompson. 1871.

Plato. **The Phaedo of Plato.** Edited with Introduction, Notes and Appendices by R. D. Archer-Hind. Second Edition. 1894.

Plato. **The Phaedrus of Plato.** With English Notes and Dissertations by W. H. Thompson. 1868.

Plato. **The Philebus of Plato.** Edited with Introduction, Notes and Appendices by Robert Gregg Bury. 1897.

Plato. **Plato's Republic:** The Greek Text, Edited with Notes and Essays by B. Jowett and Lewis Campbell. Volume II: Essays. 1894.

Plato. **The Sophistes and Politicus of Plato.** With a Revised Text and English Notes by Lewis Campbell. 1867.

Plato. **The Theaetetus of Plato.** With a Revised Text and English Notes by Lewis Campbell. 1861.

Plato. **The Timaeus of Plato.** Edited with Introduction and Notes by R. D. Archer-Hind. 1888.

Schleiermacher, [Friedrich Ernst Daniel]. **Introductions to the Dialogues of Plato.** Translated from the German by William Dobson. 1836.

Stenzel, Julius. **Plato's Method of Dialectic.** Translated and Edited by D. J. Allan. 1940.

Stewart, J. A. **Notes on the Nicomachean Ethics of Aristotle.** 1892.